SECOND EDITION

# The Computer Triangle

HARDWARE • SOFTWARE • PEOPLE

Robert L. Oakman
University of South Carolina

John Wiley & Sons, Inc.
New York • Chichester • Brisbane • Toronto • Singapore • Weinheim

*Acquisitions Editor*    Beth Lang Golub
*Marketing Manager*    Leslie Hines
*Production Editor*    Jeanine Furino
*Cover Design*    Carolyn Joseph
*Design Direction*    Karin Gerdes Kincheloe
*Assistant Manufacturing Manager*    Mark Cirillo
*Photo Editor*    Hilary Newman
*Illustration Coordinator*    Anna Melhorn

*Cover Photos:*
*Rock, pyramids (Egyptian and human), circuit board, and collage photos:*
Comstock, Inc.
*Bird:*   Art Wolfe/Tony Stone Images/New York, Inc.
*Diatom:*   M. Abbey/Photo Researchers.
*Vase:*   Erich Lessing Photography/Art Resource.
*Badge:*   David Pollack/The Stock Market.

This book was set in 10/12 New Aster by GGS, Inc. and
printed and bound by Banta Company. The cover was printed by Banta Company.

Recognizing the importance of preserving what has been written, it is a
policy of John Wiley & Sons, Inc. to have books of enduring value published
in the United States printed on acid-free paper, and we exert our best
efforts to that end.

Printed in the United States of America
10 9 8 7 6 5 4 3 2 1

# About the Author

**Robert L. Oakman** has been on the faculty at the University of South Carolina for twenty-eight years, with a joint appointment in English and Computer Science. For the past eleven years he has served as coordinator of the introductory computer literacy course for the general undergraduate population.

With the introduction of new personal computers, Oakman redesigned the computer literacy course at the University of South Carolina to switch the focus from computer concepts and programming to the uses of applications software as well as computer and society issues. The goal of his interdisciplinary course was to make technical materials interesting and relevant to a wide variety of majors—foreign languages, art, education, nursing, journalism, English, history, criminal justice. The course has been hugely successful, attracting more than 10,000 students during the past ten years.

Professor Oakman's educational background is rather distinctive: he holds a B.A. degree in mathematics from the University of Mississippi, an M.A. in numerical analysis (the early focus of computer science studies) from the University of Wisconsin, and M.A. and Ph.D. degrees in English literature from Indiana University. In addition to computer literacy, his research interests are natural language processing and educational technology, including multimedia authoring systems.

# Preface

The foundation of *The Computer Triangle* rests on the interconnections between the three main elements that make up computing: hardware, software, and people. From Charles Babbage's invention of the Difference Engine in 1822, to the punch card tabulating machines used for the 1890 Census, to the primitive computers created for military work in World War II, to the commercial mainframes of the 1950s, to the introduction of the microprocessor and the Internet about 1970—people have continuously improved hardware and software to better serve the needs of society. Hardware got better, smaller, and less expensive as software got more sophisticated and easier to use. Network connections developed to link people and places throughout the world. The most significant addition to the Second Edition of *The Computer Triangle* is the full treatment of the widespread impact of the Internet in all areas of modern technology. The personal computer of the late twentieth century has become the machine for everyone. Today the world cannot do without the computer—in the workplace, the school, and the home.

Applications of computers abound in all areas of modern life. Yet with all the benefits that computers offer people have come new worries associated with the spread of technology: impersonalization, government snooping, automation and downsizing, on-line pornography on the Internet. Hardware and software innovation brought both good and bad consequences for society. This interconnectivity of the three elements, the interdisciplinary nature of the machine and its effects on those who use it—these are major focuses of this book.

## Goals of *The Computer Triangle*

The computer constitutes a powerful educational tool for imaginative creativity and insight in all areas of the arts and sciences. The machine offers a variety of efficient methods of data analysis to probe records of human experience from the world around us in the humanities and social sciences, just as they do in the sciences and professions. Indeed, the computer is integral to study in all areas of college and university education. With the phenomenal growth of the Internet in the last few years, even people who have never turned on computers have sensed that they are missing out on its great potential as an information source. *The Computer Triangle* was written to reach this audience with the following goals in mind:

- Highlighting the place of the computer in education of students in *all disciplines.*
- Treating the computer as a *general information-processing tool,* not just a number cruncher or an accounting machine.
- Introducing the fundamental concepts of *hardware and software as a foundation for discussing particular applications.*

- Presenting a *generic treatment of all major applications software*—word processing, spreadsheets, databases, and graphics.
- Highlighting the *most important new area in computer technology*—the Internet and its extensions into all kinds of data communications.
- Including a *wide choice of examples* of the role of computers in all areas of modern life—education, medicine, media, business, government, humanities, sciences, art, and the movies.
- Understanding the *negative as well as the positive social consequences* of using the computer.

## ▶ Changes in the New Edition

All of the preceding emphases from the first edition are kept in this revision. In addition, new topics have been introduced in every chapter, including multimedia and World Wide Web materials in education, the role of computers in downsizing, rapid applications development tools, voice command systems, caller ID services, QuickTime VR, commerce and security on the Internet, implications of the Telecommunications Act of 1996, and the possibilities of network computers. The importance of the Internet in all sections is featured by a new marginal icon in the text, described below, and self-paced student exercises exploring the World Wibe Web and included with the CD-ROM Web transparencies which accompany this new edition.

## ▶ Themes of *The Computer Triangle*

The metaphor of the Computer Triangle also fits well with the themes that are woven throughout this book—social relevance, historical insights, and the growth of the Internet. Distinctive icons appear in the margins to indicate where each of these themes is exemplified in the text narrative.

### SOCIAL RELEVANCE

SOCIETY

This book contains a strong emphasis on *societal implications of computers* in modern life, both positive and negative. Underlying this treatment is the truism that technology brings with it changes in the lives of its users, not all of them planned or anticipated. Issues of privacy and personal service, computer viruses, and freedom of speech on bulletin boards suggest the many societal connections of modern computing. To emphasize points where this people side of the Computer Triangle is important, an icon for societal relevance is placed in the margin. Further exploration into the societal implications of computing is encouraged by including experiential and critical thinking questions at the end of each chapter and a list of further readings at the end of the book.

### HISTORICAL INSIGHTS

HISTORY

A second icon focuses on *the history of computing*, which is interspersed throughout the text at appropriate points rather than being set apart in a special chapter or appendix on history. Throughout the book, historical references arise naturally out of the discussion, with a special focus on computing milestones in the 25 years of the personal computer revolution. A number of famous documents of computer development are discussed in the text and included in the bibliography. Classic articles, such as Alan Turing on artificial intelligence, Edsger Dijkstra on the need for structured programming, and E. F. Codd's definition of relational databases, are presented in the context of the conditions that led to them and their implications and outcomes for the future. More recently, the successful search for the most notorious hacker by one of the world's computer security experts and the highly publicized victory of a computer chess program over Garry Kasparov bring the fascinating history of this machine up to date.

## THE INTERNET

A third icon highlights *the growing importance of the Internet,* certainly the most visible computing topic in the last several years. The multifaceted Internet, which combines computers and communications, is more than twenty five years old. When it spawned the World Wide Web in the 1990s, its possibilities for worldwide distribution of multimedia on the personal computer were suddenly apparent. The Web expands the interdisciplinary nature of computing in ways not envisioned 10 years ago. From distance education to on-line businesses, to diagnostic medicine via teleconferencing, the Internet today collects and distributes for its users the world over a wide spectrum of information in many different media: texts, sounds, graphics, digitized photography, and video. This book includes many examples of how the Internet is changing how we think of computing as a primary source of information. Because Internet developments are so widespread in modern computing, the icon shows up in many unexpected places throughout the text.

**INTERNET**

 ## Organization of *The Computer Triangle*

This book is organized somewhat differently from many other computer literacy texts, which tend to relegate the societal implications of computing to a back chapter. *The Computer Triangle* balances the human side of computing with the more technical issues of hardware and software. Consequently, the book begins by introducing the interdisciplinary nature of computers through multimedia and the World Wide Web. The second and third chapters then consider positive and negative aspects of modern computing in a variety of settings before moving to a detailed treatment of hardware and software. These topics precede presentation of word processing, spreadsheets, databases, and graphics applications. The final two chapters treat future prospects, including artificial intelligence, for all three sides of the Computer Triangle.

 ## Other Distinguishing Features

In the process of developing *The Computer Triangle,* the publisher commissioned reviews by many academics to evaluate content and presentation in the book. Also, a focus group of faculty who teach a computer literacy course provided further suggestions for refining the manuscript to meet their classroom needs. In response to their perceptive comments, some distinctive features have been incorporated into the text.

## FLEXIBILITY

Individual instructors may wish to take different approaches to the computer literacy course. Therefore, all chapters are designed to stand alone, so that materials can be taught in a different order, after the introductory chapter. Chapter 1 opens with the World Wide Web, which is treated with other aspects of the Internet in a later chapter. The first chapter also offers an orientation to computer fundamentals in the discussion of an advertisement for a personal computer system so that instructors who wish to move hardware and software forward for earlier discussion can do so. Each of the chapters on applications software are totally independent. Their discussion can be easily reordered to parallel instruction about various software packages in a different sequence in a computer laboratory. In fact, at our university we regularly rearrange the discussion of chapters as we modify the laboratory software assignments from semester to semester.

## A GENERIC APPROACH

Reviewers suggested keeping the explanation of major applications software as generic as possible. Therefore the sections on word processing, graphics, and data communications single out no particular brand of software. Even for spreadsheets and databases, where an actual commercial package is used to develop a practical example, features that different software vendors include in their products are also discussed. The generic approach fits naturally with the interdisciplinary orientation of the book.

The hardware and software discussions include the three major families of computers and operating systems in common use today: Intel/Windows, Macintosh, and Unix machines. Where appropriate, one of these may be featured to make a point about the evolution of personal computing with comparative comments to other machines. The last chapter looks at the current scene in personal and workstation computing as a means of forecasting where the next few years will lead. In addition, other kinds of computers for special needs are covered, such as supercomputers in weather research, parallel processing for genetic decoding, and inexpensive network computers for Web access. The focus is on broad inclusive coverage of hardware in all phases of modern computing.

## PERSPECTIVES

Focus group participants identified the fresh perspectives on social, evolutionary, and technological topics as one of the book's most distinctive features. Highlighted in shaded boxes, these perspectives serve to investigate a subject of particular interest in more detail. Critical Thinking Questions at the end of the chapter encourage further study of perspective topics.

**Social Perspectives** zero in on the positive and negative aspects of a subject like government databases or address an application like artificial intelligence in medicine with special focus. **Evolutionary Perspectives** tend to examine a development over time, for instance, the growth of early electronic networks into today's Information Superhighway.

Since the book is designed for the average undergraduate student, technical topics in computer science like binary coding and the storage requirements of different media files are discussed so that the nontechnical student can understand the point. Often analogies from other areas are used to clarify technological information. Some technical topics are given their own more detailed **Technological Perspectives**—for example, Boolean searches and problems with automatic spelling checkers. The text is designed to give leeway to instructors to discuss the nuts and bolts of hardware and software at several levels of detail and coverage.

## MEANINGFUL ILLUSTRATIONS

A frequent complaint about textbooks is that the illustrations have only a general relevance to the text. Visual elements in *The Computer Triangle* have been carefully chosen to enhance the understanding of the concepts and applications presented in the text. The author and publisher have made a conscious effort to make the photographs and diagrams fit naturally with the text narrative. Descriptive captions refer the picture directly to the discussion in the text.

## ▶ Strong Pedagogy

The pedagogical structure of this book has been planned to promote ease of learning. Various study aids have been included to help students understand and apply basic computing concepts.

- **Learning Outcomes** at the beginning of the chapter outline the main concepts and applications that students are expected to understand after reading the chapter.
- **Computers in Context** help readers to see immediately the importance of the topics covered in the chapter. These brief vignettes often put the main topics in a larger picture and provide an interesting background. Examples include a World Wide Web course in American literature with on-line commenting and the Human Genome Project as a current and future application of computers to better our lives.
- **Marginal Definitions** highlight key terms as they are introduced in the text. This running glossary also provides an effective review aid. A complete alphabetical Glossary appears at the end of the book for easy reference.
- **Perspectives** present social, evolutionary, and technological implications of computers for all components of the Computer Triangle.
- A **Summary** at the end of every chapter provides a quick contextual review of the major concepts covered in the chapter.
- **List of Key Terms** appears at the end of the chapter so students can test themselves on their understanding of these important terms. If they cannot define a term, they can refer back to the definition given in the text.
- **Self-Tests,** with answer keys for immediate feedback, appear at the end of every chapter. These include multiple-choice, true/false, and fill-in questions for students to confirm their learning of the material covered in the chapter.
- **Experiential Exercises** and **Critical Thinking Questions** allow students to expand their knowledge of the main concepts of each chapter and to confront societal and philosophical implications of the Computer Age. These exercises are suitable for individual projects and papers, often encouraging students to investigate personally the computing environment on their own campuses.
- **References,** at the end of the book include a number of famous documents and classic articles of computer development as well as a wealth of current resources for interested students to pursue. They also provide a good start in seeking sources to do the exercises.

## ▶ Supplements

With the Second Edition comes an extensive complement of instructional aids available on a companion **CD-ROM** for instructors, as well as their students. The highlight of the CD-ROM is a set of multimedia World Wide Web transparencies for each chapter, prepared by the author and his development team. These annotated notes for the chapters include illustrations and photographs from the text as well as many additional addresses to Web sites that illustrate and reinforce key concepts covered in the text, a glossary of all terms in the book, student Web exercises, and topical updates about current trends in computing.

The Web transparencies have two purposes. With an overhead projector attached to their computer, instructors can display them in class with browser software from the CD-ROM or from the Internet directly from a Web server at Wiley in New York. After class, students can review the materials in these transparencies anywhere that provides Web access to the Internet server at Wiley: in the computer laboratory, or perhaps in their dorm rooms on their own machines.

Another unique resource available on the CD-ROM is a full-featured multimedia authoring package called MediaLink (InterEd) and written by the author's development team at the University of South Carolina for both Macintosh or Windows computers. With MediaLink, students and teachers can create multimedia assignments incorporating all the computer media—text, sound, graphics, digitized photography, and video—without the heavy learning curve of most multimedia software. The key is flexible drag-and-drop linking of resources without the need of scripts or flowcharts found in other packages like HyperCard, ToolBook, and Macromedia Director. Included on the CD-ROM are the MediaLink software, an instruction manual, and sample lessons created with the software in a variety of disciplines. As far as we know, no other computer literacy text comes with a multimedia authoring package ready for teachers and students to use with about two hours of preparation. Instructors may find MediaLink an appropriate multimedia software application to add to laboratory components of their computer literacy courses.

Among other resources included on the CD-ROM available to teachers are the following:

- an *Instructor's Manual* with further suggestions for covering and expanding on materials in the text.
- *PassPort Multimedia Software*, a collection of multimedia programs for Windows using text, graphics, photos, animation, and sound to enhance and extend the information provided in the text. One set of lessons introduces productivity tool concepts, and another provides interesting explorations of new products and technologies.

Besides the materials on the CD-ROM, John Wiley & Sons makes available to instructors:

- Instructor's Resource Guide which includes 1) the hardcopy of the Instructor's Manual and 2) a test bank of approximately 75 questions per chapter, including multiple-choice, true-false, and fill-in-the-blanks.
- *MicroTest*, a computerized version of the Test Bank, available in both IBM and Macintosh versions.
- *Acetate Transparencies* of 50 full-color figures of key text illustrations and tables.
- *How Multimedia Computers Work*, a multimedia presentation on CD-ROM for Windows computers presenting the inside story of computer hardware in a vivid and entertaining instructional mode.

In addition, Wiley offers the *Getting Started* series, an extensive selection of applications manuals. These concise, yet complete, manuals offer readers a step-by-step, hands-on introduction to popular DOS and Windows applications programs. Most come with a data disk containing sample files and all with a wealth of exercises and screen dumps. When packaged with this text, the manuals are offered at a discounted price. Contact your local Wiley representative for specific information.

## ▶ Acknowledgments

I would like to acknowledge the extensive help and advice that I have received at all stages of preparation for this new edition. My editor, Beth Lang Golub, strongly agrees with me that there is a place for this kind of up-to-date "computers and society" textbook in the literacy field and has been foremost in making helpful suggestions in carrying out the revision. In-house Wiley people—Hilary Newman in Photo Research, Jeanine Furino in Production, Anna Melhorn in Illustration, and Leslie Hines in Marketing—are due special thanks for shepherding the project through its several stages in record time.

At South Carolina, Robert L. Cannon, Chair in Computer Science, has always supported my efforts in computer literacy and offered release time for manuscript preparation of the Second Edition on an incredibly tight deadline. Dean Jerome D. Odom assumed his post as the first edition came out and has enthusiastically supported its current revision. Members of the MediaLink development team, especially Reginald A. Riser and Jay A. Waller, have done superior work in the planning and execution of the CD-ROM supplement. Other members, including Mark Bloemeke, Clif Presser, and Michael Williamson, have helped over the years to get computer illustrations ready for publication. My graduate assistant and teaching colleague Christopher Eason has worked closely with me this time around on an improved Instructor's Manual and Test Bank. My sons, current students at Rice and Williams, helped with some of the early revisions, especially to the new instructional Web pages. Thanks are also due to colleagues at other colleges and universities who provided useful suggestions for improvement in the revision, including:

Robert Gearhart
Ithaca College

Fred Hanzelin
South Suburban College

Fred C. Homeyer
Angelo State University

Larry Lagerstrom
University of California—Berkeley

James C. Miller
Bradley University

Bradford Morgan
South Dakota School of Mines and
   Technology

Peter Wegner
Brown University

Finally I owe my family an apology for another six months of putting up with piles of books and articles on the study floor and a lot of hours monopolizing the home computer. If our experience is any guide, every family needs to have at least two computers, for personal work and schoolwork at home, and two phone lines, for personal calls and access to the Internet.

*Robert L. Oakman*

# Contents

## Chapter 3.  Computers in Society: The Drawbacks  56

## Chapter 4.  Computer Hardware  75

# CHAPTER 1

# Computer Literacy: A Current Perspective

▶ **LEARNING OUTCOMES**

*After completing this chapter, you should be able to:*

1. *Describe the uses of computers in various academic disciplines.*

2. *Trace the evolution of the term* computer: *from electronic calculator to general-purpose information processing device to multimedia machine.*

3. *Understand the jargon that surrounds personal computers.*

4. *Discuss the value of computer literacy today—in daily life, college study, and careers.*

5. *Describe analogous relationships between the computer and the human mind.*

6. *Explain how the generality and flexibility of the personal computer make it such a powerful multimedia and network tool for many areas of application.*

▶ **COMPUTERS IN CONTEXT**

*Without leaving their dorm rooms at night, students taking American literature from Professor Daniel Anderson at the University of Texas can attend "classes" on Frank Norris's naturalistic novel,* McTeague, *or Lorraine Hanberry's play,* A Raisin in the Sun. *Using a personal computer, they access the "UT Austin Lecture Hall" on the University's* World Wide Web *(called both the* Web *and* WWW) *site on the* Internet, *where a wide variety of class materials and discussion groups for many classes are available on-line at any hour of the day or night. Opening up the lesson on* McTeague, *they can read the text on the screen, see a discussion of a silent movie classic based on the book, read papers about major ideas in the novel like social Darwinism or naturalism written by their classmates, and even add their own analyses and critical interpretations. In addition to these on-line sessions on the World Wide Web, they also attend the live lectures given by Professor Anderson; but materials offered on the Web for viewing supplement the live class, especially the reactions to the literary works done by fellow students. The on-line forum provided by access to the Web Lecture Hall supports the concept of peer teaching: that students can learn from their peers just as they can from the teacher. In this interactive mode, everyone is a learner investigating the literary responses to the American experience through great works of literature. (See Figure 1-1.)*

**FIGURE 1-1** A group of three students in American literature at the University of Texas created this Web page to discuss major themes in Frank Norris's naturalistic novel called *McTeague* about a dentist. When the page was loaded onto the class Web site, all of the other students in the class could read these students' responses to the novel.

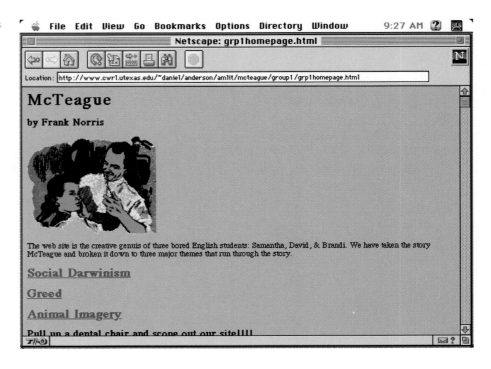

**Internet:** The largest network of interconnected computers in the world and the most common name for the Information Superhighway.

**World Wide Web (the Web, WWW):** The most popular part of the Internet today, a method of storing and distributing materials in several media over the network so that it can be viewed with browser software on a personal computer.

**on-line:** A term used to describe being connected to a computer network, often at a remote location.

The "Lecture Hall" at UT Austin is a pioneering large-scale college effort to make course materials available on the **Internet** in a variety of media and fields from chemistry to French to geography to social work, in all more than twenty-five departments. Different faculty members create course materials for distribution throughout the campus on the **World Wide Web,** including course syllabi, assignments, lecture notes, discussion circles, and even examinations. Not only can students at UT Austin view these materials, but anyone with a Web account on the Internet anywhere in the world can look in on what is being taught. A personal computer with a connection to the Internet offers unparalleled possibilities for receiving content materials and then provides a way for students to give interactive feedback to the teacher and other student colleagues. Few universities offer such diversity of **WWW** courses as Texas, but the trend toward **on-line** offerings is spreading quickly throughout higher education.

## Computers in Academia

In today's colleges and universities students are learning to use computers in all disciplines. As evidence of the increasing importance of the computer on campus, a major state university completed a survey of planning for student computing needs in the late 1990s. A faculty committee interviewed colleagues from every college and professional school on the campus and found a unanimous response. Students and faculty in all liberal arts fields from art through zoology, and in professional programs from library science and criminal justice to nursing and law, were already using computers in their educational programs. The committee found no dissent among the faculty that all students were expected to have computer experience as an integral part of their education. They would continue to have increasing needs for the machines in all subjects in the future, both in school and in the professions that follow their training.

Computers used for distribution of lessons on the World Wide Web represent only one sort of application found throughout college and university curricula. **Applications software** is a category of computer **programs** that run on personal computers for various applications; the machines themselves are denoted by the term **hardware.** The following examples are suggestive of innovative computer uses in current research and teaching projects found in many areas of higher education today. They illustrate how the spectrum of computer applications software packages can fit a variety of educational goals.

## DATABASE MANAGEMENT

A distinguished classics scholar at Oxford University inherited a massive file of index cards containing inscriptions and notes from Greek tomb monuments in ancient Asia Minor. An old scholar friend had collected this material in the 1930s, and it had languished in boxes for years. The cards contained descriptions and designs of the tombs, plus all the writings in Latin or Greek that could be read on them. There were also notes about the decorations found on the tombs.

Although little is known of kinship relationships of the Hellenistic period, the inscriptions suggest that daughters often built tombs in honor of their fathers, and sons for their mothers. The professor wanted to study this tomb culture in some detail, especially the complex kinship relations it embodies, in order to produce a book on Hellenistic tombs. Because of the size of the card file, she turned to the computer to store, sort, and retrieve the information in order to test a number of complex hypotheses about family structures. The tasks for which she was using the computer fall into the general category of **database management,** the computer equivalent of her index cards and filing system (Oakman).

## COMPUTER-ASSISTED INSTRUCTION

For English speakers, Chinese is a difficult language to read because of the unfamiliar characters which make it up. Unlike Western languages, it is not made up of letters representing sounds, which combine to make words. Individual Chinese characters stand alone as both words and pronouncible units. Beginners need to know how to recognize and write about 3,000 basic characters before they can expect to read elementary texts.

Teachers have always tried to discover successful methods to teach the basic character vocabulary. A computer program developed at Dartmouth College is helping to make this process easier. On the computer screen as they are working on a vocabulary lesson, students can choose several options: to see the character drawn by animation with proper strokes of the pen; to hear the character pronounced; to see the English definition; or to get a spelling of the word in Western letters. They work through the character lists at their own pace and choose the information embodied in the program as they want or need it. The program, which combines graphics, sound, and word processing in its presentation, is an example of multimedia software. Designed for foreign language instruction, it falls into the category of **drill-and-practice educational software,** a major type of **computer-assisted instruction (CAI).** (See Figure 1-2.)

## SIMULATIONS

Biology students often study living ecosystems in which a large number of variables interact with each other and change over time. Because such dynamic systems are difficult to examine firsthand in the laboratory, teach-

**applications software:** A program for a personal computer designed to carry out a common user need, such as word processing or a spreadsheet program.

**program:** A set of instructions that tells a computer what to do. Programs are often read from a diskette or a hard drive but sometimes are already resident in the computer's central memory.

**hardware:** Any computer machinery that performs information-processing functions.

**database management:** Software to encode, organize, manipulate, search for, and retrieve data stored in a database.

**drill-and-practice educational software:** Instructional computer programs that drill students on materials for mastery, such as foreign language grammar exercises.

**computer-assisted instruction (CAI):** The use of computers in some form for instruction, such as drill-and-practice in foreign languages.

**FIGURE 1-2** The Hanzi Assistant program from Dartmouth presents the Chinese character on the right and draws it in proper stroke order on the left. The button for voicing the character has two little dialogue symbols, male and female. Clicking this button, the user can hear the character spoken by a man's or a woman's voice or both.

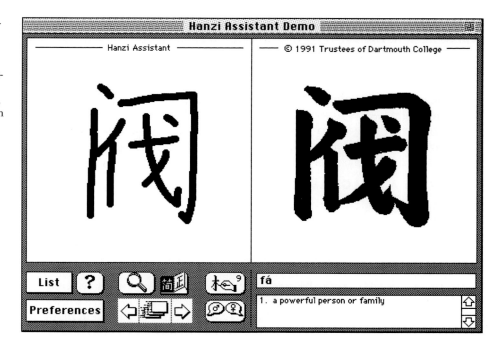

**simulation software:** A computer program that imitates a process or set of activities, such as an organic chemical reaction or an environmental disaster.

ers find that **simulation software** is particularly effective for understanding them. Simulations in biology allow students the opportunity to study the information about ecosystems, test their assumptions, explore alternative interactions, and watch the simulated results of their decisions.

A program called Environmental Decision Making, developed as a part of Project BioQUEST, includes materials about plant producers, recycling of materials, animal consumers, transformations of energy, and interactions with the human environment. With the computer, students can change the parameters, build up increasingly complex ecosystems, and simulate the activity in the ecosystems to see their function, change, and productivity. The simulation permits the students to gain understanding about how different variables interact in a global ecosystem—without leaving the computer ("Technologies for Education"). (See Figure 1-3.)

Most students today have no context for what ordinary life was like in France during the reign of the Sun King, Louis XIV. The lifestyle choices of people who lived in this age of absolute monarchy in the seventeenth century, a hundred years before the French Revolution, are very different from today. For several years, French history students of Professor Carolyn Lougee of Stanford University have been able to use a computer program called The Would-Be Gentleman (Intellimation), which simulates social conditions of life in seventeenth-century France. The simulation program is designed to give students a flavor of the different personal decisions which faced a young man of the bourgeoisie as he tried to take his inheritance from his father and make his way up in society. Questions about property and money management are balanced in the computer program with particular social decisions unique to the time: the choice of a proper wife and dowry, and the need for a powerful and influential patron to advance one's cause in society. Biographies of historical figures like Cardinal Mazarin are included in the program.

To begin, the student makes a series of choices about income, investment, and social ambition. The program then simulates the passage of time and calculates the outcomes of these decisions. The player's choices may add to his riches and prestige or perhaps adversely affect his financial and social standing. For example, if the player seeks a wife too high on the social ladder early in the game, when his financial resources are low, he will be rebuffed socially for several years and must remain a bachelor or marry below his station. As time passes, students learn from their trials how to adapt to a social system very different from modern times in a clever and entertaining historical game. They can appreciate the interactions of social forces unknown today through the ability of the computer program to interrelate social and economic decisions and show the results. Because doing is more effective than telling, this computer simulation provides a unique personal opportunity to experience aspects of a bygone era that cannot be fully understood from books or lectures. (See Figure 1-4.)

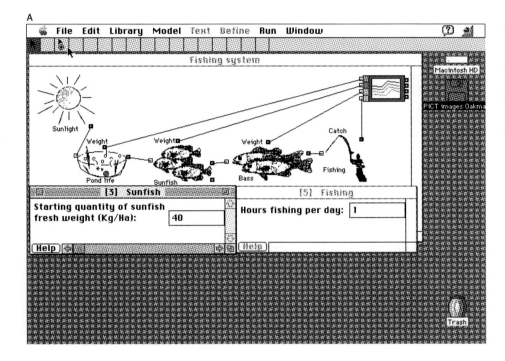

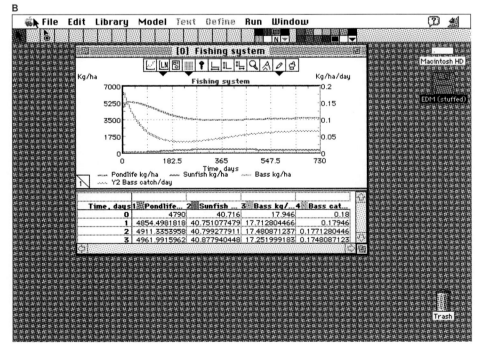

**FIGURE 1-3** The Environmental Decision Making (EDM) module of Project BioQUEST allows students (A) to change the number of fish in a lake and the number of hours that people fish there (B) to see how these factors interact to affect the equilibrium of the lake itself, including its ability to support pondlife.

**FIGURE 1-4** At this point in The Would-Be Gentleman simulation, the main character is thirty-six years old and has become the father of a son. His current wealth and investment possibilities are shown at the left.

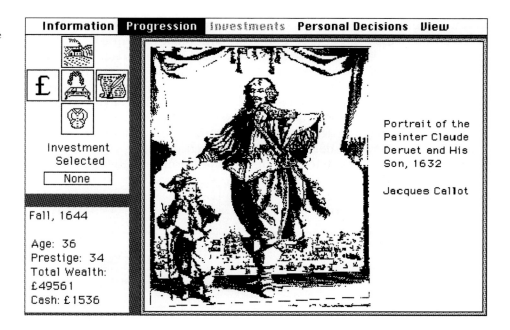

Information   Progression   Investments   Personal Decisions   View

£

Investment
Selected

None

Fall, 1644

Age: 36
Prestige: 34
Total Wealth:
£49561
Cash: £1536

Portrait of the
Painter Claude
Deruet and His
Son, 1632

Jacques Callot

## ▶ *Fundamental Concepts of Computing*

The primary computer for most users in today's world is the personal computer, first developed about twenty-five years ago. Yet the history of modern computers began more than four decades ago. Before concentrating on essential elements of modern personal computers, let us trace how ideas of what constitutes mainstream computing have changed over the years.

### EVOLUTION OF THE COMPUTER

**HISTORY**

**computer:** An electrical machine system capable of accepting data in symbolic form and processing them. The results are normally produced as output in some form.

**software:** The suite of programs that enables a computer system to process data, including both the operating system and a variety of application programs.

**special-purpose computer:** A computer dedicated to a single purpose, such as a digital watch.

**mainframe:** The first commercial computers in the 1950s: large, fast, and of general application. Today they are widely used as central or host computers in large institutions.

In 1969, *The American Heritage Dictionary* defined a **computer** as "an electronic machine that performs high-speed mathematical or logical calculations or that assembles, stores, correlates, or otherwise processes and prints information derived from coded data in accordance with a predetermined program." The emphasis was on the *mathematical nature of computer processing* carried out in the hardware under the control of the computer program, also called **software.**

The common public conception that the computer is a complex calculating machine goes back to its origins in the Second World War and continues today in the connotations of the word *computer* itself. The first computers were used to calculate mathematical firing tables for naval rockets but the modern computer is far more than a glorified calculator. In fact, the French term for computer, *ordinateur*, more accurately conveys the general concept of processing that the machine embodies. Derived from the Latin verb *ordinare*, meaning "to order," *ordinateur* emphasizes the broad sense of information processing that today's computers embody. The machine is a wonderfully fast and accurate calculator; but it can also process text, encode pictures and sound, and sense changes in movement and touch. Moreover, it can produce output of processed data in all these forms, and more.

Today computers come in all sizes and prices for all kinds of uses, from **special-purpose computers** that control cars, cameras, microwave ovens, and other commonly used devices to large **mainframe machines** in universities and scientific institutions that cost several million dollars (Figure 1-5a). Special-purpose computers are engineered to do specific jobs, like setting times and temperature ranges in the microwave, and are embedded in the appliance itself. Continually evolving from the first commercial successes in the 1950s, like UNIVAC I and the IBM 704/705 series, mainframes are the oldest kind of **general-purpose computer.** They accept a variety of programs and are typically used today for large-scale mathematical or statistical calculation or business accounting for a large organization. Smaller versions of the mainframe idea are called **minicomputers,** so-called because they were miniature mainframes when introduced in the 1960s. A typical university computer center has a staff of people who program and supervise the running of the mainframe, and many large science departments operate their own minicomputer installation.

**general-purpose computer:** A computer suitable for being programmed for a wide variety of tasks or applications.

**minicomputer:** A computer category between a mainframe and a microcomputer in terms of size, cost, and processing power.

**FIGURE 1-5A** A mainframe computer like the IBM ES/9000 is most often housed in a central computer facility and is accessible to users with terminals at remote sites.

**FIGURE 1-5B** A personal desktop computer like the Gateway 2000 can be used as a standalone machine or connected to others in a network. Notice the tower design and speakers for multimedia use.

**FIGURE 1-5C** Laptop computers, as their name implies, are small and very easy to transport.

A

B

C

**FIGURE 1-6** The overall growth of PCs in the United States has increased steadily in the last 15 years.

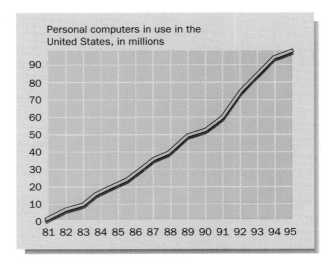

## THE PERSONAL COMPUTER

**personal computer (microcomputer or PC):** The least expensive and most common computer system in use today, built around a microprocessor and used mainly by one person at a time.

**laptop:** A portable computer: small, lightweight, and powered by either batteries or line current.

**microprocessor:** The central processor of a personal computer, often called the **chip.** In the U.S., Intel and Motorola make the most popular ones used in IBM-compatibles and Macintoshes.

Yet the computer most familiar to the public is the general-purpose **personal computer,** sometimes called the **microcomputer.** Developed after the mini in the 1970s, this computer for everybody is typically a machine small enough to sit on a desk, inexpensive enough for offices and individuals to own, and flexible enough in its design to be used for a variety of applications. Others are **laptops,** smaller and lighter with the power of a desktop model and the portability to fit into a briefcase. Prices range from several hundred dollars to several thousand, depending on machine features. All these machines are called microcomputers because they are based internally on the architecture of the **microprocessor.** Also called the **chip,** this processor forms the central core of the hardware in the modern personal computer (Figures 1-5B and C).

## COMPUTER JARGON

As the last two paragraphs suggest, computer science, like all technical fields, is filled with a wealth of terminology that is often confusing to stu-

**FIGURE 1-7** The major functional components of a computer: input, processing, storage, and output.

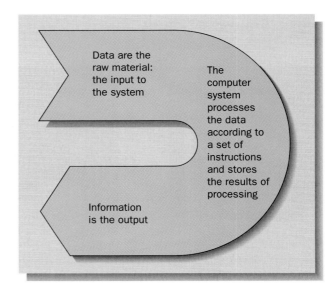

Data are the raw material: the input to the system

The computer system processes the data according to a set of instructions and stores the results of processing

Information is the output

dents and the general public. Computer advertisements in newspapers and magazines are filled with jargon and abbreviations bewildering to many readers. There is a perception that only those within the computer community should be able to understand this kind of technobabble. Yet with a little help, the average person can decipher even a newspaper advertisement for a personal computer, like the one shown on page 10, with its cryptic abbreviations. In fact, all essential elements of a personal computer system are referenced in the ad, if one knows how to decode the abbreviations.

To read the ad, one must be familiar with hardware and software concepts involved in all computer processes. For instance, **data** for analysis, whether words in word processing or figures on a graphic image, represent **input** to the computer. Inside the machine the data information goes first into **storage** and then is transferred to the microprocessor chip for **processing.** Finally the processed data are ready for some form of **output,** perhaps to be displayed on a **computer screen** (or **monitor**) or sent to a **printer.** The cycle of input, processing, and output is often called the **throughput** process. (See Figure 1-7.)

## UNDERSTANDING A COMPUTER AD

Given this background, we can examine the advertisement shown in Figure 1-8, typical of those found in metropolitan daily newspapers. It lists savings on various models of personal computers built with chips manufactured by Intel, the world leader (note the trademark "intel inside"). The first popular Intel machine was the IBM Personal Computer, or PC, based on the 8088 chip. Subsequent Intel processors, installed by many companies in computers sometimes called IBM-compatible, are identified by their numbers 286, 386, 486, and Pentium.

Both computers offered in the ad are Pentium models, though real bargains are often found on Intel 486 machines. Not only are Pentium processors considerably larger and faster than 486s, but with each processor there are models with different speeds, identified by the quoted megahertz (MHz) ranges. Megahertz speed measures the number of internal processor clock ticks (millions of cycles per second) and provides a rough guide to the number of operations the computer can carry out in a unit of time. The higher the megahertz rating, the more powerful and expensive the processor, and consequently the computer that is built around it. The less expensive Pentium in the ad has a 75 MHz rating, whereas the upgrade uses an improved processor that is almost twice as fast at 133 MHz. The differences in cost of the two Pentium systems reflect updates in configuring the chip during the design stage for added speed and performance.

## HARDWARE COMPONENTS

Other hardware in the ad is shared by both systems, but the jargon gets technical very quickly. For input the systems come with a typical 104-character **keyboard** and a **mouse,** a device used for pointing, drawing, and selecting items on the computer screen. All this is standard today. The color computer monitor, used for output of results to the screen, has a 14-inch diagonal diameter. An NI (non-interlaced) monitor produces better quality output with less flicker on the screen than less expensive models and is needed for multimedia. The decimal number .28 attached to the NI monitor refers to its dot pitch, a measure of picture quality. The lower the decimal, the more crisp the color resolution. Also included in the multimedia production kit are hardware for input and output of sounds: a special circuit board called SoundBlaster 16 for creation and playback of stereo sound and a set of stereo speakers.

**data:** A general term for numbers, letters, and other symbols processed by a computer to produce information.

**input:** The process of transferring data into a computer system for storage and processing.

**storage:** Another term for memory, a hardware device for storing binary data and programs.

**processing:** Manipulation of data by a computer that results in quick and efficient information.

**output:** Transferring data processed by a computer system to a hardware device like a monitor or a diskette for display or storage.

**computer screen** or **monitor:** A device similar to a television screen for displaying the output of a computer. Also called a video display terminal (VDT) or cathode ray tube (CRT).

**printer:** The most common output device for PCs used to create printed reports.

**throughput:** The computer cycle of inputting data, processing them, and outputting the information produced, analogous to the stimulus/response cycle in the body.

**keyboard:** A common input device for entering data into a computer; similar to a typewriter.

**mouse:** A hand-controlled hardware device that is slid around a desktop for selecting and drawing items on the computer screen, thereby reducing the need to type all commands.

**FIGURE 1-8** Typical advertisement for personal computers.

**random access memory (RAM):**
The primary internal storage device of a personal computer, where programs and data are kept during processing.

Both models come with four pieces of equipment related to the storage of data: internal RAM memory, a floppy disk drive, a hard disk drive, and a CD-ROM drive. **Random access memory (RAM)** stores data as they are being shuffled into and out of the processor. In general, the larger the RAM, the faster the results. For modern graphics applications, an Intel

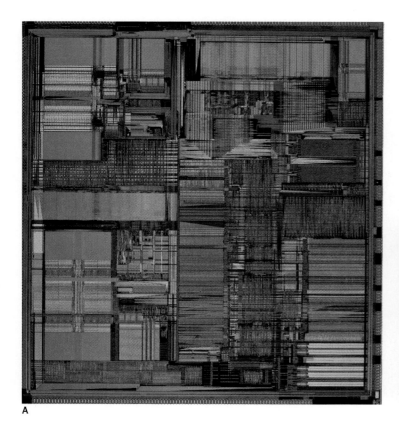

A

B

**FIGURE 1-9A** This state-of-the-art Pentium chip from Intel, used in the best Intel machines of today, holds 3.3 million transistors.

**FIGURE 1-9B** Given the size of these different versions of the Pentium chip, it is hard to imagine that they each contain millions of electronic circuits.

computer needs at least 8 megabytes (8 MB) of RAM. One **megabyte** of storage can contain a million characters of information, about 500 pages of typed text. For an additional charge users often add 8 additional megabytes of RAM on Pentium computers for a total of 16 MB, making them especially suitable for memory-intensive multimedia applications.

Users insert diskettes into the computer in the **floppy disk drive,** a slot prominently visible on the front of the machine. The computers in the ad have a floppy drive that can read diskettes holding 1.44 megabytes of data, a current industry standard. The **CD-ROM drive** can read programs and other materials, often video games and archives of information like encyclopedias, distributed on CD-ROMs, which can hold more than 600 megabytes of materials. A **hard disk drive** provides permanent storage of data when the computer is turned off. As always, the bigger the better. The machines in the ad have a massive one gigabyte (1 Gig) hard drive, not uncommon today. One **gigabyte** (one billion bytes, equivalent to 1,000 megabytes) refers to the drive's ability to store one billion characters of data.

Storage capacity of this magnitude is difficult to imagine: if 1 MB holds 500 pages, then this large hard drive could contain more than 500,000 pages, equivalent to a small library. Reflect for a moment on the meaning of these figures. Only a few years ago a 20-MB hard drive cost $300 to $400. Today the cost of a drive 50 times as large is subsumed in a total system price only about four times as much. In fact, the quantity of information that can be stored in a personal computer today dwarfs the storage of large mainframes of 20 years ago and at affordable costs.

## SOFTWARE COMPONENTS

Of course, the hardware is useless without software programs to run on it, including the **control program,** or **operating system,** that connects the user to the machine. Intel machines have always used operating systems

**megabyte (MB):** A unit of computer storage, equal to approximately 1 million bytes of storage.

**floppy disk drive:** A hardware device that can read data inserted into it from diskettes and write information out onto diskettes. Early diskettes were flexible plastic and called "floppy." Most diskettes today are no longer floppy, but the term stuck for the disk drive that reads them, as opposed to a hard disk drive.

**CD-ROM drive:** Hardware that can access digital data stored on a compact disk by reading it with a laser beam.

**hard disk drive:** A storage device that can store hundreds of millions of characters or more.

**gigabyte (GB):** A measure of main memory or auxiliary storage size, comprising one billion storage positions.

**control program (operating system):** An internal computer program designed to connect the user to the machine and monitor all activity within the machine; also called an operating system.

**FIGURE 1-10** A computer system consists of input devices, main memory and the processor, storage devices, and output devices.

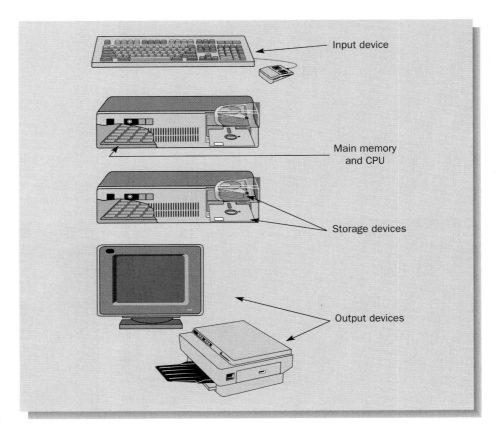

**Windows 95 (Win 95):** A new operating system introduced in 1995 into the Microsoft family of Windows software for personal computers. It includes numerous improvements over DOS-based Windows 3.1.

**FIGURE 1-11** Today's desktop computer has a variety of input and output devices. This multimedia computer has input CD-ROM and diskette drives included into the processor case and stereo speakers built into the color screen unit, allowing for sound and graphic output.

from Microsoft to communicate between user and processor. The most recent operating system for personal computers from Microsoft is called **Windows 95,** greatly upgraded from its predecessor, Windows 3.1. Today's standard for Intel computers, Windows 95 relies heavily on mem-

ory-intensive graphics and needs a large RAM memory to run efficiently. A copy of Windows 95 is loaded into the hardware, so that the customer is ready to use this very popular operating system as soon as the computer is set up.

For most users, choosing applications software for a hardware package may be the most important aspect of the purchase. In fact, one of the rules of thumb for first-time buyers of a personal computer is to look first at the software that it supports efficiently, rather than worrying about all the technical specifications of different chips and disk drives. A buyer of one of these advertised machines gets a lot of software bundled into the purchase price. Although some of the smaller programs may be distributed on several diskettes, most of this software will be encoded on CD-ROMs delivered with the purchase. Microsoft Office combines in one package the most frequent applications programs used by owners of personal computers: **word processing** for text preparation, **spreadsheets** for budgeting, and a database management package for file applications. Also included is a selection of Microsoft CD-ROMs for home entertainment and education: MS-Flight is a flight simulator, Encarta a very popular multimedia encyclopedia, and MS-Money home budgeting software. In other words, a user will be ready for productive work or leisure as soon as these systems have been set up. Other types of applications software, such as a program for user-created graphics, can also be purchased separately. They will run well on either of the computer systems offered in the ad and will make the machine an even better productivity tool.

At present, these Intel-based, Windows 95 computers (in the current jargon, **Wintel** machines) are quite typical of workaday systems offered at computer stores throughout the country, both in features and prices. Apple Macintosh computers offer similar features in the same price range, and low-cost Unix workstations are available for a few hundred dollars more. Not many years ago, Intel-based computers with much less power and flexibility cost twice as much. It seems that with every passing year, the prices of processors and memory devices are cut in half as their power is doubled. *There is no best time to buy a personal computer,* since next year's machine will offer more features, speed, or convenience for the same money. This trend has been true for at least the last decade, and is expected to continue, if not accelerate, because the technology is changing and improving so rapidly. If you are planning to buy a personal computer, look for one that will fit your personal needs for a few years. By then, something not currently designed but bigger and better will probably be available at a similar cost.

**FIGURE 1-12** Many software packages today are distributed on CD-ROMs, which hold much more information than diskettes. The CorelDRAW! graphics package includes the software and a large file of images stored on the CD-ROM, along with manuals and instructions inside the box.

**word processing software:** Any of many popular application programs designed for composing, revising, printing, and filing written documents.

**spreadsheet:** Software that can represent data in a row-and-column format and can manipulate them like an electronic ledger sheet.

**Wintel:** A modern acronym for a computer system containing an Intel microprocessor and a Microsoft Windows operating system.

## Computer Literacy for the 1990s

Knowing the elements of a modern personal computer represents only one possible aspect of computer literacy today. Twenty-five years ago courses in computer literacy almost always included a strong component of computer programming on mainframe machines. The heyday of applications software for many practical jobs lay ahead in the development of the personal computer revolution. Today the value of computing and the scope of computer literacy touch all aspects of society—daily life, college life, and all kinds of careers.

### EVOLUTION OF COMPUTER LITERACY

Asked about studying computers, many people respond that because they were never good at mathematics in school, they will surely have a rough time. Nevertheless, in recent years there has been considerable discussion of the concept of computer literacy: what it is and why it is important. What can a field initially thought of as mathematical have to do with literacy? Should the term mean the ability to read computer programs much as one learns to read a book—the definition of book literacy in current usage? Or perhaps it only implies the ability to understand a computer advertisement, like the one discussed. In the past those with the ability to create computer programs were the people who could understand and use computers. Only computer scientists, engineers, and the like were thought to be among these computer literates in the popular mind.

In the early years of the personal computer, advertisements claimed that everyone should become computer literate. National advertising campaigns of a decade ago touted the home computer as an essential appliance for every family. Many people rushed out to get their model, only to find that it sat idle in the corner most of the time. Most were used for video games or word processing, but general usage for budgets, cataloging recipes, and designing cross-stitch patterns never really caught on with the consumer public. Most of those inexpensive and limited early models have disappeared, not just because more powerful machines were developed to supersede them. In most cases, the average American household was not ready to jump wholeheartedly into the home computer revolution.

But for some people the personal computer was liberating. They not only switched from typewriting to word processing; they also computerized their tax records and used long-distance communications services to get information on stocks, airline schedules, and consumer reports. Not usually engineering types, some of them moved on to become programmers themselves or at least learned how to personalize their applications packages, like word processing, for their own needs. Some became true computer enthusiasts, perhaps even **hackers** on the Internet addicted to computing at long distance through telephone connections. Many others just found ways to integrate personal computers creatively into their daily lives at home and at work. The advent of the personal microcomputer had spawned a self-educated, computer-literate generation.

Meanwhile, much of the American public has remained unaware of the extent to which the computer revolution has been making changes in all of daily life. The automated bank teller window on the corner, the scanner at the supermarket checkout, the funny-looking numbers at the bottom of checks, and the electronic counter lying across the expressway at rush hour are all feeding information to various computers, which modify and control the way we live our lives every day. The media tout the Information Superhighway, but many people do not know what it offers. In the home, the microwave oven is controlled by a computer chip, and in new cars antilock brakes are, in fact, totally computerized. The microchip has been incorporated into most home electronics, from the compact disk player to the automated alarm system and the touch-tone telephone.

Should everyone be computer literate about how all these circuits work? What is the relationship between the microchip and the instructional computer program that Susie is using in her middle school class? Should the perennial complaint to the educational establishment, "Why can't Johnny read?" be expanded to include "Why can't Johnny compute?"

**HISTORY**

**hacker:** A computer user addicted to long-distance computing with data communications software, sometimes illegally tapping into government or industry computer systems.

## COMPUTER LITERACY TODAY

For readers of this book, the question really boils down to this: What should computer literacy mean for college students at the end of the twentieth century? How much detail about this machine should general students know? Where do we draw the line between the programmer, the amateur user of a personal computer, the student in school, the professional in the workplace, and the designer of computer chips? Why has the computer become such a pervasive influence in modern life? What are the implications of this development?

The perspective to be followed in this book is to answer these questions in several ways. Let us think of the three essential elements of modern computing as an equilateral triangle with hardware and software as the sides of the figure and the people who use them and are affected by them at the bottom. Our goal in computer literacy is not to make programmers or data processing professionals of our readers, but to make them aware of the machine, its technological nature, its societal impact, and its potential for use in their professional careers, no matter what their majors. Students can become literate about the fundamental concepts of computing and the computer's impact on all aspects of life. They should be able to open up a new program for a personal computer, read the manual, and get started with it on their own. They should also understand the advantages and disadvantages of computers, and the choices that the machines afford them and society at large, today and in the future. In fact, the metaphor of the Computer Triangle—hardware, software, and their connection to people—provides the major theme of this book.

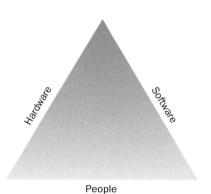

As a working definition of computer literacy, let us begin with the following goals. (The chapters in which the goals are addressed are noted in parentheses.)

- to see the broad range of computer application in all areas of academic and professional life today (Chapters 1 and 2)
- to appreciate the positive and negative effects of the computer revolution on the modern world—the so-called "computers and society" issues (Chapters 2 and 3)
- to grasp fundamental concepts of computer hardware, software, and their connection to people, the third element of the Computer Triangle (Chapters 4 and 5)
- to become familiar with a variety of applications software programs currently used with microcomputers, including word processing, spreadsheets, databases, and computer graphics, and to understand how to apply them for personal and scholarly purposes (Chapters 6–9)
- to examine the fast-developing frontier of the Internet, sometimes called the Information Superhighway, to understand how it will change the ways people receive and access information (Chapter 10)
- to identify emerging trends in computing, including artificial intelligence, to convey a sense of how the machine will continue to affect our lives in the future (Chapters 11 and 12)

In other words, a course in computer literacy should be comprehensive, up to date, and relevant to future careers and personal lives in a world filled with computers. Many students view this sort of computer awareness to be an important, indeed essential requirement of higher education in today's high-technology society. The remarks of one student majoring in exercise physiology are typical of many:

> *I see a time when all majors being taught in colleges and universities throughout the country will be a combination of whatever the particular field of study is and computer science. The reason for this will be that*

*computers will be so tied in with our society that no professional will be able to function effectively without a thorough knowledge of them. . . . It would be very wise for [students] attending college today to familiarize themselves with computers as much as they possibly can. The more you know about them, the less you will have to fear that they will someday replace you. Hopefully, everyone will one day think of them as irreplaceable tools for the betterment of society, rather than incomprehensible piles of machinery that were created to replace man.*

It is this vision of computer literacy that this book sets out to fulfill.

## ▶ The Computer and the Mind

Computers are one of the most powerful tools humans have yet devised to increase their capacity to do things they have always wanted or needed to do. Among earlier tools, Gutenberg's printing press spread ideas of the Renaissance and Reformation throughout western Europe; Galileo's telescope showed that the earth was not at the center of the universe; and Leeuwenhoek's microscope revealed secrets about how body and mind worked. Aside from the book, the computer is arguably the most important tool in the world today.

### BRAIN RESEARCH

Why is the computer such a universal and powerful tool? In order to answer this question, let us look first at the human mind and examine the current understanding of how it works. The human animal is the most marvelous machine in the universe as we know it; and it is distinguished from the rest of the animal kingdom especially by its brain. Besides managing the body's involuntary functions, like breathing and digestion, without conscious effort, the brain absorbs a vast array of sensory data—sight, sound, touch, taste, and smell—which it decodes, understands, and responds to. Some of this material is recorded in memory, while the rest is quickly forgotten.

Modern thinking divides the hemispheres of the cerebrum into the left and right brain, joined by a vast bundle of neural connections called the corpus callosum. The left brain is mostly responsible for logical and symbolic relationships, and seems to be the center for understanding written and oral language. Processing in this hemisphere takes place in a parallel fashion (neurons send out multiple signals simultaneously), even though logical processes that people normally think of as sequential or serial in nature reside there.

The more unfamiliar right brain seems responsible for decoding spatial relations, such as the visual recognition of shapes, as well as for music and emotion. It seems to work by holistic processing—that is, by forming a general overall impression. For example, people easily recognize patterns of letters on the printed page; but computers are less accurate at character recognition, a right-brain function (Crick).

Recent research indicates that neat characterizations of the brain's function (left brain for reasoning and right brain for intuition) are somewhat too simplistic. The corpus callosum is so interwoven between the two halves that each receives and communicates sensory signals to the other, and each adds its mode of interpretation to the mind's final understanding of the sensory message.

## BRAIN-COMPUTER ANALOGIES

Frequently modern writings on the brain use the computer as an analogy to compare and contrast with the workings and functions of the brain. Both process electrical signals, though those in the brain are organically produced, while the computer's are generated by power stations or batteries. Both have large memory banks, though the memory of the brain is vastly larger—perhaps 100 billion neurons and 100 trillion synapses, compared to several billion memory locations in a computer. Most computer processes take place in a serial fashion, like logic, one piece of data at a time. Often the computer is faster than the brain at these transfers. Newer computer hardware designs, however, act more like the multiple parallel processes of the brain, but with many fewer than the trillions of connections in the human mind. Of course, the brain is a living organism, whereas the computer is a created electrical device without a life of its own (Hubel). Yet scientists have predicted organic computer chips in the future that may behave like living matter.

The most complete analogy between brain and computer focuses on how the two machines process materials from the outside world, although the details of how it is done clearly differ. Both accept input from outside, process it in some fashion, and produce some kind of output, or response to what they were given to process. If you accidentally touch a hot stove, the brain quickly senses the pain and jerks the hand away. Hearing your teacher ask you to open your book to a certain page entails processing the verbal request and making the appropriate response, or output. This

The brain processes the hot sensation and removes the hand quickly from the burner.

The processor located inside the computer receives keystroke signals and displays the message.

**FIGURE 1-13** The stimulus/response cycle in perception is analogous to throughput in a computer.

**stimulus/response:** A common psychological way to describe the cycle of response in the human body to external sensations as mediated by the brain. Analogous to the throughput process in computers.

**Universal Product Code (UPC):** A bar code printed on most consumer goods that indicates the manufacturer of the good as well as the product itself. It can be read by a scanner input device for computer processing.

**binary coding:** A system for representing information in a computer with two states of electromagnetic phenomena, which can be denoted by the binary digits 1 and 0.

**computer graphics:** The methods and techniques for creating and displaying pictures or images on computer screens or other output devices like printers or plotters.

**fuzzy logic:** A field of artificial intelligence in which computers analyze logical relationships that are more or less true, in contrast to ordinary logic, where relations are more crisp.

**multimedia machine:** A term for a modern computer, a general-purpose symbol-manipulating device capable of processing and displaying a variety of output, such as sounds and video.

**artificial intelligence:** A field of computer science concerned with the possibility that the computer can carry out applications that seem to be intelligent human behavior.

process, termed the throughput process in computer science, is called **stimulus/response** in human perception.

As in the stimulus-response model, the computer scanner at the supermarket reads the strange series of lines on a can of beans (called the **Universal Product Code,** or **UPC**), looks up the price in its memory, flashes it on the register, and adds it to the running total of the bill. One input triggers several outputs. When you hit a key in word processing, the electrical signal for the character is sent to the microprocessor, which then displays it on the screen, and more importantly, puts it into working memory, which is accumulating the words of your document. In these two examples, the computer is responding differently to different types of data. Two physically similar electrical devices have been programmed to perform two different tasks.

### THE COMPUTER AS INFORMATION PROCESSOR

Of all humankind's tools, the computer has the most general application, because it works with a system that can represent any kind of information in electromagnetic form. In this system, called **binary coding,** electromagnetic information can be viewed as a series of plus and minus charges, which we shall call binary digits 1 and 0. Anything that can be coded using a set of 1s and 0s can be stored in a computer. All humankind's modes of communicating information can be symbolized in the machine's binary notation: written language, speech, mathematics, music, art, physical phenomena. (See Chapter 4 for a description of how the computer represents all different kinds of information in binary coded form.)

In terms of the brain functions, the computer is usually seen as an analytical, left-brain device. Here would reside its skills with language and mathematics. But it also has spatial capacities in **computer graphics,** including the ability to present colorful, moving visual images with proper perspective in realistic video games. The field of **fuzzy logic,** of considerable research interest in language and mathematics, even appears to give computers an intuitive, right-brain nature. Programmed with fuzzy logic, computers can analyze relationships implicit in something being more or less true—that is, sort of "fuzzy." To say that John is five years old is a crisp logical fact, whereas to call him a young boy involves fuzzy logic. He must be more than a toddler and is probably younger than 10, but exactly how old he is is a relative, fuzzy concept.

We shall deal with all these topics in more detail in later chapters. The point to be made here is that *the computer is a general-purpose symbol-manipulating device,* for which the brain analogy is particularly apt. We might call the computer the truly **multimedia machine.** Ongoing research on parallels between the brain and the computer, which falls within the realm of **artificial intelligence,** suggests fruitful insights forthcoming in both fields. Computers may eventually suggest new ways to order information about the world around us, including our own minds, that will change the way we view the process of understanding. In fact, Edward Fredkin of MIT consciously chose the organic metaphor when he called artificial intelligence "the next step in evolution" (Turkle 242).

## ▶ State of the Art: Multimedia and the Internet

Most observers would agree that the two most exciting trends in personal computing involve the use of multimedia and the growth of popular applications on the Internet. Whereas only a few years ago both were considered pioneering, these areas today are becoming standards in computing;

and the future will surely build upon their current status for more innovative applications.

## MULTIMEDIA

The mind can be viewed as a multimedia organism. Its free association of ideas is true hypermedia. Sometimes one form of sensory experience can call up another image of a different kind for further understanding or additional clarification of the original. In your mind, you might mentally associate a poem with a picture or a piece of music. Some people envision a sense of doom and foreboding when they hear a reading of Poe's "The Raven," with its repeated and haunting refrain, "Nevermore," the sound evoking a visual image. Using a *mnemonic,* an aid to memory, to help you remember something is another instance of human hypermedia. Sometimes people remember the notes on the lines of the treble clef scale with the saying Every Good Boy Does Fine (*EGBDF*) and the spaces between the lines as the word *FACE.* In this case, word examples clarify musical notation.

Modern personal computers can store and process a variety of sensory information. Formerly costly applications in sound, graphics, and video have been developed within the capabilities and budgets of the microcomputer. To refer to programs which integrate at least two media in the same application, the terms **hypertext** and **multimedia** have been coined. (Notice how many technical terms the computer revolution has added to the English language.) Hypertext programs can contain different kinds of information along with text—for instance, sound or pictures—and access them simultaneously, or jump readily from one to the other. In multimedia the base form of information can be any type of data, not just text, to which other kinds of information are linked.

Both television and movies provide forms of multimedia presentation in sight and sound, but their viewers are passive observers watching the presentation unfold. In computing, **interactive multimedia** combines the blending of different types of data—text, sound, and video—with the possibility of user interaction and response. What is to be gained by merging all sorts of media materials on a subject into a common digital format? Two advantages include the ability to link different sorts of resources in creative ways and the capacity of users to view these different sources of information in whatever way they want, which is the interactive edge. The media are integrated via links among resources, where a resource is simply an instance of a media type. A link may exist from one resource to another one, so that the latter resource can be viewed, read, or heard along with the former one by opening the link.

A hypertext document can be a wonderful multimedia tool, blending a variety of related materials into an interactive, highly visual mode of delivery. Software companies have sprung up to exploit hypertext capacities for useful commercial and educational applications. For instance, readers of a hypertext version of an electronic scientific journal, distributed on a CD-ROM for use with a computer, might, for example, open windows that display color graphic animations of experimental results or see a digital photo of a remote site or event. Electronic encyclopedias on CD-ROM, such as Compton, Grolier, and Microsoft Encarta, offer the potential for providing explanatory and enrichment resources with films and pictures not possible in print publication. Readers can move around in the document at their own pace and direction, interacting with the material to expand their knowledge of the original text. Search facilities built into these programs make it easy to find information on a specific topic.

**hypertext:** A computer application that integrates at least one other medium with text, such as sound or graphics.

**multimedia:** A term for integrating several computer media—text, sound, graphics, and video—together in one application, with some kind of navigation system among them.

**interactive multimedia:** A multimedia production produced for access on a computer so that a user can move around among its resources in any order.

**FIGURE 1-14** The entry for Franklin Delano Roosevelt in the *Grolier Multimedia Encyclopedia* offers a variety of multimedia resources besides the text: a color photograph with a voice caption and a short movie clip of an American family gathered around the radio for one of Roosevelt's fireside chats.

## A CD-ROM ENCYCLOPEDIA

Whereas there are hundreds of commercial CD-ROM products available for purchase, two will suggest the possibilities of multimedia use. Suppose you need to research the life and work of President Franklin Roosevelt and have the *Grolier Multimedia Encyclopedia*. Using the index, you discover that his name occurs sixty times in the encyclopedia in twenty-seven different articles. You discover that Roosevelt appears in the article about the actor and songwriter George M. Cohan, but clicking on the article reveals that Cohan played the president in the musical called *I'd Rather Be Right* in 1937. It would be harder to find this information in the printed version, whereas every topic on the CD-ROM is fully indexed for easy retrieval.

You can also go directly to the main entry for Roosevelt, the traditional textual description expected in the printed version. Across the top of the text window a set of icons let you know that other enrichment resources are available about Roosevelt: a sound recording of part of his first inaugural address, a short video clip on one of his famous fireside chats, and a color photograph. One might argue that these multimedia enhancements, which are not in the printed *Grolier Encyclopedia*, do not improve one's understanding of the man and his work. But you can hear Roosevelt's confident rhetoric at the first inaugural address in the midst of the Great Depression, and the newsreel clip of the fireside talk shows a family sitting around a radio listening to the president. A caption suggests the importance of this mode of communication with the American people in Roosevelt's first term. Accessing these resources is always under your control to see and hear as much as you want. The computer is the electronic delivery system that accepts all this information in multiple media from the CD-ROM, can be queried for it, and presents it in written, aural, or pictorial form.

## COMPUTER MAPPING

A small, innovative company in Virginia, called Highlighted Data, has made a business of creating hypertext programs for a variety of contexts and uses. The company has adapted massive bodies of information available from public or private sources for practical use and accessibility in multimedia. Take, for instance, the Electronic Map Cabinet, an interactive atlas for creating maps and drawings of U.S. cities and states on a variety of scales. Stored on one compact disk are **digitized** maps of the whole nation, and detailed maps of about three hundred of the largest metropolitan areas, including such small cities as Bloomington, Indiana, and Portland, Maine (see Figure 1-15). As a computer storage device, the compact disk can store more data than 500 typical diskettes (about 600 million characters). It is needed for storing the maps because the amount of information in the drawing files is so massive: about 10,000 drawing vectors are typically required to generate one map. The federal government collected all this geographical information from satellite photographs of the earth; Highlighted Data has licensed its use for easy and flexible display on a personal computer.

Program users can pick a section of a state and a scale to determine detail (from 10,500 meters down to 3 meters per drawing unit). The computer will then draw the region, including towns, rivers, highways, and railroads. Users have a choice of black and white or eight colors (roads in red, rivers in blue, and so forth), depending on the kind of computer screen and printer they have. Before printing a map, they can add features to personalize it, either words or graphics. For instance, a user might label the street names or add additional pictorial details.

Similarly, one can pick a city, zero in on the whole metropolitan region, or make the grain finer, down to street level, before customizing the map. In the California earthquake of 1989, one of the TV networks used this program to prepare maps of the affected areas within San Francisco. A few

**digitized:** A term for information that has been converted into binary digits for computer processing.

**FIGURE 1-15** A map of Madison, Wisconsin, produced with the Map Cabinet. Clearly visible are the downtown area in the center, with the State Capital square between two big lakes, and the red interstate highways on the east side of the city.

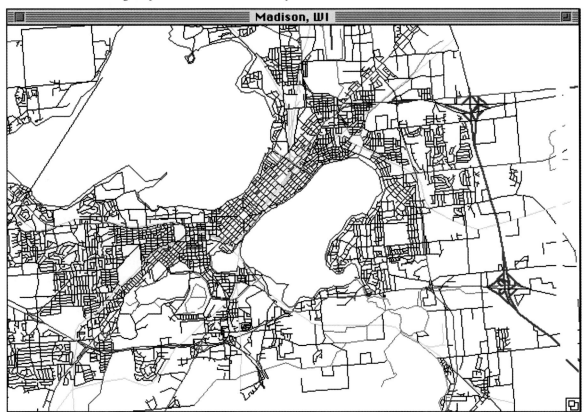

**FIGURE 1-16** Some educational publishers are now providing World Wide Web sites for their books, including instructional materials accessible by teachers and students using Web browsing software.

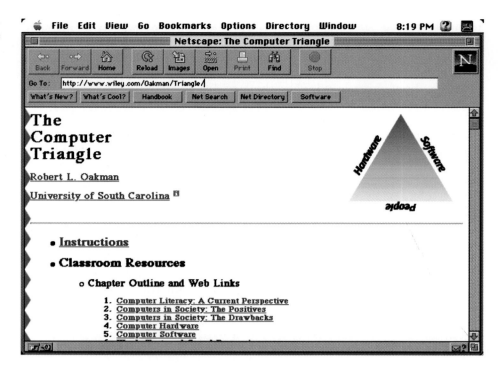

minutes after the disaster occurred, network personnel generated a color map of the area using the program, annotated it, and had it ready for broadcast within minutes of the earthquake itself. News organizations have been particularly pleased with the features of the program that allow them to add additional text or graphic materials—their own levels of hypertext— quickly and accurately to map materials covering the whole country.

## THE WEB ON THE INTERNET

Every day at colleges and universities all over the country, students and faculty sit down at their personal computers, or at terminals attached to their institutions' mainframe computers, and have a friendly browse through the exploding computer information system called the World Wide Web. After they log on, they may check the weather in their hometown, look up the current headlines from CNN on-line, find the phone number and e-mail address of a friend at an out-of-state college, sample the latest music from their favorite singing group, or check the population statistics and the election results in the last presidential election in each of the states. Perhaps like the students on the University of Texas Lecture Hall, they actually have class information prepared as Web pages where they can read, review, and add their own annotations.

Access to the Web is made available to colleges and universities, businesses, organizations like the Red Cross, and the general public through the Internet, the largest network of interconnected computers in the world. From its origins in the Cold War as a way to share technical data and messages between the Defense Department and its contractors, the Internet has over the years continued to expand as the mission and the technical power of the network have broadened. Today the Internet has connections on all continents and more than 30 million estimated users in the United States. It embraces almost all higher education institutions in this country.

Many envision the Internet, sometimes called the **Information Superhighway,** as perhaps as important for America's technological future as the interstate highway system was for an earlier era.

The phenomenal growth of the Internet among college students, businesspeople, and home computer users within the last three years can be traced to the proliferation of multimedia World Wide Web **home pages** prepared by thousands of groups and individuals. Since making a Web home page is not difficult to do, many students have already created their own customized ones. A Web document typically contains text and graphics laid out in a pleasing way, with links to other pages of related information. Users access these home pages by means of **browser software,** of which Netscape Navigator is by far the most common. Other browsers include the Microsoft Explorer, Mosaic from the National Center for Supercomputing Applications at the University of Illinois, and software extensions from commercial providers of on-line services such as CompuServe and America Online.

With browsing software, users log onto an Internet site, which may be across town, the continent, or the world, and request a home page to be sent to their local computer. The encoded multimedia document is then transferred over the Internet to them. Recent extensions to browser programs have allowed more than text and pictures to be included in home pages. In fact, Real Audio sends and plays sounds within Web documents, and the programming language called Java allows embedded animations and audio. Because telephone extensions are becoming popular add-ons, some observers envision the World Wide Web becoming the basic environment for computing and communications for most people in the next few years. Fuller information about the Internet, which offers many more services than the Web, will be treated in detail in Chapter 10.

Nevertheless, the rapid spread of Internet access, especially with local commercial providers and on-line services, has coincided with the delivery of multimedia content through the World Wide Web—all within the last few years. These two forces are changing the face of computing and information exchange in ways that are only now becoming apparent. College students in the late 1990s will find that orientation to the Internet needs to become a part of their educational experience. With the variety of resources available to them on the World Wide Web, the learning experience should be both pleasant and exciting.

**Information Superhighway:** A common term for the growth of infrastructure involving the Internet and the spread of high-speed data network services throughout the United States.

**home page:** A term used for the opening screen of a Web application, which typically will contain text and graphics. It is accessed through its own address over the Internet.

**browser software:** A computer program like Netscape Navigator which allows users to log onto remote sites on the Internet and retrieve information stored as World Wide Web documents.

## ▶ Summary

Over the years the computer has evolved from fast electronic calculator to general-purpose information processing device to a true multimedia machine connected to the world on the Internet. Computers of all kinds, especially everyday, personal computers, are now being used not only in all aspects of the workaday world, but in all educational fields in colleges and universities. Because they can encode information in all forms—written, aural, graphic, and so on—for processing and production of output, they can be used to solve problems in all areas of life. Computers are highly flexible, more like the human brain than any of humankind's earlier tools. Computer literacy today includes an understanding of the computer's parts and functions, its wide application, the specialized jargon surrounding the machine, and the multiple effects that its presence has on society at large.

## EVOLUTIONARY PERSPECTIVE

### From Single-Purpose Applications to Multimedia

A few years ago, software for most computers was single purpose. One did letter writing with word processing or financial planning with an accounting program. Later, programs like Lotus 1-2-3 IBM or Microsoft Office allowed the user some flexibility in combining data from several applications bundled together. With Lotus 1-2-3 software, one could do spreadsheet analysis, graph numerical figures, and search databases with the same package.

In today's networked multimedia environment, the kinds and quantity of data that can be interrelated and shared over the Internet have expanded enormously. People can merge information in ways never before possible. All kinds of sensory information, including touch and smell, can be captured for computer processing, inter-connected, and presented for the user's inspection. All areas of human knowledge and experience are open to organization and analysis in new and creative ways. Indeed, today's multimedia computer is beginning to resemble the brain tool that it has so often been called.

## ▶ Key Terms

applications software (p. 3)

artificial intelligence (p. 18)

binary coding (p. 18)

browser software (p. 23)

CD-ROM drive (p. 11)

computer (p. 6)

computer-assisted instruction (CAI) (p. 3)

computer graphics (p. 18)

computer screen (p. 9)

control program (operating system) (p. 11)

data (p. 9)

database management (p. 3)

digitized (p. 21)

drill-and-practice educational software (p. 3)

floppy disk drive (p. 11)

fuzzy logic (p. 18)

general-purpose computer (p. 7)

gigabyte (p. 11)

hacker (p. 14)

hard disk drive (p. 11)

hardware (p. 3)

home page (p. 23)

hypertext (hypermedia) (p. 18)

Information Superhighway (p. 23)

input (p. 9)

interactive multimedia (p. 19)

Internet (p. 1)

keyboard (p. 9)

laptop (p. 8)

mainframe machine (p. 6)

megabyte (**MB**) (p. 11)

microprocessor (chip) (p. 8)

minicomputer (p. 7)

mouse (p. 9)

multimedia (p. 19)

multimedia machine (p. 18)

on-line (p. 1)

output (p. 9)

personal computer (microcomputer or PC) (p. 8)

printer (p. 9)

processing (p. 9)

program (p. 3)

random access memory (RAM) (p. 10)

simulation software (p. 4)

software (p. 6)

special-purpose computer (p. 6)

spreadsheet (p. 13)

stimulus/response (p. 18)

storage (p. 9)

throughput (p. 9)

Universal Product Code (UPC) (p. 18)

Windows 95 (Win 95) (p. 12)

Wintel (p. 13)

word processing software (p. 13)

World Wide Web (the Web, WWW) (p. 1)

 *Self-Test*

## MULTIPLE-CHOICE

1. One of the main advantages of simulations like The Would-Be Gentleman for use in education is
   a. the opportunity to drill and practice exercise materials repeatedly
   b. the chance to act in rather than just read about unfamiliar events
   c. close interaction between teacher and student through the computer
   d. word processing capabilities for study of subjects like history

2. All of the following are examples of standard applications software currently used in colleges and universities, except
   a. multimedia
   b. word processing
   c. database management
   d. computer indexing

3. Today's personal computer can be classified as a
   a. mainframe
   b. minicomputer
   c. microcomputer
   d. special-purpose computer

4. All of the following are computer input/output devices except the
   a. mouse
   b. CAT scanner
   c. keyboard
   d. color monitor

5. Perhaps there is no best time to buy a personal computer, since a machine designed next year will typically offer all of the following for the same or less money except
   a. more features
   b. faster internal speed
   c. interchangeable processors from different manufacturers
   d. more convenient options for input/output devices

6. All of the following similarities lead to analogies between computers and the human brain except one. Which is not true?
   a. Both process electrical signals.
   b. Both have large memory banks.
   c. Both have very fast speeds of operation.
   d. Both are organically based.

7. *Grolier's Multimedia Encyclopedia,* distributed on a CD, contains what new information not available in the published version?
   a. segments of video of famous historical events and people
   b. indexes to articles
   c. illustrations
   d. articles on many subjects

8. Which of the following is not essential to a modern definition of computer literacy?
   a. the ability to program a computer in a language like **BASIC**
   b. an understanding of the parts and functions of computer systems
   c. an awareness of the wide application of computers in all areas of modern life
   d. an appreciation of "computer and society" issues

## TRUE/FALSE

9. **T   F**   The world leader in the development of computer chips today is Intel.

10. **T   F**   The common perception that a computer is a mathematical machine probably goes back to its origins in the Second World War, when it was used to calculate mathematical firing tables for naval rockets.

11. **T   F**   In order to achieve computer literacy, one must have access to the World Wide Web.

12. **T   F**   The throughput process in computers is analogous to the stimulus/response cycle in human perception.

13. **T   F**   Because the computer is a general-purpose symbol-manipulating device, today it has become a truly multimedia machine.

14. **T   F**   Computers connected to the Internet can transmit text but not multimedia.

15. **T   F**   Consumers shopping for computer hardware should pay attention to the products of Intel and Microsoft, two of the largest hardware companies in the world.

16. **T   F**   A megahertz is a measure of the size of random access memory; 1 MHz of storage equals 1 million characters of information.

## FILL-IN

17. Computer programs that run on personal computers like word processors are called applications _____, whereas the machines themselves are denoted by the term _____.

18. Drill-and-practice educational software is a major type of _____ _____, often abbreviated CAI.

19. _____ computers are engineered to do specific jobs, like setting times and temperature ranges in microwave ovens, and are embedded in the appliances.

20. The cycle of input of data to a computer, processing them, and producing some form of output is often called the _____ process.

21. A computer is useless without a control program to connect the user to the machine and monitor all activity within the machine. Such a program is called an _____ _____.

22. The relationship between computer hardware and software concepts, including their interactions with people, is sometimes called the _____ _____ .

23. The term _____ refers to computer applications that integrate at least one other medium with text, such as sound or graphics.

24. The _____, commonly called a computer chip, is being incorporated into many home electronics, such as the CD player and the Touch-Tone telephone.

## ▶ Experiential Exercises

1. Investigate at least three areas of modern life besides the microwave oven where special-purpose computers are installed.

2. Some commentators say that the popularity of the microcomputer is having the same negative effect on the development and sale of minicomputers today that the mini had on the mainframe in the late 1960s and early 1970s. Investigate why this trend might be true. Why might people choose micros over minis?

3. Find an advertisement for a personal computer system in a magazine or newspaper and try to decipher it. What parts of the ad refer to hardware and software components? You may need to consult your teacher, computer personnel at your school, or a reference book at the library in order to understand what is being offered.

4. Monitor your activities for a day or two to discover how often something having to do with computers comes up in conversation, reading, or the media. Based on your survey, write a short report on the prevalence of computers in modern life.

5. Investigate the prevalence of hypertext and multimedia tools for instruction in your college or high school. Your college's education department may be a good place to start your search. Does the library offer such tools for its users? Does your campus have a home page on the World Wide Web?

6. Pioneer "toolmakers" like Gutenberg and Leeuwenhoek opened up new frontiers of knowledge with the printing press and the microscope. It is not so easy to find one person who made such a leap in the history of computers. In the nineteenth century, Charles Babbage is a candidate; in the twentieth, John Atanasoff or Allen Turing or John von Neumann. Research one of these figures or someone else, and focus on the person's main contribution, the one that led the field forward.

## ▶ Critical Thinking Exercises

1. Have you used more instructional software in college than in high school? Speculate on why this situation is true, no matter which level of schooling is more computer intensive.

2. What does computer literacy mean to you? Be specific.

3. Argue against the proposition that the computer is the most important tool in the world today, aside from the book. What tool will you be defending?

4. Try to think of an aspect of the brain that does not fit the analogy with a computer. Can the brain really be said to be a multimedia machine?

5. Hypertext and multimedia are associative computer applications. One item of data is associated or linked with another. To what extent is the human mind also an associative organism? Discuss whether this characteristic is one of its greatest strengths.

**ANSWERS TO SELF-TEST**

*Multiple-Choice*: 1. b;    2. d;    3. c;    4. b;    5. c;    6. d;    7. a;
8. a
*True/False*: 9. T;    10. T;    11. F;    12. T;    13. T;    14. F;    15. F;
16. F
*Fill-in*: 17. software, hardware;    18. computer-assisted instruction;
19. special-purpose;    20. throughput;    21. operating system;    22.
computer triangle;    23. hypertext;    24. microprocessor

# CHAPTER 2

# Computers in Society: The Positives

▶ **LEARNING OUTCOMES**

*After completing this chapter, you should be able to:*

1. *List and give examples of five major kinds of applications software.*

2. *Describe current computer applications in education, medicine and science, the media, and government.*

3. *Discuss the benefits of these applications to society.*

4. *Discuss the outlook for the future in these technologies.*

▶ **COMPUTERS IN CONTEXT**

*A number of years ago Thomas H. Crowley, then director of Computer Science Research at Bell Laboratories in New Jersey, offered an after-hours course in computer literacy for adults. Discussing the impetus for choosing computers to solve problems, Crowley identified three main positive reasons why people turn to them for a variety of applications: (1) making a job more economical (savings of time or money) or more convenient; (2) making feasible a job that is impossible to do by any other method; and (3) using the computer to gain insight into a process by modeling or simulating it (Crowley). These three reasons for computing make the machine a powerful tool in all areas of modern life.*

One often finds that more than one of Crowley's reasons applies to a particular computer application. The three often overlap in both common and exotic applications, and it is hard to find applications in which at least one does not fit. The computer has become a positive force in most areas of life because of its characteristics: its flexibility, generality, speed, and accuracy. Even though Crowley identified them some years ago, they are still relevant to current computer usage. Let us keep Crowley's perceptive remarks in mind as we focus on four major fields of application today: education, medicine and science, the media, and government. After we look at software commonly used with positive applicability in many fields, we shall consider typical applications in each of these areas and highlight some of the frontiers of modern computer usage.

# ▶ Productivity Software and Its Benefits

**productivity software:** A general term applied to the most common kinds of applications software to increase a user's productivity: word processors, spreadsheets, database systems, graphics, data communications.

**integrated package:** Multi-functional software that combines several applications under one consistent user interface. Different application programs in the package can share data with each other.

**desktop publishing:** Using software to do page design and computer typesetting with laser printers for publications such as newsletters and magazines.

Most users of personal computers today work with several kinds of computer programs that are called collectively applications software. Users ordinarily choose them to increase their productivity in doing day-to-day work; consequently, these applications programs are also called **productivity software.** Whereas formerly packages carried out single functions, nowadays they are often bundled together in a multifunctional package that can share data among functions. Such software, called an **integrated package,** usually includes word processing, spreadsheets, and database capacity. Most people adopt applications software for economy and convenience, but both feasibility and insight often have a place in its use.

The five most common types of application are word processing, spreadsheets, database packages, graphics, and communications. After a short description here, each kind of applications package will be treated in detail in a later chapter.

Word processing is using a computer like a typewriter, to prepare documents, but it offers far more flexibility than typing. Even basic word processors make revision and editing easier than on a typewriter. And they offer features which were never envisioned for typewriters, such as the ability to elect different character fonts, stylistic options, and spelling checking. Some modern word processors even have typesetting capabilities that allow the user to do **desktop publishing.** They are now certainly more than substitutes for typewriters, and offer ease of use and features for document preparation never before feasible with personal computers.

Spreadsheets are analogous to automated accounting sheets, numerical figures laid out in rows and columns. The spreadsheet's advantage over manual accounting techniques is that it can do calculations automatically and update the ledger immediately. Suppose you are making a budget for the month and do not want to spend more than a quarter of your assets for housing. Your spreadsheet would have a slot for income and another for housing expenses, to be calculated at no more than one fourth of income. If you have put the formulaic relationship between income and housing

**FIGURE 2-1** Productivity software often has multiple uses. Many word processing packages can import spreadsheet graphs into a document.

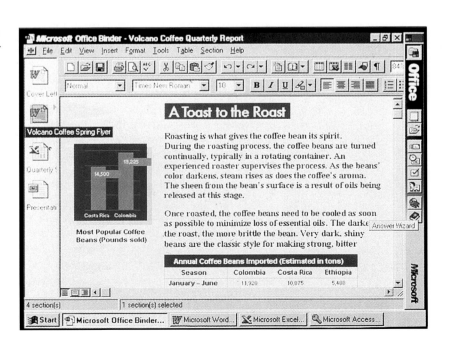

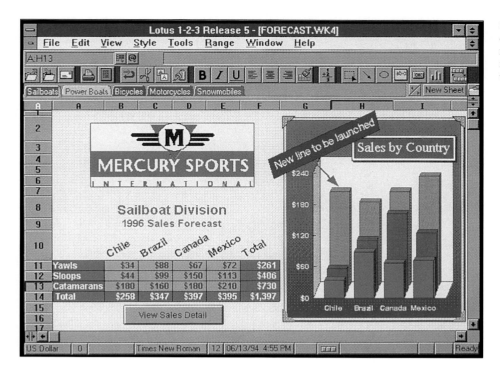

**FIGURE 2-2** Spreadsheet packages display information in column and row format and as graphs for reporting purposes and for effective presentation of numerical information.

into the spreadsheet, adjustments to income trigger the software to recalculate new housing figures conveniently and quickly. As you enter different income figures, the computer automatically refigures the housing budget to reflect the quarter-of-income allowance for that purpose. Ease of planning and insight into the budget process contribute to the popularity of spreadsheets.

In principle, database and **file management** packages are analogous to manual filing systems, such as an index card file for a mailing list of 5000 contributors to a charity campaign. The card file is probably organized alphabetically by the last names of the people on the list. Also in-

**file management:** Software for storing simple files, such as mailing lists for a small company, in which one file is accessed at a time.

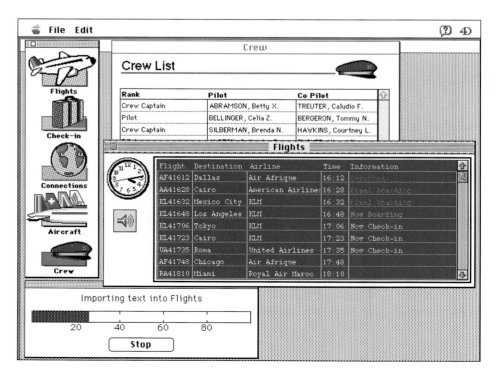

**FIGURE 2-3** Modern database software like 4th Dimension for Macintosh (ACIUS) presents tabular information in different windows with user-friendly icons on the side to select them.

**FIGURE 2-4** Modern graphics software allows designers to take photographs and add special effects for illustration and advertising.

**computer-aided design (CAD):** Using computer graphics software to aid the process of design, especially in architecture or engineering.

**killer app:** A slang term for a new and popular software application that is widely accepted and purchased by computer users.

**data communications:** Transferring data or information between computer-related devices such as electronic mail.

**modem:** A hardware device that enables data to be transmitted over telephone lines by conversion of digital computer signals to analog signals, and vice versa at the receiving end.

cluded on each name card is other associated information, such as the contributor's address, broken down into street, city, state, and ZIP code; the amount of the contribution; and the number of years the person has been giving. If the list of givers is very long, reordering the index card file to pull out all people in a certain ZIP code area who have contributed over $100 in the last three years would be tiresome and troublesome. However, when the information is put into a file management program, a one-file database of contributors, the process of sorting and searching becomes easy, for the application provides these functions as standard features. Most database packages can handle multiple files and interrelate them for powerful control over large amounts of information. Simple searches for ZIP codes, although not impossible with a set of index cards, are convenient and economical with a file management package. In addition, complex searches like the one proposed, a kind of computing for insight, become feasible.

Computer graphics packages allow the user to treat the computer screen as a drawing pallet and then print the results in black and white or color. They are commonly used either for creation of freeform art and design or for graphing numerical information. More complex graphics programs for **computer-aided design (CAD)** allow engineers to model building plans and machine tool designs directly on their screens. Today artists are using graphics packages to design logos for companies and lay out advertising copy, often in conjunction with desktop publishing packages with word processing features. Since it is often said that a picture is worth a thousand words, people regularly choose to graph their numerical or financial data to make them easier to understand—an aspect of computing for insight. Creation of line and bar graphs and pie charts are often standard graphic options in spreadsheet programs.

The increasing popularity of the Internet in recent years has led some commentators to suggest that the latest "**killer app,**" jargon for an innovative, widely adopted computer application that makes some person or business rich and famous, will be software for **data communications,** such as Web browsing tools. Yet data communications covers a wide variety of useful applications linking computers and the telephone system. Equipped with a **modem,** hardware that changes computer signals into telephone signal's and vice versa, a home computer user can access information from a variety of public and private sources or send messages throughout the world. Using the phone connection to check airline schedules and reserve tickets at home can save time and money. For a doctor seeking medical advice for an unusual condition, quick access to remote medical databases may make feasible the saving of a patient's life. **Electronic mail,** the sending of a message to another person's "mailbox" on another computer, and **computer conferencing,** multiple users commenting by electronic mail on an issue of common interest, offer extended two-way transfers of information and provide insight not readily feasible by other means.

Popular acceptance of these common kinds of applications software has been the major reason why the personal computer has been so successful. The machines that run the packages are reasonably priced; the ease of use and adaptability of their software have spurred microcomputer sales in all fields. Indeed, all areas of the professions, business, and government have incorporated these tools for a multitude of common and unusual tasks. The combination of productivity software, microcomputers, and general users represents a successful instance of the Computer Triangle. The result has been the burgeoning personal computer revolution throughout the world.

**electronic mail:** Application that enables users to electronically send and receive messages to colleagues using data communications technology with computers.

**computer conferencing:** Multiple users commenting on an issue of common interest via electronic mail. Individual members can monitor what others are adding to the conference and contribute over a set period of time.

## ▶ Computers in Education

Applications software like word processing and the increasing presence of the Internet represent only a sample of common computer uses found at all levels of education from kindergarten to college. Innovative strategies in computer-assisted instruction (CAI) include student multimedia projects, simulations in history and science, and electronic mail between students geographically dispersed throughout the world. Yet questions and debates still persist about the methods and quality of incorporating computers in education.

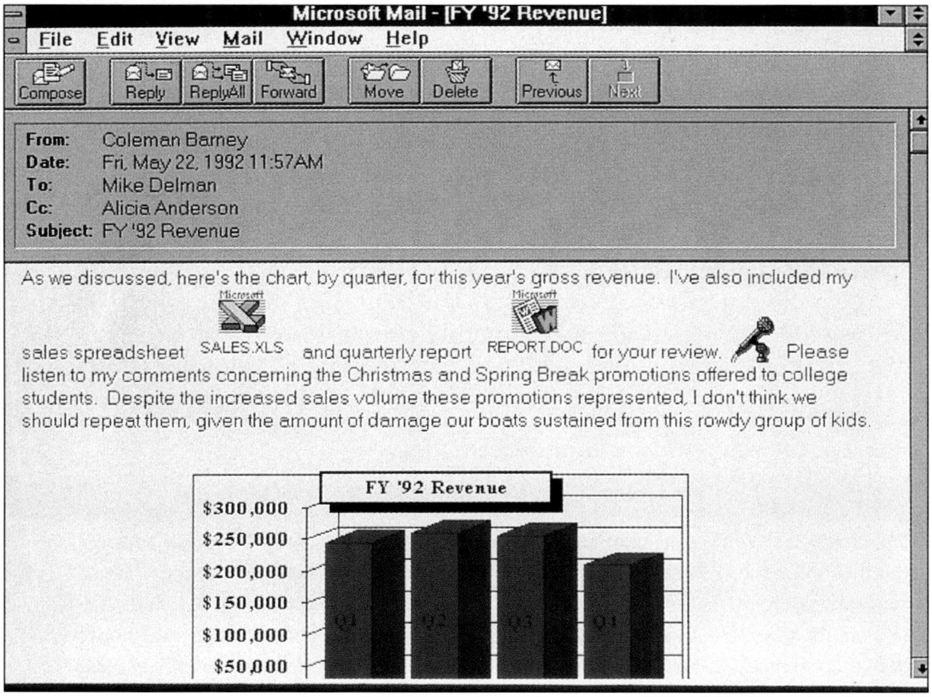

FIGURE 2-5 Electronic mail enables users to send messages to one another and to reply, forward, print, or store the messages. In this multimedia mail software (Microsoft Mail), the message itself contains a graph and voice mail, which the receiver can hear by clicking on the microphone icon.

## PEDAGOGICAL ISSUES

No one questions that computing in education is a big business. According to the Software Publishers Association, roughly $2.4 billion was spent on educational technology in public schools (kindergarten through grade 12) in 1994, and IBM Academic Consulting estimates more than $6 billion for college and university purchases in the same year. New educational paradigms, illustrated in Table 2-1, are being developed for incorporating computer support in the instruction that is two-way, collaborative, and interdisciplinary.

The traditional lecture method of delivery, with students sitting passively in a classroom, is giving way to networked classes and the teacher's becoming more of a mentor to guide student exploration of a topic. Students can communicate with each other through class networks and do team projects in a variety of multimedia (Reinhardt). Proponents of these digital, computer technologies in education argue that they make instruction more vivid and fitted to individual student needs. In addition, administrators and public officials often believe that computers will lessen the spiraling costs of education. Models of **distance learning** and consolidating resources with computer resources distributed on the Internet, such as the University of Texas WWW Lecture Hall, offer such hopes.

**distance learning:** The delivery of educational course materials offsite, formerly through videotape and closed-circuit television, now often carried out with shared content resources on the Internet.

Yet many faculty members are not convinced. A study at the University of Southern California reported in 1995 that fewer than 5 percent of college faculty members were using computers in instruction to enrich learning. Many teachers, trained in the lecture mode of instruction, report that they do not have the time to invest in learning new technology. They are skeptical of the benefits that the new modes of delivery will make in the education of their students. In many institutions personal commitments of faculty to educational computing do not lead to tenure or promotion. And faculty are even more suspicious of administrators' arguments for cost savings coming from technology (DeSieno).

Joseph Weizenbaum, long a leader in educational technology at MIT, has been a longtime critic of hastily adopted educational technology. He warns that people should not expect computers to replace the most valuable relationship in the educational process, the human contact between teacher and student. Weizenbaum thinks that going to the library and reading a novel about the Great Depression is better than gleaning loads of facts and statistics about it from a database. A multimedia database on the Depression contains an anonymous someone's selective gathering of information about a complex period, while a novel like James Farrell's *Studs Lonigan* provides a capsule reading of real life. Teachers should try to foster a student's natural talent for imagination and hold on to it as long as possible. Weizenbaum certainly agrees with much educational research that computers should be used carefully in conjunction with well-planned classroom teaching (Brady).

Few would argue that computers can replace a good teacher. But they can provide hard-to-teach supplemental dimensions or demonstrate with other methods. Let us examine how teachers are developing the new in-

**TABLE 2-1** *Changing Educational Paradigms*

| OLD MODEL | NEW MODEL | TECHNOLOGY IMPLICATIONS |
|---|---|---|
| Classroom lectures | Individual exploration | Networked PCs with access to information |
| Passive absorption | Apprenticeship | Requires skills development and simulations |
| Individual work | Team learning | Benefits from collaborative tools and e-Mail |
| Omniscient teacher | Teacher as guide | Relies on access to experts over network |
| Stable content | Fast-changing content | Requires networks and publishing tools |
| Homogeneity | Diversity | Requires a variety of access tools and methods |

## SOCIAL PERSPECTIVE

### Distance Learning

Like the American literature course at the University of Texas described in Chapter 1, Major Curtis Carver's computer science course at West Point is available at all hours of the day and night on the military academy's World Wide Web site. At West Point all cadets get a computer when they arrive, and the faculty can place assignments on the Web. Major Carver's "textbook of the future" contains more than a gigabyte of course-related resources on the Web: 200 audio files; 200 graphic files; 37 digital movies; multimedia slide shows for every lesson; student papers from earlier semesters; and definitions, search terms, and practice quizzes for each exam. Students may send queries to the teacher and take exams on-line, and the computer will do automatic scoring of objective questions. They type answers to essay questions, which are then graded later as electronic mail.

One pioneering feature of this WWW course is the learning styles quiz at the start of the course. Students answer a series of questions on the computer designed to determine what kind of learners they are—verbal, visual, aural, etc. The questionnaire is scored automatically by the machine for each student, and lesson files are then presented to them individually in the most advantageous way for their understanding. For example, verbal students will get the text documents first, whereas visual learners will be offered graphics and videos first. Although all of the material is always available, the computer presents it for each cadet in a personalized way to make it easy to comprehend. Students have control from their dorm rooms about how and when they will study the lessons outside of class (Carver).

Courses like this one suggest possibilities for the growth of distance learning and collaborative efforts among colleges and universities. The computer is the middleman dispensing multimedia and accepting responses and queries through the medium of the World Wide Web. Although the course was put together for local students at West Point, anyone with the Web address and proper access codes can view the lessons. Compared with some other sites offering a variety of materials, which may be protected by copyright law from use by others, this West Point course was developed at a public institution; and its resources are accessible in the common domain.

Other common distance learning modes include distribution of course materials on videotape or via live satellite television. Combining a computer with these methods provides for easier remote feedback between students and their teacher. For instance, MediaLink for Macintosh includes several interactive network features suitable for use on the Internet for distance learning. Students equipped with an audiovisual Mac can watch a television course live or on videotape and still have all of the multimedia capacity in lesson materials. If they log onto the Internet, they can correspond with their teacher about assignments. With their addresses, the teacher can send transmit media resources, including sounds and graphic files, directly to students. Such items as text assignments, short quizzes to fill out, or graphics for further information can be sent to all the students through their Internet addresses. Two participants can collaborate on a document in an on-line conference in **real time,** such as working on a class report at long distance. The term "real time" refers to the ability to respond to computer activity immediately, as it is happening. As each person keys text into the computer, the other party can see the typing at the other end of the Internet line. With the computer as intermediary, a number of the new learning paradigms shown in Table 2-1 can be realized. Distance learning can move from passive viewing to active two-way participation among teachers and students, a true community of learners who may be widely separated by geographical distance.

---

**real time:** A term used to describe a computer application in which the delay between input of data and completed processing is negligible. When a computer presents results as soon as the data have been received, the process is called a real-time application.

---

structional paradigms suggested in Table 2-1 in multimedia, simulations, networking, and distance learning on the Internet. In the successful cases, the three elements of the Computer Triangle—hardware, software, and people—are working together for better education.

## FROM CAI TO MULTIMEDIA

Much use of computer-assisted instruction in schools involves drill-and-practice software. These are programs designed to teach a particular kind of knowledge and to drill students for mastery. Some of this software is especially appealing to young learners, because it incorporates color graphics and sound feedback. Programs to teach the phonics approach to reading fit into this category, along with foreign language and mathematics drills and supplementary lessons for remedial students.

As students get older, drill-and-practice software tends to become boring and lose its appeal, unless it is cleverly designed to hold their interest. A multimedia program in American history called Point of View

FIGURE 2-6 West Point cadets can log onto the class Web page for Computer Science 383 and get a multimedia presentation of the topics of the course. Many include graphics, videos, and text, as well as practice exercises.

(Scholastic Software) uses a mixture of timelines on politics and popular culture, census statistics, and recorded sound to overcome the element of boredom. It takes students' interest in this important subject and their probable lack of knowledge about parts of it as a point of departure for their investigations. Students can follow their individual preferences in working through the program's materials.

For instance, students can choose to display several different historical timelines at the same time. As they view the dates of important rock music events in the pop culture of the 1960s, they can also display the political events of the Kennedy-Johnson era, including the civil rights struggle and the Vietnam War. They can play recorded excerpts of important speeches, such as Kennedy's inaugural ("Ask not what your country can do for you") or Martin Luther King's "I have a dream" speech, from the March on Washington. The possibilities for graphing census statistics are extremely varied. Students can choose to graph the numbers of white and black residents in several states. As they move through several decades on the timeline, the graphs are automatically updated and displayed on the screen. Students can save materials from the package to use in developing their own research papers with word processing programs. The package intentionally embodies a flexible, interactive learning environment to encourage students to develop their own research strategies and to learn more about American history than their textbooks contain.

## MULTIPURPOSE COMPUTING

Creative teachers at all levels of education have always found ways to incorporate innovative teaching aids and strategies in their classes. Computers add new capabilities not available by other means. One positive example is the "computer-infused classroom" in a middle school in Shoreham, New York. There a creative teacher, Robert Vlahakis, includes three computing components in an American history course: simulation, telecommunication, and standard software packages (Vlahakis).

Using data communications software, Vlahakis's students correspond with peers in other schools by electronic mail and extract stories from a public on-line news service about current events related to class materials. They are learning how to *gather and use information*, a skill that will be more important than memorization of facts in the next century, when massive databases on all subjects will be accessible from computer keyboards. With their word processors and desktop publishing software, students work in teams to prepare their own newspapers of important historical periods. They gather textual and pictorial materials, type or scan them into the computer, and compose newspapers such as the *Jamestown Memo* or the *Plymouth Bay Sun* for the Revolutionary period. For them the computer has made American history come alive.

Simulation software also provides these students with insight into the historical process which they experience vicariously. Having to make decisions based on the available evidence shows students that the answers to real world problems are usually open ended. It forces them to use higher-level thinking skills, like logic and deduction, to solve a problem. Shoreham students use a simulation package called The Other Side (Tom Snyder Productions) to negotiate a peace between two nations, and they rate the experience a highlight of the course.

To Vlahakis, "Computers have added another dimension to the teaching style that I have always employed—*an experiential, problem-solving approach* that encourages students to question, discuss, and analyze history. The computer has made it more efficient for me to *focus on the individual needs of my students* in a more diversified learning environment." All three of the positive reasons for computing are involved in this class: efficiency, insight, and the feasibility of trying individual teaching strategies not available in other ways.

**FIGURE 2-7** A cover for a newspaper of the Revolutionary War era, produced by a middle-school student in a social science class, using inexpensive software and hardware.

## MULTIMEDIA TERM PAPERS

With the availability of easy to use authoring software, some students have begun making their research investigations as multimedia presentations. An eighth grader in Montreal used a program called HyperStudio (Roger Wagner Publishing) in the fall of 1995 to present the issues of the controversial and divisive referendum on secession of the province of Quebec. Included in this impressive presentation were the text arguments of both sides, the Oui and Non parties, as well as video clips of newsfilm presenting rallies on both sides as short videos. The student also used a camcorder to present his own views on film. Using the capability of the software to access the World Wide Web, the production included a number of links to national government opinion and the editorial stands of important Canadian newspapers in Montreal and Toronto. The viewer of the lesson was able to leave the program to see the viewpoints of major opinion organs on this important vote and return to the student's presentation with only a few clicks of the mouse. This middle school student was too young to vote in the election, but through his exploration and multimedia production he was probably as qualified as many adults to make an informed choice.

Similar multimedia term papers were created in a freshman literature course on the novels of Raymond Chandler, coordinated by Professor Matthew Bruccoli at the University of South Carolina. Under Bruccoli's guidance, the students chose a chapter of one of Chandler's California detective novels to annotate for the modern college reader. According to Bruccoli, "these were a bunch of students born . . . thirty years after these novels were published. The cars meant nothing to them, the brand names that were . . . assumed to be recognizable to the reader of the 1940s and 1950s. Packard—the kids had never seen a Packard—and Los Angeles, Hollywood of the early 40s and 50s , are about as remote from them as the planet Mars. If . . . the kind of literature known as social history . . . is going to survive, ways must be found to make the material accessible."

To prepare their annotations, the students did library research on the reality of Chandler's California—historical personages, events, maps, fauna and flora, etc., and used a program called MediaLink (InterEd) to add hypertext links to their chapters. One student annotated a footnote on the modern German composer Paul Hindemith with a biographical note and segment from his symphony in E flat. Another focused on the area of Los Angeles called Central Avenue and discovered that this was the neighborhood that eventually fed the Watts riots of 1965. Of her multimedia presentation, this student said, "I liked it better than doing a normal term paper because you learn so much more. . . . When people come to view your work, they're actually seeing examples of what's going on." (Van Gelder)

Such projects exhibit several of the new educational methods described previously, including individual exploration and diversity in presentation of materials in various media. The teacher had the students investigate unfamiliar topics under his guidance, and the computer allowed them to explain it to others, in color with sound and images attached to their traditional footnotes. The ease of use of the authoring software permitted the students to create multimedia term papers on their own. The computer gave them the ability to present various media resources that otherwise would not have been possible, and both the students and their audience gained insight into the richness of literature through the hypertext assignment.

## SIMULATIONS IN MATHEMATICS AND SCIENCE

Teachers report that simulations are especially useful in teaching mathematics and science. Mathematics is hard to teach partially because many complex functions are difficult for students to visualize. The highly respected mathematical package called Mathematica (Wolfram Research)

**FIGURE 2-8** In this MediaLink (InterEd) multimedia term paper, two links have been opened to expand the reference to "Tarzan on a big scooter": the student's explanation of the quotation and a created image of Tarzan from the 1950s standing on a scooter, generated with a computer graphics program.

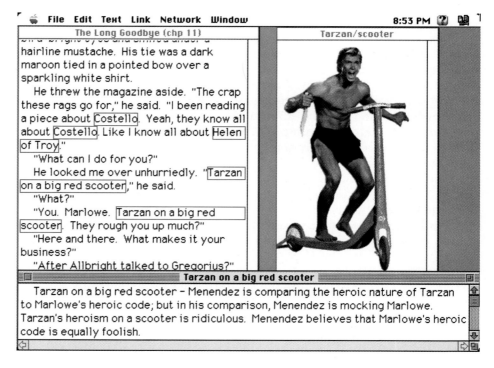

overcomes this problem (Grady). It can carry out almost any kind of mathematical operation—numerical, symbolic, or graphical. For instance, it will take an expression like $x^2 - 1$, factor it into $(x - 1)(x + 1)$, and graph it. It can do differentiation and integration in calculus or graph functions in two or three dimensions. Formerly such capabilities were available only on large systems and were clumsy to use; this program makes them easy to use on large personal systems used in many schools and colleges, like 486s and Pentiums and larger Macintoshes. Math educators are beginning to re-think their assignments to catch up with Mathematica's potential to enliven the teaching of mathematics, especially for college students.

In the experimental sciences, educational simulations often meet several needs. Perhaps the subject is hard to understand without experiment, or unsafe for students to experiment with in real life, such as infectious disease. The high cost of equipment required for an experiment may preclude having it available for student use. Sometimes a simulation cuts out a long delay in waiting for a reaction, or shows something impossible to observe, such as what happens at the atomic level (Trollip). Simulation packages in mechanics, electromagnetism, and modern physics, produced at Stanford by Blas Cabrera, present animated results on the computer screen so that students can visualize not only the processes in progress but the final result. Students can try 16 experiments on their own, several times if necessary, in order to understand the complexities of topics like planetary motion or rocket ballistics. They learn at their own pace and can grasp the interrelationships of the physical variables at work.

## Computers in Medicine and Science

SOCIETY

Accurate information and speedy access to it are probably more important in medicine than in most fields, given the life-and-death situations that doctors and nurses face every day. **Medical databases** of current research findings and treatments, well indexed by categories, were one of the first major uses of on-line databases. In *Computers and the Information Society*, James Radlow tells the story of a California doctor in the 1980s who was able to save the life of a patient with uncontrolled bleeding by tapping into MEDLINE, a well-known medical database, from his home in the middle of the night. Among summaries of 19 articles on this type of bleeding, he found an English translation of a German case which seemed to match his patient's symptoms and described a new blood replacement therapy. The doctor ordered the treatment to begin immediately and found the patient much better in the morning. Access to knowledge through data communications and up-to-date on-line medical databases saved the patient's life.

**medical database:** A specialized database of current medical research findings and treatments, such as MEDLINE.

### COMPUTERS FOR DIAGNOSIS

Today "telemedicine networks" allow specialists in large medical centers to do diagnosis at long distance through computerized two-way **videoconferencing,** using high-speed data communications. Small towns have access to the knowledge of big-city physicians on-line, whereas they could never afford to have such doctors in their communities. For instance, in May 1994, a woman in rural Georgia had a rotting skin lesion on her leg that was not responding to treatment by local doctors. Rather than sending her to Atlanta or Augusta, the hospital beamed up a specialist at the Medical College of Georgia in Augusta, whose examination of the lesion via videoconferencing identified the problem as a staph infection. He prescribed a

**videoconferencing:** A system of computer-monitored two-way video transmission using phone lines that allows viewers at both ends of the session to see and hear each other.

FIGURE 2-9 In telemedicine, specialists in urban medical centers can examine patients at long distance and offer advice to local doctors in small communities.

long dose of antibiotics, and the woman did not have to lose her leg. Although the 1980s doctor in California found the answer to his problem with a computer database, in this case the medical school dermatologist was able to see the wound and make a quick diagnosis in real time. The computer brought the contact between patient and doctor at a distance up close and personal (Cowley et al.).

Patients themselves are getting in the act of understanding their symptoms and drugs with so-called "doc-in-a-box" software kits and on-line support groups and forums. A woman in Wisconsin having complications from breast cancer surgery joined the growing CHESS (the Comprehensive Health Enhancement Support System) computer network at the suggestion of her hospital and found lots of advice from fellow patients with similar problems regarding her illness and medicines. CompuServe, an on-line computer information service, has a forum where patients can log on and ask questions, which are often answered by doctors.

"Doc-in-a-box" software CD-ROMs, expected to be a $500 million industry by 1996, package information in multimedia that can be accessed after a patient types in a set of symptoms. The program then responds with a set of possible diagnoses and an encyclopedia article on each condition. Also included is information about thousands of drugs and medical procedures. As a cost-saving measure, some HMO plans are training nurses to use software of this kind to make preliminary diagnoses over a toll-free phone line. With computer assistance patients get advice in an impersonal and anonymous way, and studies indicate that those who have logged on tend to like it. Yet software creators and forum organizers emphasize that these approaches are meant to supplement regular medical care, not replace it (Cowley).

## HOSPITAL APPLICATIONS

Keeping accurate records on hospital patients is essential; but for nurses, the load of paperwork can be overwhelming. Many hospitals have installed a portable computer in patient rooms for encoding data like temperature and pulse rate as they are gathered. Using a barcode scanner, nurses can

FIGURE 2-10 Workstations at the patient's bedside allow hospital personnel to encode and receive health care information at the point of treatment.

FIGURE 2-11 Computers are used for scanning the body and displaying images used by doctors for making diagnoses.

read drug and food requirements encoded on patients' armtags. Because the workstations are networked throughout the hospital, medical departments like radiology can file test results electronically as they are completed, and they are instantly available in any room. Treatment documentation and accounting records are also on-line. Errors due to illegible handwriting or verbal misunderstandings can be avoided, since the patient's master record is stored in typed form in the hospital's main computer. Not only does the networked hospital have more accurate records quickly accessible, but recordkeeping is more economical as well.

Hospitals routinely employ **computer monitoring** of critically ill patients when nurses are otherwise engaged. In intensive care units, for example, patients are wired with electronic sensors that monitor their vital signs, such as heartbeat and temperature. This information is collected continuously and automatically transmitted to the nurses' station, where it is displayed on a computer screen. If some vital sign falls outside the normal range, the machine beeps a warning. For example, if a heart patient's pulse falls suddenly, the machine alerts the nurse on duty, who can then respond immediately. In applications like this, the computer allows an instant diagnosis not available by other methods and can truly be a lifesaver.

Medical technology based in computers has added new diagnosis tools unimaginable only a few years ago. The most well-known one is probably **computerized axial tomography,** better known as the **CAT** or **CT scanner.** Today hospitals regularly use such devices to find brain tumors and other cancers and later to check for recurrence after surgery or chemotherapy. The equipment blends x-ray with computer graphic imagery techniques. The machinery takes a series of x-ray photo cuts through the bodily area under study, at slightly different angles. The computer then merges these separate images and displays them graphically on a color screen, showing different kinds of body tissue in different colors. **Magnetic resonance imaging (MRI scanning)** employs a similar technology using the interaction of radio waves with hydrogen nuclei in water and fatty tissue in the body to get safe and reliable computer images of the internal organs (Redington and Berninger). With both machines, doctors have a picture of the body through computer imaging that was not possible with earlier diagnostic tools.

## PROSTHETICS AND THE HANDICAPPED

Computers are being used creatively to assist handicapped people through **electronic prosthetics,** or the replacement of missing body parts with artificial limbs or organs. Programming a computer to control artificial limbs falls into the category of **cybernetics.** The early computer pioneer and mathematician Norbert Wiener, of MIT, coined the term from the Greek word *kybernetes,* meaning "pilot" or "helmsman," to refer to the study of control mechanisms, both in animals and machines. Suppose a person has been in a car accident and lost the lower part of her left leg; yet the nerve endings are still active. Medical researchers can produce an artificial leg with computer chips that sense nerve signals to move or bend the leg. When the woman wants to walk, her brain signals the sensor on the prosthetic leg; it receives the message and moves the appropriate parts of the leg and foot. Research in cybernetics is producing wonderful progress in prothetics, helping handicapped persons and accident victims to restore bodily functions like walking and talking.

Ordinary personal computers are already working wonders for handicapped people. Voice synthesizers, chin switches, head pointers, and

**SOCIETY**

**computer monitoring:** Employing a computer system to monitor the vital signs of critically ill patients automatically and to display the results on a computer screen at the nurses' station.

**SOCIETY**

**computerized axial tomography (CAT):** Using a CAT (or CT) scanner to combine x-rays with computer graphic imagery techniques to offer fine-quality images for medical diagnosis of conditions like brain tumor.

**magnetic resonance imaging (MRI):** A modern medical imaging technology for diagnosis. MRI employs reflected radio waves to get safe and reliable computer images of internal body organs.

**electronic prosthetics:** Computerized devices developed to replace or bypass missing or inoperative body parts.

**cybernetics:** The study of how control mechanisms work, both in the nervous system of animals and in automation for machines.

**SOCIETY**          **HISTORY**

**FIGURE 2-12** André Alm, paralyzed from his shoulders down, develops computer systems for the handicapped in Sweden so that people like him can control their home environments automatically.

**supercomputer:** The fastest and most expensive type of computer designed for massive mathematical calculations necessary for much high-level scientific research. Supercomputer speeds today are measured in gigaflops (one billion floating-point mathematical operations in a second) and soon in teraflops (one trillion such operations).

**graphical workstation:** A computer designed specifically to produce complicated graphics speedily and efficiently.

**gigaflop (GFLOP):** A billion floating-point (mathematical) instructions per second, a measure of the speed and power of current supercomputers, which could carry out this many operations in one second.

**teraflop (TFLOP):** A trillion floating-point computer instructions per second, a measure of the enormous number of operations carried out by the most advanced supercomputers today (tera = trillion).

**HISTORY**

**SOCIETY**

braille printers have opened up communications for handicapped students not even imagined a few years ago. The mouse, which users roll around on the table to select items on the computer screen, has become an input device for people who cannot use a pencil or a keyboard. A Swedish computer science student paralyzed from the shoulders down uses a head pointer, which monitors his head movements, to choose options on Macintosh menus. He then activates the option he wants with a puff switch, into which he blows a puff of breath. On a special machine that emulates a keyboard, controllable from his head pointer, he picks out a character and types it with the puff switch. The student has already developed a typing speed of 100 keystrokes per minute.

Hypermedia tools that open windows and present text, graphics, and sound with the click of a button are now accessible to people who do the clicking with a chin switch and a nod of their head. Speech recognition packages allow blind students to control their machines with their own voices. Many of these hardware options can be added to standard machines without enormous cost. Liz Vantrease, an active composer of opera and other music who has slowly debilitating Lou Gehrig's disease, has called the computer "an empowering device" for the disabled: "It can give you back some of the things that were so unfairly stolen from you by illness, accident, or birth defect" (Meng). The computer extends a handicapped person's sensory and motor abilities and thus makes life more truly manageable.

## COMPUTERS IN THE EXPERIMENTAL SCIENCES

In the traditional sciences we find a variety of applications that depend first on the computer as a very fast and accurate calculating engine and then as a powerful graphic imaging system. These fields apply principles of mathematics to real-world applications, often using differential equations to model natural processes. Today **supercomputers** and high-powered **graphical workstations** are the staple tools of the research scientist. Supercomputers, the most expensive computers in the world, come in different configurations, but they share one common trait: the ability to do repetitive mathematical calculations at incredible speeds. Their speed and power is usually measured in **gigaflops (GFLOPs),** billions of floating point (mathematical) instructions per second. Newer supercomputers have now reached peak speeds of a trillion floating point operations per second, called **teraflop (TFLOP),** a thousand-fold improvement over a gigaflop machine.

Weather forecasting is an everyday instance of supercomputing. Accurate weather prediction depends on the collection of temperature, wind velocity, and air pressure readings from many stations. For decades scientists have known that solving a series of complex mathematical equations containing data from thousands of weather stations will give an accurate forecast. The problem has been that the number of calculations required to solve the equations is so large. By the time they are solved by ordinary methods, the weather has changed. In the early days of computing, the first practical use of the formulas became possible. Accurate one-day forecasts were calculated with the computational power of mainframe computers of that era. Nowadays we expect accuracy about five days in advance, because supercomputers have increased calculating power so dramatically. In an earlier time natural disasters like Hurricane Hugo (1989) would probably have been more damaging, because forecasters would

**FIGURE 2-13** Modern Doppler radar systems for weather forecasting use computer visualization techniques to display their data in real time.

**FIGURE 2-14** Overhead and depth views of temperature simulation in Lake Erie from Toledo, OH (on the left), to Buffalo, NY (on the right), created at the Ohio Supercomputer Center. Green color indicates a water temperature of 8 degrees Celsius, whereas red is warmer, about 15 degrees Celsius. One notices the coolest temperatures at the east end of the lake, where the water is deepest.

have been unable to make accurate predictions well in advance of the storm.

Current weather research at the National Center for Atmospheric Research in Colorado combines the resources of a Cray supercomputer, for computation, with full-color graphical workstations, to model the behavior of thunderstorms. Researchers at the Ohio Supercomputer Center are combining weather data with water level and flow data to model the hydrodynamic conditions in Lake Erie. A few years ago this polluted, almost dead body of water was little understood. Now supercomputer modeling allows forecasts of water conditions about every six hours—roughly the same frequency as weather forecasts ("Visualization News").

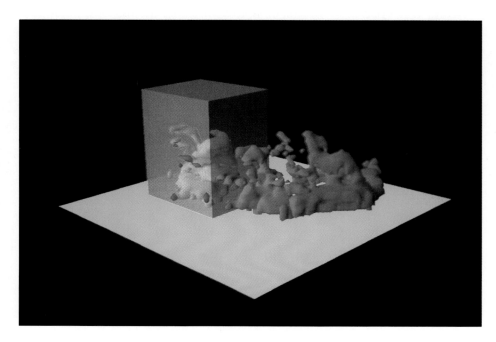

**FIGURE 2-15** A three-dimensional simulation of a thunderstorm created on Unix workstations working with a Cray supercomputer at the National Center for Atmospheric Research in Boulder, CO. In this scientific visualization method, the area in the red box has been selected to be rendered in more detail.

## COMPUTATIONAL SCIENCE

**computational science:** A partnership between computer science and the laboratory sciences. It combines the computer's ability to do massive amounts of mathematical calculations quickly and to represent the results as graphic images to solve problems in the physical and biological sciences.

**scientific visualization:** A process associated with computational science to represent as graphic images the results of complex simulation computations, sometimes involving millions of items of numerical data.

What is evolving is a new field called **computational science.** It is based on **scientific visualization,** which Donna Cox of the National Center for Supercomputing Applications has called "the process of representing, as computer graphic images, the results of simulation computations initially expressed in numbers." First the numbers are generated through supercomputing, and detailed graphic images are created. Then graphic workstations present the results for close analysis. Much of the natural phenomena displayed cannot be well understood without a visual image. As Cox has asked, how can one understand the billions of numbers that come from a supercomputer? Visualization helps to solve the problem of "numerical overload" (Cox).

In 1987, the National Science Foundation issued a report on the importance of visualization in scientific computing. In 1989 the Federal High Performance Computing Program listed 21 "Grand Challenges for which solution is likely to be possible using systems developed under this initiative." It calls for massive research funding in such areas as human genetics, the molecular basis for disease, prediction of biochemical effects in the design of new drugs, simulation of ocean currents, aerodynamic transportation design, and the study of ozone depletion in the upper atmosphere. It envisions a close working partnership between computer scientists and their colleagues in all fields of the physical, biological, and earth sciences.

In computational science, then, the scientist can now gain insight into real-world processes not possible with earlier technologies. In this new endeavor, computer science is viewed as more than a service field that produces powerful pictures. It is central to the initial mathematical modeling of real-world phenomena and to the visual understanding of the numerical outcomes. Suppose a scientist wants to display a moving color image on a computer screen made up of more than 1 million spots of color, called **pixels,** that change shade at least 15 times a second. The computational power required to calculate 15 million changes and send them to the screen in one second is a job for a supercomputer or a high-end workstation. Without such capability the researcher cannot see what is happening in real time, as the event is happening. With the computer imaging, the response seems instantaneous to the user, because human speeds of perception are much slower than computer calculations.

**pixel:** A term made from the words *picture element* to describe a spot on a computer screen capable of changing color or shade. Modern graphical screens may have more than a million pixels.

This sort of scientific computing is very expensive. In fact, the National Science Foundation program of funding five National Centers for Supercomputer Applications (at Carnegie Mellon, Princeton, Cornell, University of California at San Diego, and University of Illinois at Champaign-Urbana) had a budget of about $100 million a year through 1995 (La Breque). Supercomputing centers tend to be joint projects of universities and research institutes, which share the computational resources and costs. Thus the third of our reasons for computing, economics, joins the other two, insight and feasibility, in the explosion of scientific research through supercomputers and visualization.

## ▶ Computers in the Media

**HISTORY**

Television viewers of the mid-1980s remember the clever series of Coca-Cola ads featuring the talking head Max Headroom, a personality who existed only as a disembodied image on a TV screen. Max became so popular that an ABC series was built around his adventures "twenty minutes in the future" (Fisher). The show featured hip humor, quick cinematic cutting and music, and, for the first time on network television, integrated computer graphics. Computer-generated images moved behind Max, who appeared himself to be a computer image, but was in actuality an actor made up to look like a digital creation. The result was a series about a telegenic society of constant, multiple intrusions of media into daily life. Max Headroom was not the first use of computer video in movies, but it did break ground in network television. Today even local TV stations employ easy-to-use video graphics technology for special effects in production and advertising.

## PRINT JOURNALISM

Computers are now an integral part of journalism and the print media. In fact, desktop publishing has changed forever the production of newspapers and magazines. "Hot type" newspaper pages, produced in the past with Linotype machines and cases of leaded type, have been replaced with **cold type,** the production of typefonts and pages on computer screens. Printed by laser and xerographic processes, cold type is not limited to black and white, but appears increasingly in color. The costs are lower, the range of printing possibilities is far greater, the time lag is shorter from layout to printing, and the whole enterprise can be controlled in an editorial office.

Newspaper reporters regularly carry portable laptop computers on assignment. Thousands of reporters write their stories in the field and send them back to the home office via the built-in modem and communications software in the computer. In the newsroom, staff reporters use networked terminals to check facts and produce their stories. The managing editor can call up their stories on his terminal and edit them for final printing.

## COMPUTER GRAPHICS

In the layout department, workers use desktop publishing software to set up the pages of the paper, including the mix of stories, graphics, and digitized photographic images that make up a newspaper page. By 1990 the *Dallas Times Herald* included between 20 and 30 illustrations a day created on a Macintosh, along with advertising photographs that had been computer-enhanced with graphics packages. The director of computer imaging reported a doubling of computer-produced illustrations in one year, at no increase in labor or production costs (Matazzoni).

The *San Francisco Examiner* went high-tech when Soviet President Gorbachev visited the Bay Area in June 1990 to meet the very short deadlines of its midday and afternoon editions. Technicians videotaped Gorbachev's arrival at the Russian consulate from a television set; transferred a single frame of the tape to the newspaper's "electronic darkroom" software, run on a Macintosh; enhanced the image to print quality; and in a few minutes had the color photo on press. For later editions a reporter snapped pictures with a new Sony digital camera, which records photos on floppy diskettes rather than print film. These were easily processed in the electronic darkroom, and the final afternoon editions carried photos of Gorbachev taken that morning, before he left the area. Both technologies achieved record speed for color photography in the production process (*San Francisco Examiner*).

## USA TODAY

Surely one of the most well-known high-tech success stories for computers in the newspaper business is *USA Today*, the flashy national paper delivered daily across the country. Since it began in 1981, *USA Today* has been

**FIGURE 2-16** Max Headroom was the first computerized human image to have his own TV series.

**cold type:** Setting type and producing pages on computer screens. The resulting computer typesetting files can be printed by laser and xerographic processes. Older Linotype methods set what was called hot type.

**HISTORY**

**FIGURE 2-17** The final edition of the *San Francisco Examiner* for June 4, 1990, included a photograph of Mikhail Gorbachev's visit to the city taken with a Sony digital camera which was ready for the presses a few minutes after it was snapped. Whereas this process was very "high tech" in 1990, it has become standard in metropolitan newspapers.

**FIGURE 2-18** A satellite receiving dish like those at the printing sites for *USA Today*.

**FIGURE 2-19** *USA Today* has been a pioneer in computer applications in newspaper production, including desktop publishing and the use of colorful computer graphics.

produced with computer graphics and four-color printing. Like the *San Francisco Examiner*, the paper began capturing photo images from television in 1990, using software called Adobe Photoshop, developed by the company that led the rush to laser printing with its PostScript software (Adobe Systems). Before printing, these digital TV photos can be edited and enhanced.

More amazing is the paper's nationwide printing process, based on satellite distribution of digitized pages. Copy for the paper is sent out every night from Washington headquarters to printing locations all over the nation. First the print pages are digitized with computer hardware; then the digitized images are sent out to the printing sites via satellite. A black-and-white page takes 3 minutes to transmit; color pages, richer in digitized information, take about 6 minutes. The printers receive the images from the satellite dishes and recreate and print the pages between midnight and 2 a.m., and the paper is available all over the country that morning. Here is an application not feasible without computer technology for digitization of images and data communication by satellites. The result is the first truly nationwide daily English language newspaper (Korzenlowski).

## ▶ Computers in Government

**HISTORY**

**punch card:** Invented for compiling the Census of 1890, an early means of encoding data for computers and other data processing equipment using a code made up of patterns of punched holes on a card.

In a society as large as the United States, computers have been used since their earliest days to keep track of data of all kinds. Herman Hollerith, working for the Census Bureau, invented the **punch card** to carry out the 1890 census; UNIVAC I, the first commercial computer, helped with the 1950 count. Based on 1980 census figures, Kenneth C. Laudon described the massive numbers of people about whom records are now being kept by government and quasi-governmental agencies:

*At last count there were 50 million Social Security beneficiaries, 95 million individual and 75 million business taxpayers, 21.2 million recipients of food stamps, 10.6 million recipients of Aid to Families with Dependent Children (AFDC), 24 million criminals and 60 million civilians with fingerprints at the FBI, 3.9 million elderly receiving Supple-*

## EVOLUTIONARY PERSPECTIVE

### Cyberspace Journalism

Instead of just using the computer to produce a printed version of newspaper or magazine, why not create and distribute the product directly on the Internet? Since 1994, the growth of the World Wide Web sites and their increasing number of users have led both small and large media outlets—newspapers, magazines, and television networks—to jump onto the Web with flashy home pages offering a variety of news features. The pioneers were smaller papers like the *Raleigh News and Observer* (NandoNet) and the *San Jose Mercury News* in the heart of Silicon Valley, the center of the American computer industry. When they stepped out and showed what could be done, the bigger players followed rapidly. Today all the major television networks are there (CBS, NBC, ABC, CNN, ESPN, etc.) along with major national newspapers like the *New York Times* and the *Los Angeles Times-Washington Post* News Service; *Time* and *U. S. News;* and popular computer magazines such as *PC Magazine* and *MacWorld*.

**FIGURE 2-20** Whereas the print version of the *New York Times* has always been a black-and-white newspaper, the Web version features color photography and graphics highlighting its on-line features.

Users can spend hours on the Web just browsing the variety and quantity of information available at newspaper sites alone. What they find varies somewhat, but typically there are local, national, and world news stories, often in digest form, and a selection of features and classified advertising. Someone who wants to place an ad can often do it directly by filling out a Web form on-line and paying by credit card. On the Web, browsing the headlines is free, but at the *San Jose Mercury* one must subscribe for about $5 a month to see full-length articles. Only then can one have access to a full file of Dave Barry columns, for example. While registration to the *New York Times* on-line version was free in early 1996, there were charges for downloading articles. Even its famous crossword puzzle was available on-line, accessible with a program that allows the user to fill it out directly on the computer and check the answers. At NandoNet, hundreds of homes for sale can be viewed on the computer; in fact, the paper advertises that it provides the largest collection of real estate information available on the Internet for its area of North Carolina. In browsing mode *USA Today* offers a host of polls and lists of information about each state, much like its published version, and full text of its articles for a subscription fee.

In truth, the role of news media on the World Wide Web is in its formative stages, and what will be available in the future is not certain. All kinds of commercial media are testing out what users want and are willing to pay for. When Microsoft, the giant software firm, announced that it was going to offer an electronic journal in late 1995, regular media outlets got nervous. No one yet knows who will be the winners or losers in this evolving service. Because everyone wants to provide enough content to find viewers, users today have lots of choices to "surf the Net" for up-to-date news, sports, and weather. Can the media continue to make their services freely accessible through the subsidy of advertisers and small subscription charges for users? One can only stay tuned on-line and watch the action (McGinn and Colley).

*mental Security Income (SSI), 21.4 million recipients of Medicaid, 61.8 million people covered by private health plans, more than 500,000 doctors and dentists who generated 1.1 million office visits, 49.8 million public school students, 9.5 million arrests, 294,000 people in jail, 5.8 million defense industry workers, 2 million members of the armed forces, 36 million living veterans of all wars, 51 million credit card holders, 62 million credit records held in private credit data systems, 154 million registered motor vehicles, and 140 million licensed drivers.*

In 1987 a government report listed 26,682 big mainframe computers with a total of 173,069 terminals, as well as a growing number of personal computers (99,087) in federal service (Wilk). Computer spending and usage has continued to spiral upward in the intervening years, as illustrated by the graph in Figure 2-21. Whereas a little more than $15 billion went into federal information technology in fiscal year 1987–88, the latest figures for 1994–95 show an investment of about $25 billion a year. Certainly the

**FIGURE 2-21** The federal government continues to invest in computers and information technology. In the 1980s, government reports listed the federal departments of Defense, Justice, and Treasury as using the largest number of terminals, with Energy and Defense having the largest number of micro-computers in service.

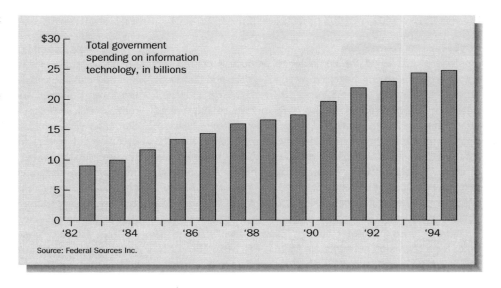

Total government spending on information technology, in billions

Source: Federal Sources Inc.

SOCIETY

number of microcomputers the federal government owns continues to grow, but we have no current figures for state and local jurisdictions.

Governments at all levels use computers to function more efficiently, effectively, and even more democratically. Computers seek out waste and fraud in government programs. They help to streamline operations by merging information collected from different agencies, for better planning, allocation of resources, and distribution of services. They work to collect taxes fairly and to discover cheaters, as well as to distribute monies to the less privileged members of the society. They use information collected about the economy and the society to make plans for future growth and development. They monitor criminal activity and seek out lawbreakers.

In addition, the federal government uses computers for our collective defense. Federal agencies reporting the most computers in 1985 were the Defense Department (66 percent of the mainframes and 39 percent of the micros in the federal government), the Department of Energy, including nuclear regulation (10 percent of the mainframes), the Justice Department, including the FBI (10 percent of the micros), and the Treasury Department, including the Internal Revenue System (4 percent of the mainframes and 6 percent of the micros).

## CONSTITUTIONAL QUESTIONS

SOCIETY

Studies of the effects of increasing computer usage in government have focused discussion among constitutional scholars on the shifting divisions of power among the three branches of the federal government, and on the power relations between the federal government and the states. One question concerns the computer's role in bringing about unequal parity in the historical checks and balances embodied in the Constitution among governmental bodies. The agencies that possess most of the federal government's computers are departments of the executive branch, controlled by Cabinet members. With this massive control over computer information resources, the president and the executive branch seem to have an unfair advantage in the distribution of power.

Congress, since the early 1970s, has added its own considerable computer resources—for example, for modeling the federal budget process in the Congressional Budget Office. It regularly requires the executive branch to share its computer-produced materials for consideration in the legislative process. Nevertheless, after passage of the Gramm-Rudman-Hollings law requiring automatic deficit reduction, Congressman Michael Synar of Oklahoma brought suit questioning its constitutionality. He felt that Congress had unwisely given over its constitutional responsibility for budgeting not to the President but to a computer (Kraemer and King).

Since the election of 1994, the continuing battle between the Republican Congress and the Democratic White House has reached onto the Internet. Before the election, the White House went onto the World Wide Web with one of the most popular home pages: http://www.whitehouse.gov. Visitors can not only view photos of the mansion but also position papers from the Clinton administration. Similarly most executive department agencies have added Web sites with the strong encouragement of the Clinton-Gore administration. In early 1995, Speaker of the House Newt Gingrich unveiled his rival service for the Congress called Thomas (named for Thomas Jefferson): http://thomas.loc.gov. This site offers the full text of pending legislation and the *Congressional Record*. Both groups believe that getting the word (and in some cases, the picture) out about the government can only improve communication with the voting public. Taxpayers paid for the development of the Internet over the last 25 years, and they can now log on and actively watch the struggle between the two most visible branches of government (Weingarten).

The judiciary, the least computerized of the three branches, can also require information from the executive departments, and has the power to rule ineligible whatever evidence it chooses. In other words, the judiciary can decide in particular cases whether information is or is not relevant and thus may stymie the executive branch's arguments by ruling its massive data files inadmissible to the case at hand. Computers have only intensified the continual tug of war for power between the branches of the federal government.

## WELFARE AND LAW ENFORCEMENT

In relations between the federal government and the states and cities, the evidence is more mixed. Especially in social welfare and law enforcement, the federal government has more presence on the local level now than ever before. With the provision of welfare funds from states and national agencies to cities and counties come mandates about how the programs must be administered and monitored. This degree of governmental control is made possible with computers; whether it is desirable is a controversial political issue.

Federal incentives for law enforcement funds can require standardization and sharing of information at all levels through such agencies as the National Crime Information Center. NCIC was formed in 1967 to collect and distribute criminal information: files on stolen property and firearms, lists of wanted criminals and missing persons, and criminal histories of people arrested for or convicted of serious crimes. Gradually state and local police departments have merged their records into NCIC and coordinated their computer hardware to allow almost instant access to these massive criminal files. David Nemecek, director of NCIC, reported in August 1990 that the agency got more than 1 million queries a day for criminal information from more than 64 thousand law enforcement agencies (Boyd). Without such centralization and standardization of criminal records and the ability to access them through communications links, there could be no effective nationwide coordination of law enforcement. On the other hand, critics allege that NCIC is vulnerable to abuse. Computer Professionals for Social Responsibility has, in fact, persuaded the FBI to spell out policies prohibiting the use of NCIC to track "suspicious" individuals.

**The Effect of Computers on Government**

No level of government can exist today without computers for data processing and much more. Machines produce efficiency and savings in the ordinary tasks of government, and simulations offer valuable insights for better social planning, cost control, and management.

No part of the federal system seems in danger of losing its constitutional mission because of the growth of computer technology. New relationships, both competitive and cooperative, are evolving between the three federal branches and state and local governments. Questions of the invasion of personal privacy and the possibility for encroachment on the freedoms of individuals have not been adequately addressed.

In defense research, computers suggest the possibility of a peaceful world based on weapons that come right out of science fiction. But the role of the armed services in this technological, robotic world is still not settled.

## COMPUTERIZED FINGERPRINT SEARCHES

**SOCIETY**

In recent years, using digitized imaging, computer programs have been developed to compare fingerprints automatically, replacing the time-consuming process of checking fingerprint cards manually. In one case reported in the *Christian Science Monitor* (9 June 1988), a burglar who murdered a woman in San Francisco in 1978 and left behind his fingerprints was caught when the police department got the software eight years later. A police inspector was able to find the man's prints in less than 4 minutes—a job he had been unable to accomplish in almost a decade of checking records visually. The murderer was picked up, admitted the crime, and is now in jail.

In 1988 these digitized fingerprint records had not yet been incorporated into NCIC, for two reasons. Several competing encoding standards from different software producers were in use, and the FBI did not have the funds to encode its more than 20 million criminal fingerprints—that is, more than 200 million individual prints, 10 per person. While the FBI worked to complete this job by 1993, states had been buying the same software and sharing data among themselves. With their own computers and budgets, local jurisdictions have kept control over their own criminal data, and with microcomputers approaching the power of mainframe machines this trend will grow.

## COMPUTERS IN DEFENSE

**Strategic Defense Initiative (SDI):** A defense system nicknamed "Star Wars" that combined computerized radar monitoring of incoming missiles and shooting them down with automated interceptor missiles. Controversial from the start, the program is being dismantled in the 1990s.

**smart weapons:** Military hardware, like the Tomahawk missile from the 1991 Persian Gulf War, that incorporates computers in its design to carry out its mission.

Certainly the most massive use and expenditure on computers in the U.S. government has been in defense of the nation. The famous and controversial Star Wars weapons program of the 1980s, properly called the **Strategic Defense Initiative (SDI),** was based on the use of computers to monitor attacking missiles and automatically deploy defensive missiles to destroy them. The program has been vilified by some computer professionals as too expensive and unworkable, and credited by supporters with helping to end the Cold War (because the Soviet Union had neither the technology nor the finances to mount a credible alternative). Some critics alleged that SDI was far more than a defensive system and could be used for a preemptive first-strike nuclear attack.

Star Wars aside, modern warfare was changed forever by the so-called **smart weapons** that aided soldiers, sailors, and pilots in the 1991 Persian Gulf War, which has been called "the first information war" by author Alan Campen. High-tech successes included Tomahawk stealth missiles, which sought out and destroyed their targets with pinpoint accuracy, and Patriot missiles, which used computer-generated trajectories to intercept

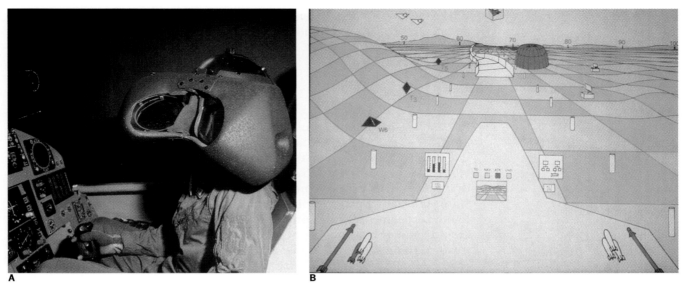

**FIGURE 2-22** Pilots wearing this protoype helmet (A) in the supercockpit of future fighter planes can see the area ahead of them as in a video game (B) and fly the plane with verbal and touch commands.

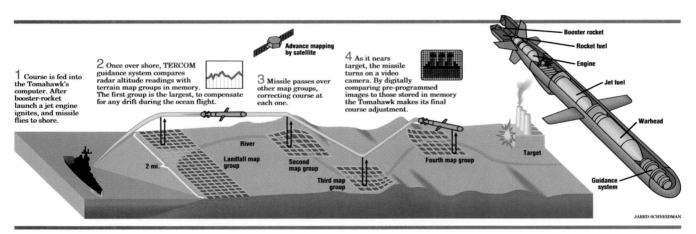

**FIGURE 2-23** Note the places in which the computer is involved in helping a Tomahawk missile seek out its target.

incoming Iraqi Scuds. In a continuing research project called the **super-cockpit,** pilots wear "virtual reality helmets." As in a video game, computers in the helmets show pilots the terrain ahead of them, the enemy weapons approaching, and the evasive actions they can take. Research includes voice-control systems that allow planes to be flown by speech commands. If the pilot is unable to fly the plane, the computer, dubbed the "pilot's associate," takes over (Thomas and Barry).

War is becoming depersonalized; the enemy is not seen by the soldier or the pilot, but found and destroyed electronically. Even in the ranks of defense analysts, critics contend that General George Patton was right when he said, "Wars may be fought with weapons, but they are won by men. It is the spirit of men who follow and of the man who leads that gains the victory." A lot of faith and federal research money have been invested in the Strategic Computing Program of the Defense Department and in the workability of automated weapons. Whether defense budgets will be able to keep pace with the 1980s in these times of federal deficits and the end of the Cold War, in order to sustain the research required by

**supercockpit:** A Defense Department research project to create a computerized helmet that resembles a video game and automates many functions for the pilot of the plane.

**SOCIETY**

these new computing systems, remains an important question for national debate among Congress and the American people.

## ▶ Summary

For individual computer users, as well as in education, the medical and physical sciences, the media, and at all levels of government, the computer is a positive technology that offers economy, insight, and applications that would be impossible to do otherwise. It enables its users to be more productive and to do enormous good. It gives reality to the old slogan Information Is Power for individuals and organizations alike. For some handicapped people, the computer is literally empowering, and for government it makes possible the exercise of power for social good in a complex, modern mass society. Yet like any technology, computers bring inevitable costs, not all of them monetary. We must turn now to the other side of the equation, the societal consequences of the computer age.

## ▶ Key Terms

cold type (p. 45)

computational science (p. 44)

computer-aided design (CAD) (p. 32)

computer conferencing (p. 33)

computerized axial tomography (CAT or CT scanner) (p. 41)

computer monitoring (p. 41)

cybernetics (p. 41)

data communications (p. 32)

desktop publishing (p. 30)

distance learning (p. 34)

electronic mail (p. 33)

electronic prosthetics (p. 41)

file management (p. 31)

gigaflop (GFLOP) (p. 42)

graphical workstation (p. 42)

integrated package (p. 30)

killer app (p. 32)

magnetic resonance imaging (MRI scanning) (p. 41)

medical database (p. 39)

modem (p. 32)

pixel (p. 44)

productivity software (p. 30)

punch card (p. 46)

real time (p. 35)

scientific visualization (p. 44)

smart weapons (p. 50)

Strategic Defense Initiative (SDI) (p. 50)

supercockpit (p. 51)

supercomputer (p. 42)

teraflop (TFLOP) (p. 42)

videoconferencing (p. 39)

## ▶ Self-Test

### MULTIPLE-CHOICE

1. All of the following characteristics make the computer a powerful force in many areas of application except
   a. its flexibility
   b. its speed
   c. its accuracy
   d. its compatibility among different models and manufacturers
2. Applications software that is called "integrated"
   a. works on black-and-white screens only

b. has several programs that can interact with each other's data

c. is handled in character mode

d. can be run only on a mouse-driven computer

3. Which of the following computer strategies represent new methods of educational pedagogy?

a. distance learning

b. network classrooms

c. team projects in multimedia

d. all of the above

4. All of the following are reasons for the popularity of computer simulations in the natural sciences except one. Identify it.

a. Students gain experience in on-line networking in the laboratory.

b. Sometimes experiments are not safe for students to do in real life.

c. Equipment for some experiments is too costly for many laboratories.

d. Simulations cut down on delay in waiting for reactions.

5. Which of the following does not characterize modern scientific research in business and universities?

a. supercomputers

b. graphical workstations

c. dissection of laboratory animals with robots

d. scientific visualization

6. The era of computerized journalism is characterized by all of the following except

a. reporting with laptop computers equipped with modems

b. cold type publishing

c. voice-activated typesetting

d. on-line versions of newspapers and magazines

7. Which of the following is not a reason that governments at all levels use computers to carry out their business?

a. to function more efficiently

b. to discourage dissent

c. to manage governmental services more effectively

d. to spread their benefits more democratically

8. Choose from the following list a project that exemplifies computers used for national defense.

a. SDI, the Star Wars project

b. supercockpits

c. the Patriot missile

d. all of the above

## TRUE/FALSE

9. **T  F**  Word processing is simply typewriting using a computer keyboard for input and a printer for output.

10. **T  F**  The chief advantage of a spreadsheet over manual accounting techniques is its capacity to do arithmetic calculations automatically.

11. **T  F**  A major reason why the personal computer has become so popular is that various kinds of applications software which run on it can do so many useful jobs.

12. **T  F**  In the future experts expect computers to become a primary replacement for the human contact between teacher and student.

13. **T  F**  One of the main reasons why *USA Today* could become America's first national paper, delivered throughout the country daily, was satellite distribution and printing of the downloaded text at local sites.

14. **T  F**  Studies show that by the year 2000 as many Americans will get their news from the World Wide Web as from printed newspapers.

15. **T  F**  Most of the computers in the federal government are in departments of the legislative branch controlled by Congress.

16. **T  F**  Military leaders unanimously agree that future armies will have few ordinary foot soldiers, whose role will be taken over by a technological, robotic force.

## FILL-IN

17. Computer programs for common applications like word processing or spreadsheets, which users choose to increase their day-to-day productivity, are often called _____.

18. _____ packages are analogous to manual filing systems, such as using index cards for a mailing list.

19. Electronic mail and computer conferencing represent two instances of the burgeoning applications software field called _____.

20. _____ is a well-known medical database of current research findings and treatments, well indexed and suitable for on-line searches.

21. Computers are being used frequently in the field of _____, the replacement of missing body parts with artificial limbs or organs.

22. The new field of _____ combines two major computer capacities, the ability to do massive amounts of mathematical calculations quickly and to represent the results as graphic images.

23. When a computer calculates the results of an experiment and presents the results as soon as the data have been read, the process is called a _____ application.

24. The _____ was created to collect and distribute criminal information, such as the names of wanted criminals and missing persons and criminal records of people convicted of serious crimes.

## ▶ Experiential Exercises

1. Go to the administrative office of your academic department or college to see what kinds of applications software are used there. For what sorts of jobs are specific kinds of software used? What particular brands are favored and why?

2. Investigate the role of computer-assisted instruction in your college or university. Are writing courses taught with computers? Do the social sciences use on-line databases? What kinds of simulations are found in the social and physical sciences?

3. Do writing teachers recommend spelling and grammar checkers at your college? Are calculators encouraged in mathematics classes? If not, what reasons are given for discouraging such computer aids?

4. American health care remains the most expensive in the world. For a

recent year, research the extent to which economists credit expensive high-tech computer devices like CAT and MRI scanners with increasing overall health costs.

5. Look up the 21 Grand Challenge problems identified by the Federal High Performance Computing Program in 1989. Find out whether natural scientists at your institution do research related to those problems, and write a report on the role of computing in the effort.

6. Investigate the role of computers in journalism on your campus or in your community, including both print and radio and television.

7. Take a topic like Bosnia, the Super Bowl, or something else current, and see what sorts of information you can find about it on World Wide Web versions of newspapers, magazines, and television networks. Is the depth of coverage suitable for writing a report, or would you be better off using traditional sources in the library? How easy is it to use the indexing systems available on the Web?

8. Given the widespread use of NCIC crime files, go to a local police station and see if they are queried, for what purposes, and how often. How reliable do officials think that NCIC information is?

9. The Tomahawk and Stealth missile technologies that were used in the 1991 war with Iraq were really developed in the 1970s. Investigate the computer component of some current weapon system under development.

## ▶ Critical Thinking Exercises

1. With increasing use of CAI, how is the role of the classroom teacher changing? Are computers in education generally a positive trend?

2. What effects will health care reforms discussed in Washington have on the spread of high-tech medicine? Would Americans want cost controls to hold back the growth of medical technology?

3. The growth of "big science" involving supercomputers is thought by some to be too expensive for continued support by the federal government, at least at levels sustained in the Cold War. Discuss.

4. Because print and broadcast media are merging materials into common digital formats, the media industries of the future will probably coalesce into giant newspaper/TV/movie conglomerates. Discuss this statement.

5. Most of the computers in the federal government are used in the departments of the executive branch, such as Defense, Treasury, and Justice. As a result, the computer contributes to unequal parity in favor of the president *vis-à-vis* the Congress and the Judiciary in terms of the checks and balances embodied in the Constitution. Defend or refute this point.

6. Wars in the future will be automated with computerized weapons systems. The days of the foot soldier are rapidly ending. Discuss this statement.

### ANSWERS TO SELF-TEST

*Multiple-Choice*: 1. d;   2. b;   3. d;   4. a;   5. c;   6. c;   7. b;
8. d
*True/False*: 9. F;   10. T;   11. T;   12. F;   13. T;   14. F;
15. F;   16. F
*Fill-in*: 17. productivity software;   18. database;   19. data communications;   20. MEDLINE;   21. prosthetics;   22. computational science;   23. real-time;   24. National Crime Information Center (NCIC)

# CHAPTER 3

# Computers in Society: The Drawbacks

▶ **LEARNING OUTCOMES**

*After completing this chapter, you should be able to:*

1. *Discuss the personal and individual issues, such as loss of individuality and personal service, that have arisen because of computerization.*

2. *List and discuss the harmful effects of computers on the workplace.*

3. *Assess the positive and negative aspects of the government's need for information about citizens.*

▶ **COMPUTERS IN CONTEXT**

*The old Chinese proverb "May you live in interesting times" certainly applies to the late twentieth century, including the many beneficial applications of computers and their associated technologies, which enrich so many aspects of our lives. But the connotations of the proverb are not all positive. The slogan is a paradox, a double-edged sword. When someone in China greeted you with this aphorism, he or she usually meant it as a negative comment—a curse—for interesting times hold great potential for unhappy consequences in daily life and society. The same can be said for the world of modern computing. The pervasive intrusion of the computer into so much of life has had some negative effects on us and even seems a threat to some members of our society. Sometimes the Computer Triangle seems over-balanced in favor of hardware and software to the detriment of society, presumably the most important element.*

This phenomenon should not be surprising. Just as the invention of printing brought to an end the era of beautiful medieval manuscripts, and the invention of the automobile effectively ended the carriage trade, the introduction of any new technology has its negative effects on current ways of life. The introduction of packaged cake mixes and frozen vegetables had a strong negative effect on home baking and gardening in the postwar period. And microwave cooking has not only shortened the food preparation time for two-person working families, but has also cut down on the number of stews and soups lovingly simmered on low all day in an earlier era. One could argue that all-day cooking wasted a lot of energy and valuable time for the cook who stayed in the kitchen all day. Certainly the process of freezing foods made vegetables and fruits available to consumers regardless of geographical location or season. Whatever one's perspective on such changes, the principle remains the same. *The technology may be neutral, but its effects on the people who use it have never been.*

Many of the negative effects that the computer revolution has had on modern life can be classified into three broad categories: personal, economic, and governmental. In each area a variety of changes brought on by the computer can be seen as drawbacks. Many of them are interrelated and cannot be discussed in isolation. In such cases as personal privacy and government use of personal data, the boundaries between the three categories are not rigid, nor the issues simple.

## ▶ Personal and Individual Issues

A lot of people are not happy with the steady invasion of computers into everyday life. Often complaints fall into two categories, loss of individuality and personal service. The demands of the organization and the marketplace sometimes conflict with personal dignity and convenience.

### LOSS OF INDIVIDUALITY

In the mid-1960s, before the massive demonstrations of the Vietnam era, the most serious threat to the stable climate of university life was the student rebellion at the University of California at Berkeley. Sociologists who studied the event have characterized it as a way for students to strike back at what they perceived as an unconcerned system. They protested the impersonal way in which they were treated by the factory of higher education, called the multiversity. Students complained that they were treated like faceless numbers in large lecture classes that robbed them of personal attention. Centralized record keeping, made possible with data processing computers, had replaced the personal touch of earlier days. The university, and the machine which was its embodiment, were perceived as being unconcerned about individuals.

**SOCIETY**

A persuasive symbol of the protest was the **punch card,** the most popular input medium for large computers of that time and widely used for college records and registration. Punch cards came with a printed warning not to fold, spindle, or mutilate them, so they could be read into computers automatically by card readers. Responding to students' feelings of impersonality, another large state university of the same era allowed students to vent their frustrations with the system humorously by sponsoring a "fold, spindle, and mutilate" day. Thousands of punch cards were handed out at the student union, so that students could fold, spindle, and mutilate them as they wished—and in the process make a statement on the importance of the individual.

**punch card:** Invented for compiling the 1890 census, an early means of encoding data for computers and other data processing equipment using a code made up of patterns of punched holes in a card.

### PERSONAL SERVICE VERSUS ECONOMY

Even though the punch card is seldom seen today, many people still feel that they are treated more like numbers than human beings. Supermarkets have installed scanners at the checkout counter to read Universal Product Codes (UPCs), the product numbers embodied in the bar codes printed on almost all packages. In the process, they have ceased to put price stickers on individual items on the shelves. Prices are quoted only on the edge of the shelves, where they are presumably in clear view when customers are making their choices among products. Once customers have taken an item, they have no record of its price until they get to the checkout

**FIGURE 3-1** (right) A cartoon about the 1960s illustrating student discontent at being treated like numbers on a punch card. Punch cards often carried a message not to fold, spindle, or mutilate them.

**FIGURE 3-2** (below) A scanning device at the supermarket checkout counter reads the UPC on packages. The computer then looks up the price and computes the total cost of a purchase. Items rarely still have individual price labels.

SOCIETY

counter. Of course, they can keep count of what they are spending with a small calculator as they pass through the store, but few people bother to do so. Many shoppers sense a loss of personal service with this UPC-coded, numerically controlled philosophy of more and more stores today.

Although supermarket executives probably received a few consumer complaints when the systems were installed, issues of economy dominated in the decision to make the switch. Using UPC bar codes that can be read by a scanner on the shelf and on the product speeds reordering, checkout, and inventory. Clerks no longer need to attach price labels to cans and boxes, and are thus freed for other jobs. Productivity increases, but some personal service is sacrificed. Gone forever in most places are the small, family-run stores that ran a tab for families and billed by the month. Where they do survive, their costs for items are inevitably higher than those of big stores, for service costs are factored into their prices. Here we have a dramatic illustration of the tradeoffs that the introduction of technology often entails in a changing marketplace. The personal service and convenience of the corner store have been replaced by the greater selection and lower prices of larger, more impersonal stores with centralized record keeping.

## MACHINE OR HUMAN ERROR?

SOCIETY

People also feel victimized when an error is made in some form of computerized billing, typically managed by a program running on some large and remote mainframe computer. Their complaints to local stores or agencies are often met by staff responses that "the computer made the error." The employees who handle the complaints are often uncomfortable with computers and technology. They do not work with the machines directly and do not understand how they work. Both customer and clerk feel a sense of **computer phobia.** It's the machine's fault. Blaming the absent and mysterious machine allows everyone to feel free of responsibility for the foul-up.

Perhaps the computer program was poorly designed, and inefficiency and error did creep into the billing process. Some years ago a subscriber to a popular national magazine sent a check with an order form, but did not receive any copies of the magazine for several months. The subscriber

**computer phobia:** A sense of unease and helplessness around computers sometimes felt by people unfamiliar with them. Taking a computer literacy course should help to relieve this condition.

wrote two letters to the publisher but got no response, nor any magazines either. In desperation, the customer decided to telephone the subscription office collect to register an indignant complaint. A pleasant voice at the other end of the line informed the caller that the magazine never accepted collect calls for subscription inquiries. If the customer was willing to pay for the call, the clerk would try to help him.

Exasperated after repeated attempts to get satisfaction, the subscriber agreed to pay for the call, and straightened the matter out on the phone in a short time. The operator admitted that the computerized subscription system for the magazine was terribly messed up. Unable to cope with hundreds of letters from irate subscribers every month, the company consciously decided just to ignore them and not to answer any mail about subscription problems. Saddled with a computer program which needed replacement, executives chose to let customer service go, except for phone calls paid for by customers themselves. Certainly the company did not advertise the policy, and only those who were victims of the system became aware of it.

More often than not, problems of this kind are caused by human error on the part of the people who work with computer systems. Remember that the Computer Triangle consists of hardware, software, and the people who interact with them. This interconnection is often called the **human–computer** (or **man–machine**) **interface**—technical terms coined to describe the points of connection and interaction. Just as software "interfaces" with hardware when computer programs turn on printers, so people who work at banks, stores, and airlines interface with computers and their underlying programs, even if they never see the machines. If a clerk encodes an erroneous figure into a billing record, the faulty information gets into the computer and eventually comes back to the customer.

A true, everyday example shows the absurd lengths to which such situations can be carried. A few years ago, a computer scientist paid a friend with a $20 check. When the friend cashed it at the local branch of another bank, the teller made an error in posting it by adding an extra 0 to the magnetic numbers in the lower right-hand corner of the check, an area reserved for the value of the check. The check was read into the banking system by a scanner and eventually cleared through the check writer's home bank. The man's account was debited not for $20 but for $200, because of the extra 0 added accidentally at the other bank.

A few days later the man received a statement showing not only the $180 error, but an overdraft on the account. Two service charges had been levied, one for the overdraft and another because the balance had fallen below the minimum necessary for free checking. Meanwhile, another check written in the interim had been returned for insufficient funds.

Then began six weeks of headaches to get the error cleared up. First, the local branch bank could not handle the transactions; the customer had to go to the main office downtown. After a few minutes, the officer there understood the problem. (Remember that the check was clearly written for $20.) The two service charges had been automatically assessed by the computer accounting program when the account balance hit minimum and later dropped below zero. The officer disappeared into the data processing section to rectify the account. The bank corrected the error, refunded the service charges, reprocessed the bounced check, and sent a letter to the creditor to explain that the overdraft was not the customer's fault.

However, the hour that the man took off from work to correct the error had not permanently cleared up the matter. Because the monthly balance had been below minimum at the beginning of the current accounting period, the officer explained, the computer program would apply an automatic service charge to the next month's statement. When the man asked if the charge could be short-circuited at this point, the bank officer answered

SOCIETY

**human–computer (man–machine) interface:** Term coined to refer to the points of connection and interaction between people and computer systems. Problems caused by human input of bad data to computers represent a breakdown at the interface point between people and the system.

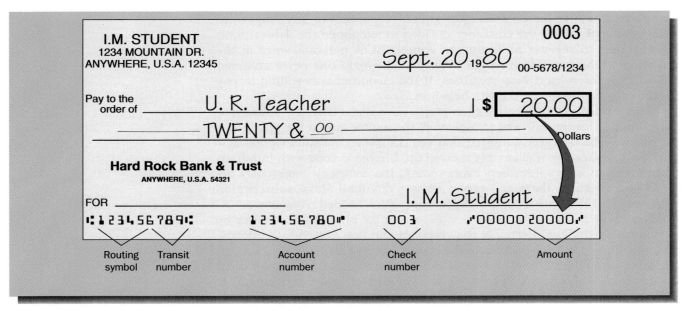

**FIGURE 3-3** This $20.00 check was erroneously encoded for computer processing as worth $200.00, denoted by the extra zero in the computer-readable numbers inadvertently typed at the bottom right corner. From then on, processing by computer systems involved a $180.00 error.

with a polite "no"; the customer would have to come back when the new statement came. The customer returned to the main branch the next month, explained the situation once again, and finally got the new service charge refunded and the account balanced correctly.

The fact that the customer worked with computers and understood what had taken place at each stage of the automated process, from scanner to the computer accounting program, did not eliminate his frustration or prevent his taking two hours' leave from work to correct the records. No wonder that people who are unfamiliar with computers feel threatened and helpless against such eventualities. Such mix-ups are a classic cause of computer phobia. Of course, the computer does not talk back, and it gets blamed even though it is only carrying out its programmed instructions. In the good old days, a kindly clerk could have rectified everything in a few minutes. In this case; however, as soon as the teller at the other bank had encoded the extra zero, several computer systems automatically were set in motion. Nowhere in the ensuing chain of events was there another person who could reverse the process until it had been played out. Often unaware of the automated procedures, bank personnel are glad to blame the problem on the impersonal machine.

### GARBAGE IN, GARBAGE OUT

Computer professionals have coined a phrase, "garbage in, garbage out" (abbreviated GIGO), to describe situations of this kind. The smooth interface between human and machine in computerized banking became hostage to an innocent keying error at the beginning of the chain. Today accounting programs should be flexible enough to allow bank personnel to stop the second automatic service charge at the same time they correct the original error. In this case, the original human error reverberated through an automated system and cost both the customer and the bank staff time and money to rectify. Given faulty data to process, the computer compounded the error—an extended case of GIGO.

## ▶ Computers in the Workplace

The increasing presence of computers affects the workplace from Main Street to the major centers of the global economy. High technology brings changes in the job mix both locally and throughout the world. Issues like job displacement and global competition are complex and interrelated. Put into perspective, they are difficult to analyze in black-and-white terms.

### JOB DISPLACEMENT

Early in the nineteenth century, in northern England, where the Industrial Revolution began, workers in the mechanized textile industry were laid off when factory owners introduced faster weaving machines needing fewer workers. Groups of the unemployed weavers roamed the countryside, destroying factories and equipment. These civil protests against changes in the way textiles were manufactured are known as the **Luddite riots,** named for an early protester, Ned Ludlam. The government did not condone destruction of the property of factory owners and meted out strong penalties to the rioters. The case is remembered as the first in which the introduction of a new technology led to social disruption as a result of unemployment (see Richard Altick, *Victorian People and Ideas*). Today the term *Luddite* is still applied negatively to someone who opposes technological change.

The first years of the computer revolution brought cries from the labor movement that the introduction of automation would lead to massive unemployment. Some industries, like textiles, did get by with fewer employees when they introduced automated methods and robotic machines. But simultaneously a whole new industry, the computer field, was developing and adding new possibilities for the uses of computers and allied devices like communications and telephones. Early studies indicated that at least as many jobs were created from computing as were replaced. But often these new jobs did not go to the workers who were replaced. The losers tended to be unskilled workers with few adaptable skills and older people less able or willing to relocate or retrain. Whenever a new technology is introduced, displacement of some workers and readjustment in the conditions of employment are bound to occur.

The current term for job displacement is **downsizing,** which has affected middle-aged, middle-class managers as well as unskilled and older workers. The media and politicians have advanced a number of reasons to explain why even middle managers with twenty years of experience in a prosperous corporation fear loss of job security. Although some politicians blame global trade agreements such as NAFTA and GATT, many who have studied the subject see a major transition taking place in the American economy, which must be explained by a complex series of interrelated developments. Columnist Trudy Rubin thinks that "changing technology—in which America is a leader—bears much of the responsibility" (Rubin). The replacement of work by computing technology has even resulted in the downsizing of such companies as IBM and AT&T, whose business is based in these technologies.

Besides technology, major factors contributing to downsizing include global competition, rising health-care costs, and deregulation of industries (Montague). Jeffrey Rifkin, author of *The End of Work*, speaks of "near-workerless factories in such industries as insurance and banking—and not just because the machines are more efficient" (quoted in Raspberry). A small, highly trained work force keeps health insurance and pension costs down and helps to make the bottom line on profits look better to the stockholders. One cannot blame NAFTA or computers for all the woes of down-

**Luddite riots:** Early nineteenth-century revolts by weavers in northern England when the introduction of weaving machinery into factories led to their being laid off. A famous instance where the introduction of new technology led to unemployment and social unrest.

 **SOCIETY**    **HISTORY**

**downsizing:** A term for the shrinking size of modern corporations and the subsequent loss of jobs, including many middle managers.

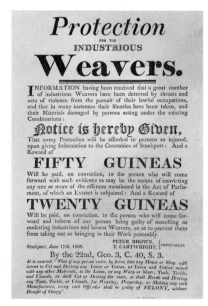

**FIGURE 3-4** An 1808 poster from England offers rewards for witnesses who help to convict Luddites of breaking weaving machines and attacking factory weavers.

sizing. Different trends work together to play their part in the economic transition of the 1990s. Like the Computer Triangle, the interplay of technology and other societal factors must be considered in trying to explain the phenomenon of downsizing.

## IMPORTANCE OF EDUCATION

Those best able to cope with technological change are those with education and the ability to retool. Certainly our society is consumed with the need for students to stay in school and complete at least their high school education, to meet the challenges of the twentieth-first century and of high technology. The state and federal governments are working to upgrade the standards of general education at all levels. College faculties are full of arguments about what subjects will best enable students to adjust to the changes and challenges of the next century. Along with the rise of required courses in computer literacy, many colleges are returning to the basic standards of the old liberal arts curriculum. They are focusing on writing and communications skills; mathematics and quantitative reasoning; and humanities, sciences, and foreign languages.

SOCIETY

More than ever before, students are not likely to be doing the same jobs in 20 years that they prepared for when they left college. We see the importance of skills that are adaptable to new jobs and new work situations, rather than narrow professional training. Continuing education, already a fact of life in many professional fields like education and medicine, is becoming the norm in more and more professions. Newspapers are filled with ads for evening and weekend seminars on the latest strategies for improving productivity. As we have seen in Chapters 1 and 2, computer education can work hand in hand with traditional subjects in the college curriculum. Not only is learning to program a computer excellent training in rigorous thinking and logical reasoning, but computers offer a variety of methods for data analysis, to probe diverse problems in all areas of human experience.

## EMPLOYEE INVOLVEMENT IN CHANGE

In offices where clerical workers still do much keyboarding and word processing, we have seen some harmful side effects of the computer revolution in recent years. Although some older employees feel threatened by the changes, in most places in America an almost universal transition to modern office technology has been accomplished. Studies have shown that the transition has been most successful where the affected employees themselves are actively involved in the changeover. That is, they are apprised of the proposed changes—new machines and new working arrangements—and are given an opportunity to comment and make suggestions about the most suitable ways to make the transition. Along with their supervisors, they feel a part of the change; their input is sought and is taken into account. On the other hand, when managers make all the decisions and only inform workers that the office will be shifting to computers, they often experience an increase in reported personnel difficulties—illness, job stress, injured feelings—during and after the transition period. Here we have a clear case of technology transfer with a human dimension. Taking account of the human–computer interface at the outset smoothes the whole process.

**FIGURE 3-5** Recent studies indicate that some computer terminals give off harmful electromagnetic radiation. Experts advise that people not sit too close to the screen for long periods, especially pregnant women.

## HEALTH RISKS

Even with computers, physical working conditions can lead to health problems. The workplace has always been linked to various physical and emotional problems, whether in mines, on the assembly line, or in the office. The computer office is clean, well lit, and not typically filled with machines that cause damage to their users. However, people who sit at computer keyboards or stare at computer screens all day sometimes report wrist pain similar to tennis elbow or eyestrain and fatigue. In 1988 the Bureau of Labor Statistics reported an alarming increase in the number of incidents of **repetitive stress injury (RSI),** a syndrome that is attributed to long hours at a computer keyboard. Some people have such severe pain in their arms that they have difficulty with ordinary routines like opening doors or brushing teeth (Kantrowitz and Crandall).

Even more disturbing is recent research into the possible harmful effects of **low-level electromagnetic emissions** from computer screens, especially for women in their childbearing years. For years government and industry have said that radiation from computer monitors is within safe levels for workers. In 1984 the Computer and Business Equipment Manufacturers Association said that pregnant women asking to be transferred away from work on terminals was "like asking to be transferred away from a light bulb." Yet scientists in Sweden, Canada, and the United States questioned these safety claims in their research into the effects of the special kind of sawtooth magnetic radiation emitted by computer screens. In 1990, when the issue reached the public press, no clear link could be definitely proved between miscarriages, cancer, and computer emissions. But with more than 40 million terminals at use in the workplace, the questions raised by recent research can no longer be ignored (Brodeur).

The whole issue of healthful working conditions in the computerized office has led to the development of **ergonomics,** the subject of machine and office equipment designs that minimize health problems. A glance at ads for keyboards, computer screens, and office furniture shows a growing concern for ergonomics. Desks that lower the keyboard; nonglare screens that are low in emissions; chairs with a variety of positions for better back support, including new designs with back and leg support but no actual

**repetitive stress injury (RSI):** A medical condition resulting in severe arm pain, thought to be caused by sitting long hours at computer keyboards.

SOCIETY

**low-level electromagnetic emissions:** Small amounts of radiation emitted by electronic equipment such as computer screens that may be hazardous to the health of people who work with computers for many hours.

**ergonomics:** The study of how to adapt machines and working conditions to people to minimize health risks.

**FIGURE 3-6 (A)** Ergonomically designed workstations are intended to make the user comfortable and to reduce health problems.

**FIGURE 3-6 (B)** This office furniture is designed for the comfort and health of the employee, including an ergonomic chair and a keyboard lower than desk level.

A

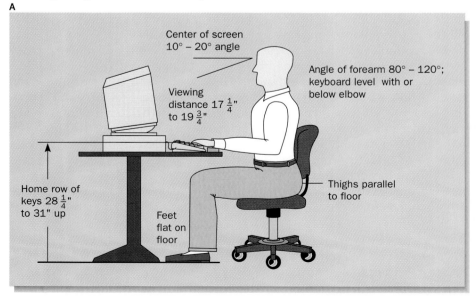

B

**FIGURE 3-7** Graffiti sprayed on a wall in East Germany soon after the Berlin Wall came down. What does "software" mean in this context? Was the graffiti artist possibly a disgruntled communist?

SOCIETY

SOCIETY

seat (see Figure 3-6)—all these are indicative of the ergonomic movement in design brought about by the presence of computers in the office.

## GLOBAL ECONOMIC CHALLENGE

In the last two decades the electronics and textile industries have moved many of their production facilities overseas because labor costs are lower there. Some parts of the data processing industry have done the same. Large banks with massive numbers of checks to clear have gone "high tech" with long-distance communications. They ship their checks by air to data processing centers in the Caribbean, where wages are much lower than in the United States. Typing clerks there carry out the data entry job offshore and produce the records needed to update the bank's accounts at home. When the records are ready to send back to the United States, they are transmitted electronically by satellite, and quickly and accurately, in a matter of minutes, they move directly into the input stream of the bank's computers. Later a magnetic tape or disk is mailed back to the bank for storage, as a permanent record of the transactions. Of course, hiring key-boarding employees in low-wage countries displaces the jobs of workers in the United States.

More significant than the loss of jobs to other nations is the extent to which high technology itself, including the computer industry, has become the current battleground of economic competition among nations. As the 1980s ended, the Berlin Wall, the most visible symbol of the Cold War, came down, and the countries of Eastern Europe began to move toward democracy and integration into the economic and cultural life of the Western world. Most analysts now believe that the Cold War, which dominated American foreign policy for more than 40 years after the end of the Second World War, is over. Although much uncertainty remains, conditions in the former Soviet Union and Communist bloc nations have changed so drastically that a return to the sorts of international tensions common in the last decades seems unlikely.

The decade of the 1990s, then, is seeing a shift from military to economic growth and competition on a global scale. The creation of the European Common Market in 1992 and the growing power and influence of the Pacific nations—preeminently Japan, but also Hong Kong, Singapore, Taiwan, and South Korea—represent formidable economic competition for American high-tech industries. Already much of the home electronics industry has moved to Asia. These countries also produce high-quality computers and allied hardware at cheaper prices than American suppliers, and their governments fund research into future needs heavily.

For example, Japan in the early 1980s put a lot of government money into artificial intelligence research in order to develop the so-called Fifth Generation of intelligent computers. Historically, the United States government has not seen fit to encourage private business to carry out industrial research with government funds, except in the military and space fields, where the national interest was threatened. Compared to Japan, we have far less government planning for economic development. We have a tradition of private capitalism, unfettered by government regulation and control, that has been successful for a long time.

Relevant for discussion here are the following remarks by Akio Morita, former chairman of Sony Corporation, quoted in a *USA Today* interview:

*Last summer a friend of mine (in the USA) who is always criticizing Japan for being "unfair" invited me to his summer home to play golf. After the game, he invited me to his house and while his wife was prepar-*

## SOCIAL PERSPECTIVE

### The Two-Edged Sword of International Competition

The point is that *the computerized workplace of today and tomorrow is being affected by global economic trends.* The old concern for unemployment caused by the introduction of a few computers in the office takes on added significance if they all are being manufactured overseas rather than at home. International competition is a two-edged sword. Consumers benefit from lower-priced, higher-quality goods, while workers may suffer when their jobs are lost to foreign competition. Free trade, which many Americans support, should be fair trade on the world stage. Japan's economic strength has come not only from government support of industrial research but also from protecting its industries at home from outside competition. China is notorious for blatantly copying American high-tech products, including music

and video CDs and software, and selling them throughout Asia (Simons and Zielenziger).

Ultimately, however, a nation's workers can be paid higher wages only if they produce and sell an increasingly higher value of goods. The United States has always led in computer advances and is far ahead of the world in the burgeoning growth of the Internet. Many people feel that the ability of American business to compete successfully in the market for computer systems and other high-tech, high-value goods is crucial to providing a better quality of life for future generations. Advances in computers, transportation, and communications have produced the "global village," and economic decisions made both here and overseas will continue to have a greater impact on our work and daily lives than ever before.

*ing dinner, he showed me around. In the garage, I saw a Kawasaki snowmobile. . . . Next to it was a Japanese motor boat. . . . In the house, I saw a Sony TV and numerous other Japanese-made products. I said, "You criticize us all the time for not buying American products while it's obvious that you prefer Japanese products. Are you asking us to buy something you won't buy yourself?"*

*We are focusing on business 10 years in advance while you seem to be concerned only with profits 10 minutes from now. At that rate, you may well never be able to compete with us.*

Much is being implied here about differences in social and governmental policy between the two countries, including issues of competitiveness, free trade, corporate accounting, and governmental planning. We can argue that the American lead in the computer field has been fostered by freedom from government regulation and unrestrained economic competition between hardware and software companies. Moreover, over the years, Japan has been less an inventor of computer technology than a marketer of quality products, whose ideas were first perfected elsewhere. Yet neither of these statements is the whole story. The National Science Foundation in recent years has had a conscious mission to sponsor research in supercomputers, parallel processing, and high-speed data communications—all frontier areas in computing—to keep the United States in the forefront of technological development. Moreover, some of the most important consumer computer products in this period were first developed in Japan, including the laser printing process and the optical disk reader, for massive storage of data on a compact disk.

**FIGURE 3-8** Akio Morita, the former chairman of SONY, is known for his controversial remarks about Japanese–American business relations and practices.

**SOCIETY**

## ▶ Government Invasion of Privacy

A few years ago the world successfully lived through 1984, the target year of the famous novel of the same name by the English novelist George Orwell. In this novel of the future, written in 1949, the world had become a global totalitarian state in which personal privacy and other rights had been usurped by government. The slogan "Big Brother is watching you" was embodied in the giant television screens in homes to monitor private life and behavior. Much public discussion of the novel has centered on the relevance of its predictions, including the role of computer data banks in the invasion of privacy.

## LARGE PUBLIC DATA BANKS

Fortunately we are not even close to the societal control and supervision suggested in Orwell's dark vision. Through an irony of history, totalitarian societies that might wish to monitor their citizens electronically have also been hopeless failures at everyday computer technology. Freedom to exchange information and ideas seems to be a necessary ingredient for technological innovation.

SOCIETY

Computerized data banks do contain enormous quantities of information about every citizen of the United States. In 1982 it was estimated that the government held an average of 15 personal files on every man, woman, and child in the country. That data collection is acknowledged to have grown greatly in the last decade (Boyd). Public institutions from city hall and the courthouse to the state capitol and the federal government in Washington, D.C., are all collectors of these materials, along with several national credit rating services. Private citizens' income and debt levels, welfare payments, driving and court records, and census data—these and much more are collected, stored, retrieved, and in some cases merged and transmitted from agency to agency. The Internal Revenue Service (IRS), the Selective Service System, the Federal Bureau of Investigation (FBI), the Census Bureau, and the U.S. Department of Health and Human Services (HHS) are only a few of the numerous federal agencies that hold data on private citizens. States and communities add many more agencies and data banks.

Supporters of data banks say that these days of computer files are not much different from the old days of the grapevine. In rural America people knew a lot about their neighbors' personal lives, even though the information was not kept on computer. A person's "secrets" were often general knowledge in the community.

Civil libertarian critics of government data banks disagree. As Janlori Goldman of the American Civil Liberties Union said, "You could move away from a small town and start over. . . . You can't do that any more. The information follows you" (Boyd). *Local information is now available at the national level.* With today's centralized data banks, your credit rating in Ohio is instantly retrievable when you move to Arizona and apply for a credit card at a local department store. Critics worry about an unwarranted invasion of privacy and the possible lack of security in the collection, storage, and transmission of sensitive information about private citizens. They are especially concerned about information gathered for one purpose being used for another. They base their concerns on the Fourth Amendment to the Constitution, which guarantees freedom from unwarranted search and seizure of "person, house, papers, and effects" (Shadduck).

Let us consider one horrifying case in detail. Most states routinely sell their computerized driver's license records to members of the public, such as direct mail advertisers, for a small fee. In 1989 Robert J. Bardo, a 20-year-old Arizona fan obsessed with the television actress Rebecca Schaeffer, of "My Sister Sam," hired a detective to find out where she lived. The detective paid for Schaeffer's California driving record and turned the address over to Bardo, who sought her out in West Hollywood, then shot and killed her when she opened the door but refused to talk to him (Rothfeder). The frightening possibility looms that nobody's privacy is

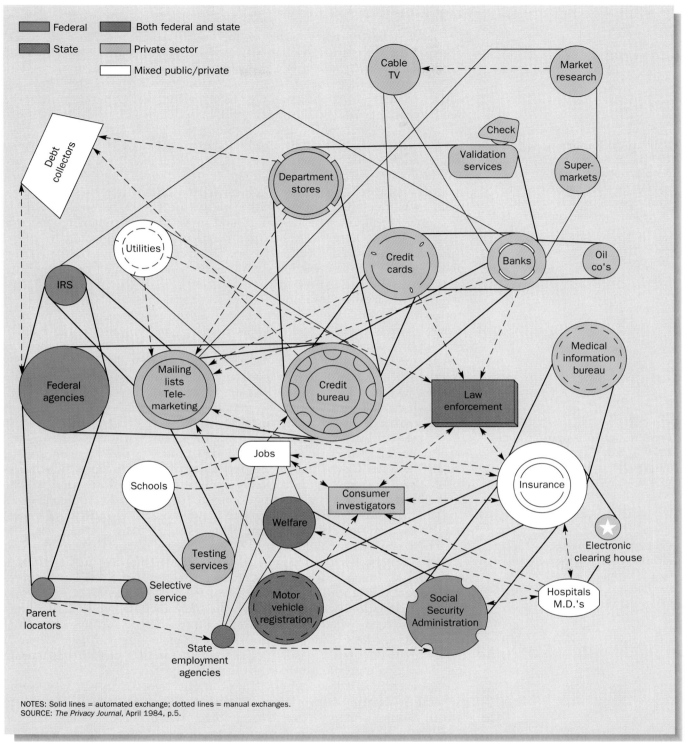

**FIGURE 3-9** Complex linkages of government databases at all levels including connections to the private sector.

safe from kooks and crazies. As Marc Rotenberg, an authority on computer privacy, put it, "States are literally wholesaling their data bases. . . . Information that is gathered for one purpose, say a driver's license, is being used for totally different purposes." In fact, a detective in Texas published a book telling how to access all sorts of public databases using a personal computer and a telephone (Boyd).

## THE RIGHT TO PRIVACY

The legal right to privacy, based on the Fourth Amendment and other sections of the Constitution, was affirmed by the Supreme Court in 1965 (*Griswold* v. *Connecticut*). But the right is not absolute and must be balanced with society's need for information. Given the possibilities for abuses of the right in the computer information age, Congress during the last 20 years has spelled out privacy rights in detail. Four federal laws deal with various aspects of the question (Slotnick et al.).

One federal law, the **Fair Credit Reporting Act of 1970,** was enacted to give individuals the same access to their credit ratings as companies. The law allows citizens to challenge materials included in their credit records, because sometimes the information contains errors that cause them to be denied credit without explanation. Credit bureaus now hold data on 150 million Americans and add more than 24 billion records per year. In 1990, Congress scheduled hearings about updating this law. Improvements would specify that credit bureaus clean out obsolete complaints and make their written summaries understandable to ordinary citizens who question their records.

The conservative columnist James Kilpatrick has come out in favor of outlawing the practice of "prescreening" in the new legislation. Currently credit bureaus compile and sell "prescreened" mailing lists containing financial information from their records. For instance, makers of detergents can get the names of customers who recently purchased washing machines on credit. Kilpatrick disagrees that the cost effectiveness of this marketing scheme justifies the resulting loss of privacy and increase in junk mail: "My own thought, for whatever it may be worth, is that our privacy is sufficiently invaded already" (Kilpatrick).

The **Freedom of Information Act of 1970** guarantees citizens the right to see all of the information held about them by federal agencies like the IRS and the CIA. A person can request any files on record by addressing each federal agency individually, in writing. The information will be forthcoming unless it is vital to national security or invades someone else's privacy. Similar legislation may have been enacted by individual states, but the 1970 law covers only federal agencies.

The **Crime Control Act of 1973** was passed because criminal arrest records can be very damaging to a person if they are not accurate. According to this law, when an arrest record is sent from one law enforcement agency to another—such as from the FBI to the NCIC (National Crime Information Center)—the data file must include, along with details about the arrest, whether the person was prosecuted, and if so, the final verdict. As in the Freedom of Information Act, people can get access to their files if they have reason to believe that the files contain inaccurate and damaging material, so that the errors can be corrected.

Apparently this law has not been too effective, for in April 1990, the General Accounting Office informed Congress that "the data quality problem in criminal history records is serious." When one considers that the NCIC receives about 1 million requests for information a day, the possibilities for error and abuse are enormous. Because more than a million users in more than 64,000 law enforcement agencies are authorized to access NCIC files, data security is also a big problem (Boyd).

The **Federal Privacy Act of 1974** was enacted into law after flagrant violations of personal privacy in the Watergate scandal. This act limits the information-gathering activities of the federal government (not the states) to that which is "relevant and necessary," and whenever possible, to information supplied by individuals themselves. The government must tell peo-

**Fair Credit Reporting Act of 1970:** U.S. federal law allowing people to inspect their credit records so that they may challenge erroneous information included in the computer files.

**SOCIETY**

**Freedom of Information Act of 1970:** U.S. law that guarantees citizens the right to see information collected about them by federal agencies like the IRS.

**Crime Control Act of 1973:** U.S. federal law that allows citizens access to criminal records about them that may be in error in order to correct them.

**SOCIETY**

**Federal Privacy Act of 1974:** U.S. law enacted after government invasions of privacy during the Watergate era that limits the kinds of information the federal government can gather on private citizens to that which is "relevant and necessary."

ple why the information is wanted, how it is to be used, and under what legal right the agency is requesting it. When the information has been collected, the agency must get the citizen's consent to disclose it, except for "routine use." What constitutes "routine use" is the really tricky legal question.

One disturbing aspect of "routine use" is the ubiquitous adoption of the Social Security number (SSN) as a personal identifier. A government-sponsored report called *Records, Computers, and the Rights of Citizens* (1973) specifically recommended against using a universal number in government data files. Yet the trend has continued and even accelerated. Until a few years ago, the Selective Service System had a separate number for young men registered for the draft; now it uses the Social Security number. The tax reform laws of 1986 stipulated that every person over five years old claimed as a dependent on a federal income tax return had to have a Social Security number. Today babies are getting numbers, though they do not earn money or collect benefits. The number has, in effect, become a universal identification number for U.S. citizens. A person with access to the right databases can get a lot of information about an individual through this single nine-digit number.

**FIGURE 3-10** Today a policeman in a squad car can tap directly into NCIC files to check on an individual's driving record, even though critics charge that many NCIC records are in error.

SOCIETY

## COMPUTER MATCHING

We have seen that a large number of government data banks contain information about citizens, identified with either their Social Security numbers or their driver's licenses. Thus the "routine use" of personal data without one's knowledge has become a controversial issue in recent years in cases of **computer matching.** Legally the question is whether government agencies should be allowed to use information collected for one purpose for a totally different purpose (Shadduck). Once it was difficult to merge data banks containing information about the same person, because they were organized differently and keyed by different codes, such as the draft number or the census plot. Now, because files are increasingly coded by Social Security number or driver's license, they can be matched much more easily.

As a society we believe in the apprehension of spouses who renege on their child support payments or of people who abuse the welfare system by claiming unwarranted benefits. Computer matching of different government records is being used to ferret out cases like these and bring them to account. Suppose a divorced father has disappeared and quit sending support payments for his children. Using his Social Security number, officials can match his divorce record with his tax records. Not only can they find his address; his income shows his financial resources for meeting his parental obligations.

An everyday example outside federal jurisdiction illustrates the difference between computer matching and ordinary data checking. When you write a check at the supermarket and the clerk enters your driver's license number on the checkout terminal, the computer will make a search to see if you have written bad checks to that store chain. That information belongs to the supermarket chain; it has not been gotten from a credit bureau. Your current check is not being matched with your record on auto loans or credit purchases at department stores.

The first application of computer matching was designed to catch welfare fraud. It compared federal employees listed with the Civil Service Commission with the rolls of Aid to Families with Dependent Children, kept in HHS files. Other applications have included merging addresses in

**computer matching:** The controversial practice of merging records collected by different government databases to find suspected criminals, such as people who have reneged on alimony.

SOCIETY

**Individual Rights Versus Social Needs**

Issues of right and wrong regarding privacy versus governmental oversight in computer matching are not clear-cut. More than 200 different computer matches were carried out in the first seven years of using the technique. Legally a federal agency is required only to publish its intention to do a match in the *Federal Register* before proceeding, and most searches go unnoticed. Critics claim that often these fishing expeditions turn the presumption of innocence into the presumption of guilt. They invoke images of Big Brother in Orwell's *1984*: people's private lives are being scrutinized without their knowledge, they charge.

On the other side, defenders of matching note that the practice is the only way the government can save billions of dollars per year by weeding out fraud such as double billing, welfare cheating, or defaulted student loans. Every year billions of dollars are paid out to millions of people in various kinds of government benefits. The government contends that one of the best ways to monitor waste and fraud in these massive programs, all of which depend on computer processing, is to do matching. The computer is used only to do fast and accurate screening of records and to flag those that may be suspect. The staff, not the computer, decides whether a person has been involved in fraud or lawbreaking. No one argues that the government should not investigate possible fraud. Computer processing of files makes the process of investigation far more wide ranging and cost-effective (Kusserow).

We as a people accept the legitimate need of government and private agencies like lending institutions to collect information for social planning and administrative purposes. In these times of high crime rates and a national drug crisis, public opinion polls show that citizens are willing to accept some loss of privacy for safety and economic reasons (Boyd). Yet Congress has consistently refused to allow different presidential administrations to set up one national data bank on all citizens, based on some universal code like the Social Security number.

IRS records with birthdays to find males who have not registered for the draft. Comparing Labor Department lists of people eligible for Black Lung benefits with Medicare bills from HHS has identified cases of medical fraud involving double billing for services. To look for tax evasion, the IRS has developed one of the most complex matching schemes, involving the merging of IRS records with motor vehicle registrations showing car makes and census data containing information about a person's home and community. Computer analysis of these detailed personal profiles is intended to flag possible anomalies in individuals' reported incomes (Shadduck).

**FIGURE 3-11** Data entry operators at the IRS key personal financial data into computers. Some IRS offices process tens of thousands of income tax returns a day before the tax is calculated and automated auditing is done.

## ▶ Summary

Like most innovations, technological change has its positive and negative sides. Individuality and personal service are challenged by the automation of records and computerization of the marketplace. The computer represents one factor in the changing complexion of employment, not only in the local office but in the larger global economy. Computer matching of government records has raised questions about invasion of privacy. The machine, neutral in itself (except for its possible health risks, which are not yet fully understood), opens up the potential for both great public good and private evil. Citizens and legislators must keep in mind the delicate balance between the government's need for information and the citizen's right to privacy.

## ▶ Key Terms

computer matching (p. 69)

computer phobia (p. 58)

Crime Control Act of 1973 (p. 68)

downsizing (p. 61)

ergonomics (p. 63)

Fair Credit Reporting Act of 1970 (p. 68)

Federal Privacy Act of 1974 (p. 68)

Freedom of Information Act of 1970 (p. 68)

human–computer (man–machine) interface (p. 59)

low-level electromagnetic emissions (p. 63)

Luddite riots (p. 61)

punch card (p. 57)

repetitive stress injury (RSI) (p. 63)

## ▶ Self-Test

### MULTIPLE-CHOICE

1. The bar-coded products scanned in most grocery stores today represent which of the following trends?
   a. Some shoppers feel they are treated more like numbers than human beings.
   b. Many shoppers feel a loss of personal service, since there are no price tags on individual items.
   c. Bar codes and scanning have produced economies in the costs of stocking the shelves, checkout, and inventory.
   d. All of the above.

2. Health hazards associated with computers in the workplace fall into the area of
   a. computer phobia
   b. ergonomics
   c. automation and unemployment
   d. personal privacy

3. A unique code used on most goods today to make them suitable for processing by computers is called
   a. UPC
   b. MICR
   c. SSN
   d. GIGO

4. Problems that ensue when a clerk types an incorrect figure into a charge account record represent

a. an example of computer phobia
b. a case of job displacement
c. a loss of individuality
d. a mistake in the computer–human interface

5. When managers make decisions about automation without worker input, certain effects may be expected during the transition period. Which of the following is least likely in such a situation?
a. more illness
b. job stress
c. an increase in wages
d. injured feelings

6. Which of the following seems the least likely cause of downsizing in the workplace?
a. global competition
b. fluctuations in the value of the dollar
c. rapid technological change
d. rising pension and health care costs

7. Which of the following federal laws would be broken if colleges sold students' data files to advertisers?
a. Fair Credit Reporting Act
b. Freedom of Information Act
c. Federal Privacy Act
d. Crime Control Act

8. All of the following have been advanced as advantages of computer matching except
a. Finding welfare cheaters
b. Saving federal dollars currently lost through fraud
c. Cost-effective screening to eliminate waste in government programs
d. Protecting the privacy of individuals

## TRUE/FALSE

9. **T  F**  Because technology is value-neutral, people should not be concerned with its effects on society.

10. **T  F**  The common response "The computer made the error" usually is a proper explanation of mistakes in computerized billing systems.

11. **T  F**  The Luddite riots are often discussed in computer texts because the workers were victims of technological change.

12. **T  F**  One of the main applications of computer matching has been to find auto thieves.

13. **T  F**  Possible health risks from exposure to computer screens show that the effects of technology on people are not neutral.

14. **T  F**  The computerized workplace of today is more affected by global economic trends than the unautomated office of yesterday.

15. **T  F**  Because so many law enforcement agencies access NCIC files regularly, the security and accuracy of NCIC data is a big problem.

16. **T  F**  Examples of GIGO in NCIC files will probably not be a problem for criminal investigations.

## FILL-IN

17. Employees in automated offices who do not themselves work with computers directly and do not understand how they work often feel a sense of _____.

18. ____ is a phrase used to describe situations in which there is a breakdown in the interface between people and machine. If bad data are put into the computer, the results will also be bad.

19. It seems increasingly probable that World War III will be an _____ conflict rather than a military one.

20. The worldwide growth and expansion of services involving computers, transportation, and communications have led social commentators to say that we live in a _____, where decisions made overseas impact our lives daily.

21. The legal right to _____, based primarily on the Fourth Amendment to the Constitution, was affirmed by the Supreme Court in *Griswold* v. *Connecticut* (1965).

22. Credit bureaus often practice _____ of mailing lists compiled from their records in order to market them to advertisers.

23. The _____ was enacted into law after flagrant violations of personal privacy in the Watergate scandal; it limits federal information-gathering activities to that which is "relevant and necessary."

24. _____ involves the merging of data files from different government agencies to find people who may have defaulted on their alimony payments or gotten unwarranted welfare benefits.

## ▶ Experiential Exercises

1. Ask an older supermarket shopper whether it makes any difference to him or her that grocery items no longer bear price labels. Do shoppers regularly do comparison shopping by reading the shelf labels? Can they keep up with the approximate amount they are spending as they go through the store?

2. Have you, your family, or a friend ever had a problem with computerized billing? Can you identify where in the computer-human interface the error was introduced?

3. In 1989 President Bush and the nation's governors agreed on broad targets for educational improvement called Goals 2000, and President Clinton continued the initiative to seek ways to meet these goals by the end of the century. Investigate the status of the program today, its successes and failures, paying particular attention to the role of computer technology in these plans.

4. Research the idea that the Soviet empire lost out to the West economically because it never moved past the Industrial Age into the Information Age, a description often used to characterize current Western industrial society.

5. Research the limitations written into federal laws on privacy and use of government data files. Does your state have similar safeguards in its code of laws? Is computer matching common at the state level? Perhaps some state provisions go beyond federal protections.

6. Many people mistakenly believe that the right to privacy is a basic constitutional right. Look up the background of *Griswold* v. *Connecticut* (1965), and research some of the areas besides government data banks in which its precedents have been applied.

## ▶ Critical Thinking Exercises

1. Consider these milestones in the history of technology, and comment on their effects on history: the printing press, the steam engine, the automobile.

2. In the 1960s concerns about the impersonality of large university classes where students were treated as numbers led to campus rebellions such as the Berkeley riots of 1964. With declining monetary support for higher education in the 1990s, large classes, especially at state schools, are more and more common; and many of these 1960s issues are reappearing. How does the mindset of today's student compare to that of students of the 1960s faced with similar situations?

3. Automation has kept retail prices down, even if it has sometimes meant a loss of personal service. Discuss.

4. Continuing education after graduation will probably be more important to your career than your bachelor's degree. Discuss.

5. Japan is more successful at cooperation between industry and government in worldwide business competition than the United States. Discuss.

6. Because the United States leads the world in computing and Internet usage, it will remain the world's technology leader for the foreseeable future. Discuss.

7. The United States needs one central database of information on its citizens for better social administration. Discuss.

**ANSWERS TO SELF-TEST**

*Multiple-Choice*: 1. d;   2. b;   3. a;   4. d;   5. c;   6. b;   7. c; 8. d
*True/False*: 9. F;   10. F;   11. T;   12. F;   13. T;   14. T; 15. T;   16. F
*Fill-in*: 17. computer phobia;   18. "Garbage in, garbage out";   19. economic;   20. global village;   21. privacy;   22. prescreening;   23. Privacy Act of 1974;   24. computer matching

# CHAPTER 4

# Computer Hardware

▶ ## LEARNING OUTCOMES

*After completing this chapter, you should be able to:*

1. *Name and describe the five fundamental functions that underlie all modern computers.*

2. *Relate how these five functions fit together as hardware in a personal computer.*

3. *Describe the role of the microprocessor in a personal computer.*

4. *Explain how data of all kinds are represented in an electronic digital computer.*

5. *Distinguish between primary and secondary data storage devices.*

6. *Describe the wide variety of input and output devices available for modern computing.*

7. *Explain how specific types of hardware fit different tasks and data types.*

▶ ## COMPUTERS IN CONTEXT

*Suppose you want to write a letter home from college in the first weeks of your freshman year, describing what you have been doing and listing your initial expenses for your parents. You would get out a piece of paper; compose the letter by hand; include details of your activities; sum up all your expenses, such as tuition and room and board; put the letter in an envelope; and mail it. Without overburdening the obvious, we can identify several elements of this process that parallel the throughput process in a computer: input of data, storage and processing, and output of the results.*

*In writing your letter, the input is your words, written by hand but composed in your head. The paper provides storage (or memory) for your thoughts in a permanent form, so you can remember them later, if you need to revise them. Paper also is the eventual output medium—the finished letter ready to be mailed home. Writing itself, the forming of the words, is a learned process, though for adults it is almost automatic. The summing up of your college expenses is another process, addition, also learned in childhood. Throughout the whole activity your mind determines what you do first, the order of the operations (getting out the paper, composing the letter, putting it in an envelope), and how you do it, including the conscious processes of writing and addition. Your mind serves the* control function *of coordinating all these activities in an almost unconscious fashion. You do not give much higher-level thought to most of the separate processes, except the composing of your text and the addition of your expenses.*

**FIGURE 4-1** Most personal computer systems come equipped with a CPU for processing and memory, a keyboard and mouse for input, and a monitor for output.

U sing a hand calculator, an inexpensive special-purpose computer, also involves the five functions mentioned above: *input, storage, processing, output,* and *control.* Of course, the mind coordinates the whole process and thus performs the control function. The numbers that a person enters by hitting the keys are the input information. The buttons are the input devices, and the arithmetic operations like addition and subtraction are processes the machine offers. When the arithmetic buttons are punched, the operations are carried out on the numbers that have been keyed in. The little screen displays this input data, stored in memory for processing, and later shows the results of the calculations.

Hardware forms one corner of the Computer Triangle, with people and software the other two. People run computer software such as word processor programs on their hardware in order to do useful things like writing letters. The hardware consists of the electronic devices that make up a computer system. Their size may vary from a room full of equipment in a large university mainframe installation to a personal computer and screen sitting on a desk to a compact portable that will fit in a briefcase. Prices of hardware range from millions of dollars for supercomputers and mainframes to several hundred for a small PC.

Using a personal computer to produce a letter incorporates the same five functions as using a calculator or writing a letter by hand. In fact, *these are the five functions all computer systems must perform.* Let us put together the necessary components of hardware needed to write a letter.

## ▶ Hardware and Its Functions

To write the letter, you switch on the computer, a human control function, and the computer boots itself up for applications use. You open the word processing program by choosing it with an input device (probably a mouse) from a list of applications stored on the internal hard disk drive. The program is then read from the drive and stored in the central memory of the computer. The word processing program now takes over the control function. You can then begin to compose the text at the keyboard, another piece of hardware used for input. As you type, the program stores the text internally in the computer's central memory, located on memory chips inside the main computer.

Meanwhile, you can see what you have typed because a copy of your work is being displayed on the computer screen for your inspection. This output device is sometimes called the monitor or **CRT** or **VDT** (for **cathode ray tube** or **visual display terminal,** both fancy terms for a TV screen). The process of adding up your expenses is carried out in one part of the internal processor of the machine, which is called the **arithmetic/ logic unit.** If you need to make corrections, they also are done in the processor. Corrections are then stored in memory; meanwhile, you can always see what you have written on the monitor. To produce a printed copy of the letter, you send the final stored copy of the text from internal storage to another output device, a printer. Control mechanisms are built into the microprocessor, or chip, and are located on the main circuit board of the machine, called the **motherboard.** They monitor all the other processes, including the display of your typed characters on the screen and the sending of text to the printer at the end of the session.

The most important element of any computer is the **central processing unit,** also called the **CPU.** This is the essential core of the computer, the foundation of the system. Normally the CPU contains on its micro-

**cathode ray tube (CRT) or visual display terminal (VDT):** The most common type of computer screen or monitor.

**arithmetic/logic unit:** The processor unit in the CPU that performs arithmetic and comparison operations.

**motherboard:** The main circuit board of a computer containing the microprocessor, memory chips, and other components.

**central processing unit (CPU):** The core of a microcomputer system. It contains both the arithmetic/logic unit and the control unit.

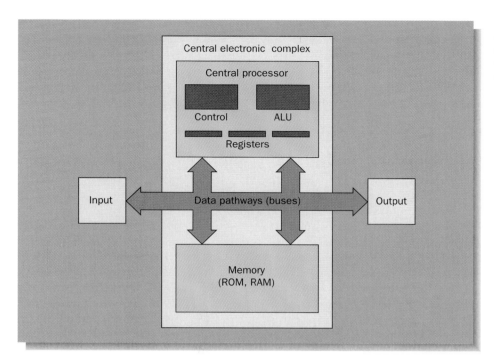

**FIGURE 4-2** A general computer system with the CPU and memory at the center of the hardware. All parts of the CPU are included on the microprocessor chip.

processor chip two of the middle elements of the computing process—processing and control. This microprocessor is placed on the motherboard, along with several memory chips for internal storage of data. The actual design and layout of these electronic circuits and memory chips differs from machine to machine and is referred to as the **computer architecture.**

The original IBM PC and its compatibles were built around the 8088 microprocessor, developed by Intel Corporation. Later improved versions of IBM PCs and a host of compatibles from Compaq, Gateway, Dell, and many others have all been based on bigger, faster, and more powerful versions of Intel chips (80286, 80386, 80486, and the Pentium, which could be called 80586). A Motorola chip, the 68000, formed the basis for the original Apple Macintosh; later, upgraded versions of the Macintosh machines used larger, improved versions of Motorola microprocessors (68020,

**computer architecture:** A term to describe the design and layout of the electronic components of a computer system.

**HISTORY**

**FIGURE 4-3** The architecture for the Macintosh 9500 includes two system boards: (A) the main logic board with the major components and (B) a daughterboard, which actually holds the PowerPC 604 processor. This design allows for later upgrading of the system by swapping out the processor board.

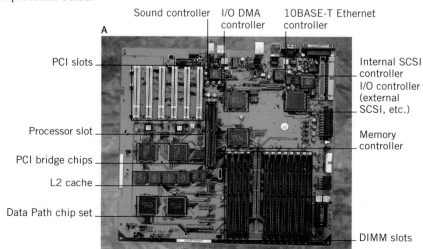

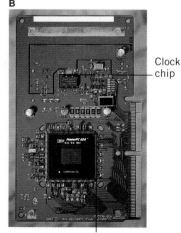

**FIGURE 4-4** The iCOMP Index provides a simple relative measure of Intel microprocessor performance. It is not a benchmark, but the results from industry-standard benchmarks measured on well-designed commercially-available systems rolled into a simple-to-use number.

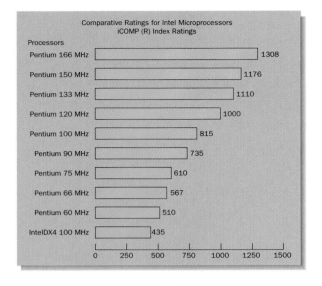

68030, and 68040). Today's Power Macintoshes are based on a newer, more powerful Motorola/IBM chip family called the PowerPC, introduced in 1993. The original microprocessor was called the PowerPC 601, and the most advanced chips (603, 604) closely parallel the speed of the best Pentiums (see Table 4-1).

The newer and more powerful the chip, the faster its internal processor's clock speed, measured in megahertz (MHz). A processor that is clocked at 100 MHz has 100 million clock cycles per second. Since the internal operations of the processor are keyed to the clock ticks, the higher the MHz rating, the faster the job can be done—and the more costly the computer. Because other considerations in addition to MHz rating complicate the picture (such as the amount of internal memory available), a better measure of processor speed and efficiency is the amount of work per cycle that the processor can do. To do such ratings on processors, comparisons are made on millions of instructions per second, the **MIPS** rating. Figure 4-4 compares average efficiencies over many brands for selected Intel processors, of which the MIPS rating is an important component, and one easily notes the rising efficiency with better processors. The average Pentium/120 system has more than twice the effective performance of the fast DX4/100 and consequently costs considerably more. The MHz number and the MIPS rating of a particular computer together provide a quick way to measure the speed and throughput capacity. A shopper can make performance comparisons between two machines using these two published measures.

**MIPS (million instructions per second):** One measure of a computer's processing speed, sometimes used to compare how many instructions different microprocessors can execute in a second.

## ▶ *Electronic Representation of Data*

We have seen how a real-world computer system is built around the five essential functions of input, storage, processing, output, and control. But how does the machine store and manipulate information from the outside world? What are the possibilities for input of information, internal storage, and output of the results?

To begin with, the computer is a magnetic and electrical device. Elementary physics discusses both of these physical phenomena in terms of polarities, or changes in direction. A magnet is charged with either north or south polarity, and opposite charges attract each other. Electricity is represented as a directional stream of electrons flowing through a conductor, such as a copper wire. The speed of transmission of electricity depends on the nature of the conducting medium. Yet it is one of the fastest physical processes that we know. Measured in hundreds of thousands of miles per second, electrical transmission approaches the speed of light, 186,000 miles per second.

Suppose, for example, that your power has gone out because of an electrical storm. When the power company has repaired the lines and flips the switch on at its main plant, the lights go on almost immediately throughout the network. To ordinary people, transmission seems instantaneous. The modern computer takes advantage of the incredible speed of electricity, as well as the benefits of miniaturization offered by chip technology. Because electricity goes very fast and does not have far to go in tiny computer circuits, personal computers' internal speeds are measured today in billionths of a second or **nanoseconds.**

But people do not think of information as electronic charges flowing in chips and wires connected to them. What relation is there between the words, numbers, pictures, and musical notes we know and use every day and the electrical and magnetic media that make up the computer? Computers use binary coding to represent information, to match the two-part nature of electricity. The word *binary* comes from the Latin prefix *bi-*, for "two." The notion of binary choice is not totally unfamiliar, for a number of other binary conditions occur in ordinary life: yes and no, on and off, true and false, left and right. If we can develop a way to represent information in binary form—with two symbols represented by 0 and 1—then a computer can store and process those symbols at incredible speeds.

**nanosecond:** A billionth of a second, the unit of magnitude that personal computer internal speeds are measured in today.

## BINARY TECHNOLOGY IN PROCESSORS

Processor chips are built to process so many binary digits at one time. One can think of storage of binary materials on a chip as the two states of a switch, off and on, representing 0 and 1. In fact, the first mainframe computers in the 1940s actually had electromagnetic relay switches for binary representation. In the 1950s, the invention of the transistor created smaller, more reliable switches; and modern microprocessor chips are essentially miniaturized versions of transistor. They are the physical embodiment of the electronic information, the binary codes 0 and 1.

**HISTORY**

A single binary digit is referred to as one **bit**—an amalgam of the words *binary* and *digit*. The more bits the hardware can push through the microprocessor at one time, the more work the computer can get done in a

**bit:** An abbreviation for *binary digit*, which can be either 0 or 1.

**TABLE 4-1** *Comparing Microprocessors*

| COMPANY | PROCESSOR | WORD SIZE (BITS) | ADDRESS BUS (BITS) | I/O DATA BUS (BITS) | MAX RAM (BYTES) | MAX SPEED (MHZ) | MAX SPEED (MIPS) |
|---|---|---|---|---|---|---|---|
| Intel | 8088 | 16 | 20 | 8 | 1 MB | 8 | 0.3 |
| Intel | 8086 | 16 | 20 | 16 | 1 MB | 12 | 0.3 |
| Intel | 80286 | 16 | 24 | 16 | 16 MB | 16 | 2 |
| Motorola | 68000 | 32 | 24 | 16 | 16 MB | 20 | 2 |
| Motorola | 68020 | 32 | 32 | 32 | 4 GB | 33 | 7 |
| Motorola | 68030 | 32 | 32 | 32 | 4 GB | 50 | 12 |
| Intel | i386SX | 32 | 32 | 16 | 4 GB | 33 | 8 |
| Intel | i386DX | 32 | 32 | 32 | 4 GB | 33 | 8 |
| Motorola | 68040 | 32 | 32 | 32 | 4 GB | 50 | 20 |
| Intel | i486DX | 32 | 32 | 32 | 4 GB | 66 | 20 |
| Intel | Pentium | 32 | 32 | 64 | 4 GB | 100 | 166 |
| MIPS | R4000A | 64 | 36 | 64 | 6 GB | 75 | 100 |
| Motorola/ IBM | PowerPC 601 | 32 | 32 | 64 | 4 GB | 100 | 300 |
| Digital | Alpha | 64 | 64 | 64 | 16 GB | 150 | 300 |

**TECHNOLOGICAL PERSPECTIVE**

**Symbolic Coding of Information**

All of us use several different codes a day, without even thinking about it. Coding systems we typically use for representing information include the Roman alphabet and punctuation marks, for language text; the decimal number system, for arithmetic; and musical notes, for recording sound on paper. We also transmit information as pictures, incorporating color and line, and as sound, through sound waves of varying frequency. Educated people have no difficulty distinguishing among letters, numbers, or musical notes, because they know the notation. What we learned as children, we use without thinking.

There is nothing inherent in these representation systems, which we take for granted, that determines them as normal or naturally correct. For instance, the sequence of letters *chat* means different things to speakers of English and French. The French word for "cat" has nothing in common in meaning with the English word for an informal conversation, though the spellings are the same. Given the context, however, one should not get confused. Or take Chinese, a written language based on characters rather than the Roman alphabet. Words in English and Chinese may represent the same sound, though they look quite different.

HISTORY

unit of time. A measure of throughput related to the number of bits engineered into a processor is its MIPS rate. Early personal computers of the 1970s were limited to 8-bit processors, but today's advanced chips, like the Pentium and the PowerPC, have 64-bit processors. In theory, that means that the newer chips can do as many as eight times the number of operations per second as the early chips. In fact, these numbers are only rough figures, since a number of other technical innovations of the last 20 years also contribute to the MIPS ratings.

## BINARY CODING OF CHARACTERS

In computers we must represent information in binary notation, as a series of bits, so that the electromagnetic hardware can store our information. For the alphabet and other characters found on a typewriter keyboard, two well-known codes have been developed and accepted for use in machines around the world. The most widely used coding scheme is called **ASCII** (American Standard Code for Information Interchange), adopted universally for personal computers in the 1970s. The original ASCII scheme consisted of seven bits for coding letters, numbers, punctuation marks, and special symbols like the dollar sign; but an Extended ASCII code with eight bits per character is the standard today. Inside the computer, a bit is a spot in storage capable of holding only one of two possible magnetic states or voltages at any given time, which we know as 0 and 1.

**ASCII (American Standard Code for Information Interchange):** The most common character code used for microcomputers and data communications. Standard ASCII consists of seven bits per character; Extended ASCII of eight bits.

**TABLE 4-2** *Number of Unique Binary Symbols as Bit Strings*

1 Bit:  0 1
2 Bits: 00 01 10 11
3 Bits: 000 001 010 011 100 101 110 111
4 Bits: 0000 0001 0010 0011 0100 0101 0110 0111 1000 1001 1010 1011 1100
        1101 1110 1111

In general, for a string of length $n$, there are $2^n$ possible, unique binary symbols.

The seven-bit ASCII code represents $A$ as 1000001 and $B$ as 1000010. If you take the time to work it out, you will find that in seven bits, there can be 128 different codes. This relationship can be stated mathematically as the following principle:

For $n$ binary digits, one can create exactly $2^n$ possible, different, and unique binary symbols.

For example, in seven bits there are $2^7$ (that is, 128) unique binary codes.

Ordinary typewriter keyboards have about 100 different characters; thus seven-bit ASCII, with its 128 codes, can accommodate everything people type with a different and unique symbol. It can have different codes for the letters of our alphabet, both capital and lowercase (56 codes), for decimal numbers (10 codes), for the standard punctuation marks (period, comma, colon, and so on—about 20 codes), for mathematical operators ($+ - = / < >$), and for other special-purpose signs ($ @ %), and still not use up all its possibilities. The extended version of ASCII uses an additional eighth bit, thus expanding the possibilities to 256 ($2^8 = 256$). Extended ASCII includes the common accents of European languages, like the French grave and the German umlaut. But for most people and applications, understanding the seven-bit ASCII coding scheme is sufficient.

An older eight-bit coding scheme called **EBCDIC** (Extended Binary Coded Decimal Interchange Code) was developed in the early days of large IBM mainframe computers. With its 256 codes, EBCDIC allows coding of all the Western languages, including classical Greek, and all the symbols needed in the arts, sciences, and business. Yet it does not have enough different codes for Chinese or Japanese, which have thousands of different characters. (Encoding the characters of Eastern languages is complex; some solutions will be discussed in Chapter 6.)

In today's world we need many languages, and a new standard coding scheme called **Unicode** is beginning to be accepted. Unicode has 16 bits to code a character, allowing 65,536 different binary codes ($2^{16} = 65,536$), so that many characters common to Chinese, Japanese, and Korean can be included along with the Roman alphabet, Cyrillic, and Arabic. By 1992, more than 28,000 characters had been defined; Extended ASCII, with its European accent marks, is treated as a subset. Most experts think that computer manufacturers in the next few years will adopt Unicode as the standard coding scheme for their machines (Dvorak).

**HISTORY**

**EBCDIC (Extended Binary Coded Decimal Interchange Code):** A standard character code using 8 bits per character devised for IBM mainframes in the 1960s but less frequently used today than ASCII.

**Unicode:** A new standard coding scheme that allows 65,536 different binary codes because it uses 16 bits to code a character.

## BINARY CODING OF NUMBERS

The binary system must be adapted for all other kinds of data that are to be stored and processed in the computer. In fact, before the development of the coding schemes we have just discussed, early computers used binary coding for the numerical operations they were designed to process. There are two standard coding conventions for numbers, one for **integers** (whole

**integer:** Any positive or negative whole number, including zero.

**TABLE 4-3** *Extended ASCII Codes in Eight Bits*

| CHARACTER | BINARY CODE | DECIMAL | CHARACTER | BINARY CODE | DECIMAL | CHARACTER | BINARY CODE | DECIMAL |
|---|---|---|---|---|---|---|---|---|
| 0 | 0011 0000 | 48 | C | 0100 0011 | 67 | O | 0100 1111 | 79 |
| 1 | 0011 0001 | 49 | D | 0100 0100 | 68 | P | 0101 0000 | 80 |
| 2 | 0011 0010 | 50 | E | 0100 0101 | 69 | Q | 0101 0001 | 81 |
| 3 | 0011 0011 | 51 | F | 0100 0110 | 70 | R | 0101 0010 | 82 |
| 4 | 0011 0100 | 52 | G | 0100 0111 | 71 | S | 0101 0011 | 83 |
| 5 | 0011 0101 | 53 | H | 0100 1000 | 72 | T | 0101 0100 | 84 |
| 6 | 0011 0110 | 54 | I | 0100 1001 | 73 | U | 0101 0101 | 85 |
| 7 | 0011 0111 | 55 | J | 0100 1010 | 74 | V | 0101 0110 | 86 |
| 8 | 0011 1000 | 56 | K | 0100 1011 | 75 | W | 0101 0111 | 87 |
| 9 | 0011 1001 | 57 | L | 0100 1100 | 76 | X | 0101 1000 | 88 |
| A | 0100 0001 | 65 | M | 0100 1101 | 77 | Y | 0101 1001 | 89 |
| B | 0100 0010 | 66 | N | 0100 1110 | 78 | Z | 0101 1010 | 90 |

**real number:** A positive or negative number, including zero, that can be expressed with fractions, called **floating point** in computers because they are represented with a floating binary point similar to a decimal point.

**place system:** The basis of any number system, such as decimal or binary integers. A digit in a certain place means that the digit is raised to the power of the base number for that place. For instance, the 2 in the "tens" place in the number 20 must be multiplied by 10 to get its value.

**binary integer:** A whole number, either positive or negative, composed of binary digits 0 and 1 representing powers of 2.

numbers such as 4) and another for **real numbers** containing a fractional or decimal part, such as *pi* (3.1416). Real numbers are often called **floating-point numbers** in computer terminology, because they have a decimal part.

One can count in binary just as one counts in decimal. Just as the decimal number system probably developed because people have 10 fingers, so the binary number system works well with the physical basis of electricity in computers. In the decimal system, the number 129 really means

$$(1 \times 100) + (2 \times 10) + (9 \times 1)$$

We use a **place system** to read this decimal number. The number 291 has the same digits, but they are in different places, and thus represent different values:

$$(2 \times 100) + (9 \times 10) + (1 \times 1)$$

The places themselves are powers of 10: the units column ($10^0 = 1$), the tens column ($10^1 = 10$), the hundreds column ($10^2 = 100$), reading from right to left. This foundation in 10 is why we call the system the decimal system (*decem* means "ten" in Latin).

In an analogous way, **binary integers** use a place system based on powers of 2: the units place ($2^0$), the "twos" place ($2^1$), the "fours" place ($2^2$), the "eights" place ($2^3$), and so on. Thus the sequence 1101, in binary, stands for

$$(1 \times 8) + (1 \times 4) + (0 \times 2) + (1 \times 1)$$

In the decimal system, this is the number 13. That is, 1101 (base 2) is the same as 13 (base 10). It is possible to represent all the integer numbers, both positive and negative, in binary notation, though the concept is unfamiliar to most people.

Computers use a different system for encoding real, or floating-point, numbers. Floating-point notation is much like scientific notation for decimal numbers. For instance, the sun is 93 million miles from the earth; in scientific notation, that number can be written as $9.3 \times 10^7$. The decimal point has been moved (or floated) seven places to the left; the power (or exponent) of 10 shows how far to the left it has moved. Similarly, this large figure can be encoded in binary notation using a fraction and the base number 2 raised to an exponential power: $93,000,000 = 1.386 \times 2^{26}$. Using floating-point notation, computers can encode all ranges of numbers, from very large figures to very small fractions, and recover them to standard form by moving the point.

Let us stop for a moment and reflect that the same two binary digits, 0 and 1, can be used for three different coding schemes: the alphabetic characters on a keyboard, integers, and floating-point numbers. Take the seven-bit binary sequence 1001001. Is it the ASCII code for capital I or the binary integer equal to the decimal number 73 $[(1 \times 64) + (0 \times 32) + (0 \times 16) + (1 \times 8) + (0 \times 4) + (0 \times 2) + (1 \times 1)]$? Remember that each column represents a multiple of 2. Such confusion is no different from the problem of interpreting the word *chat* in English or French. As long as you know the correct context, you can properly interpret the information that is being conveyed.

Numbers especially can cause confusion. For instance, the numbers 419 in an address (419 Elm Street) and 419 in a count of marbles look the same, but in fact, they are not. The number in an address is not used for counting, whereas the number of marbles is: we might get two more marbles and add them to get a total of 421. Inside a computer, these two versions of the sequence 419 would be stored in different ways. The address would be stored as **numeric characters** in ASCII, along with the ASCII codes for the street name. The number of marbles would be stored as a binary integer. Many computer programs ask users to specify what form data should be in—character, integer, or floating-point—so that the machine will know what binary form to use in its internal coding.

**numeric character:** A number stored as ASCII codes inside a computer, rather than being stored as a binary integer or floating-point real number. A street number or ZIP code as part of an address is an example.

## BINARY CODING OF GRAPHICS AND SOUND

Computers can also store graphic images and digitized music and voice in binary notation. The method for pictures is really not difficult to understand. Think of a grid of points like a piece of graph paper, maybe 10 squares to a side. If you blackened in certain points to show your initials, you would use only a few of the 100 squares and leave the rest unfilled. When we store the whole grid (or **matrix**) of points inside the computer, every point will take up one bit of storage. If you have filled in a square, the computer will store a 1 in that bit; for the empty squares, it will store 0s. The computer's memory will contain a record of the entire matrix as a series of bit patterns.

**matrix:** An arrangement of data in a grid of rows and columns suitable for storing the pixel layout of a bit-mapped character or graphic in computer memory.

Change the size of the grid to many thousands of points, called pixels, and the **resolution** on the screen can be very fine. For instance, a Sony Trinitron 17-inch screen is made up of more than 786,000 pixels, consisting of 768 rows and 1024 columns. The computer keeps an internal image of the entire screen in the form of a very large binary record of which bits are blackened and which are not. Any pixel on this **bit-mapped** screen can be filled to make graphical images of characters, lines, or whole pictures. Using more than one bit per pixel allows each pixel to be assigned a grayscale value ranging from pure black to pure white, or a value from a large palette of colors. Chapter 9, on graphics, treats these pictorial representations in more detail.

**resolution:** A term referring to the number of pixels on a computer screen. The higher the resolution, the better the characters or images on the screen appear.

**bit-mapped:** A term used to describe images composed of patterns of dots and displayed on graphics computer screens.

Storage of sound records in computers is done exactly the way digital sound is stored on compact disks. All sound, including music and voice, takes the physical form of a sound wave, measured in **kilohertz (kHz)**—so many thousands of cycles per second. As the sound is made, the computer takes samples of the sound waves. The resulting samples are combined to

**kilohertz (kHz):** A measuring unit for a sound wave, representing a thousand cycles per second.

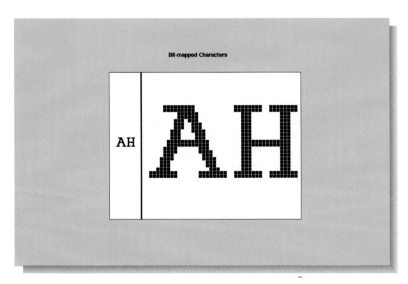

**FIGURE 4-5** Enlarged bit-mapped patterns of pixels for uppercase A and H. The way the letters will appear on the screen is shown at the left.

**FIGURE 4-6**   The software called LanguageWriter (Research Design Associates) presents digitized sound as a graph. Here both the soundwave for *fourscore* and the typed word are highlighted.

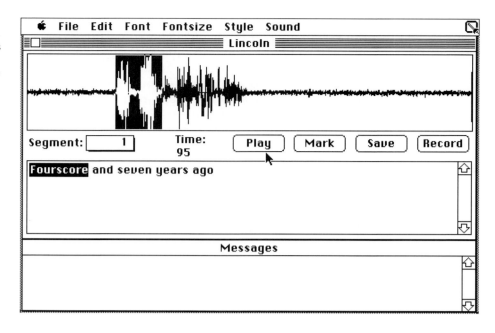

make an approximate representation of the wave itself. The more samples that are taken per second—perhaps about 22,000 (described as sampling at 22 kHz)—the more accurate the approximated sound wave will be. These sound frequencies are **digital** (or **numeric**) **data,** and therefore are easy to store as binary numbers. Later, when the sound is played back, a sound synthesizer receives the digital information and voices it as a clean, clear copy of what was recorded.

Because digitizing equipment samples so much sound, typically between 7000 and 22,000 samples per second, the quantity of digital information that is stored in a computerized sound record of even moderate length is very large. Compared even to pictorial data, in which every pixel of a large computer screen is stored as a bit, a sound record is usually larger. Sampling 20 seconds of stereo music at 22 kHz, which will capture it quite accurately, requires about 3.2 million bits of internal storage. One can see that a full composition several minutes in length will use up computer storage very rapidly. Nevertheless, as with all the other kinds of data we have discussed, the computer will record the information in binary form for further processing or output.

## ▶ Primary Storage of Information

We now have a sense of why and how a computer represents information of all types in binary notation. Let us return to our original project, the letter home from college, and see how the hardware would accomplish that task in binary notation. Normally we would type the letter at a keyboard. As we depress each key, the circuitry in the keyboard converts the alphabetic characters to ASCII binary symbols and sends them to the CPU to be stored. The **memory** in the CPU, also called **primary storage,** can be divided into two categories, random-access memory and read-only memory.

### RANDOM-ACCESS MEMORY (RAM)

Random-access memory (RAM) chips are typically used on the motherboard for primary storage. These are **semiconductor memories** made of silicon which can hold two electronic states, conducting and nonconduct-

**digital (numeric) data:** A term that applies to forms of data that can be expressed in numeric terms, and thus can be readily processed by digital computers.

**primary storage:** The functional component of a computer where programs and data are stored for processing, normally RAM in PCs.

**memory:** The functional component of a computer that stores programs and data before they are processed by the CPU.

**semiconductor memory:** Another term for RAM chips, based on a semiconductor technology similar to that of microprocessor chips.

**FIGURE 4-7** Different sizes of random-access chip memory take up approximately the same space. From right to left, they hold 1 megabyte, 4 megabytes, and 16 megabytes. Of course, the greater their storage capacity, the costlier they are.

ing, matching the binary states of 0 and 1. Since ASCII and EBCDIC are seven- or eight-bit codes, RAM is organized in groups of eight bits, called **bytes.** Since one byte equals eight bits, each byte of memory holds one typed character.

The storage capacity of typical RAM memories installed in today's personal computers may be difficult to comprehend. Someone who has a computer with 4 megabytes (4 MB) of central memory, small for many modern systems, has a machine with about 4 million bytes (or 32 million bits) of primary storage. In other words, the computer's memory can store about 4 million ASCII characters at a time. How much is that? Let us assume that a typed page of text has 35 lines, each holding 80 characters. The page, then, has 2800 characters on it, including the spaces between words. At this rate, we could store more than 1400 typed pages in the computer's memory (4 million divided by 2800), assuming nothing else were there! It is hard to imagine that all that storage can fit on several small RAM chips.

Compared with other media, text files are not really greedy of memory. By contrast, the 20-second sound mentioned earlier would need 3.2 million bits of RAM (or .4 million bytes, since eight bits equal one byte). Thus a 4 MB RAM could store only about 10 such sounds. Because pictures and movies also require very large memories, multimedia computers are often configured with at least 32 MB of central storage. As a rule of thumb, multimedia developers try to load their systems with as much RAM as they can afford. Meanwhile, a number of technically complicated schemes have been devised using hardware and software to compress large sound, graphic, and video files so that they can be stored in less space than uncompressed raw data.

**byte:** A unit of memory in the computer consisting of eight consecutive bits, often used to store one character of data or information.

**FIGURE 4-8** The word CAB stored in RAM memory. Note that the three letters differ in only one bit.

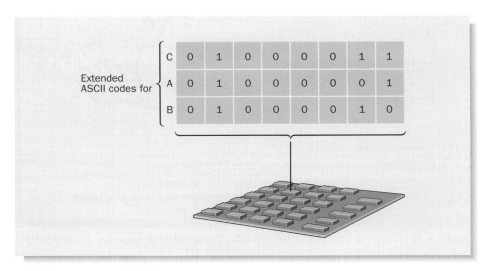

Extended ASCII codes for

| | | | | | | | | |
|---|---|---|---|---|---|---|---|---|
| C | 0 | 1 | 0 | 0 | 0 | 0 | 1 | 1 |
| A | 0 | 1 | 0 | 0 | 0 | 0 | 0 | 1 |
| B | 0 | 1 | 0 | 0 | 0 | 0 | 1 | 0 |

**FIGURE 4-9** Core memory, used on early mainframe computers, was larger and slower of access than to-day's RAM memories, but it had one positive characteristic they lack. If the power failed, core memories held their charge, thus retaining their binary information.

**core memory:** An older kind of random-access memory (RAM) device that held its magnetic charge even when the power was off. RAM memory chips replaced core memory because core was more expensive to produce, larger in size, and slower to access.

**read-only memory (ROM):** Memory chip that permanently stores instructions and data. Because it can be read from but cannot have new information put into it, manufacturers store important control programs in ROM chips.

RAM chips have four characteristics that are desirable in primary memory: (1) small physical size for large storage capacity; (2) quick access to information; (3) an inexpensive price; and (4) reliability. Chips certainly do hold great quantities of information for their cost. The term *random access,* embedded in the RAM name, refers to the computer's ability to store information in and retrieve it from different parts of memory. No matter where a byte of information is stored on the chip, the control unit can locate it and access it directly.

Reliability means that the memory will hold its information safely while the machine is in use. As long as the power is on, the RAM memories will retain their contents. Earlier central memory technology, called **core memory,** held its charge in magnetic form (positive and negative charges), even when the power was switched off—a very useful safeguard against power failures. However, core memory was more expensive to produce, larger in size, and slower to access than modern semiconductor memory chips, and eventually was replaced by RAM in most machines.

### READ-ONLY MEMORY (ROM)

Some of the central memory inside a computer is of the **ROM** type, or **read-only memory.** Because the term ROM looks like RAM, the two are often confused. Both are usually made of silicon, but ROM memory cannot accept new information. Bytes of ROM memory can be read out, but they cannot be written over. Control procedures stored in the central computer and other proprietary information put into memory by the manufacturer are normally stored in ROM chips. Sometimes computer languages are put into ROM before a machine is shipped. They can be read by the user innumerable times but cannot be destroyed when new materials are read into the machine.

As you write your letter to your parents, the software shifts information back and forth between primary storage in RAM and the processor chip during word processing and summing up of your early expenses. These processes are controlled by your word processor program and calculator program. Both of these functions fall into the category of software, to

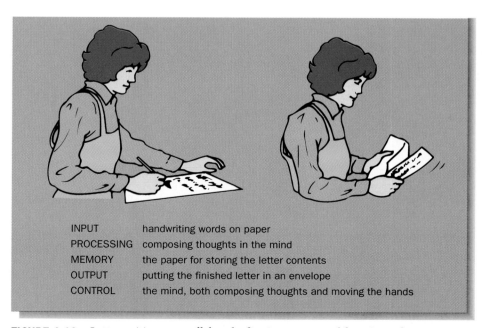

| INPUT | handwriting words on paper |
| PROCESSING | composing thoughts in the mind |
| MEMORY | the paper for storing the letter contents |
| OUTPUT | putting the finished letter in an envelope |
| CONTROL | the mind, both composing thoughts and moving the hands |

**FIGURE 4-10** Letter writing as parallel to the five interconnected functions of a computer.

be discussed in detail in Chapter 5. Suffice it to say that the control mechanisms of the machine carry out these processes as needed and place the correct information back into primary storage for output. When your letter is ready for printing, the control program sends the text character by character—that is, byte by byte—to the printer.

To accomplish your letter-writing task, then, you have used a series of devices that move information around in binary form, from keyboard to RAM to processor to RAM to printer. Indeed, we have followed a common pattern for combining the five computer functions: input to memory to processor to memory to output. Given that memory and processor reside together on the motherboard, the heart of the computer, we have followed the standard throughput cycle, input to internal processing to output.

## ▶ Secondary Mass Storage

Both programs and data can be saved and stored in electronic form on secondary devices such as diskettes, hard drives, compact disks, and magneto-optical disks.

### DISKETTES

Small magnetic **diskettes** are perhaps the most widely known storage medium associated with personal computers. They are classified as **secondary mass storage,** for one does not input directly onto a diskette. Prepared software is often sold already encoded on diskettes. For instance, the word processing package you used to create your letter probably came on a diskette. Blank diskettes are useful for storing data that have already been keyed into a computer. You will likely keep a copy of your finished letter on a diskette, for your records. From then on, the letter can be read back into the machine, for inspection or correction. Thus, diskettes can serve both input and output functions.

Information is encoded onto diskettes in circular tracks on the flexible disk inside the case. Binary information is stored on diskettes as a series of

**diskette:** The most common form of secondary storage—small, inexpensive, and portable—which records data as magnetized bits that are read by a disk drive.

**secondary mass storage:** A term that applies to the medium in which computer programs and data are stored while not in use, such as on diskettes or magnetic tape.

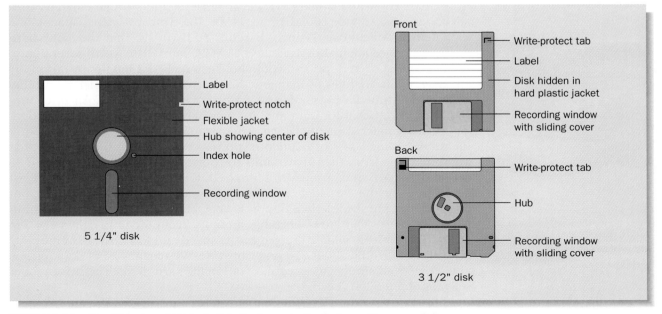

Front
— Write-protect tab
— Label
— Disk hidden in hard plastic jacket
— Recording window with sliding cover

Back
— Write-protect tab
— Hub
— Recording window with sliding cover

Label
Write-protect notch
Flexible jacket
Hub showing center of disk
Index hole
Recording window

5 1/4" disk

3 1/2" disk

**FIGURE 4-11**   The 5¼-inch and 3½-inch diskettes have similar features. However, sliding panels and a hard case give the 3½-diskette more protection.

tiny charged magnetic spots representing the binary codes 0 and 1. When a diskette is put into a disk drive, the hardware reads the encoded data as it rotates under a read/write head at very fast speed. Or it writes new information onto the diskette at the user's command.

Most diskettes come in two sizes, 5¼ and 3½ inches. The larger, older type is often called a floppy disk, because it is encased in cardboard or vinyl and is bendable. The smaller type, popular with most current machines, is not, strictly speaking, a floppy, because its case is hard plastic. The disk itself inside the hard case is made of the same flexible Mylar material as the floppy diskette.

For their size and price, magnetic diskettes can store very large quantities of information. Older 5¼-inch floppies held 360K of information—about 100 typed pages of double-spaced text; but newer ones can store 1.2 MB. High-density 3½-inch diskettes can store 1.44 MB of data, or about four times as much as the older large format. They can be carried in a shirt pocket and cost only a dollar or two. For the money and convenience, diskettes are clearly the world's most popular storage medium.

## OTHER TYPES OF MASS STORAGE

Many similar devices hold much more massive amounts of information than diskettes, notably hard disk drives, read-only compact disks, and the newer read/write magneto-optical disks. Unlike Mylar floppies, metallic plates in hard disks capture the binary data as they rotate very rapidly under a read/write head. Because speeds of access with magnetic hard disks are much faster than with floppy disks, hard disks provide ideal secondary storage when one works closely with central memory. Some hard disk packs that are designed for use with mainframe computers are removable and transportable. In personal computers, hard disks are either mounted in the cabinet or purchased separately and plugged into the computer.

Personal computer hard disks come in various sizes, from 200 MB to more than 2 **gigabytes** (2 billion bytes, or 10 times as much as 200 MB). The larger the storage capacity, the higher the price, from several hundred to about a thousand dollars. To get a sense of the storage capacity of a small hard disk, divide 200 MB by 1.44MB, the typical storage capacity of a high-density Macintosh 3½-inch diskette. You will see that the small hard disk can replace about 135 diskettes. A big 2G hard disk, worth several hundred dollars at current prices, would hold as much as 1350 floppy disks.

Several alternatives to magnetic hard drives exist for easier portability of large multimedia presentations with movies and sound. All offer random access retrieval for data and are rewritable. SyQuest drives are popular in the smaller capacity range. They are similar to large diskettes—3½ inches or 5¼ inches—but made of rigid platters encased in cartridges that are removable from their drive units for portability. They hold between 88 MB and 270 MB and cost several hundred dollars for the drive and almost a hundred for the cartridge. Bernoulli boxes are similarly removable, but the diskettes are flexible like floppies. They come in sizes and prices similar to SyQuest. The latest portable memory technology is called the Zip drive from Iomega, widely praised for its speed and low cost. Its removable cartridge costs only about $20 and can store 100 megabytes of data retrievable at a speed similar to a regular stationary hard drive. The drive reader sells for about $200 (Leeds).

For several years CDs have been used for storing massive quantities of information. A typical **CD-ROM** disk can store 600 MB of data—more than a 500MB hard disk. The data stored on a CD-ROM disk can be read directly into primary storage of a personal computer and displayed on a CRT

**FIGURE 4-12**   Internal hard drives are made of rigid material and hold many times more data than a diskette.

**gigabyte (GB):** A measure of main memory or auxiliary storage size, comprising one billion storage positions.

**FIGURE 4-13**   These external CD-ROM drives have drawers for insertion of the CD-ROMs. Older models had removable caddies into which CD-ROMs had to be inserted before being placed in the drive.

**CD-ROM:** A compact disk on which large volumes of information are stored digitally and accessed by laser beam.

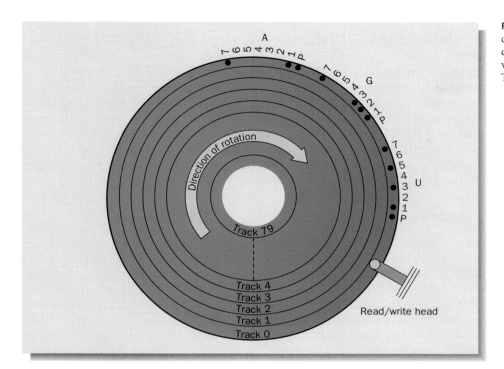

**FIGURE 4-14** Illustration of how characters are recorded on a hard disk drive in tracks. Note that the letters will be read off in order: U, G, and A. The spots stand for binary coding.

screen. Unlike the hard disk, however, CD-ROM disks are compact and easily removable. Users can keep a library of dozens of disks. They are often slower to read than equivalent hard-drive disks; but newer models that sample 2, 4, and 6 times normal speeds have eliminated much of the wait time associated with early CD-ROM drives. Information is stored in digital form and read by a laser beam through the same process used in compact disk players.

CD-ROM disks provide an inexpensive way to distribute large commercial databases such as dictionaries and encyclopedias. Home computer users can get complete libraries, containing thousands of volumes, on just a few disks. CDs can also be used to store pictures and sound, which require more storage than can be economically kept with current magnetic disk costs. All the entries, appendixes, pictures, and even word pronunciations in Webster's *Ninth New Collegiate Dictionary* will fit on one CD-ROM. The text and pictures can be read directly from the disk into primary storage in the personal computer and displayed on the CRT screen. The pronunciations are sent to the computer's microphone. Because ordinary CDs are read-only media, a dictionary sold in this format cannot be corrupted accidentally by a careless computer user.

**Magneto-optical drives**, often called **MO** technology, share features of both hard drives and CD-ROMs. Like their hard drive descendants, their information is stored in magnetic form, but it is read by a laser, somewhat like a CD-ROM. Their advantage is massive storage for the price (up to 2.3 gigabytes on one cartridge in 1995). Because the methods for storing data and then reading them back are more complex than other devices, MO drives have slower access times (sometimes a liability) than hard drives. MO cartridges are very safe means of storage. One does not run the risk of a hard drive crash, and the data will be intact indefinitely (Shatz-Akin). As with most computer decisions, choosing a mass storage medium depends on which characteristics are most important: portability, size, cost, safety, and access speed. No longer are cost or capacity the limiting factors that they were only a few years ago.

**FIGURE 4-15** Many alternative technologies exist for disk storage of massive quantities of information in portable form: SyQuest drives, Zip drives, and MO drives.

**magneto-optical (MO):** Mass storage that combines magnetic and laser technology for safe, portable storage of massive amounts of information in gigabyte quantities.

## ▶ *Input and Output*

Although the keyboard is the most common input device, we have a number of other options for getting information into the machines. The punch card and paper tape were once very popular media for encoding data. Prepared at a keypunch machine, the cards bore punch patterns that were read by a card reader, which converted to the internal binary representation. Nowadays most of the data formerly encoded on punch cards or paper tape are input directly by keyboarding—the process of typing at a keyboard—or is read by some automated method.

### DIRECT INPUT

We are familiar in daily life with several methods of scanning data directly into computers. Optical scanners read the magnetic ink numbers at the bottom of a check more accurately and much faster than an operator can type them; the process is called **magnetic ink character recognition (MICR).** The numbers have fixed shapes, so that they can be read without confusion by machines—a necessity in **optical character recognition (OCR).** Another example is the OCR scanner at the supermarket counter, which can recognize the Universal Product Code printed almost universally these days on retail products. The popular **flatbed** and **slide scanners** that digitize photographs and drawings as a set of pixel dots represent another category of optical scanning today. Desktop scanners that read text documents directly into computer memory provide popular alternatives to keyboarding and are available in many models and prices. They offer varying degrees of accuracy in capturing text automatically.

Another method of direct input is the magnetically coded strip on the back of the credit card used at **automated teller machines (ATMs).** The strip is made of Mylar, which can carry binary information in the form of positive and negative magnetic charges. The customer's account information and security code are stored on this strip. When the customer puts the

**magnetic ink character recognition (MICR):** An input process used by banks to read the digits and symbols printed in magnetic ink at the bottom of checks.

**optical character recognition (OCR):** An input process that scans a printed character in a book or reads a number on a check and translates them into computer-readable codes.

**flatbed scanner:** An input device to digitize photographs and drawings as a set of dots, called pixels, so that they can be processed by computers.

**slide scanner:** An input device for digitizing color slides directly so that they are suitable for storage in computers.

**automated teller machine (ATM):** An interactive input/output device for banking where customers gain access to the machine by means of a PIN (personal identification number). Normally they can then make deposits, withdraw money, and get other information about their accounts.

**FIGURE 4-16** Scanners digitize both text and images and can be of different types. The hand-held one in (A) is reading letters and presenting them as Braille characters in the device on the left. The one in (B) is a popular desktop model often used for capturing graphics or photographs.

A

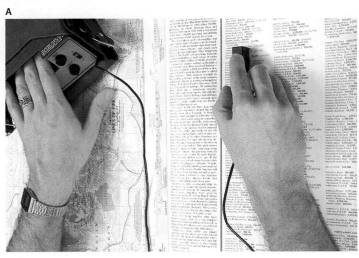

B

**A**

**B**

**FIGURE 4-17 A AND B** Mice pointing devices come in several different forms. The standard one rolls around on the table, whereas the trackpad on many laptop computers is controlled by the user's finger.

card into the ATM, the machine reads the customer's information and then asks for the security code. If a person enters an incorrect code, the machine will not work and may even keep the card—one way to discourage theft and unauthorized use of these popular cards.

## MOUSE INPUT

Besides the keyboard, most personal computers come equipped with a mouse, trackpad, or trackball for input. By moving the mouse around on the table next to the computer, users are able to move a pointer around on the CRT screen. They can then control various software functions by pointing with the mouse and clicking its buttons. First popularized by the Macintosh, the mouse is associated with a control philosophy called the **graphical user interface (GUI),** a fancy way of saying that control functions can be carried out by pointing at pictures and sections of the screen called **menus** and **windows.** Today most makers of personal computers, as well as manufacturers of larger, more powerful workstations, are offering the GUI interface as a standard option on their machines. Users of these machines do less keyboarding and more "mousing" to get the computer to carry out tasks like saving files to diskettes, sending data to printers, or shutting down the computer itself.

The mouse and similar devices work on the principle of **analog/digital input,** which means that some physical measurement is sensed (such as the direction of mouse movement) and digitized (converted to binary data) by the input hardware before being sent to the computer. Placement of the mouse on the table refers to some section of the screen, whose coordinates are identified internally by row and column measurements stored in binary form. The computer monitors movement of the mouse, left and right, up and down, and moves the location of the pointer, sometimes called the **cursor,** on the CRT in the same direction.

## OTHER ANALOG/DIGITAL INPUT

Many less familiar input methods also use the analog/digital principle. Large maps and architectural drawings can be encoded for computer processing using a digitizing draft table. As the user slides the digitizer around the boundaries of a map, it notes the coordinates of the borders. The computer stores them for later use in reconstructing the graphic image on screen. The wire stretched across the highway to count the traffic at rush

**graphical user interface (GUI):** A computer interface, commonly accessed with a pointing device like a mouse, that uses pictures, graphic symbols, windows, and menus to represent commands, choices, and actions.

**menu:** A list of choices displayed on the screen from which a user can select program operations. A computer with a GUI often presents menus in pull-down form.

**window:** A resizable rectangular display area of a computer screen, prominent in systems having a graphical user interface.

**analog/digital input:** Hardware that senses a physical measurement, like the directional movement of a mouse, and converts it to digital data for input to the computer.

**cursor:** A small blinking arrow, vertical line, or underline on a computer screen to indicate where the next input will be displayed.

**FIGURE 4-18** A digitizer table is used for converting illustrations, such as maps, into machine-readable form.

hour; the sensor of radiation levels in a nuclear reactor; and the monitor worn by the heart patient in the hospital are other examples of analog/digital input devices in everyday use.

Another analog/digital input application is the **touch screen,** which senses the presence of your finger. Touch screens look somewhat like a CRT. Travelers often use them to get precoded information about hotels and restaurants. At EPCOT Center in Florida, for example, visitors interact with an automated reservation system for booking tables at restaurants by making choices at a bank of touch panels. Many museums provide touch screens in their exhibits, to offer visitors hands-on control of what they see.

Today some computers even allow people to input hand-written characters on a special touch screen. The computer must recognize these markings as letters and numbers, in effect processing an analog signal before storage. Developments of this kind include the use of a stylus to write

**touch screen:** An input/output device that allows a user to control the computer by touching the screen, which then displays the output.

**FIGURE 4-19** Using a touchscreen to make a move, a user can play tic-tac-toe with the IBM Ultimedia PS/2 computer.

**FIGURE 4-20** An insurance adjuster is using a pen-based computer designed to take notes about car wrecks. She has a wireless model, which can send data back to the home office via cellular phone technology.

## SOCIAL PERSPECTIVE

### The Kurzweil Scanner for the Blind

It seems appropriate to close the discussion of input devices by looking at one that was developed to meet a special social need: an optical scanner for blind people. More than ten years ago, Raymond Kurzweil, a young engineering genius, introduced a scanner that had learned to "read" books to the blind. That is a more difficult task than you might think. Modern typesetting methods offer several thousand typefaces for the production of books and magazines. Yet people rarely think about these variations in type. Every day you see capital and lowercase letters in many sizes and shapes, but you have no difficulty classifying them. However, scanners have great difficulty recognizing letters and numbers with style and shape differences.

The Kurzweil scanner for the blind was one of the first that could read and learn new typefaces and styles. A blind person puts a book down on a glass screen that looks much like a copier screen, and the machine finds the first line and begins to read and voice the letters and words. The process combines optical character recognition of the letters and then voicing them through a synthesizer. Sometimes word recognition is not perfect. Hearing a word that makes no sense, a blind person can stop the scanner and back it up using a control panel with Braille buttons. The user then instructs the machine to spell out the word letter by letter. After finding the error, the user types in the correct interpretation, and the scanner learns to recognize that shape correctly and stores it for later use. Gradually the machine comes to "know" the letters and characters of the book's typeface, and begins to read the text with some facility.

Although it may not be perfect, the Kurzweil blind reader is a computer application with great positive social value. Subsequent versions of this optical scanner and similar desktop models from other manufacturers have shown tremendous commercial potential in converting typeset materials directly into machine-readable files.

**FIGURE 4-21** The Kurzweil optical scanner recognizes words and voices them for a blind reader.

on the small screen of a "digital assistant," such as the Apple Newton, introduced in 1993.

Voice input, a digitizing process, also holds much potential for the future. Currently researchers are working on hardware that users train to their voices, so that they can give spoken instructions to the computer. The

| | |
|---|---|
| A a *A* **A a** | Avant Garde |
| A a *A* **A a** | Courier |
| A a *A* **A a** | Helvetica |
| A a *A* **A a** | Syntax |
| A a *A* **A a** | Times |
| *A a A A a* | *Zapf Chancery* |
| A a *A* **A a** | Optima |

**FIGURE 4-22** Versions of the letter A in several well-known fonts for laser printing. The first two A's in each line are plain text, the next italic, and the last two are boldface. Whereas people recognize all of these as A, optical character readers like the Kurzweil scanner have a tougher time.

**voiceprint:** An audio signature of a person in digital form, useful for allowing a computer system to recognize a person's voice commands.

**soft copy:** Computer output presented on a CRT screen rather than being printed.

**hard copy:** Output printed on paper.

**monochrome screen:** A computer screen offering one color, typically white, green, or amber, against a black background.

**RGB (red-green-blue) monitor:** A term for a color monitor, with the letters of the name standing for the three primary additive colors that combine to make color images on the screen.

**HISTORY**

**near letter quality (NLQ):** Fine-quality printing produced by dot-matrix printers in their best resolution, which is almost as good as that produced by fully formed characters.

**ink-jet printer:** An inexpensive nonimpact printer in which tiny dot patterns are sprayed onto paper to form characters.

**laser printer:** A popular nonimpact printer that creates high-quality output by using a laser beam to create an image on an electrically charged drum.

hardware must develop a **voiceprint** of the user, with all his or her sound patterns, including pitch, accent, and inflection, in order to be able to understand verbal commands.

## SCREEN OUTPUT

CRT screens are the most popular and familiar kind of output hardware. Output on a screen is called **soft copy,** as opposed to **hard copy,** or paper output. Information in soft copy remains in electronic form suitable for being examined on the screen. Users can see and correct their data on screen, then send the output from central storage to the printer for a finished hard copy or have a permanent copy on a secondary storage medium like a diskette. Screens come in **monochrome** or color. Color screens are sometimes called **RGB monitors,** for red-green-blue, the three basic colors on both TV screens and color monitors. (Chapter 9 treats the graphical aspect of CRT screens in more detail.)

## PRINTED OUTPUT

Printers come in many different kinds and sizes, but they are usually categorized as impact or nonimpact, depending on whether a keystroke actually hits the paper. Today's users of personal computers are likely to encounter three common types: dot-matrix, ink-jet, and laser printers. A few years ago the least expensive and most popular printer for home use was the dot-matrix, an impact printer. Like the dot patterns that make up the characters on a bit-mapped graphics screen, dot-matrix characters were printed as a series of dots based on grid patterns. The more dots per character, the higher the resolution of the printer. Quality dot-matrix printers offered several levels of resolution, from draft mode to **near letter quality** (abbreviated **NLQ**). In the latter, the printer produced enough dots per unit to fill in the gaps visually, and the result was a pleasant-looking, readable document. Today dot-matrix printers are being replaced by **ink-jet printers.** They use a nonimpact process to spray dot patterns on the paper and produce a high-quality image for a reasonable price. More expensive models of these two printers can be equipped to produce color output, based on a four-color process. Both can create graphic images like figures and graphs as well as headlines in selected typefaces.

The **laser printer** is the Cadillac of printers, and of course, it costs more—sometimes double the price of other printers. The technology is similar to that of the copy machine. A laser beams an image of the characters or graphics onto an electrically charged drum. Toner ink sticks to the drum, transferring the image to the paper passing over the drum. Laser printers intended for the personal computer market create high-quality output based on image patterns of 300 to 600 dots per inch. Similar but much more expensive devices for high-quality commercial printing have a resolution of several thousand dots per inch. The print in a book like this

**TABLE 4-4** *Desktop Printers*

| | TYPE | CATEGORY | QUALITY | SPEED | COST |
|---|---|---|---|---|---|
| Impact | Dot-matrix | Serial | Draft to near letter quality | 30 to 500 cps | $100 to $300 |
| Nonimpact | Ink-jet | Serial | Near letter quality | 35 to 400 cps | $300 to $1500 |
| | Laser | Page | Letter | 8 to 28 ppm | $500 to $10,000 |

*cps = characters per second; ppm = pages per minute; 48 cps = 1 ppm*

**FIGURE 4-23** Most printers use patterns of dots to create letters and symbols. The higher the density of dots, the closer the characters approach the appearance of fully formed characters. Shown are enlarged illustrations depicting dot matrix, ink-jet, laser, and fully formed characters.

one is produced by commercial laser printers that cost tens of thousands of dollars. Nevertheless, the quality one regularly finds in low-end laser printers more than satisfies most office and home computer users.

## VOICE AND GRAPHIC OUTPUT

We have already mentioned voice output based on digitized speech and music. Digitized sound waves are passed through a **synthesizer** to create these sounds. The Kurzweil blind reader incorporates such hardware. After the scanner recognizes the letters on a printed page, it generates a series of digital sound patterns and voices them as words and sentences.

A common kind of graphic output device is the **plotter,** used to produce maps, engineering drawings, and architectural blueprints from stored digital images. Plotters work like large dot-matrix printers with high resolution. The drawings are created by connecting the coordinate points along the curves of an image. The result is a high-quality graphic image in black and white or color.

**synthesizer:** A device that can electronically generate sound, either music or voice, from digital information.

**plotter:** An output device that creates a graphic image by controlling the motion of a pen on paper.

## ▶ Summary

Thus we come to the end of our discussion of how computers store and process information as binary data by combining different hardware devices in a typical general-purpose computer. All kinds of printed and sensory data can be captured in digital form, converted to binary codes, processed internally, and output in many forms and media. Even special-purpose computers in appliances based on microprocessors exhibit the throughput functions. They also accept input commands but produce predictable, preprogrammed responses (processing and output functions). For example, you punch a series of buttons on a microwave console (the input stage), and the result is a certain level of cooking power for a specified period of time (the process controlled by the chip). The cooking time is also displayed on the small screen that resembles one on a hand computer (the output). As long as readers understand the five essential elements of the computer cycle—input, memory, processing, output, and control—they should have no trouble adapting to new hardware devices which perform these functions in faster, cheaper, more reliable, and even more innovative ways.

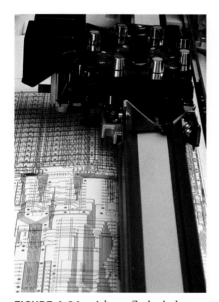

**FIGURE 4-24** A large flatbed plotter can be used to create complex engineering drawings in several colors.

## ▶ Key Terms

analog/digital input (p. 91)

arithmetic/logic unit (p. 76)

ASCII (American Standard Code for Information Interchange) (p. 80)

automated teller machine (ATM) (p. 90)

binary integer (p. 82)

bit (p. 79)

bit-mapped (p. 83)

byte (p. 85)

cathode ray tube (CRT) (p. 76)

CD-ROM (p. 88)

central processing unit (CPU) (p. 76)

computer architecture (p. 77)

core memory (p. 86)

cursor (p. 91)

digital (numeric) data (p. 84)

disk drive (p. 76)

diskette (p. 87)

EBCDIC (Extended Binary Coded Decimal Interchange Code) (p. 81)

flatbed scanner (p. 90)

gigabyte (GB) (p. 88)

graphical user interface (GUI) (p. 91)

hard copy (p. 94)

ink-jet printer (p. 94)

integer (p. 81)

kilohertz (kHz) (p. 83)

laser printer (p. 94)

magnetic ink character recognition (MICR) (p. 90)

magneto-optical (MO) (p. 89)

matrix (p. 83)

memory (p. 84)

menu (p. 91)

million instructions per second (MIPS) (p. 78)

monochrome screen (p. 94)

motherboard (p. 76)

nanosecond (p. 79)

near letter quality (NLQ) (p. 94)

numeric character (p. 83)

optical character recognition (OCR) (p. 90)

place system (p. 82)

plotter (p. 95)

primary storage (p. 84)

read-only memory (ROM) (p. 86)

real (floating-point) number (p. 82)

resolution (p. 83)

RGB monitor (p. 94)

secondary mass storage (p. 87)

semiconductor memory (p. 84)

slide scanner (p. 90)

soft copy (p. 94)

synthesizer (p. 95)

touch screen (p. 92)

Unicode (p. 81)

visual display terminal (VDT) (p. 76)

voiceprint (p. 94)

window (p. 91)

 *Self-Test*

## MULTIPLE-CHOICE

1. All of the following are terms for the output screen that comes with a personal computer system except
   a. OCR
   b. monitor
   c. VDT
   d. CRT

2. Sometimes computers use a seven-bit code to encode characters like letters, numbers, and symbols. How many different symbols can be represented with seven bits?
   a. 7
   b. 77
   c. 128
   d. $7^2$

3. Older IBM mainframes encode characters in a code called EBCDIC, but most personal computers use a code called
   a. MIPS
   b. ASCII
   c. hexadecimal
   d. Intel

4. ROM is a special type of computer memory that can
   a. change when the power is turned off
   b. never change
   c. change only during reads
   d. be written to by programs

5. All of the following are advantages of diskettes for storage of data except
   a. small size
   b. portability
   c. low cost for the amount of storage that they contain
   d. fast access speed compared to hard disks

6. CD-ROM disks provide a convenient way to store
   a. dictionaries and encyclopedias
   b. digital photographs
   c. archives of spoken sound
   d. all of the above

7. All of the following represent forms of direct input except
   a. optical scanning
   b. an ATM cash card
   c. punch cards
   d. a flatbed scanner

8. Which of the following input methods is not analog to digital?
   a. a 3½-inch diskette
   b. a mouse
   c. a monitor worn by a heart patient
   d. a sensor to detect nuclear radiation levels

## TRUE/FALSE

9. **T   F**   When a program is running on a personal computer, the active binary representation of the program is located in RAM memory.

10. **T   F**   As a rule of thumb, the newer and more powerful the chip, the faster its clock speed.

11. **T   F**   Examining the MHz numbers and MIPS ratings of two computers provides a quick way to compare their speed and throughput capacity.

12. **T   F**   Binary codes were invented for storing letters and numbers in a computer, but graphic images are not stored using binary notation.

13. **T   F**   A 5¼-inch floppy diskette with 1.2MB capacity does not have the storage capacity to encode 200 pages of English text (30 lines per page, 80 characters per line).

14. **T   F**   Soft copy is information in electronic form, suitable for being read on a CRT.

15. **T   F**   Ink-jet printers that spray dot patterns on paper to produce a fine-quality image for a reasonable price fall into the category of impact printers.

16. **T   F**   The technology of a laser printer is similar to that of the cassette tape.

## FILL-IN

17. The five functional elements of any computer system are input, output, memory, _____, and _____.

18. The _____ is the basic component of the CPU and the key to its architecture.

19. The binary number 101 is equivalent to the value ___ in the decimal system.

20. Eight bits of binary data comprise one ____.

21. _____ is the most common binary coding scheme for representing letters, numbers, punctuation marks, and special characters like the dollar sign in personal computers.

22. The picture elements that allow the presentation of graphic images on a computer screen are called _____.

23. Reading the numbers at the bottom of checks, or the barcodes on items at the supermarket, falls into the input category called _____.

24. An inexpensive printer for the casual personal computer user that sprays ink on the paper is called _____.

## ▶ Experiential Exercises

1. Analyze several activities in terms of the five general functions of a computer system: adding numbers on the blackboard, lining up for the start of a 10K race, making a cake from scratch. Try to isolate the five components: input, memory, process, output, and control.

2. Some computer science applications are based on an octal system, using the eight decimal digits 0–7. Others are based on the hexadecimal (hex = 6 + decimal = 10), with 16 symbols (0–9 plus the letters A, B, C, D, E, and F). Investigate both these numerical coding schemes. What do the octal numbers 10 and 20 translate into in the decimal system? What are the decimal equivalents of the hexadecimal numbers 2A and BA? (Hint: review how both the decimal and binary number systems work. Octal is base 8, hexadecimal, base 16.)

3. Distinguish between RAM and ROM memory. Research the sorts of program code that are often stored in ROM by manufacturers.

4. Sometimes segments of a diskette are bad, and the computer tells the user that they are unreadable. Find out what can cause this. In what cases can the bad parts be recovered with diagnostic software?

5. Estimate the number of characters in a typical 20-page term paper or a 300-page novel. How many 1.44MB diskettes would be needed to store the term paper? How much storage in megabytes in a hard disk would be needed to store the novel?

6. Investigate forms of direct input other than those discussed in this chapter—for example, those used in an intensive care unit at a hospital, for logging in letters for shipping, or for counting items on supermarket shelves. How typical are analog/digital hybrid input systems in these settings?

7. Find out more about the growing field of color printers by reading a computer magazine like *Byte*, *PC World*, or *Macworld*. How do color printers work, and what are the costs?

# ▶ Critical Thinking Exercises

1. Discuss the parallels between stimulus and response in human perception and in the computer in terms of the five functional elements discussed in the text.

2. In the natural world, binary states occur more frequently than decimal states, and not just in electromagnetic phenomena. Why then did early humankind not develop a binary number system instead of one based on the number 10? Discuss.

3. Discuss everyday symbols that have different meanings dependent on their context. For instance, what meanings are associated with the color red or the number 7 in different situations?

4. People recognize characters in many typefaces much better than scanners like the Kurzweil blind reader and many commercial models. Discuss reasons for this phenomenon.

## ANSWERS TO SELF-TEST

*Multiple-Choice*: 1. a;    2. c;    3. b;    4. b;    5. d;    6. d;    7. c;
8. a
*True/False*: 9. T;    10. T;    11. T;    12. F;    13. F;    14. T;
15. F;    16. F
*Fill-in*: 17. processor, control;    18. microprocessor;    19. 5;    20.
byte;    21. ASCII;    22. pixels;    23. optical scanning;    24. an ink-
jet printer

# CHAPTER 5

# Computer Software

▶ **LEARNING OUTCOMES**

*After completing this chapter, you should be able to:*

1. *Explain why the algorithm is fundamental to all computer processing.*

2. *Express basic algorithmic processes in flowcharts and pseudocode.*

3. *Explain the principles of structured programming, top-down design, and systems analysis.*

4. *Describe the evolution of computer programming from machine language to compiler languages.*

5. *Describe the user interfaces commonly found on personal computers and workstations.*

6. *Describe the characteristics of computer viruses and other software hazards and explain how to cope with them.*

▶ **COMPUTERS IN CONTEXT**

*Suppose you save some money by buying a mountain bike unassembled and delivered in the carton. Anxious to try it out, you get out a screwdriver and a wrench or two to put its parts together. Inside the carton are all of the components and a set of instructions for assembling them. Some people will not bother to read the instructions and jump right into the process. Others, more careful, will follow the labeled steps of ordered assembly. The instructions may say that the brakes should be put together before being mounted on the rear wheel. If the wheel is attached to the frame before attaching the completed brake, it may be difficult to screw all of the components together. Maybe an important bolt cannot be tightened with the wheel already in place. Following the instructions would have avoided this problem.*

*Manufacturers include the instructions to make the assembly job easier and faster, for they have thought through the steps about how best to put the bike together. Their instructions represent a logical, orderly process, a road map for achieving the goal of assembling the bike in the simplest and most convenient way. If the instructions are well thought out, those who follow their advice will be ready for a first ride quicker than those who experimented with assembly using trial and error.*

Like the road map of instructions, control over the logical processes of a computer is a central element among the five components of a computer system. Calculator users are exercising control, for example, in punching the buttons in the correct order to add a column of figures. Young children can play with the buttons of a calculator; but without conscious control of what they are doing, the results will be nonsense.

In computers, software usually fulfills the control function. The term *software* was coined as an afterthought in the early days of computing, which were dominated by hardware developments. Starting in the 1950s, computer scientists devised programming languages to adapt computers for a variety of applications. Since the programs were not actual hardware devices, they were distinguished from machines by calling them "software." Hardware carries out the actual work, but it is not very useful without people and software, the other two components of the Computer Triangle, to tell it what to do.

Software as a general category includes (1) applications software, (2) video games, (3) programming languages that let users write their own programs, and (4) operating systems that control the functions of computers. We will begin with programming languages, then take a look at operating systems and the applications software that runs on computers.

## ▶ Algorithmic Processes and Structured Program Design

To understand the role of software, think back to putting together the mountain bike. In this task, some things had to be done before others. First you gathered the tools, then opened the carton and followed directions in assembling the components. In computer terms, you followed a straightforward **algorithm**—a logical sequence of steps—to carry out the task. The notion of algorithms is central to the problem-solving philosophy of computers. Given a goal, people think through the series of steps required to achieve it and come to an algorithmic solution to their problem. By contrast, children playing with a calculator lack an algorithm in their random pressing of the buttons, and the results have little or no meaning.

Many processes in everyday life incorporate the principles of the algorithm: using a recipe to bake a cake from scratch; obeying the rules of a game like Monopoly to navigate a token around a playing board; or following a set of instructions for assembling a toy. Algorithms provide useful ways to break up complex processes, like cake baking, into simpler components that make up the process. Sometimes recipe instructions are poorly written and hard to follow. To avoid such pitfalls, a proper algorithm should be unambiguous and should lead to the solution by a clear, concise process.

**algorithm:** A predetermined series of instructions for carrying out a task in a finite number of steps.

### FLOWCHARTS AND PSEUDOCODE

Two common ways to display the steps of an algorithm are the flowchart and pseudocode. A **flowchart,** or **flow diagram,** uses pictorial symbols and arrows to represent the relationships of the parts of an algorithm. **Pseudocode** is a structured English description of the operations. If you were going to write a computer program, your teacher would probably suggest that you design the solution using one of these problem-solving strategies.

For example, a portion of an algorithm for one player's moves in Monopoly might look like the flowchart in Figure 5-3. Ovals start and stop flowcharts, and rectangles stand for operations that follow each other in linear order, one after another. When the flow reaches a diamond-shaped box, called a **decision box** or **branch** (the fourth step in the diagram), a question must be answered or a decision made. The next operation to be carried out depends on the answer or decision that went before. If the token lands on the Go to Jail square, the player must go directly to jail (without passing Go and collecting $200); she follows the Yes arrow. Otherwise, the No arrow leads the player to another question, about landing on a

**flowchart (flow diagram):** A graphic representation of an algorithm, often used in the design phase of programming to work out the logical flow of a program.

**pseudocode:** A kind of structured English used to describe the algorithmic steps needed in a program, analogous to a flowchart as a planning tool for programming.

**decision box (branch):** One of the fundamental building blocks of flowcharting, offering a choice between alternative directions to continue, analogous to selection in structured programming.

**FIGURE 5-1** An algorithm for baking a cake. Carrying out the instructions in another order will not get the same results.

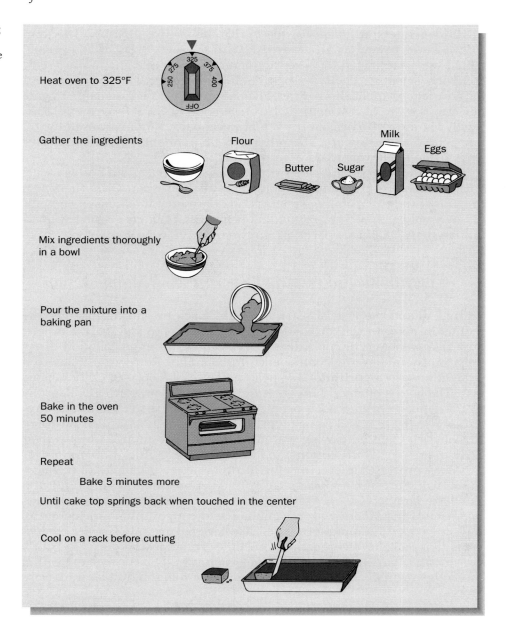

Heat oven to 325°F

Gather the ingredients

Flour    Butter    Sugar    Milk    Eggs

Mix ingredients thoroughly in a bowl

Pour the mixture into a baking pan

Bake in the oven 50 minutes

Repeat

    Bake 5 minutes more

Until cake top springs back when touched in the center

Cool on a rack before cutting

Chance or Community Chest square. Again the movement through the flowchart branches. Often, as in this case, the branches are two-way, yes-or-no binary choices, like so many things associated with computers. No matter which of the several routes the player takes through the two decision boxes, she eventually follows the arrows to the end of her turn and passes control over to the next player. Because we do not have the whole Monopoly flowchart, we never reach an oval for "Stop." The flowchart presents visually the moves and choices that must be considered after each throw of the dice by one player.

The equivalent algorithm in pseudocode might look like the following:

Procedure Monopoly_Move

Begin one's move.

Throw the dice.

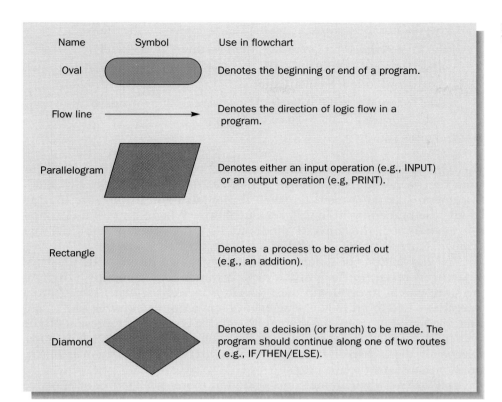

**FIGURE 5-2** Common flowchart symbols and their meanings.

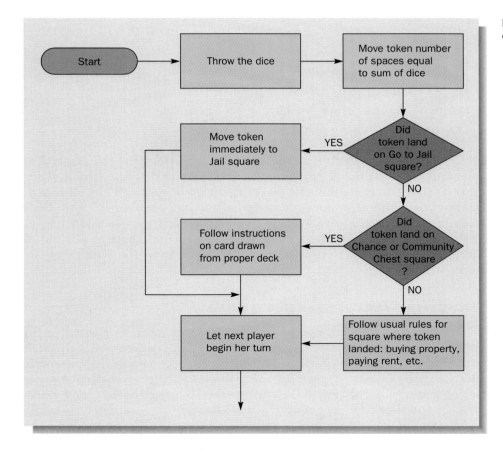

**FIGURE 5-3** A flowchart of one player's move in Monopoly.

Move the number of spaces on the board shown on the dice.

If the token landed on Go to Jail, then go there immediately.

Else if the token landed on Chance or Community Chest, then draw a card and follow its instructions.

Else follow the usual rules for the square (buying property, paying rent, collecting $200 for passing Go, etc.).

End one's move.

**if/then/else condition:** A branching condition in both pseudocode and structured programming.

**structured program design:** The process of designing the components of a computer program as a set of individual self-contained modules that can be interrelated.

**loop:** A series of program instructions performed repeatedly until a certain condition is satisfied, embodying the structured programming construct of iteration.

**sequence:** The structured program construct for a series of statements that are carried out in linear order, one after another.

**selection:** The term used in structured programming for the choice represented by a decision box or an if/then/else condition.

**iteration (looping):** One of the four main constructs in structured programming for executing a series of steps repeatedly in a program, often called looping.

**transfer:** Programming statements, like the "go-to" in nonstructured programming languages, that allow program code to be transferred into and out of modules.

This kind of structured English is not hard to read. The only unfamiliar construct is probably the set of sentences of the "If/else if/else" kind. Statements like these, usually called **if/then/else conditions,** are used to handle the branching in logical sentence form. Whenever an if/else condition is satisfied, the move is made, and all the other possibilities are skipped. Only one of the possibilities can be satisfied in any move.

The conventions of sentence indentation shown in this code illustrate **structured program design,** the most common way computer programmers are taught to divide up their jobs into logical segments for solution. Operations within an indented segment form a unit, somewhat like a self-contained module. Here the several if/then/else conditions represent all the possibilities of action determined by the square on which the token lands. Except for the if/then/else conditions, the flow of the algorithm is linear, from one statement to the next.

To illustrate algorithmic construction in more detail, we can reference the pseudocode for Monopoly_Move from another set of instructions that represent the whole game. Consider the following pseudocode:

Main Procedure Monopoly_Game

Hand out each player's initial money.

Decide which player goes first.

Repeat

Call Procedure Monopoly_Move for next player.

Decide if this player must drop out.

Until all players except one have dropped out.

Declare the surviving player to be the winner.

This main procedure outlines the start and end rules for the game. The rules indented within the repeat/until structure constitute a **loop.** They must be repeated until only one player is left in the game. Within the looping structure, the separate procedure for one person's move (Procedure Monopoly_Move) will be called repeatedly until everyone except one player has gone broke. Finally the condition in the until statement at the end of the loop has been met, and the survivor is declared the winner of the game.

## STRUCTURE VERSUS SPAGHETTI CODE

**HISTORY**

Edsger Dijkstra, a Dutch computer scientist, was largely responsible for the concept of structured program design. In a famous letter (March 1968) to the *Communications of the ACM,* one of the best known computer science journals, Dijkstra argued for using three structures—**sequence** (a series of steps in linear order), **selection** (the if/then/else idea), and **iteration,** or **looping** (the repeat/until idea)—for writing computer software, and for avoiding a fourth kind of step, called **transfer** (the go-to idea). The first three structures form modular units intact within themselves, with only one entry point and one exit each (such as Procedure Monopoly_ Move). Thus parts of a large program can be built of these smaller, separate modules, each free of the other. Transfer statements, on the other hand, allow programmers to transfer in and out of modules with the go-to command. The result has been dubbed "**spaghetti code**," a term which describes the look of a program with many go-to's. In structured design, independent units follow each other in linear fashion or nest inside each other like Chinese boxes. With go-to's, transfers from one unit to another may point anywhere, backward or forward, like the haphazard arrangement of spaghetti in a bowl.

Keeping structures separate allows for modular development of software, called **top-down design.** The guiding principle is to divide and conquer: start at the top, break up a big task into a series of independent sub-

**spaghetti code:** A term for a computer program not following structured programming principles, with many "go-to's" that allow unlimited transfer of control between modules.

**top-down design:** An approach in structured program design that breaks up a general task into a series of more detailed subtasks, which are further divided until no more detail is necessary.

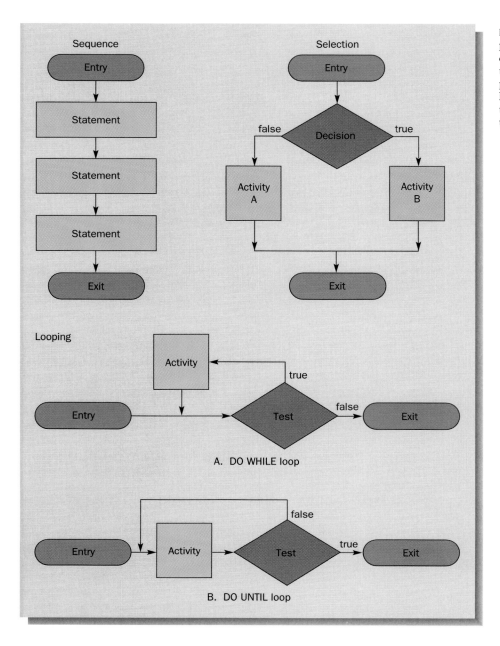

**FIGURE 5-4** The three most common programming control structures: sequence, selection, and looping. Note that all of them have only one entry point and one exit and thus are modular structures. Change within a structure will not affect others before or after it.

**procedure:** In structured programming, one of a series of independent subtasks that stand alone and can be performed one at a time in a modular fashion.

tasks, called **procedures** in programming, and solve them one at a time in modular fashion. In the case of Monopoly, the Main Procedure is the design for the whole game. The call to Monopoly_Move from the Main Procedure illustrates modular program design. The Monopoly move has been encapsulated as a separate procedure, which is called for in every person's turn, within the larger repeat/until loop.

To achieve a modular design, software designers first break up a top-down design into separate procedures, to be coded and tested independently. When these individual modules are complete and have been checked for accuracy, they can be put together to make the whole. Think about a modular stereo system. If the tape drive fails, you can replace it or add a new piece of equipment, like a CD player, without affecting the amplifier and speakers. Similarly, mistakes made within a program module can be found and corrected, and the rest of the modules are unaffected. Because there are no transfers between modules, programmers need not worry about a ripple effect, in which one change messes up other parts of an algorithm. Programmers working on a large project can be assigned individual parts of the job and can work independently of others. After all the programming subtasks are complete, the solutions can be brought together to form a solution for the entire project.

**HISTORY**

The famous case of indexing *The New York Times* in the early 1970s was a compelling argument for the efficiency of top-down design and the structured approach (Baker 1972a, 1972b). The job involved writing software to index articles from the paper, build a database of content terms for the articles, and allow users to access appropriate articles. The *Times* software project lasted 22 months and required 132 months' worth of work on the part of programmers. Yet it was completed ahead of schedule and under budget. In the first year of the indexing system, users found fewer than fifty errors in the software—an amazing statistic for a series of programs containing over 80,000 lines of program code. In saving time and money, this case is always cited as a landmark for the success of the structured approach, which has become the most common method for teaching beginning programmers today.

Top-down design applies not only to producing software, but to organizing whole systems of machines, programs, and people to accomplish a task in the most efficient, timely, and least expensive way possible. The field of **systems analysis** looks at applications top-down and tries to put the three elements of the Computer Triangle together into a coordinated system. In general terms, systems analysis is a way of looking at the whole picture in several steps: (1) assessing the feasibility of coordinating hardware, software, and people; (2) proposing and implementing a solution; (3) getting feedback about whether the solution works; and (4) making corrections where needed. Without looking at the whole process as a complete system, one may make a decision in one area that will lead to problems at a later stage. Such flaws should be revealed at the feedback stage in time to be corrected. Thinking about the whole enterprise as a joint effort of people, hardware, and software—the essence of the Computer Triangle— cuts out duplicated effort, saves time and money, and takes into account human factors involved in computing change.

**systems analysis:** A field of analysis that looks at a proposed computer application from the top down and tries to put together an efficient, coordinated system made up of hardware, software, and people to achieve the desired goal.

## ▶ The Evolution of Software

Because a computer has binary electrical hardware, it is no wonder that the internal software codes that run the hardware are recorded in binary. To implement the throughput process requires a partnership of hardware and software working together in the **processing cycle.** A minimal set of basic binary instructions for all general-purpose digital computers must include facilities for reading information into memory, transferring it to the processor, storing the new results again in memory, and sending them from memory to output.

The arithmetic/logic unit is designed to carry out binary operations on data that are read from memory. These operations include at least the four **arithmetic functions** (addition, subtraction, multiplication, and division) and the full set of **logical comparison operators** (equal to, less than, greater than, not equal to, greater than or equal to, and less than or equal to).

## THE STORED PROGRAM CONCEPT

Before it is executed, a program of computer instructions must itself be read into the memory of the machine. The principle that the program (the software) is stored in memory along with the data to be processed is called the **stored program concept.** Proposed in 1946 by the Princeton mathematician John von Neumann, the idea is that computer programs can be stored as binary data in memory and even modified like data in the arithmetic/logic unit. Previously programs were wired into the computer using a **plugboard;** modification of the program required stopping the machine for rewiring. The stored program concept brought generality of application to the digital computer and led directly to the first commercial model, the UNIVAC I, in 1951.

## THE PROCESSING CYCLE

To get some sense of the processing cycle, recall from Chapter 1 that a microprocessor chip has an **internal clock speed** measured in megahertz. Retrieval of binary instructions from memory and processing of them inside the chip are triggered by the regularity of the clock ticks. First, the instruction is moved across a **data bus** into an **instruction decoder** in the control unit of the chip. Then the microprocessor sets out to implement the instruction. Suppose we want to check to see if a name is in a data file stored on a hard disk. The software must instruct the computer to retrieve a list of names, one name at a time, from the disk file and move it into sequential locations in RAM memory. Then each name can be moved to the arithmatic logic unit (ALU), one at a time, and compared to the name in question, to see if the two are "equal"—that is, the same. The retrieve-and-compare process is repeated for each name in the list. Names that do not match are filed again in memory; a matching name can be printed on the screen for the viewer's perusal. Every small step of the process is controlled by the instructions in the computer program, which are moved from memory, decoded, and carried out step by step.

This search method of looking up a name in a file is called **sequential search** and is considered a "brute force" way of operating. It may be adequate for small data files but is too time consuming for many practical applications, for which more efficient search strategies have been devised. Remember, however, that internal operations in a computer take place in billionths of a second. In one second, several thousand names can be searched even at personal computer speeds; larger, faster machines can search hundreds of thousands of names in the same amount of time.

**processing cycle:** The implementation of the throughput process from input to output, which requires a partnership of hardware and software in carrying out the five functions of all computer applications.

**arithmetic function:** One of the arithmetic operations—addition, subtraction, multiplication, or division—included in most programming languages.

**logical comparison operator:** One of the common logical operations—less than, greater than, equal to, not equal to, etc.—included in most programming languages.

**HISTORY**

**stored program concept:** The storage of data and instructions in central memory so that instructions can be treated like data. Von Neumann proposed this principle in the 1940s, so that the computer did not have to be hard-wired each time a specific task was to be performed.

**plugboard:** Before programming languages were invented, programs were individually wired for one application using such a wiring board, and modification required stopping the machine for rewiring.

**internal clock speed:** Measured in megahertz, the speed of the CPU clock determines how quickly binary instructions are retrieved from memory and processed.

**data bus:** An electrical path to transfer data and instructions back and forth between internal memory devices and the processor.

**instruction decoder:** A part of the control unit of the CPU which receives machine language instructions, interprets them, and carries them out.

**sequential search:** A programming strategy of searching for an item in a data file by examining items in the order in which they are stored, often not the most efficient searching method.

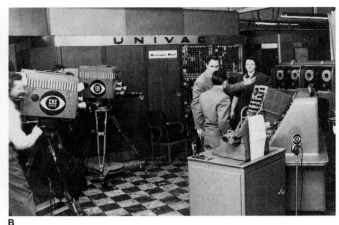

A                                                          B

**FIGURE 5-5** (A) John von Neumann introduced the concept for a stored-program computer in 1945. (B) The UNIVAC I (1951) was the first commercially available stored-program electronic digital computer.

**HISTORY**

**machine language:** The basic set of binary operations, specific to each computer brand, that constitute its main power.

**assembler:** A program that translates assembly language code to binary machine language before it is run by a computer.

**assembly language:** A computer language of symbolic instructions and addresses that convert into binary machine language codes on a one-to-one basis.

## MACHINE LANGUAGE AND ASSEMBLY LANGUAGE

The binary instruction set of a computer is called its **machine language.** Typically about 100 such operations are built into any particular computer. Users of the first digital computers in the 1940s and early 1950s had to instruct the machines to do their work by coding the commands directly into them in binary. They were programming the computer to work in its own language; there were no shortcuts to make the task easier. This incredibly slow and tedious task of binary coding limited the use of the first machines to highly trained specialists.

Soon, however, programs called **assemblers,** the first software advances, were devised to make it easier for people to write and correct instructions. These computer programs translated **assembly language** code to binary machine language. It is important to stress that before *any* computer program is run, it must be in the binary form the machine requires. If one is not going to code in binary—and today no one does—a translation process must take place.

Here is a simple assembly-language program that instructs a computer to read two numbers, add them up, and print out the answer. It is annotated to show the small steps involved in assembly-language programming. The annotations themselves are like pseudocode for the job:

| | |
|---|---|
| RD A | Read a number into memory location A. |
| RD B | Read a second number into memory location B. |
| CLA A | Clear the ALU and add the number in A to it. |
| ADD B | Add the number in B to the ALU. |
| ST SUM | Store the result from the ALU in location SUM. |
| PRT SUM | Send the number in SUM to the printer. |
| HALT | Stop processing. |

This program deals with three pieces of data: the two numbers to be added and the sum that is created, stored, and printed. Note that each programming statement is rather elementary; very little happens with each. Imagine the length and complexity of an assembler program to calculate a complex payroll for a large company with many employees! The program also does not specify the values of the two numbers to be added. A general

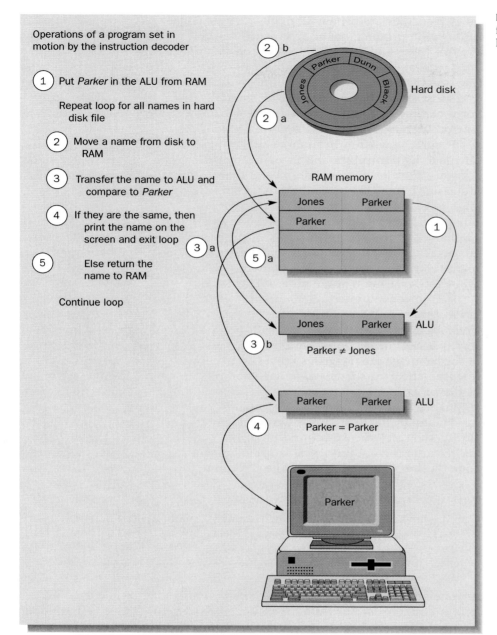

**FIGURE 5-6** The processing cycle for finding a name called "Parker" in a hard disk file.

Operations of a program set in motion by the instruction decoder

1. Put *Parker* in the ALU from RAM

   Repeat loop for all names in hard disk file

2. Move a name from disk to RAM

3. Transfer the name to ALU and compare to *Parker*

4. If they are the same, then print the name on the screen and exit loop

5. Else return the name to RAM

   Continue loop

solution, it adds up whatever numbers are read from an input device like the keyboard; it will work for any two numbers. *Striving for generality,* rather than designing a specific solution for specific data, adds flexibility to programming.

## HIGH-LEVEL LANGUAGES

Assembly languages are an advance over machine language, but they are still difficult for most people. Very little gets done in each step. In the late 1950s a newer, easier-to-use type of programming language was developed, now called **high-level language.** When people today refer to programming

**high-level language:** A programming language that is more like English than it is like assembly language, and thus easier to use in writing programs. Compiler and interpreter languages are all high-level languages.

**compiler:** Software that translates a program written in a high-level language into lower-level language instructions. As an additional benefit, it searches along the way for grammar errors in the program.

**interpreter:** A computer program that translates a high-level instruction to machine language, line by line, and then executes it before considering the next instruction.

**source code:** The statements that make up a computer program in a high-level programming language, ready for an interpreter or a compiler.

**object code:** The binary version of a program, originally written in a high-level language, having been created as machine language code by the translation process.

**syntax error:** An error found in a computer program in the compiling stage because a statement violates the grammatical rules of the programming language.

**logical error:** A bug in a computer program in which the logic is faulty—for instance, in which instructions are not in proper sequence or the wrong instructions are used.

languages, they are usually thinking of this category of software. Almost all of the programming that goes on in the world is done in one of several hundred of these high-level languages. The first was FORTRAN (1957), still a very popular language for scientific programming, and the second popular one was COBOL (1960), still commonly used for business data processing. The most common language for teaching beginning programming on personal computers is BASIC (1964), developed originally at Dartmouth as an interpreter but also available in compiler versions.

Programs written in high-level languages are translated to machine language by **compilers** and **interpreters.** Compilers and interpreters are software that let programmers code their applications in languages that are easier to read, write, and correct than machine or assembly languages. High-level languages embody abstractions that are lacking in brute-force binary coding. Often statements in these languages look like algebra or English. The translation process of programs written in high-level languages, called **source code,** to binary code is handled by the compiler or interpreter program inside the computer. Then the computer runs the job in the binary version of the program, called **object code.**

Compilers and interpreters differ in the way they accomplish the translation process. A compiler translates the whole finished program at one time; an interpreter translates it as it is being executed, line by line. In either process, instructions that do not make sense as properly formed rules of the language are flagged, so that the programmer can correct them. This feature—checking for mistakes in the grammar (or *syntax,* to be technical) of the programming language—represents another attraction of high-level languages.

The following program is written in True BASIC, a modern version of BASIC that includes structured program ideas. Notice how much shorter and clearer the addition problem looks in high-level language. (Pseudocode for the process appears in the column to the right.)

| | |
|---|---|
| Input A, B | Read two numbers A and B. |
| Let SUM = A + B | Add them up and call the result SUM. |
| Print SUM | Print the value of SUM. |
| End | Halt the process. |

Anyone who knows high school algebra can understand this code; in fact, it is a condensed, formulaic version of the pseudocode. Once having planned their applications with a flowchart, pseudocode, or some other modern design tool, programmers find it convenient to write them in high-level languages that offer ease of use, readability, and syntactic error checking in the translation process.

We have seen that high-level language offers programmers help in identifying **syntax errors**—mistakes in typing or even in the proper grammar of their statements. For example, the read statement above cannot be written "Input A and B" in True BASIC. That language does not recognize *and* for a series, but requires a comma. A programmer will get an error message for such a statement and an opportunity to correct it. It is worth noting that a **logical error,** such as placing the print command before the add command, will not be caught by True BASIC. The computer will print the current value of SUM, which is nil, before it adds A and B, and their sum will never be printed. Program statements that are arranged out of order contain a logical flaw and will produce bad results, even if they are properly formed.

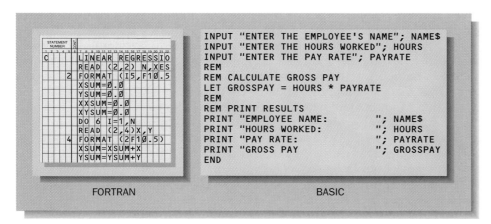

```
         STATEMENT
          NUMBER
 C           LINEAR REGRESSIO
       2     READ (2,2) N,XES
             FORMAT (I5,F10.5
             XSUM=0.0
             YSUM=0.0
             XXSUM=0.0
             XYSUM=0.0
             DO 6 I=1,N
             READ (2,4)X,Y
       4     FORMAT (2F10.5)
             XSUM=XSUM+X
             YSUM=YSUM+Y
```

FORTRAN

```
INPUT "ENTER THE EMPLOYEE'S NAME"; NAME$
INPUT "ENTER THE HOURS WORKED"; HOURS
INPUT "ENTER THE PAY RATE"; PAYRATE
REM
REM CALCULATE GROSS PAY
LET GROSSPAY = HOURS * PAYRATE
REM
REM PRINT RESULTS
PRINT "EMPLOYEE NAME:        "; NAME$
PRINT "HOURS WORKED:         "; HOURS
PRINT "PAY RATE:             "; PAYRATE
PRINT "GROSS PAY             "; GROSSPAY
END
```

BASIC

**FIGURE 5-7** Two early algorithmic programming languages: FORTRAN developed for scientists and engineers in 1956, and BASIC from Thomas Kurtz and John Kemeny at Dartmouth in 1964. BASIC was intended as a first language for teaching programming to students.

## A SAMPLING OF PROGRAMMING LANGUAGES

The selection of programming languages is wide and varied. Literally hundreds of languages are available today, for a host of applications areas. FORTRAN, COBOL, and BASIC, the early favorites among programming languages for science, business, and education, are algorithmic in design. Featuring mathematical operations and file handling capabilities, they are easy to code from flowcharts and pseudocode. Before the adoption of structured programming, around 1970, all these languages used the go-to instruction liberally, and the result was "spaghetti code," difficult to correct when it contained **bugs.**

The origin of the terms *bug* and *debug* in reference to mistakes in computer programs makes an interesting story in itself. In the Second World War at Harvard, early military computers used relay switches. When one computer failed, operators found that a moth had been crushed in the relay and had crashed the machine. Thus the first bug to cause a computing error was a real one! **Debugging** the machine literally meant removing the moth; today it means finding and correcting programming errors.

Recent versions of the early languages, such as True BASIC, have replaced go-to's with modern algorithmic structures. Newer languages like

**bug:** A term for a program error, usually in software, that causes it to crash or malfunction.

**HISTORY**

**debugging:** The process of correcting errors in a computer program, often helped by error diagnostics from the compiler.

A

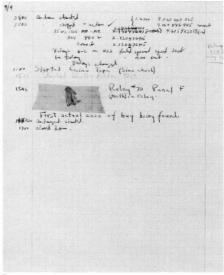

B

**FIGURE 5-8** (A) Grace Hopper was one of the first programmers; (B) she actually found a bug (moth) in the computer, which she affixed to her lab manual.

**FIGURE 5-9** A Logo turtle draws patterns on the floor according to instructions programmed into the computer in the Logo language.

**string-handling language:** A category of programming languages like LISP and SNOBOL appropriate for lists and textual data, such as natural language.

**logic programming languages:** A category of languages like Prolog very similar to symbolic logic, especially applicable to artificial intelligence research and expert systems.

**expert system:** A category of computer software in artificial intelligence designed to model the behavior of human experts in some field and frequently coded in logic programming language.

PL/I, Pascal, Modula2, and C were designed intentionally as structured algorithmic languages. When computing was dominated by large IBM computers, PL/I was popular with computer science departments, but today Pascal or C are the favored first languages for computer science majors. Pascal is named for the French mathematician and philosopher who invented the hand calculator. Niklaus Wirth, the Swiss inventor of Pascal, hopes that Modula2 will become its successor. The language C has a growing number of followers. Faced with a need to standardize U.S. military software, the Defense Department in 1979 introduced its own standard algorithmic language, called Ada. Contractors now produce Ada programs that will run on all Defense Department machines. The name honors Ada Lovelace, the first programmer of Charles Babbage's Analytical Engine, a nineteenth-century forerunner of the modern computer.

**String-handling languages,** including SNOBOL and LISP, are especially adept at pattern matching for lists and language texts. Programmers use them for code breaking, linguistic and literary analysis, and artificial intelligence. For instance, one can use SNOBOL to find all the instances of death and dying in a computerized version of *Hamlet*. LISP has been popular for writing chess-playing programs, which involve the assessment of hundreds of chess patterns before the program chooses the most advantageous move. Code breakers seek to match repeated patterns of letters or symbols to crack difficult codes. Seymour Papert's Logo, a derivative of LISP that is easy to code and has features for graphics and calculation, is intended for young children. They learn how to think logically by instructing a robot turtle to move in geometrical patterns around the floor or by commanding a cartoon turtle to do its tricks on a computer screen.

In recent years a new category of languages, called **logic programming language,** has appeared for research in artificial intelligence and **expert systems,** computer programs that try to model the behavior of human experts. Prolog, a current favorite, incorporates the features of symbolic logic directly into its codes. Using Prolog, one can easily define relationships between entities and query them logically. For example, con-

**FIGURE 5-10** Two computing pioneers for whom programming languages are named: (A) the French mathematician Blaise Pascal and (B) Augusta Ada, Countess of Lovelace, the daughter of Lord Byron. Pascal invented the first adding machine, and Lovelace is the person credited with the idea of programming. She worked with (C) Charles Babbage on his design of the Analytical Engine in the 1830s.

A

B

C

sider the following short segment of annotated Prolog about people and cats:

| Code | Meaning |
|------|---------|
| cat(fluffy). | Fluffy is a cat. |
| cat(blackie). | Blackie is a cat. |
| owns(john, fluffy). | John owns Fluffy. |
| owns(mary, blackie). | Mary owns Blackie. |
| ? – owns(X, fluffy). | Query: Find the owner of Fluffy. |
| X = john | Prolog response: John owns Fluffy. |
| Yes | The search for an answer succeeds. |

The first two statements define Fluffy and Blackie as cats. The second two set up the ownership relations between people and their pets, the entities in this example. The power of Prolog logic is seen in the fifth statement, with its question mark: it asks for the owner of Fluffy the cat (the variable X). The computer responds with the next two lines. It looks for the relationship "owns" that includes Fluffy and finds John. The last line prints "Yes" to show that the machine has found a solution to the question. Note how Prolog's statements and questions seem more like natural language than mathematics. Logic languages, which model human thinking directly, promise more intelligent computer programs in many fields in future years.

##  Operating Systems

Every computer has an **operating system,** a complex piece of software provided by the manufacturer that serves a control function. In large mainframe machines it is sometimes also called the **executive,** or **monitor, program.** The operating system is a sort of super software, the computer's own program for monitoring all its operations. For example, when a programmer submits a BASIC program to a personal computer, the machine has to recognize that the programmer is using BASIC code (and not something else) and get ready to compile (or translate) the BASIC statements to machine binary code. The user first invokes the BASIC compiler with commands to the operating system and then types in BASIC code on the keyboard. When coding is complete, the operating system transfers the program to the BASIC compiler, oversees the running of the program, and turns on appropriate output devices, such as the diskette drive or the printer. Mainframe users also must tell the operating system which compiler is needed and where to find input files and send output files.

### DOS

Most personal computers in recent years have been based on two common operating systems: IBM-compatible DOS and Macintosh. A major difference between the two, several years ago, was the way that users interacted with the machine from their keyboards or with their mice. **DOS** stands for Disk Operating System, and describes the way that users controlled the IBM PC and its clones. Microsoft developed DOS (another name, MS-DOS, refers to its origin at Microsoft) originally to handle input and output of files with disk drives on the IBM PC; hence its name, Disk Operating System. At first users interacted with the operating system by means of the keyboard, typing in their command lines. The command "format a:" in-

**operating system:** The computer's own system software for monitoring all of its operations, such as moving data into and out of storage and coordinating the running of application programs.

**executive (monitor) program:** Other terms for an operating system.

**DOS:** An abbreviation for Disk Operating System, the popular operating system developed by Microsoft and found on IBM-compatible computers.

**HISTORY**

```
C:\>format a:
<this formats a disk to make it readable by the computer>
Insert new diskette for drive A:
and press ENTER when ready...

Checking existing disk format.
Formatting 1.44M
Format complete.

Volume Label (11 characters, ENTER for none)? mydisk

   1457664 bytes total disk space
   1457664 bytes available on disk

      512 bytes in each allocation unit.
     2847 allocation units available on disk.

Volume Serial Number is 415E-14E9

Format another (Y/N)?n


C:\>dir
<shows the files in the directory>
 Volume in drive C is C_DRIVE
 Volume Serial Number is 1C62-8132
 Directory of C:\

AUTOEXEC BAT        417 08-01-94  11:47p
CONFIG   SYS        287 08-01-94  11:40p
DOS          <DIR>      07-30-94   9:55p
      3 file(s)          704 bytes
                    179650560 bytes free


C:\>copy *.* a:
<copies all of the files from the c: drive to the a: drive>
AUTOEXEC.BAT
CONFIG.SYS
      2 file(s) copied
```

**user interface:** The way a user communicates with the computer.

**menu-driven:** A technique of presenting command choices in the operating system by giving the user several different options, recently in pull-down menus.

**function keys:** Shortcut keys on the keyboard that are set up to send commands to the operating system, especially in MS-DOS systems.

**template:** A cardboard or plastic pattern sometimes packed with software for placement on a keyboard, listing the most common commands in the package.

**pull-down menu:** A menu of command options that is hidden from view until revealed by a combination of keystrokes or depression of a mouse.

**desktop:** The background of a computer screen with a GUI on which icons and windows appear.

structed DOS to format a new diskette on the A disk drive. "Type a: letter" meant that DOS was to display on the computer screen the contents of the file called "letter," stored on the A drive.

Over the last 10 years of machine evolution, DOS software has expanded enormously to incorporate many other features, including the primacy of hard disks over diskettes for storage. The command-line DOS **user interface**—a computer term which refers to how the user communicates with the computer—first became mainly **menu-driven.** This means that software was written to give the user a choice of actions from a menu of options shown on the screen: perhaps using the operating system for formatting diskettes; saving files or deleting them; or choosing features of an applications software package, such as a word processor. Having decided on a choice, the user typed some combination of keystrokes or **function keys;** the operating system recognized the commands and carried out the action. For example, a person using a word processor got used to a variety of keystrokes to mark underlined passages, italics, boldface letters, and sections of text to be moved around. Often the software package came with a cardboard or plastic **template** to lay down on the keyboard, showing the most common key combinations as a reminder.

## THE MACINTOSH GRAPHICAL USER INTERFACE

The Macintosh was the first popular machine to use an operating system based more on the mouse than the keyboard. Called a *graphical user interface* (GUI), it features **pull-down menus** and files presented in windows on a **desktop.** Instead of a menu of keying choices, the Macintosh user is

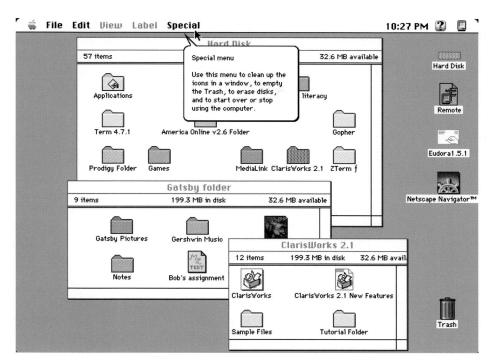

**FIGURE 5-12** The Macintosh graphical user interface, with its windows and icons. Balloon Help is active to give advice about features of the desktop, in this case the Special menu.

shown a pictorial screen with **icons** for the disk drives, a **trash can** for deletion of files, and a set of word choices (the pull-down menus) at the top. Choosing items presented in a graphical mode by clicking a mouse is favored on this machine over typing at a keyboard. Depressing the mouse on one of the menu bars opens up a window of more choices; releasing the mouse over one of the menu options activates that action, such as saving or printing a file. Files are opened as a series of stacked windows on the desktop somewhere in the middle of the screen. In addressing the operating system, use of the mouse takes precedence over using the keyboard, although that also remains possible.

Although a Xerox research group in Palo Alto pioneered the icon-driven GUI, the Macintosh gained it wide acceptability. Today most computer manufacturers are adopting the idea. DOS machines based on Intel chips (386, 486, Pentium), along with larger workstations based on the Unix operating system, have joined the GUI bandwagon. The IBM operating system called **OS/2** and the Microsoft operating environment called Windows, upgraded in 1990, have adopted the graphical or pictorial approach. All indications are that GUI will continue to dominate operating systems in personal computers.

### MICROSOFT WINDOWS ENVIRONMENTS

Bill Gates and Microsoft Corporation are associated today with an operating environment called Windows, currently the most popular in the world. By 1992 the wealthiest man in America, with estimated assets of $6.3 billion at 37 years of age, Gates got his start by licensing the DOS operating system to IBM for their first PC in the early 1980s. In 1990, Microsoft stepped out on its own with the introduction of Windows 3.0, a popular GUI that works with DOS machines and Intel chips. Apple claimed that Windows was copied from the Macintosh interface, and IBM was unhappy that Windows was a direct competitor to its OS/2, which had itself been originally commissioned from Microsoft.

**icon:** A picture on a computer screen with a graphical user interface that represents a physical object, such as a file folder, a program, or a trash can.

**trash can:** An icon common with graphical user interface systems used for getting rid of files. "Emptying the trash" means deleting files stored there.

**HISTORY**

**OS/2:** An acronym for Operating System/2, a powerful GUI personal computer operating system owned by IBM.

Windows soon became the most popular GUI in the world, and software developers were scrambling to develop their applications programs to run under Windows, especially Version 3.1. But this version of Windows was really an overlay to the DOS operating system, not a truly rewritten one, and still had a number of features from early DOS days that were cumbersome, such as the requirement that file names be limited to 8 characters, including a 3-letter extension. Being forced to use file names like file1.exe or docum.txt often created lots of file directories in which the names often were not suggestive of what they contained. Compared to the Macintosh, many reviewers found it clumsy, not a full-featured GUI.

Much changed with the introduction of the heavily publicized new operating system called **Windows 95** (abbreviated **Win 95**) in the summer of 1995. Users can use long file names and easily configure their machines for a variety of hardware devices. Whereas adding new devices such as laser printers, sound cards, and CD-ROM readers had alway been tricky in earlier Windows, Win95 features "plug and play," which means that the operating system will do configuration automatically. Sharing of files among computers is made much easier, and moving files among windows with the "drag and drop" process popularized by the Macintosh is fully implemented. Win 95 offers **multitasking,** a term for the concurrent running of two processes at once. This makes it much faster and more efficient in the running of multiple applications. Windows 95 is a true GUI operating system, but it takes a lot of memory to run efficiently. Although Microsoft says that it will run on a 386 Intel computer with 4 megabytes of RAM, in actuality one needs at least 16 MB of RAM and a Pentium processor to take full advantage of its power and versatility.

Windows 95 represents the latest personal computer version of Microsoft's grand strategy for a family of GUI operating systems collectively called **Windows NT.** More than a GUI, Windows NT is a full operating system designed to network together all kinds of computers and office equipment, including telephones, copiers, and fax machines—in effect, to be the universal controlling program for the next generation. The goal is the **paperless office,** where all documents and communications are

**Windows 95 (Win 95):** A true operating system introduced in 1995 into the Microsoft family of Windows software for personal computers. It includes numerous improvements over DOS-based Windows 3.1.

**multitasking:** a powerful feature of modern operating systems that allows processors to work on more than one application at a time to achieve faster, more efficient operation.

**Windows NT:** The upgrading of Microsoft's Windows environment into a full operating system that can be used by all kinds of computers and communications devices.

**paperless office:** A term used to describe a totally computerized office where all communications will be handled electronically in soft copy.

**FIGURE 5-13** Microsoft Windows, today's most popular interface for DOS computers, presents the user with typical graphical user interface features: windows, icons for files, and pull-down menus.

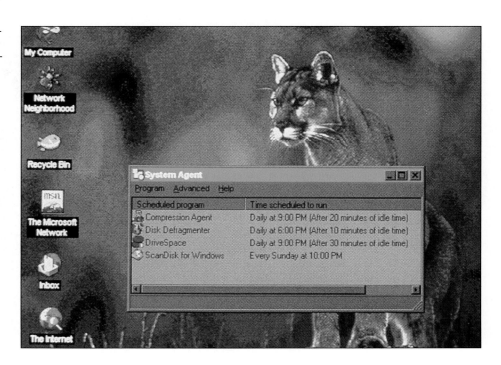

routed around effortlessly through the auspices of NT. New generations of office equipment would have NT built in, with license fees paid to Microsoft (McCarroll).

Microsoft even plans some version of the evolving NT software to work with cable systems and the whole gamut of computers, including small, pen-based devices and large-scale networks of workstations. The promising innovation of NT is that it is no longer hardware-bound to Intel processors; it can be delivered for all kinds of computing platforms and office machines—a strategy that has been called "Windows everywhere." According to Microsoft, the prospect for NT is seamless integration among a variety of equipment types. How compatible will all these versions of NT be as machinery evolves? Critics are skeptical about true compatibility among the various dialects of Windows NT and wonder if the Windows interface will ever be universal.

## UNIX

One reason that Windows may not dominate operating systems in the future is that another, older operating system, called **Unix,** has been widely adopted throughout the world. Because of its portability—that is, its ability to run on many hardware platforms—Unix has become popular on machines of all sizes, from microcomputers to supercomputers. Unix began in the 1970s on large time-sharing machines at Bell Laboratories. Addressed by commands at the keyboard, Unix offers a very large set of possibilities for its users to control their machines; in fact, one commentator has called it the "Swiss army knife of software" (*Fortune* 1984). Its approximately 200 utility programs can be combined for jobs like fancy formatting of output or indexing, which would be very cumbersome to do in other operating systems. Unfortunately, Unix in pure form is also much harder for most users to learn than Windows or the Macintosh operating system, a problem which has restricted its use primarily to the scientific and technical community.

A variety of scientific **workstations**—single-user machines that are usually faster, more powerful, and more expensive than personal computers—have adopted the Unix standard. Machines of this type include Sun, Apollo, the DECstation from Digital Equipment, and more advanced models from Apple and IBM. Starting in the late 1980s, several graphical user interfaces have been developed for Unix. The most important of these are Open Look from AT&T and Sun Microsystems, and Motif from the Open Software foundation, an industry consortium that includes Apollo, Digital Equipment, and IBM. Both Open Look and Motif are based on the X Windowing System developed at MIT. "User-friendly" **front-end systems** like X Windows relieve users of learning many short command abbreviations for the utility programs available since the early days in Unix. The result is an easier-to-use, very powerful portable operating system. Because the UNIX community has heavy strength in the workstation market and a lot of powerful corporate hardware supporters, it can be expected to remain popular in the future, especially in its GUI forms.

## APPLICATIONS SOFTWARE AND OPERATING SYSTEMS

Most people use personal computers for running applications software rather than for writing computer programs in languages like BASIC or C. They may think that all this talk about operating systems and programming languages applies to computer specialists rather than to them. However, every time someone turns on a personal computer to create a

**Unix:** An operating system designed for portability and flexibility among a variety of computers, from microcomputers to supercomputers.

**HISTORY**

**workstation:** A category of desktop computers targeted for high-performance specialized applications such as computer-aided design and publishing, modeling, and visualization. Bigger, faster, and until recently more expensive than a typical personal computer.

**front-end system:** "User friendly" software developed to stand between the user and a complicated operating system. Examples include Microsoft Windows for DOS and X Windows for Unix.

**FIGURE 5-14** An X Windowing System running Unix on a Silicon Graphics scientific workstation allows multiple windows and processes—experimental data, graphics, e-mail, etc.—to be active at the same time.

```
# Determine the current directory.

% pwd
/acct/william/tmp

# List the files in the current directory.

% ls
Imakefile       file_browser.c  proj            takehome
Makefile        final           show_pix.c      twosrl.c
error           myproj          tags

# Rename a file.

% mv final exam.paper

# List the files in the current directory.
Imakefile       exam.paper      proj            takehome
Makefile        file_browser.c  show_pix.c      twosrl.c
error           myproj          tags

# Mail a file to user 'hellmann'

% mail hellmann < exam.paper
```

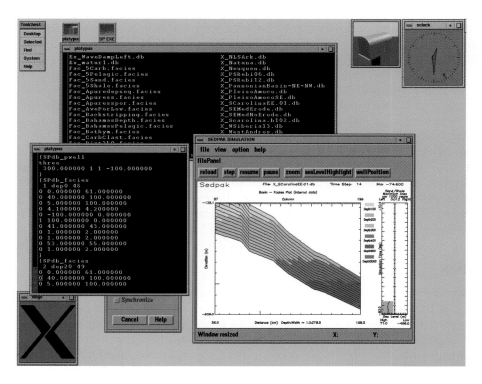

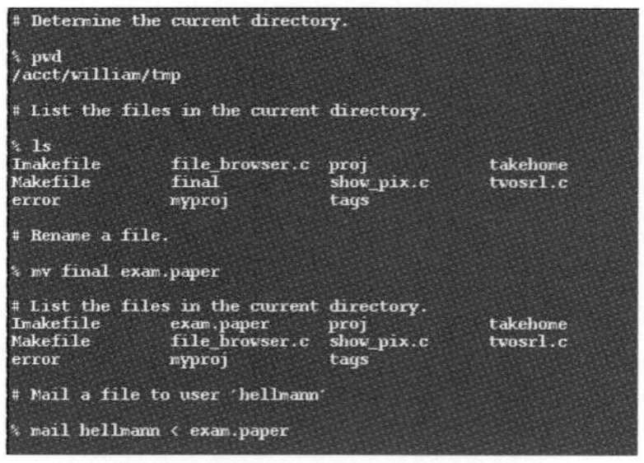

**FIGURE 5-15** A few Unix commands, made up of two or three letters, such as ls (for list) or mv (for move). What they do is explained in the lines beginning with a pound sign (#).

spreadsheet or write a letter, both activities are involved. The people or software company that wrote the spreadsheet or word processing package coded it originally in some programming language. When it was debugged and ready for sale, they compiled it into machine-language object code, the binary form needed by the computer to run the program, and copied it onto diskettes or CD-ROMs for distribution. All the translation processes involved in program development have already been carried out when the package is distributed.

As they use the software, users are running the program in its binary form. They must first access it, however, with the aid of their operating systems. Often they choose a file folder on their desktop or click the program icon to open it with the mouse. The operating system accepts their choice, retrieves the program code from storage (probably on hard disk), and opens it for use. No matter what its interface with the user looks like, the operating system always stands between the user and the computer and controls the functions needed by the package, such as reading data files and storing or printing results. Applications software would not exist without programming or operating systems.

**object-oriented programming:** A popular, recent programming technique which offers users a set of predefined objects or tools to construct applications, illustrated by such languages as Smalltalk.

**object:** In software engineering, an instance of data encapsulated with all its features and possible uses in constructing program applications, like an interchangeable part in manufacturing.

## OBJECT-ORIENTED DESIGN

Allied with the growing popularity of the graphical user interface is a movement in programming called **object-oriented programming.** Pioneered in a language called **Smalltalk,** this approach is probably best known in the HyperCard authoring language, for Macintosh, and ToolBook, for Intel machines, and the programming language C++. Object-oriented programming offers users a set of **objects,** or tools, with which to construct applications. The concept is moving beyond the procedural approach of structured programming and toward a software environment analogous to the concept of interchangeable parts for car repair.

We replace an old battery with a new one without worrying about the consequences to other parts of the automobile.

In other words, the object-oriented environment comes with a lot of very complex programming built in to make software construction easier. The user has a set of building blocks, or tools—the objects—to use in developing a new application. HyperCard, for example, provides windows and buttons with which to link text, graphics, sound, and video for multimedia presentations. For instance, a menu object contains procedures to open or close the window, drag it around the screen with a mouse, define its menu options, and so on. Software developers can resize, rearrange, or reshape these tools and decide whether they should contain text or pictures. They do not have to be concerned with writing program code to generate menus or windows or create linkages among them. Students in high school can create jazzy, animated HyperCard applications, called **stacks,** without extensive computer training, though complex applications require more experience with programming in procedural languages.

Traditional languages like Pascal, Ada, and C are appearing with object modules that can be assembled and linked in the programming process. The most popular choice is C++, a version of the C programming language beefed up with a class of objects that users can assemble and link into their programs. With object-oriented design, programmers get used to reusing earlier program modules treated as new objects for faster software development.

Meanwhile, a whole new category of **rapid applications development (RAD)** tools have appeared that incorporate object-oriented components added to tried-and-true language backgrounds and superior graphical user interfaces. The most well-known ones for Windows are Delphi, from Borland, based in Pascal, and Visual BASIC, from Microsoft, built on their Quick BASIC language. These tools have helpful features to allow users to move quickly from design of an application through prototyping to final deployment. Much of the work formerly involved in programming has been automated with objects, templates, excellent graphical support, and

**FIGURE 5-16** The user of Visual BASIC is offered a set of components for the design of a custom application. The Component Manager catalogs these resources: who created them, when they were created, and where they were located. This sort of programming help supports rapid application development.

**stack:** A term for an individual HyperCard application, analogous to a file.

**MULTIMEDIA**

**rapid applications development (RAD) tools:** Programming environments with objects, graphical interfaces, and superior debugging features for rapid prototyping of applications. Both Delphi and Visual BASIC fall into this category.

**FIGURE 5-17** A student-produced HyperCard stack. Clearly visible are the button to go on to the next card and fields containing the title and information about setting up a personal goldfish tank.

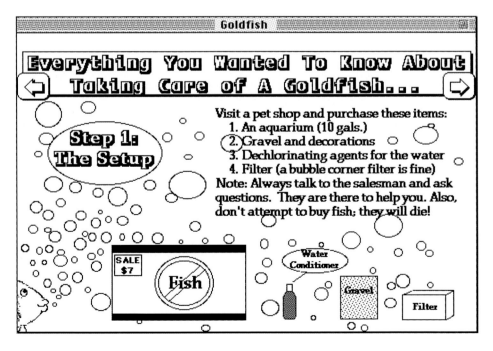

helpful debugging features. Productivity goes up as programming time goes down. Some studies indicate that Visual BASIC allows programmers to cut out between 33 percent and 80 percent of the code that would be required for the same application created with a traditional approach (Stern and Stern). Certainly object-oriented concepts are making the programming cycle simpler and easier to use in all kinds of software environments.

## ▶ Software Hazards

Software programs hold almost unlimited application possibilities. Yet unscrupulous individuals have found ways to build hazards into software that can cause major difficulties for users.

### COMPUTER VIRUSES

**computer virus:** Software that invades operating systems or application programs through contact with corrupted files. It may seriously damage computer files if not eradicated.

**virus checker:** Computer software that monitors the system, looking for computer viruses and correcting or deleting them if they show up.

**bulletin board:** A dial-up computer network site typically offering news and programs that may be downloaded to one's computer.

**pirated software:** Programs that have been copied illegally rather than purchased legally.

**bomb:** A crash of a computer system caused by a virus, which may cause a hard disk or diskette to be erased or permanently damaged.

The Achilles heel in software today is surely the **computer virus** and associated hazards with colorful names like worms and Trojan horses. Many people remember the scare of March 6, 1992, the birthday of Michelangelo and the day that a destructive computer virus called Michelangelo was set to go off worldwide. Intel-based computers all over the world were expected to come down with the virus, a software time bomb, and have many of their files ruined. For weeks newspapers, magazines, and television stations warned people to prepare by getting a **virus checker** (and killer) to disinfect their files, especially those on hard disk. Sales of these protective programs were brisk; some vendors gave programs away. Because the virus was widely publicized, people saved their files and secured their systems. On M-day itself, the virus hit as forecast, but only a few scattered losses were reported throughout the world. Many thought that the threat had been overblown, overstated, and oversold. Some wondered if people would ever take dire warnings of virus harm seriously again after such a fizzle (Markoff 1992).

Computer viruses behave much like their biological counterparts. They depend for their spread on computer networks, computer **bulletin boards,** or **pirated software**—that is, programs that have been copied illegally rather than purchased. Large systems running on mainframes and small personal computers alike may be corrupted by viruses that are sent throughout the world by some prankster or evil programmer. The virus is actually a hidden software file that has infected programs on the network. Assume that a user logs onto an infected network and copies one of the files to a personal computer. The virus comes along too, and infects the operating system of that computer and all subsequent diskettes that are inserted into it. If one of these now corrupt diskettes is put into another machine, the virus spreads into the new operating system and proceeds to infect other diskettes inserted into that host. The virus spreads quickly and silently. At some future time it may cause a hard disk filled with important files or applications software to **bomb**—that is, to be erased or permanently damaged.

In a typical instance, a few years ago a faculty member was word processing at home. Suddenly the computer crashed: it crackled with electronic static, and the screen filled with vibrating lines. Her machine had bombed because of a hidden virus. Not only was her letter permanently lost, but her word processing program was erased from her diskette. A

**FIGURE 5-18** A warning about the danger of the Michelangelo virus at the New Jersey Institute of Technology.

backup copy of the word processing program had to be reinstalled before the machine could resume work. The diskette containing the letter and word processing program had also contained a video game, which had been legally copied from a computer network. The game was infected and had corrupted the diskette. Why it crashed the system when it did remains unclear. Perhaps, like the Michelangelo virus, it was set off by the computer's internal clock reaching a certain day or time; or it may have been triggered after so many thousands of cycles of data passed through the processor.

## TROJAN HORSES

Logic bombs are called **Trojan horses** if they hide in a program that normally performs a useful function. Just as the Greek army used the gift of a statue of a horse filled with soldiers to get behind the walls of Troy, a Trojan horse program lies in wait, ready to do some malicious task, as the host program is performing normally. In 1987, for example, a HyperCard application called Sexy Ladies presented racy pictures to the viewer while its hidden Trojan horse was busily erasing portions of the user's hard-disk files. Presumably the author of the virus intended to punish those who opted for prurient pictures. Unlike viruses, Trojan horses do not ordinarily reproduce themselves, but are confined to the application in which they carry out their nefarious deeds.

Some computer hazards are written as serious jokes. In fact, the editor of *Macmag* in Canada and a programmer in Arizona created a Trojan horse program that flashed a "universal message of peace" on Macintosh screens in March 1987 in order to show the dangers of pirating software. Despite the fact that a Canadian software group gave them an award for

**Trojan horse:** An unauthorized program hidden inside a legitimate program, usually doing some harm to the computer system while the host program appears to be performing normally.

**Computer Fraud and Abuse Act (1986):** A U.S. federal law that makes accessing a federal computer without authorization and causing damage greater than $1000 a felony; aimed at hacker invasions of public computers.

this ploy, most people whose program files are corrupted, erased, or just inconvenienced by viruses do not see them as harmless. Laws are appearing in some states against the creation and distribution of viruses and the like; the crime is punishable by fines and jail sentences. The federal government in 1986 passed the **Computer Fraud and Abuse Act,** which makes it a felony to "intentionally access a Federal interest computer without authorization" and cause damage of over $1000 (Hafner).

For individual users, the best strategy for the forewarned is to be forearmed against viruses. Despite the overblown claims of doom with Michelangelo, software users should be aware that viruses are often on the loose, especially in programs copied from somewhere else. They can cause disruption and loss of valuable personal files. On a regular basis people should archive copies on diskettes or backup tapes of computer files kept on hard disks. They should also keep a copy of a virus checker program on their computers and run it often on all software copied from elsewhere. Many free or inexpensive programs of this type are updated regularly for all the latest viruses. They check diskettes inserted into a

---

## SOCIAL PERSPECTIVE

### The Internet Worm

**FIGURE 5-19** Robert Morris, the creator of the Internet worm, leaving court in 1990 after his conviction for violating the federal Computer Fraud and Abuse Act.

The most famous test case for the 1986 federal law on computer fraud and abuse began in November 1988, when a computer hazard called a **worm** invaded computers attached to an international scientific network that became the modern Internet. Between 3000 and 6000 machines were estimated to have been infected—about 5 percent of Internet users. The worm spread through Unix machines and copied itself relentlessly. It did not, however, delete files, destroy information, or hide Trojan horses for later mischief. Like a virus, the worm invaded all of the active machines on the network; but unlike a virus, it did not ruin files or cause any apparent damage (Denning).

Eventually authorities fingered Robert T. Morris, Jr., a Cornell graduate student, as the source. Ironically, Morris's father was a respected security expert with the National Computer Security Center. Presumably intended to show the vulnerability of networks to attack, the Internet worm got out of hand. Even Morris's corrective message, sent out to tell victims how to cripple the worm, went unread, because the machines were totally tied up with making copies of the worm. Serious research was shut down for several days, until the worm code could be purged from infected machines. Time and money were lost to stamp out the problem (Hafner).

To some programmers, Morris became a folk hero. But the Justice Department compared him to a terrorist and sought his punishment under the new law. Convicted of a felony in Syracuse, New York, Morris was sentenced in May 1990 to three years probation, fined $10,000, and ordered to do 400 hours of community service (Markoff).

Meanwhile, computer professionals demanded that experiments designed to show the vulnerabilities of networks to corruption must be done under controlled circumstances. Too much is at stake in business or governmental networks, they argued, for them to be vulnerable to pranksters or criminals releasing viruses. While some government officials advocated stricter access controls to networks, *Business Week* (4 December 1989) argued that that policy would choke the free interchange of information so important to the technical and scientific community.

---

**worm:** A program that reproduces itself by creating copies of itself and worming its way into alien operating systems. The infamous Internet worm infiltrated several thousand Unix systems in 1988.

personal computer automatically for hidden virus files or codes, then disinfect the diskettes when a problem is found. Stopping a virus in its tracks protects one's own programs and files and keeps it from spreading to others.

## SOFTWARE PIRACY

When someone copies a piece of purchased software that was borrowed from a friend onto a personal diskette, then goes home and loads it onto another computer, the borrower has committed an act of **software piracy.** In effect, this person has stolen a copyrighted work and is using it without paying the developer for the privilege. The practice is illegal but hard to trace. Because this sort of genteel crime is rampant among all segments of software users, computer software designers and public interest groups have developed several strategies to cope with it. Big software houses sometimes add **copy protection** to their program codes. Perhaps after a certain number of authorized copies of the program have been made for use and backup, the software has been preprogrammed to become disabled and not function properly. Yet clever programmers have always found ways around copy protection.

More popular practices in colleges and universities, where so much software is used for education, are **software licenses** and **shareware** and **freeware.** Many departments and institutions pay software developers a license fee—either a one-time charge or an annual stipend—for use of the program by students without restriction. The shareware/freeware phenomenon accepts the easy copying of software as a fact of life. The au-

**software piracy:** Illegal or unauthorized copying of software.

**copy protection:** A software strategy employed by program developers to make it difficult to copy software illegally.

**software license:** Paying a license fee to software developers for access to a program by a number of users without restriction, common in businesses and institutions.

**shareware:** Software distributed free of charge on a trial basis through bulletin boards or among friends. Those who like it are expected to pay a nominal fee in order to receive additional documentation and news of upgrades.

**freeware:** Software often made available free of charge on electronic bulletin boards and through user groups.

---

## EVOLUTIONARY PERSPECTIVE

### The Increasing Importance of Software

Today software holds as important a place in the computer world as hardware. The popular news media turned out to cover the 1990 introduction of Microsoft Windows 3.0, a software environment with a flexible graphic interface for DOS machines, with much speculation about how it would affect sales of both IBM-compatibles and Apple Macintosh machines. By 1993, Windows was a great success, and Microsoft was the world's largest software company. It was doing well while hardware giants IBM and Apple, which make machines on which Microsoft's various programs run, were having financial problems.

Even more publicity accompanied the introduction of Windows 95 in the summer of 1995. After an extensive media blitz, customers were waiting at midnight at many computer stores to get the first copies. Clearly superior to its earlier Windows cousin, the new Microsoft operating system was expected by many analysts to sweep the world. How it compares to the Macintosh operating system or IBM's powerful OS/2 for Intel-based machines was a topic of much analysis in computer magazines and columns for several months. Some say that the success of Microsoft indicates

that software is now the most important element of the Computer Triangle. People, the third element of the Computer Triangle, have continued to adopt the hardware of computing because of an explosion of software useful for a variety of interests and professional needs.

From the user's vantage point, the software layer has come a long way from the binary codes at its base. As operating systems become more complex in terms of their features, one hope for object-oriented languages is that software development itself will become more "user friendly" for the average computer user. Artificial intelligence and computational linguistics, addressing the relationship between human languages and computer languages, are promising areas of research. Many people predict that in the coming years computer users will be able to program new applications just by addressing their machines with their requirements in ordinary spoken English. Between them and the binary machine language inside the computer, the software interface will fill a bigger and far more commanding role in the technology of the future. Wherever the software frontier moves by the end of the decade, we can assume that user friendliness and power will be two of its hallmarks.

thors of shareware encourage copying by users, but ask for a token fee with registration. Those who send the fee get information about improvements and upgrades; others may use the program as they wish, without penalty. Freeware is just what the name implies. Someone has written a piece of software that he or she wants to share without charge with the computing community. The author does not guarantee that it is error free, but makes it freely available. Local on-line computer bulletin board services typically offer a variety of shareware and freeware programs to their users.

## ▶ Summary

Nobody's computer would be worth anything without the software that makes it such a powerful tool. The GUI of current operating systems exemplifies the tendency to think of the computer as more than hardware. The computer is no good without people to use it, and software is the vital control link between the person and the chips. Software is exploding in all areas; computer languages are becoming more user friendly. People are becoming used to analyzing their problems as systems. Students of programming are learning to use structured design principles in their first courses. Hypertext authoring tools are making it possible for inexperienced programmers to develop their own personal applications. Along with the good have also come inevitable pitfalls and abuses, like computer viruses and software piracy.

## ▶ Key Terms

algorithm (p. 101)

arithmetic function (p. 107)

assembler (p. 108)

assembly language (p. 108)

bomb (p. 120)

bug (p. 111)

bulletin board (p. 120)

compiler (p. 110)

Computer Fraud and Abuse Act (p. 122)

computer virus (p. 120)

copy protection (p. 123)

data bus (p. 107)

debugging (p. 111)

decision box (branch) (p. 101)

desktop (p. 114)

DOS (p. 113)

executive (monitor) program (p. 113)

expert system (p. 112)

flowchart (flow diagram) (p. 101)

freeware (p. 123)

front-end system (p. 117)

function key (p. 114)

high-level language (p. 109)

icon (p. 115)

if/then/else condition (p. 104)

instruction decoder (p. 107)

internal clock speed (p. 107)

interpreter (p. 110)

iteration (looping) (p. 104)

logic programming language (p. 112)

logical comparison operator (p. 107)

logical error (p. 110)

loop (p. 104)

machine language (p. 108)

menu-driven (p. 114)

multitasking (p. 116)

object (p. 118)

object code (p. 110)

object-oriented programming (p. 118)

operating system (p. 113)

OS/2 (p. 115)

paperless office (p. 116)

pirated software (p. 120)

plugboard (p. 107)

procedure (p. 106)

processing cycle (p. 107)

 Self-Test

## MULTIPLE-CHOICE

1. Of the five elements of a typical computer system, software fulfills which function?
   a. input
   b. processing
   c. control
   d. memory

2. All of the following illustrate the concepts of an algorithm except
   a. listening to music
   b. deciphering a coded message
   c. assembling a Christmas toy
   d. working toward a college major by taking certain courses

3. According to Dijkstra's structured programming principles, which type of programming step is to be avoided?
   a. sequence (a series of steps in a linear order)
   b. selection (the if/then/else idea)
   c. iteration (or looping, the repeat/until idea)
   d. transfer (the go-to)

4. All of the following are characteristic of modern structured programming except
   a. top-down design
   b. modular coding
   c. machine language
   d. programming with procedures

5. Which of the following represents the proper evolution of programming languages?
   a. compilers, assemblers, interpreters
   b. interpreters, machine language, assemblers
   c. machine language, assemblers, compilers
   d. machine language, compilers, assemblers

6. Computer programs are written in high-level languages for all of the following reasons except
   a. ease of coding
   b. readability of the program
   c. syntactic error checking
   d. similarity to binary object code

7. All of the following are popular operating systems in use today except
   a. Windows 95
   b. Macintosh
   c. Pentium
   d. Unix

8. All of the following can be classified as software hazards except
   a. copy protection
   b. computer viruses
   c. Trojan horses
   d. worms

## TRUE/FALSE

9. **T  F**  A flowchart uses graphic symbols and arrows to depict the relationships of parts of an algorithm.

10. **T  F**  Before a person writes a computer program, he or she must first create a flowchart or pseudocode for the process.

11. **T  F**  Spaghetti code is exemplified by a computer program with too many go-to's.

12. **T  F**  Desktop publishing at *The New York Times* is often cited as a landmark for the success of the structured programming approach.

13. **T  F**  The machine language instruction set of a computer typically contains several hundred operations.

14. **T  F**  Source code must be translated into object code before the computer can execute it.

15. **T  F**  Logic programming languages like Prolog are popular today for research in artificial intelligence and expert systems.

16. **T  F**  By adding copy protection to their computer programs, small software developers have been able to stop all unauthorized copying of their products.

## FILL-IN

17. An _____ can be defined as a logical sequence of steps to carry out some task.

18. _____ is a structured English description of the operations embodied in an algorithm.

19. _____ is the latest Windows development for personal computers, a new and powerful operating system introduced in 1995.

20. The principle that program software is stored in memory along with data to be processed is called the _____.

21. The incorrect statement "Input A and B" in True BASIC represents a _____ error that will be caught by the compiler or interpreter.

22. The _____ is a kind of super software, the computer's own program for monitoring all its operations.

23. _____ offers users a set of objects or tools to construct applications, analogous to the concept of interchangeable parts in manufacturing.

24. Many colleges pay software developers a _____ fee to allow students to use computer programs legally without individually purchasing them.

## ▶ Experiential Exercises

1. Write out an algorithm for making your favorite recipe. Then using the symbols illustrated by Figure 5-2 create a flowchart for assembling the recipe. Finally, try to structure your recipe in pseudocode, and see how this written form resembles your recipe.

2. Investigate the difference between spaghetti code and structured programming. You might begin by finding Dijkstra's famous letter, "Go To Statement Considered Harmful," in the *Communications of the ACM* in 1968. You want to understand what go-to's are in an algorithm, how using them leads to spaghetti code, and why that is bad. On the positive side, what are the advantages of structured programs or algorithms?

3. Look up the history of the computers built in the 1940s to see how they were programmed for single jobs in Second World War defense work. Then study the contribution of John von Neumann in coming up with the idea of the stored program concept, which is seen as fundamental for developing the first commercial computer, the UNIVAC I, in 1951. Learn how von Neumann's concept of storing programs in computer memory opened them up to being general-purpose machines, not limited to performing single-purpose functions.

4. Ask your teacher, or find a textbook survey of computer programming languages, to see how the commands of several of them look. For example, a comparison of early BASIC with FORTRAN shows how it was modeled on many of FORTRAN's principles. It will be instructive to look at simple COBOL also, to get a feel for the file processing orientation of that still popular language. For more recent languages, try to find some code for Pascal or C and, for a change, SNOBOL, LISP, or Logo. You want to sense the flavor of different programming languages.

5. Investigate different types of operating systems, including DOS and its modern descendants, the Windows family; OS/2; Macintosh; and Unix. If possible, try to get a chance to look at the interfaces that they present to the user. How many are GUIs? Is the keyboard or the mouse more commonly used to access the features of the operating system?

6. Investigate the differences between Trojan horses, worms, and viruses. What are some famous cases of each not mentioned in the text? Ask people at your computer center or the computer science department whether any of them have ever been harmful at your institution. How common is it for student diskettes to become infected with viruses? What is done to kill viruses?

7. The trial history of Robert Morris and the Internet worm is famous for being the first big case to apply the Computer Fraud and Abuse Act of 1986. Magazines and newspapers of 1989–1990 were full of arguments on both sides of the case, for the government and for Morris. At the trial, some famous computer professionals argued for leniency for Morris. Research the case to see the whole spectrum of discussion at the time. What did the judge say when he sentenced Morris to a large fine but no jail term? Did the trial lay down precedents for later cases?

## ▶ Critical Thinking Exercises

1. Compare the flowchart and pseudocode algorithms you wrote for exercise 1. Look carefully at them to see whether you have included branches or loops. How are these main programming constructs represented in the flowchart? What are they called in pseudocode? Remember that both these representations of the recipe algorithm should be equivalent. A person should be able to follow either of them in making the recipe.

2. The top-down approach is only one aspect of the systems approach to solving a problem—that is, looking at the whole problem as a collection of interrelated parts. The human body or a marine ecosystem are both instances of natural biological systems. What does it mean to speak of either of these as a system? You may want to look up principles of systems analysis in the library to explain the body as a system.

3. Why are programming languages named for Ada Lovelace and Blaise Pascal and a chain of computer software stores for Charles Babbage? Do these names have more significance than the name of another computer chain, Egghead Software?

4. The Internet worm was an inconvenient invasion of several thousand computers for several days but destroyed no valuable data. Which was more important in the long run: the breaking of federal law or the warning of Internet's vulnerability to corruption?

5. With Microsoft, the world's software leader, making more money than most hardware companies, argue for the primacy of software over hardware in the Computer Triangle of the 1990s.

## ANSWERS TO SELF-TEST

*Multiple-Choice*: 1. c;    2. a;    3. d;    4. c;    5. c;    6. d;    7. c;
8. a
*True/False*: 9. T;    10. F;    11. T;    12. F;    13. F;    14. T;    15. T;
16. F
*Fill-in*: 17. algorithm;    18. pseudocode;    19. Windows 95;    20.
stored-program concept;    21. syntax;    22. operating system;    23.
object-oriented programming;    24. software license

# CHAPTER 6

# Word, Text, and Sound Processing

▶ ## LEARNING OUTCOMES

*After completing this chapter, you should be able to:*

1. *Explain why word processing is more than typewriting.*

2. *List and describe the essential features of all word processing programs.*

3. *Describe a variety of additional text processing features, like spelling checkers, style checkers, and thesauri.*

4. *Discuss the larger issues of text processing, such as literary analysis and desktop publishing.*

5. *Explain the connection between text and sound applications, including the composition and printing of musical scores.*

6. *Discuss the difficulties of applying conventional word processing concepts to character languages like Arabic, Chinese, and Japanese.*

▶ ## COMPUTERS IN CONTEXT

*In 1964 IBM introduced a new electronic typewriter that could save a typed text on magnetic tape; later the text could be retrieved from the tape, corrected, amended, or printed again. As part of their advertising campaign, IBM coined the term* word processing *to describe these additional features of the typewriting process. In an age when computers were mathematical mainframe machines, applying computer concepts like data preparation, storage on magnetic media, and printout of stored material to text materials like words and documents was a revolutionary idea. Little could IBM have known how the concept would mushroom in the ensuing years.*

*Probably the single most important software application for the spread of the personal computer has been word processing. Originally an advertising name, word processing invented a whole new software field and market for computers. People afraid of touching a computer have learned to do word processing and found their work easier, faster, and more attractive. Word and text processing have spawned a whole array of computer applications in writing, publishing, and even sound and graphics. Of all the major areas of applications software today, it is appropriate to turn first to word processing and its allied fields.*

**H**ow does **word processing** differ from traditional typewriting? When the typewriter replaced the pen and pencil as the favored writing instrument of business organizations and many individuals, its attractions included speed of production; uniform formatting capabilities (margins and tabs); and the polished look of the final document, usually produced in one of two type sizes (elite and pica). Letter and document formats became more standardized and easier to read than handwriting. Yet correction of keying mistakes remained a problem that had many solutions: special typing erasers, opaque liquid correction fluids, and the self-correcting ribbon. Checking for spelling errors meant looking up words in a dictionary or a list of common misspellings.

**word processing:** Popular applications software designed for composing, revising, printing, and filing written documents.

## ▶ From Dedicated Word Processor to Personal Computer Software

Following the introduction of IBM's enhanced typewriter, special-purpose computers called **dedicated word processors** were developed in the 1970s and early 1980s to carry out features of word processing. A version of the text was kept on a binary medium, like magnetic tape or a magnetic card. The typist could bring the saved text back to the keyboard and print it again, either on the typewriter itself or on a separate printer. In computer terms, these early magnetic typewriters were input, storage, and output devices, with processing capabilities mainly limited to text preparation. They were especially good for the creation of form letters. The secretary typed the new name and address at the top and let the machine print the body of the letter.

**dedicated word processor:** A specialized computer typewriter designed only for word processing.

**HISTORY**

Machines soon added possibilities for addition and correction of text. A few years ago these were large, expensive systems, but today they are what one buys as a typewriter in any office supply store. They often look like older electronic typewriters but have many expanded features not formerly available, including a window showing a line or two of text available for correction before final saving and a built-in spelling checker. Many have two memories, so that a list of addresses can be prepared separately from the text of a form letter and then merged with the letter at the keyboard. This capacity is called **mail-merge.** Perhaps there is a choice of several fonts and type styles, such as roman and italic letters. The cost of the machine determines the extent of the features provided. Not general-purpose computers, these dedicated word processors are machines designed to do text preparation only: typing, correction, editing, and final printing.

**mail-merge:** A word processing feature that permits personalizing a form letter by merging the letter document and a name and address file before printing.

**HISTORY**

Although the personal computer did not create word processing, in a sense word processing created the mass market for the personal computer. About 1980 dedicated word processors were expanding their features by adding many special-purpose keys to the keyboard. Meanwhile, general-purpose personal computers began appearing, with programs that let them do word processing with the same features as the dedicated machines. In addition, these PCs offered other applications, like spreadsheets and database management. Because they cost no more than special-purpose machines, their soaring sales cut into the market for stand-alone word processors in the last several years. In fact, the availability of popular software fueled the personal computer hardware revolution. These two Computer Triangle elements worked together to create the dominance of personal computers. Today word processing is the most common application for personal computers. High school typewriting courses have been transformed into courses on general word processing on personal computers, and many elementary schools regularly teach keyboarding as a basic skill for young people to learn at an early age.

## ▶ Essential Features of Word Processing

The basic features of all modern word processing software can be broken down into five different categories: text preparation, editing, formatting, document storage and retrieval, and printing. Text preparation includes both what an old typewriter offered and the file-handling capacities required in creating and saving a document. The writer opens the software and begins a new piece of writing. As the characters are being typed, the cursor, a darkened or blinking spot on the CRT screen, shows the current position of the keying. The cursor automatically moves down to another line when the next word to be typed exceeds the margin setting, a convenient word processing feature called **word wrap.** Older typewriters monitored line length by ringing a margin bell; the typist had to hit the carriage return for each new line. Only when a paragraph is complete in word processing does the typist have to hit the return or enter key to overrule word wrap and skip down to a new line.

After a few minutes the writer should save the document as a new file, with its identifying file name, on a diskette or hard disk. If some glitch in the electric power supply, such as a thunderstorm, were to disrupt the computer, text being encoded into the machine's RAM memory would be lost. The version of the document safely stored in a permanent magnetic form, on an external storage medium like a diskette, can be retrieved and continued, edited or corrected. Later upgrades to the file can then be saved under the same file name, which always contains the most recent version of the text. These file-handling features are not unique to word processing, but are typical of all types of applications software.

### KEYBOARD LAYOUT

The actual typing of the document parallels the process on any typewriter. Computers come equipped with a traditional **Qwerty keyboard** (pronounced "kwerty"), one in which the first six alphabetic letters on the top row are *q, w, e, r, t,* and *y,* arranged in left-to-right order. In the 1930s A. Dvorak researched the frequency of English letter combinations and the easiest fingerings for them, then suggested a new keyboard arrangement for the most efficient use of the keys. However, the Dvorak scheme has never caught on, and most touchtyping instruction is carried out on the Qwerty keyboard. Many keyboards also come with **numeric keypads,** useful for keying numbers quickly, and a section of special-purpose function keys, whose roles change with the software.

### INTERFACE ISSUES

Word processors handle such features as marking special characters in different ways, depending on the interface between the user and the software. If the interface between the user and the machine is command-driven, common in early MS-DOS software, the computer combines menus, keystrokes, and function keys to trigger specific actions in the word processing program. Keystroke choices given on a menu are often used for filing

**word wrap:** A feature of word processing that allows a person to continue typing beyond the end of a line without pressing the return key. The computer program automatically reformats the material within the margins set by the user.

**Qwerty keyboard:** The standard typewriter keyboard layout, named for the first six letters on the top line of characters.

**numeric keypad:** The section of a keyboard containing an arrangement of numbers in a square for easy input of numeric data.

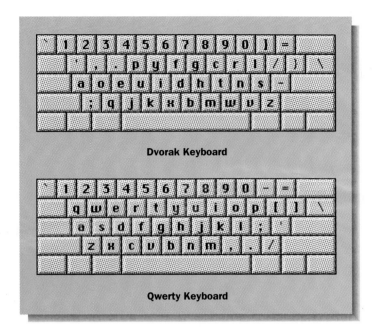

**FIGURE 6-1** Compare the differences between the Dvorak and the Qwerty keyboard layouts. Note that on the Dvorak the most common keys tend to be placed on the middle row, where the fingers rest.

and retrieving documents. Special keystrokes also mark sections of text to be printed in special ways: italics, boldface, underlined letters, footnotes, or foreign accents (such as the acute accent in French or the umlaut in German).

For example, suppose you want to type the following sentence:

> For my independent reading in American literature, I read "The Raven" by Edgar Allan Poe and <u>Moby Dick</u> by Herman Melville.[1]

You need to indicate in the keying process that the title of Melville's novel is to be underlined and the footnote raised. Before the first letter of *Moby Dick*, you would type a particular keystroke code for underlining, and another before the numeral 1, to signal a superscript. As you key these characters, the software adds the underlining and raises the footnote. Having invoked these special character treatments, you must then turn them off with another set of keystrokes to return to normal text mode.

With a GUI—found on the Macintosh and on current Intel machines running OS/2 or Microsoft Windows—the mouse replaces keystroke coding with highlighting of characters for underlining and footnote superscripts. For instance, you drag the mouse across the already typed text for the title, then choose the underline option on a pull-down menu. The word processor then underlines your regularly typed text. Pull-down menus also handle common filing and editing functions. With a graphical user interface, the screen presentation is called **WYSIWYG** ("What you see is what you get," pronounced "wizzywig")—an acronym that means that the screen shows word-processed text exactly as it will be printed later. Older word processors often inserted characters on the screen to mark special features. Keystrokes denoting underlining or superscripting might show up on the screen, although they would not appear in the printed version of the text. Most users prefer WYSIWYG word processors, because they can observe in the preparation stage what the printed output is going to be like, note situations that need additional treatment, and preview the results.

**WYSIWYG (What you see is what you get):** The display of information on a computer screen in a form that closely resembles what will eventually be printed, characteristic of word processing or desktop publishing software on computers with bit-mapped screens.

**FIGURE 6-2** Word Perfect for Windows 95 (Corel Corp.) provides users with help windows, offering advice about how to use its full set of features and functions.

## EDITING FEATURES

In editing their work, *writers can make additions, deletions, and corrections to text much more easily* with word processors than with old typewriters, because in conventional typewriting the text is printed as it is keyed. Even newer typewriters with correction windows cannot display much text for editing at one time. In word processing, the user is making a magnetic record of the document, which is still fluid and available for change. Only when it is ready is it sent off to the printer. Meanwhile, it can be saved as a

**FIGURE 6-3** A word processor designed for a WYSIWYG screen, such as Microsoft Word for Macintosh, allows a user to try out a variety of fonts, styles, and spacings on the screen during document creation. The document will look the same when it is printed.

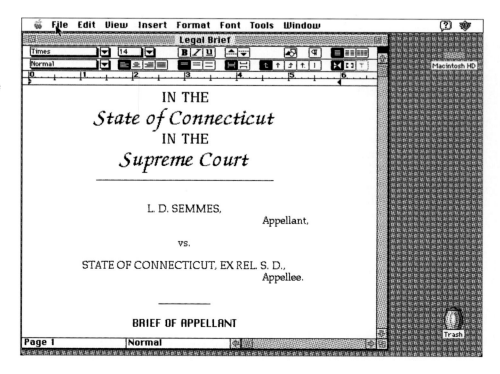

file and retrieved at will, and whole sections can be cut out or paragraphs added.

Any keying process involves the possibility of inserting errors into a document, but in word processing, corrections can be made whenever they are discovered. The user can type over a section of a sentence that needs rewriting, or open up a draft of a letter and insert a "canned" piece of text, such as a previously prepared set of company rules stored in another file. Canned text, often used by lawyers and insurance companies, is called **boilerplate.** Before word processing, rekeying of such repeated materials took lots of time and opened the possibility of introducing more errors in the final document. Now such texts can be created once, stored away, and called up as needed for insertion into a new document.

One of the most useful and convenient features of word processing, not available in typewriting, is called either **block move** or **electronic cut and paste.** Suppose that in editing a long term paper you saw that a paragraph would read more smoothly if it were moved ahead of another one. You can mark or highlight it, then move the cursor (which always shows where current processing is taking place) to the preferred location. Invoking the block move option, you are then able to rearrange the paragraphs. The affected text is shifted ahead to its new location, and the hole left by the cutout is closed up. You have literally moved a block of text or carried out the equivalent of the cutting and pasting process used in the layout of newspaper pages—hence the name for the process. Of course, the text to be moved could be a single word or a sentence, not just a larger unit like a paragraph.

Because a whole text file can be queried in its magnetic form, word processors offer a convenient **search and replace** function. Perhaps you wrote in the first draft of a twenty-page term paper that an author's name was John Hammond, but found out later that his first name was James. You can search the document quickly for the name "John Hammond" and replace it with the proper name without having to scan all of the text by eye. If you want to look at all the words that begin with the Latin prefix

**boilerplate:** A block of standard text, such as formulaic parts of a legal document like a will, that are saved and inserted in many documents with a word processor.

**electronic cut and paste (block move):** A standard word processing feature that allows selecting a letter, word, or section of text; deleting it from its current location; and moving it somewhere else in the current or another document.

**search and replace:** A word processing feature that searches for a specific pattern like a word or a phrase and replaces it with another, either automatically or after the user approves the change.

**FIGURE 6-4** A typical menu in a word processor for the search and replace function.

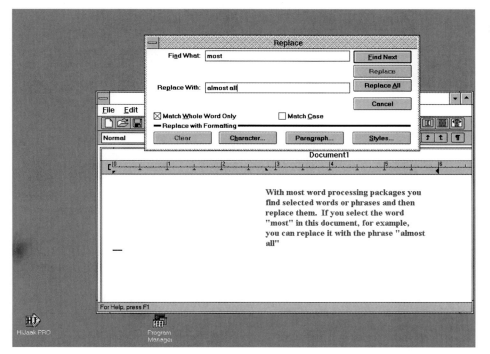

**TABLE 6-1** *Some English Words That Begin with* Ante

| | |
|---|---|
| anteater* | antediluvian |
| antebellum | antelope* |
| antecedent | antenna* |
| antechamber | anterior |
| antedate | anteroom |

*The Latin prefix is not involved.*

**pattern matching:** A computer technique for finding a predetermined pattern, such as a phrase in a long list of clichés.

**ruler line:** A section of some word processor screens for setting options such as margins, tabs, and spacing between lines of text, resembling a ruler in inches or centimeters.

**centering of text:** A cumbersome practice in typewriting that is standard with word processing.

**justifying of lines:** The ability of a word processor to align both left and right margins, such a tedious process with a typewriter that it is never done.

*ante,* like *antebellum* or *antechamber,* the search function allows you to look for particular letter patterns, not just complete words. The software scans through the text looking for the four-letter prefix *ante,* but will also highlight for your inspection any word that contains that letter sequence (such as *anteater*), not just those with the prefix *ante.* The machine is just looking for a **pattern match;** it does not "know" whether a letter pattern is a prefix or not. Whether to replace a pattern or word when it is found is your choice.

## FORMATTING OPTIONS

Although typewriters have always offered a variety of formats for presentation of a document, word processors are even more flexible. Like their predecessors, all word processors offer several settings for margins, tab keys for indentation, and a choice of spacing between lines (single, double, or triple). Often this is done on a **ruler line,** a section of the screen where the user chooses among several options. New options include **centering of text** and **justifying of lines** on the right margin or on both left and right, as in most books. Traditionally, typed documents are lined up (or justified) on the left margin only; the right margin is not straight—the so-called ragged-right margin. Because word processors keep up with the number of characters typed in relation to the line width (for word wrap), they can also line

**FIGURE 6-5** Margins in a document can be ragged right or right justified. The latter has the effect of squaring up the page.

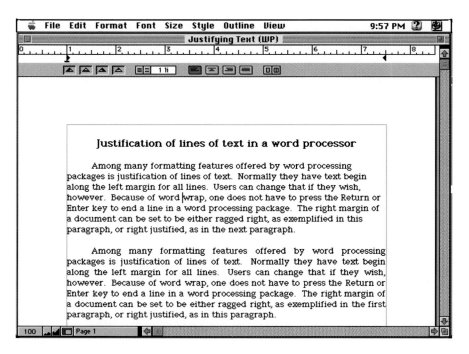

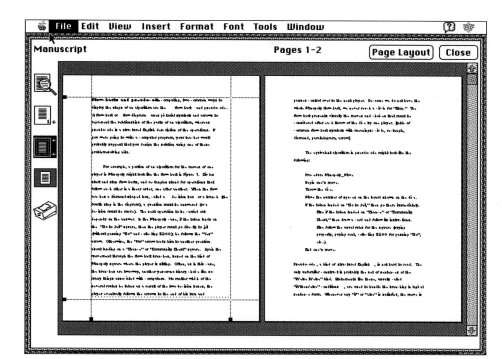

**FIGURE 6-6** Microsoft Word for the Macintosh features the page preview feature for inspection of the document for formatting before printing.

up the text on the right margin and even fully justify the line, making the margin straight on both sides of the paper. This latter option makes an attractive squared printed page, unless the additional spaces inserted between words are noticeable. This situation sometimes occurs in lines with lots of long, unhyphenated words. If a long word will not fit at the end of the line, it gets moved to the next line. The justification software must then fill in a lot of the letter spaces with blanks distributed throughout the first line.

In addition, many word processing programs offer the user **automatic numbering of pages,** either at the top or bottom of every sheet. Page numbering was bothersome on older typewriters, and full justification was impossible. Some programs even allow for **automatic renumbering of footnotes** after a note has been inserted or deleted. Others offer a popular formatting option called **page preview,** an alternative to the WYSIWYG feature. Given a formatted document, the program shows a visual outline, either miniature or full size, of how full pages will look when printed. The user can note single lines or headings that stick out at the bottom or top of a page and adjust the text accordingly.

Some word processors have bundled other helpful features suitable for special environments. Many come with a **label maker** for addresses and an easy way to print envelopes, usually accompanied by the mail-merge feature. Others offer easy setup and printing of data in columns, such as financial figures. **Automatic formatting of tabular data,** perhaps lined up on the decimal point in monetary figures, is useful for producing tables of figures. A typist does not have to examine every dollar amount and count back a certain number of characters for proper alignment of a column of figures on the decimal point. As each number is keyed, the software waits for the decimal point before placing the figure on the line.

## TYPE FONTS, STYLES, AND SIZES

The type of screen that the computer has determines the number and variety of type fonts and styles that word processing software can display. Older

**automatic numbering of pages:** A standard word processing feature of numbering pages at the top or bottom as the text is being keyed.

**automatic renumbering of footnotes:** A convenient word processing feature that renumbers when a revision has been made and footnotes have been added or deleted.

**page preview:** A convenient graphical addition to a word processor which shows a small image of what the layout of a word processed page will look like when printed, useful for noting single lines at the top or bottom or adjusting margins.

**label maker:** A word processing feature making it possible to create labels easily with software and a printer.

**automatic formatting of tabular data:** A feature of full-featured word processors which lines up monetary figures under the decimal point, useful for producing tables of figures.

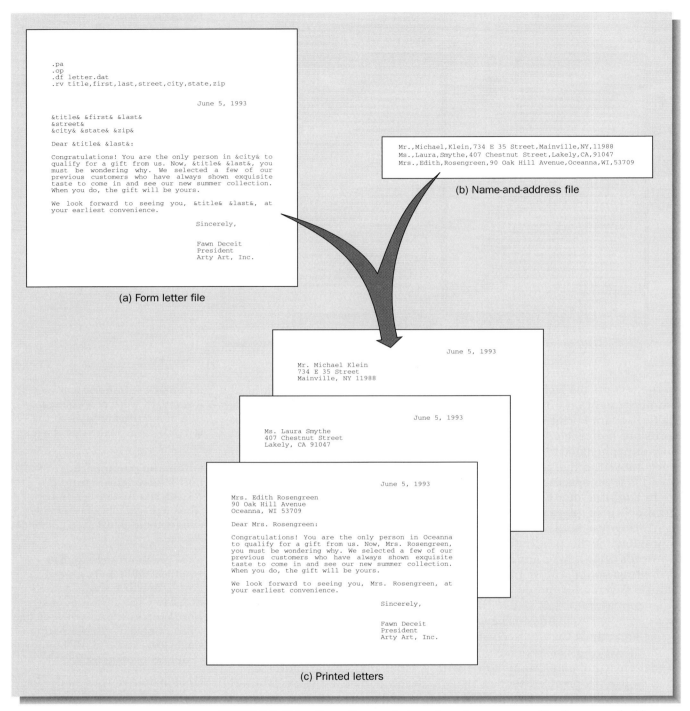

```
.pa
.op
.df letter.dat
.rv title,first,last,street,city,state,zip

                                     June 5, 1993

&title& &first& &last&
&street&
&city& &state& &zip&

Dear &title& &last&:

Congratulations! You are the only person in &city& to
qualify for a gift from us. Now, &title& &last&, you
must be wondering why. We selected a few of our
previous customers who have always shown exquisite
taste to come in and see our new summer collection.
When you do, the gift will be yours.

We look forward to seeing you, &title& &last&, at
your earliest convenience.

                    Sincerely,


                    Fawn Deceit
                    President
                    Arty Art, Inc.
```

(a) Form letter file

```
Mr.,Michael,Klein,734 E 35 Street,Mainville,NY,11988
Ms.,Laura,Smythe,407 Chestnut Street,Lakely,CA,91047
Mrs.,Edith,Rosengreen,90 Oak Hill Avenue,Oceanna,WI,53709
```

(b) Name-and-address file

```
                                     June 5, 1993

Mr. Michael Klein
734 E 35 Street
Mainville, NY 11988
```

```
                                     June 5, 1993

Ms. Laura Smythe
407 Chestnut Street
Lakely, CA 91047
```

```
                                     June 5, 1993

Mrs. Edith Rosengreen
90 Oak Hill Avenue
Oceanna, WI 53709

Dear Mrs. Rosengreen:

Congratulations! You are the only person in Oceanna
to qualify for a gift from us. Now, Mrs. Rosengreen,
you must be wondering why. We selected a few of our
previous customers who have always shown exquisite
taste to come in and see our new summer collection.
When you do, the gift will be yours.

We look forward to seeing you, Mrs. Rosengreen, at
your earliest convenience.

                    Sincerely,


                    Fawn Deceit
                    President
                    Arty Art, Inc.
```

(c) Printed letters

**FIGURE 6-7** Using the mail merge feature of word processors, a file of names and addresses can be merged with a letter file to create personalized letters.

**Super Video Graphics Adapter (SVGA) monitor:** A common type of color computer monitor for graphics display in better IBM-compatibles.

screens displayed characters in set character positions, like typewriters, and could present a limited number of styles—usually roman, italic, underlined, and boldface—in one font and size. Most modern screens also have graphic capabilities and can produce bigger or smaller type sizes in their graphics mode. As an integral part of its graphical user interface, the Macintosh pioneered the bit-mapped screen and was thus free to offer a full range of type fonts, styles, and sizes. Intel computers using Windows also utilize the bit-mapped output screen, such as an **SVGA (Super Video Graphics Adapter)** monitor. Today most personal computers and all scientific work-

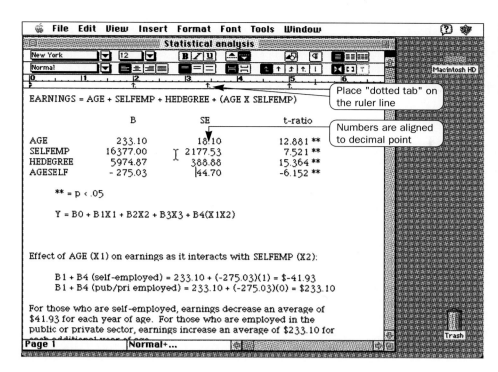

**FIGURE 6-8** Before creating a table of numerical figures, a user of Microsoft Word (Macintosh) can set "dotted tabs" on the ruler line, so that numbers of different lengths will be properly aligned under the decimal points.

stations feature this kind of screen. A bit-mapped screen is one in which everything displayed is viewed as a picture or graph. To the machine, there is no difference between a picture of a tree, a logo for a company, or a fancy type font. Each is just a set of many small, blackened pixels.

Designers are free to develop pixel representations for any traditional font or to invent new ones. It is not uncommon for word processors to support more than 100 fonts stored on the hard disk of the computer. They can all be drawn in a selection of type sizes from 4-point to 127-point. With 72 points to the inch, these sizes range from very small print to very large—large enough for signboards. Pixel-based type fonts can also be presented in many styles: roman, italic, bold, underlined, outlined, or shadowed. Some word processors offer **proportional spacing** between letters, as in typesetting; that feature was never available with typewriters, which had set print positions for both wide and narrow letters. Proportional spacing puts less space between the letters *f* and *l* than between *m* and *a*, for a more aesthetically pleasing look. With all these print capabilities, word processing has moved far beyond the capacities of typewriting.

**FIGURE 6-9** Most modern word processors can display and print documents using a number of different type fonts and sizes.

**proportional spacing:** A fine printing option of variable spacing between letters for a pleasant visual effect, common in typesetting and available with some full-featured word processors.

## ▶ Additional Features of Modern Text Processing

In addition to allowing flexibility in how a document will look, modern software also makes it easier to perform some of the more cognitive tasks of text processing.

### HYPHENATION AND SPELLING

Given a version of a text in magnetic form, software can carry out a number of additional manipulations on it that formerly could only be done by people. Some word processors offer **automatic hyphenation** to split long multisyllable words at the end of the line. Built into the program are the standard rules for hyphenation. When the typist chooses this formatting option, the computer applies those rules to the text. Microsoft Word for

**automatic hyphenation:** A feature of some word processors, which can be set to let the program automatically divide words at the end of a line according to the rules of hyphenation of the language or suggest a division and wait for user confirmation.

## TECHNOLOGICAL PERSPECTIVE

### The Pitfalls of Automatic Spelling Checkers

Compared with doing proofreading or looking up words in dictionaries, users who do automated spell checking save time and hassles in editing their work. Yet this helpful aid does not always work perfectly. If someone types the word *thy* when she meant *the,* the checking program will not catch the error. Based on a search for correct patterns, it only knows what are legitimate words, not whether they make any sense in context. Technical Support Services, a government agency in South Carolina, has reported that an early spelling checker for Microsoft Word did not flag any of the following nonsense words: *ave, mo, pf, rd.* The program took them to be acceptable abbreviations for *avenue, month, preferred,* and *road.* The designers of the program chose to include those abbreviations without periods in its lists, with the result that such sequences of letters are skipped in the checking process. Subsequent versions of the Word spelling checker caught *ave* and *mo,* but let *rd* pass unnoticed.

Sometimes the results are surprising and even humorous. Since spell-checking software is only looking for correct sequences of letters that form words, it does not understand whether they make sense or not. The Coastal Corporation in Houston a few years ago pointed out this problem with the following poem:

> I have a spelling checker.
>
> It comes with my PC.
>
> It plainly marks four my revue
>
> Mistake I cannot see.
>
> I've run this poem threw it,
>
> I'm sure you're please too no
>
> It's letter perfect in it's weigh
>
> My checker tolled me sew.

(quoted in the *Raleigh News and Observer* 1992)

All the words are properly spelled forms, but the mistakes in usage are numerous and glaring.

Equally troublesome are new words, perfectly acceptable but not yet included in the computer lists that make up the checking software. Microsoft Word 6.0, the current version of the program and presumably politically correct, does not recognize Newt Gingrich's name and suggests as an alternative "Jingoish" (Tanaka and Rogers). With the new terms of the Information Age, Microsoft Word and its great rival Word Perfect (Corel) are both often baffled. For the word *Internet,* Word 6.0 proposes that the writer means *interment,* whereas Word Perfect 6.1 , released in November 1994, accepts it. However, Word Perfect thinks *interactivity* should be *underactivity* and wants to change *terabyte* to *thereabouts.* Both are clueless about the terms *cyberspace* and *netsurfing,* a term for surfing the Internet. Designers at Word Perfect report that they update their dictionaries every year, but in a field creating as much new jargon and slang as computing, they will always be behind (Manes).

Sometimes the careless user of spell checking software will accept the results without question and get into real trouble. In December 1994, an editor for the *Dallas Morning News* accepted all the alternative spellings in an article on technology and ended up with references to Intel and Microsoft corporations coming out as "Until" and "Microvolts" (Rigdon). People, third parties in the Computer Triangle, must be wary of total reliance on automated spelling checkers in their word processing. Having the computer to assist with spelling does not replace the need for careful proofreading by a document's creator.

the Macintosh, for example, offers hyphenation either automatically or semi-automatically. In the latter mode, the program displays a suggestion for splitting a word at the end of a line and asks the typist for a confirmation or change. With confirmation, the program splits the word and reformats the remaining lines before proceeding.

More common than hyphenation are **spelling checkers,** which today are considered standard features of word processors for English. Based on the principles of search and replace, most have built-in dictionaries of 60,000 to 120,000 words and work on an already typed text file. At the user's request, the computer looks up every word in the document in its dictionary and displays those that *may* be misspelled. Proper names, acronyms like MS-DOS, and foreign words like *monsieur* are often not in the dictionary, and show up just like common keying errors, such as *teh* for *the* or double words like *and and.* The checker usually displays a list of correctly spelled alternatives to the typist. If the word is incorrectly spelled, the user either fixes it or chooses the proper spelling from the list offered by the software. Then the typist invokes the replace function to correct the word in the document. Most checkers allow the user to customize the dictionary with acronyms or proper names used frequently, so they will not stop the search unnecessarily.

**spelling checker:** A computer program that checks a document for misspellings and offers suggestions for correction.

In spell checking, the computer is carrying out search operations through thousands of words at fantastic speeds and quickly flashing up words for the user's consideration. Some checkers even beep after the typing of a word that may be misspelled or miskeyed. In this case, lists of words are literally being searched as the typist is hitting the keys. Having sensed the keystroke for the space bar, the software notifies the user that the letter sequence just typed may not be a word. Before proceeding, the user is prompted to reconsider what has just been keyed.

## THESAURI AND INDEXES

Some word processing programs provide **on-line thesaurus** help. A thesaurus is a dictionary of synonyms and words with similar meanings. Automated ones work like spelling checkers but offer a different kind of editorial guidance. Rather than using the same word repeatedly, the typist can consult the thesaurus to vary the vocabulary of the document. First the user highlights the word, and the thesaurus calls up synonyms and related terms on the screen (the search function). If one of the words works well in the context of the passage, the software can substitute it automatically for the word under review (the replace function).

By comparison, automated help with **indexing,** offered by some word processors, usually involves the active assistance of the preparer. An index presents a text's important terms in an alphabetical list along with their locations in the form of page numbers. Suppose you want to provide an index to your document. While typing the text or later in the editing stages, you would select the terms to be indexed and highlight them with the cursor. Typically the software encodes some kind of embedded characters into the text alongside the terms. Later it collects them and creates and formats the index with page numbers. The embedded characters do not appear in the printed version of the text.

Automated schemes for picking out index terms were developed two decades ago, but none have proved successful enough to be included in

**on-line thesaurus:** Computer software including a thesaurus to offer a list of synonyms that can be substituted for a word while the writer is using the word processor.

**indexing:** A text processing application to index a text, which works best when the user is actively involved in the process.

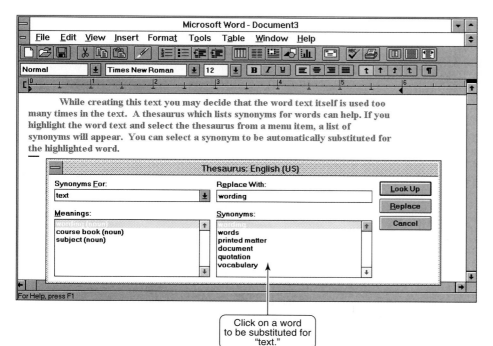

**FIGURE 6-10** Most word processing packages have a thesaurus from which you can select synonyms for highlighted words. You can select an alternative word and replace it in your text.

**FIGURE 6-11** With a computer-assisted indexing program, editors of the Thomas Jefferson Papers were able to prepare a cumulative index to the first twenty volumes, a monumental task that could not have been considered with traditional indexing practice. This page of the index shows references to Alexander Hamilton in most of the Jefferson volumes.

**style and grammar checker:** A software program that checks for punctuation errors does limited grammar checking, flags awkward usage, and suggests revisions.

word processors. To illustrate the problems, suppose only proper nouns—that is, names beginning with an initial capital letter, which do not begin a sentence—are to be indexed automatically. Any word that starts with a capital is a candidate; unless it is at the beginning of a sentence, it is likely to be an index term. Eliminating a list of sentence openers like pronouns (*she, they*), articles (*the, a*), and introductory elements (*when, from, before*) narrows the list of possible index terms to be found among introductory words, but it will not be foolproof. The resultant index will not be perfect, and will need editing before final printing. Getting the computer to "understand" the text and decide on its index terms still falls into the realm of research in artificial intelligence. Developers of word processors have decided to rely on human assistance in choosing index terms: people pick their own items as they do input or editing.

## SCHOLARLY INDEXING

A scholarly edition of the letters and papers of a famous person like Thomas Jefferson needs a very complete and cross-referenced index, because often people look up one topic rather than reading the book directly. The edition is a source book for all kinds of searches for subjects that may be covered there. Computer-assisted indexing programs developed by the Henry Laurens Project at the University of South Carolina let editors decide on the index terms as they complete editorial work. Editors encode the terms and cross-references along with the pages on which they occur; then the computer compiles and formats the index for final printing. An indexing job for a 400-page volume that used to take the staff at least half a year per volume using index cards has been reduced to a one- or two-month job, with no loss of accuracy.

In the past, editors could not consider publishing a cumulative index to an edition like the Jefferson papers because of the prohibitive cost, time, and trouble. With computer assistance, the published index to the first 20 volumes of the *Papers of Thomas Jefferson* (1983)—an ongoing project begun in the 1940s at Princeton—has become a scholarly model. The editors encoded each of the long separate volume indexes with a Kurzweil optical scanner; merged the files alphabetically with the computerized indexing programs developed by the Laurens Project; combined similar terms listed differently in different places; and formatted the resulting index for computer typesetting—all in a year's time. Without the computer, this monumental reference work would not have been possible at all. With the computer, it will have a merged index for all the Jefferson papers when they are complete sometime in the next century.

## STYLE CHECKING

Today one also finds a wide choice of **style and grammar checkers** for English that work with word-processed files, though they are not always incorporated into word processing programs themselves. All are indebted to the principles of the Writer's Workbench (WWB), developed in the late 1970s for use by technical writers at Bell Telephone Laboratories. Based on the famous *Elements of Style* by William Strunk, Jr., and E. B. White, WWB is intended to foster generally agreed-upon principles of good writing: that it be grammatically correct, correctly spelled, and not too wordy. The Strunk and White book suggested specific refinements: cutting down on passive verbs; using short, concrete diction; and preferring verbs to nouns made from them ("orient the students" rather than "have an orientation for them"). Scholars at Colorado State have used WWB to train college writers for more than a decade, and their research shows that giving this kind of stylistic advice makes a measurable positive difference in student writing (Kiefer and Smith).

Most checkers take a prepared document and run a variety of stylistic, usage, grammar, punctuation, and statistical tests on it. Given the results, the writer can go back later into the editing mode of a word processor and make corrections or changes to the paper. The current generation of style checking programs allows writers to run the checks while in the editing mode, and then to make changes immediately if they like the improvements suggested by the program. None of the programs correct mistakes automatically, without the user's approval. Grammatik 6 (Novell), Correct Grammar (Lifetree Software), and Edit! (McGraw-Hill) fall into this category.

Typical of the stylistic options that these programs provide, the Edit! program combines editing and checking into one integrated, interactive process. The program organizes the types of advice it offers into a hierarchy of levels (Word, Sentence, Paragraph, and Overall Paper). Users choose the checks they want to run against their document, and the program figuratively taps them on the shoulder with information about what it has found in the paper. It assumes that writers can assess its advice, and even provides an on-line handbook if needed. If writers decide to change their texts, they can make corrections at any point by entering the editing mode, then return to checking with one keystroke.

To get a sense of the way software like Edit! works, consider the following sentence:

*Irregardless of the principals involved, it was decided that all of the nerds would perform his job normally at this point in time.*

The program finds a number of problems with this very faulty sentence. The incorrect usage of *Irregardless* should be replaced by the correct form, *Regardless*. The writer should note the correct spelling from the confusing pair *principal/principle* based on the meanings and examples given by the program:

principal: the main person, place, or thing

ex. The president is the principal officer of most organizations.

principle: a basic guideline for conduct or action

ex. His main principle was that business should be conducted ethically.

Edit! flags the passive verb *was decided* and advises writers not to use the construction too frequently. The pronoun *his* is singular and does not match

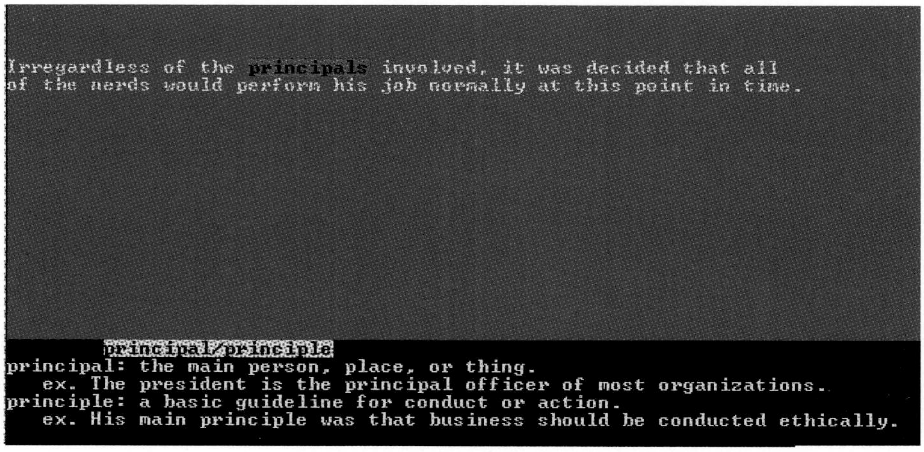

**FIGURE 6-12** Stylistic advice offered by the Edit! program (McGraw-Hill) is shown to the user below the text.

the reference word *all,* which is plural. *His* also is noted as a masculine pronoun; the program prompts the writer to watch out for sexist language—advice probably ignored in this sentence. The program tags the term *nerds* as slang that may offend, but the decision to revise, as always, is left to the author. Finally, Edit! marks the phrase *at this point in time* as a wordy cliché and suggests that it be revised. Among other features, Edit! also shows the lengths of sentences; comments on proper transitional words; looks for offensive racist terms; and offers a variety of statistics about the paper. Some of the advice is based on grammar rules, some on preferred usage.

Like spelling programs, no style or grammar checker works perfectly. The extent to which these programs offer correct advice depends primarily on how much **grammatical analysis**—the actual **parsing** of sentences—is included. Some things can be handled with pattern matching of lists of words; others depend on more grammatical "understanding" of what is going on in the discourse. For instance, consider the search for a passive verb in the following two sentences:

> *The book in the cupboard was red in color.*
> *The book in the cupboard was loaned to Joan.*

**grammatical analysis:** An area of linguistic application of computers in which the machine is programmed to parse sentences, an area of research that needs improvement before it will be widely used in practical applications.

**parsing:** A linguistic term for breaking up a sentence in a natural language into its syntactical components, such as noun and verb phrases; today a lively subject of computer research.

Pattern-matching software might include a rule that passive verbs are signaled by words ending in *-ed,* the usual mark in English for the past participle, an essential element of the passive voice. Of course, *red* is neither a verb nor a signal of the passive; yet *loaned* is a true passive form. Resolving problems of this sort, common in all languages, requires more sophisticated grammatical analysis than computer programs with pattern matching allow. Much research in the computational analysis of languages is addressing these complex problems, and current programs include various levels of help based on this research.

Just as the South Carolina state agency advised its clients to proofread when using spelling checkers, they advised that programs like Grammatik, which they had reviewed, were also not currently foolproof: "The English language is simply too quirky for such software to be able to handle it 100 percent of the time. PROOFREAD!" Writers can get valuable advice from available style and grammar checkers, as long as they realize that the programs do not analyze all of the language correctly. Since the software does not correct automatically, the user has a chance to consider the advice before deciding to take or reject it. The people element of the Computer Triangle ultimately gets to make the final decision.

## ▶ Beyond Word Processing

Using computers to process, edit, and style documents is only the first level in utilizing the powers of the computer for more sophisticated applications. Computer hardware and software enable people to teach writing skills, do literary analysis more efficiently, produce publications on their desktop, and creatively combine text, sound, and graphics.

### COMPUTERS FOR WRITING

**writing center:** A laboratory found in many colleges and schools offering advice about writing improvement. Today many writing centers are using computers for tutorials and conferencing with students.

Many schools today have **writing centers** where personal computers and word processing are used in the teaching of composition. Research like that at Colorado State with Writer's Workbench suggests that students learn to write as well and as easily with computers as they do by the traditional methods, and many teaching techniques have been developed to facilitate the process. Many writing classes are using word processors equipped with spelling checkers and style and grammar checkers. Professional debates about letting students use spelling and grammar checkers resemble similar debates in mathematics about whether students should have access to calculators. If these aids help the student to gain comprehension and mastery of a subject, many teachers allow them. Certainly students have access to these electronic tools in their work and in their after-school activities.

**Networking** of machines is becoming popular in writing classes. A series of machines interconnects with network hardware and software so that students can share programs and files and send messages to one another. Because writing teachers have found that students often accept advice from their peers more readily than from the teacher, **on-line conferencing and commenting systems** have been popular in some universities. Carnegie Mellon students have access to such an on-line writing system and are expected to read and critique the work of other students in their class. They log onto the system at their leisure, read each other's papers, and file their comments electronically as a kind of e-mail. Extended on-line dialogues and debates about a paper are not uncommon. Similar possibilities for electronic commenting are available on the World Wide Web literary forum at the University of Texas (described in Chapter 1).

MediaLink for Macintosh (InterEd) allows live on-line interaction between teacher and student or peer groups of students during a writing class. For instance, teachers can find the names of their students on a list of active network users and then log on with them one at a time to comment, answer questions, and offer editorial advice. The students would probably be in the networked classroom at the time, but they could be somewhere else on the Internet. The software supports interaction in a classroom network or distance learning on the Internet. With MediaLink, teachers are collaborating with students in real time—responding to their computer activity immediately, as it is occurring. Of course, in any class a teacher can always walk around the room and comment on individual papers. In the networked writing class, editing with the teacher's advice, such as inserting a new sentence, becomes easier, faster, and more convenient because of the interactivity of software like MediaLink.

When the teacher is linked through the Internet with students at long distance, the learning environment is sometimes called the **virtual classroom.** With MediaLink, teachers can send out assignments and carry on real-time dialogues with students about their writing. Different students can be paired and work in peer groups on joint assignments, even if they are not at the same site. By contrast, support for distance students in composition without computer networks is, however, strictly off-line, probably by mail, but certainly not live. The development of a genuine writing community—a dialogue between teacher and student writers—has become possible with software such as MediaLink within the hands-on, networked classroom, whether it is on campus or extended to distance learning.

## LITERARY ANALYSIS

Even before the era of word processing, computers were helping to answer a number of literary questions that formerly had been impossible to handle, or pure drudgery to deal with. The **computer concordance** to literary texts pioneered the use of the machine for text applications in the 1950s. A concordance is an alphabetical word index to a text, which shows not only the location of each word in the text by page or chapter, but also the word within its context. Readers get a sense of an author's themes and word choice from a concordance.

**FIGURE 6-13** Students at Carnegie Mellon have networked writing labs where they may read each other's papers and leave comments for their classmates.

**networking:** The process of connecting computers together on a network so that they can communicate among themselves and share resources, such as papers in a writing class.

**on-line commenting system:** Similar to computer conferencing, a networking setup used for education so that students can read and comment on each other's written work.

**virtual classroom:** A distance learning environment in which students and teachers can be physically separated but in contact via a technology supporting remote access like computer networking or videoconferencing.

**HISTORY**

**computer concordance:** The use of computers to make indexes of words within their context for classic literary texts, the first literary application of computers, begun in the 1950s.

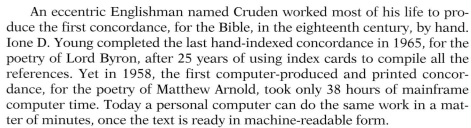

## Index Words in Order of Frequency

| | | | | |
|---|---|---|---|---|
| 1682 I | 232 DAY | 143 HEAVEN | 114 OUT | 87 PUT TAKE UP |
| 980 AS | 230 KNOW | 141 DEATH FACE SUCH | 112 EVERY FAR SUMMER | 86 BEE HOME LOOK THY WITHIN |
| 755 MY | 226 LITTLE | 140 WITHOUT | 110 NATURE | 85 DOWN |
| 719 BE | 223 THEE | 135 TELL | 107 ANY MINE | 83 FEET |
| 616 ME | 218 SHE | 130 GOD TIME | 106 FIRST LOVE UNTO | 82 LIGHT OH |
| 579 HER | 216 AWAY | 128 BEFORE | 102 BIRD | 81 LAST |
| 563 WE | 202 US | 127 COME | 100 SAY | 80 KNEW MYSELF OLD |
| 521 HIS | 191 NEVER | 125 SOUL | 96 SWEET | 79 BECAUSE HAND LET MIND OWN |
| 462 HE | 189 MORE | 124 HEART | 94 DIE | 78 UNTIL |
| 378 YOU | 178 SOME | 123 YOUR | 93 MAN | 77 SKY |
| 354 ALL | 174 TILL | 122 SEA | 92 EYE | 76 DOOR NOON PLACE WENT |
| 352 ONE | 170 SUN | 121 NIGHT | 90 MEN | |
| 349 LIKE | 156 LIFE | 119 ONLY | 89 MAKE | |
| 252 HIM | 152 GO | 117 STILL THOU | 88 EYES | |
| 248 OUR | 151 YET | 115 WAY | | |
| 244 JUST | 146 SEE | | | |

**FIGURE 6-14** An appendix to the computer-generated concordance of the poems of Emily Dickinson lists the occurrences of her most frequent words, after the most common words like *the* and *an* have been removed. The list shows her preference for personal pronouns and heavy use of words like *heaven* and *God*.

SOCIETY

An eccentric Englishman named Cruden worked most of his life to produce the first concordance, for the Bible, in the eighteenth century, by hand. Ione D. Young completed the last hand-indexed concordance in 1965, for the poetry of Lord Byron, after 25 years of using index cards to compile all the references. Yet in 1958, the first computer-produced and printed concordance, for the poetry of Matthew Arnold, took only 38 hours of mainframe computer time. Today a personal computer can do the same work in a matter of minutes, once the text is ready in machine-readable form.

A list of an author's most frequently used words gives a rough estimate of the preoccupations of the writer. As an illustration of the usefulness of a concordance, consider the most frequent content words in the short but deceptively complex lyric poems of Emily Dickinson. Dickinson relied heavily on first-person pronouns in her very personal poems (*I* occurs 1682 times, *my* 755, and *me* 616). Common among nouns of content are natural phenomena like *day* (232) and *sun* (170), as well as many words with religious connotations: *life* (156), *heaven* (143), *death* (141), *God* (130), *time* (130), *soul* (125), and *heart* (124). Dickinson stressed the ordinary person's relation to God and nature, as a cursory glance at her frequency list shows. In the concordance the reader can see every occurrence of a word like *God* in the context of the line in which it occurs, along with a reference to the poem's title (Oakman). Because of the computer, more than a thousand writers and great works have been concorded, from St. Thomas Aquinas to the *Koran* to F. Scott Fitzgerald's novel *The Great Gatsby*. Programs like WordCruncher (Brigham Young University) and Micro-OCP (Oxford Concordance Program, from Oxford University Press) allow individuals to concord any text encoded in roman letters on their own personal computers.

## AUTHORSHIP STUDIES

Disputed authorship problems that have vexed scholars for centuries are natural candidates for computer analysis. In the 1950s two statisticians at Harvard, Frederick Mosteller and David Wallace, attacked the question of whether Alexander Hamilton or James Madison wrote the 12 anonymous *Federalist* papers, for which history left no evidence in letters or diaries. These articles in a New York newspaper were important public arguments for the ratification of the Constitution. Mosteller and Wallace looked at a number of stylistic variables, but in the end found that common words like *enough, upon,* and *whilst* versus *while,* rather than content words like nouns and verbs, provided the telltale clues that distinguished Hamilton from Madison. Their finding that Madison was the author led to a rush of computer studies to analyze style in many cases of dubious authorship, including some works of Plato, the two "authors" of Isaiah in the Old Testament, and some Renaissance plays partially written by Shakespeare. Every case is unique; the stylistic fingerprints used to crack the authorship in one case often do not work in another (Oakman).

In recent years authorship methods have found their way into the law courts. In the United States, the trial of Patty Hearst was one of the most celebrated cases of the 1970s. In the early 1970s the newspaper heiress was kidnaped by political radicals and presumably forced to commit robberies against the state. At Hearst's trial in 1976, F. Lee Bailey, her famous attorney, tried to get expert testimony from scholars of computerized authorship problems to prove that travel diaries she wrote in Europe and exam papers from Berkeley were not written by the same person who sent revolutionary statements from captivity with the Symbionese Liberation Army. However, the trial judge refused to consider such evidence, and the scholars were never allowed in the courtroom. This has been the usual American practice (Bailey).

EVOLUTIONARY PERSPECTIVE

**From Print Shop to Desktop**

The old days of the dirty print shop and Linotype composition have been transformed by the technology of the bit-mapped image and the laser printer. With desktop publishing, we have a revolution in the world of printing. Yet in any technological revolution, there are inevitably advantages and disadvantages. Production costs come down, time is saved, and editorial control is in the hands of the people with the software. The old mimeographed newsletter of the Girl Scout troop or the small academic or professional society takes on a whole new face. Professors who own a personal computer, a word processor that handles several alphabets, including Greek, Cyrillic, and Arabic characters, and a laser printer can edit and publish a journal of good appearance in their offices. The technology is there for an explosion of new journals and books.

Yet questions of quality concern more than the look of the production. Scholars and newsletter editors are not usually people with layout experience, and some early results of the democratization of the publishing process have been clearly amateurish in format and appearance. People cannot acquire years of design skills with a computer program costing a few hundred dollars. The mixing of type fonts and sizes without regard for typographical convention can be noticeably distracting to the reader. Traditional publication methods also include an important peer review process, which serves to weed out inferior work. With desktop publishing, people can set up vanity presses to turn out second-rate work that has found no outlet in the world of traditional commercial publishing. The quantity of publications which already threatens to inundate libraries will undoubtedly increase—but not necessarily the quality. Becoming a Gutenberg in your office does not make you automatically a first-rate author or designer, even if what you print has a professional appearance.

In Britain and Australia, however, defendants who claim that police have falsified confessions used against them in court have successfully gotten judges to allow authorship studies in their defense. Scholars like the Reverend Andrew Morton in Scotland have often been asked to attest whether statements submitted by the police are, in fact, written by the defendants. The Morton method, a simple computer process of stylistic analysis and graphing of the results, was instrumental in reopening the case of the Birmingham Six, sent to jail for a suspected IRA bombing (*The Edinburgh Scotsman*). Whether this controversial method will prove to be foolproof, or become standard in American courts, remains an open question. Nevertheless, what started out as scholarly analysis of historical and literary questions is becoming important in circles far outside the computer centers and libraries of academe.

## DESKTOP PUBLISHING

Today desktop publishing constitutes the hottest area of text processing. The appearance of bit-mapped screens as standard hardware, now generally available, meant that both text and graphics were treated by the computer in the same way—as a series of dot patterns. Shifting type fonts, styles, and sizes became a process of redrawing the pixel patterns on the screen. Printing reproduced these patterns first on dot-matrix printers and later on laser printers, with their superior resolution. Letters and technical documents could carry graphs and pictorial materials side by side with text. This possibility exists with word processors that create characters not in defined character slots, but as bit-mapped images.

Add the invention of laser printers, with their fine production, to the intermingling of text and graphic images, and desktop publishing was born. Software designers soon began creating packages that made layout and makeup of print pages containing both media easy and comfortable to do. Users of such packages as Aldus PageMaker have complete control of the printed word and associated graphics. They can edit their documents, include illustrations, lay out a page with headlines and text, examine the look of a two-page spread, and print the final copy without need of a commercial typesetter. Pages can be set up on screen in two or more columns.

**FIGURE 6-15** Desktop publishing software like PageMaker (Adobe) can lay out pages and produce typeset quality output. Note how the inserted text material is wrapped around the map in the page under construction.

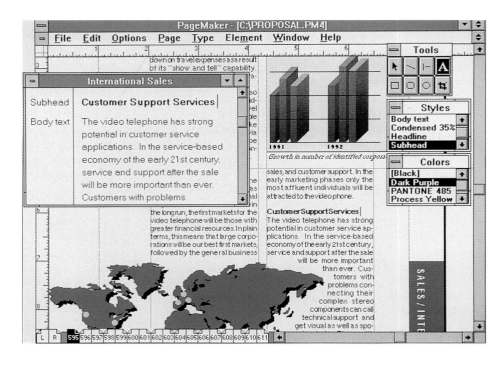

**kerning:** A fine printing feature that overlaps the placement of letter combinations for a pleasant visual effect, available in some full-featured word processors.

Graphics in black and white and color can include illustrations that artists have drawn, computer-produced graphs, or photographs captured as bit-mapped images with a laser scanner. In the text itself, the designer can mix different fonts and type sizes in the body of the article, headings, and titles, and even wrap text around a small picture in the middle of a column. Some programs offer such fine printing features as **kerning,** a process of adjusting the placement of letters for a pleasant visual effect. For instance, kerning the combination of capitals *TA* puts the foot of the *A* underneath the bar of the *T*. Word processors that put characters in defined slots, like typewriters, cannot create such effects.

All of this can be done quickly, in a matter of minutes or hours, under the control of the author and designer, who may be the same person. In many places people have set up small businesses to do business printing with only a personal computer, a laser printer, and software for word processing, graphics, and desktop publishing. In the 1980s, many large businesses which had standardized on MS-DOS machines in their offices, for routine applications software, added a Macintosh in the print department for desktop publishing. Although early laser printers did not have the resolution of fine computerized typesetters, the quality of their output was sufficient for such purposes as advertising flyers and in-house memos. New hardware for laser scanning can digitize a color photograph with fine resolution; and improvements appear every year. Because laser printing today offers color production and greater resolution than early models, desktop publishing is increasingly being used in newspaper and magazine production.

## TEXT AND SOUND

Now that the printed word has been married to the visual image by the computer, the next frontier for text processing has already appeared on the horizon: the text-sound connection. Most personal computers come with built-in microphones. In 1990 personal computers—first in the Macintosh, the multimedia pioneer—began to appear with special sound chips for the capture and reproduction of sound of CD quality. Intel computers soon followed, and the era of multimedia CD's on variety of topics was born.

Mixing of sound and print material in the same application holds enormous promise. **Voice mail** software allows a person to send an electronic letter to a colleague along with a spoken version or a question about it. When the mail is read, the computer plays the sound file at the reader's workstation. World Wide Web files containing text and graphics can now also include sound extensions of radio quality such as RealAudio (Progressive Networks) and StreamWorks (Xing Technologies). Foreign language software from many companies offers hypermedia lessons in French, German, Spanish, Italian, Russian, Chinese, and Japanese, incorporating text, voice, and graphics. And CD-ROM encyclopedias routinely add sound files to their text articles, such as the example of Roosevelt's fireside chats presented with materials about his life and work in the Grolier Multimedia Encyclopedia in Chapter 1. Sound applications combined with text and graphics can be taken for granted in modern personal computer multimedia systems.

## MUSIC

Computer-produced musical composition combines the machine's capacity to voice multiple sound tracks with the ability to produce a printed record of the score. Sound reproduction with the microphones included in inexpensive computers works on the same principle as the popular keyboard synthesizer. Attaching the musical keyboard to the computer for output produces even better sound through the standard interface for digital music called **MIDI (Musical Instrument Digital Interface).** The digital codes for musical notes are produced by the computer and transferred through the MIDI device to the synthesizer, where they are realized as sound. MIDI interfaces can also capture synthesized keyboard music for input to the computer.

Software like Encore (Passport Designs) and Music Prose (Coda Music Software) allows the composer to see the score of a Beethoven symphony and listen to it, then modify its timing or change its key, and play back the results immediately. Composers can create new works at a MIDI keyboard, and the software creates the musical notation for them on the screen. They then edit the notes or add lyrics to the music. When a composition is complete, the computer plays it back on the MIDI keyboard and outputs the score on a printer, for distribution to human players. As in desktop publishing, the multimedia computer is greatly affecting traditional habits of composition (Deutsch).

## VOICE COMMANDS

One of the most ambitious developments in combining text and voice was the experimental Kurzweil Voice Writer. Described in 1986 by Raymond Kurzweil, the designer of the optical scanner a decade earlier, the Voice Writer is a word processor which accepts voice dictation and creates a printed document directly. In simple terms, it is an automated secretary that types out what one dictates to it. Kurzweil envisions its use by deaf people on the telephone. As the caller speaks, a screen at the deaf person's end of the line displays the conversation. The system combines multiple "expert" processors to decipher speech with a dictionary of about 5000 words and a program for understanding grammar and syntax. It trains on the user's voice and learns the person's frequent vocabulary; then it automatically adds those terms to the dictionary and eliminates others not often needed.

**FIGURE 6-16** Graphics software can take a digitized photo and enhance it for special effect before using it in a desktop publishing project.

**voice mail:** A technology which allows a person to send a digitized spoken message to a colleague. The message is stored in a computer and later played back to the recipient when the mail is retrieved.

**Musical Instrument Digital Interface (MIDI):** A technology for connecting electronic music instruments and computers. The information that passes between MIDI devices is a condensed description of the composition. On playback, MIDI controls the generation of sound on a synthesizer.

**FIGURE 6-17** Software like Free Style (Mark of the Unicorn) makes it easy to play different instruments as MIDI input files on computer, mix them for effect, and create musical scores directly.

**automatic speech recognition (ASR):** A lively research area in speech processing to recognize a person's voice and respond to voice commands or type out what has been said.

**FIGURE 6-18** This musician has attached a MIDI keyboard directly to a computer. As he composes, the computer will create the musical score.

**FIGURE 6-19** A person dictating to the Kurzweil Voice Writer, which creates the typed text on the screen. Because the process is not perfect, the typed material will probably need editing before printing.

Kurzweil quotes Hamlet's famous line to suggest the tough problems involved in **automatic speech recognition (ASR):** "To be or not to be, that is the question." Each of the first six words has at least one homonym—a different word that sounds the same:

to, too, two

be, bee, *b*

or, oar

not, knot

Combining all the possibilities gives 324 interpretations of these six words that sound alike. Acoustically all are correct, but only one is linguistically correct. Kurzweil solves these dilemmas by analyzing context and identifying word classes that can occur together. The system also allows the person dictating the text to punctuate or format the document with voice commands. Like imperfect grammar checkers, the system does not obviate the need to edit and proofread the result before printing. Kurzweil's expert language understanding and word processing system suggests how automated speech recognition can revolutionize the world of writing (Kurzweil).

By 1993 continued research led Apple Computer to introduce an addition to its Macintosh operating system that could understand simple English-language commands on the menus of popular software. A research team recorded thousands of English speakers, male and female, from all the dialect areas of North America, reading the menu commands in their accents. They then created "intelligent" voice recognition software called PlainTalk that allows English speakers to give voice commands to the operating system and common software packages. For instance, the computer can understand the Save and Print commands, no matter whether they were said by a Boston dowager or a Southern gentleman. If one asks the computer to save a document, the computer recognizes the command and in a synthetic voice asks the user to type in a file name. Although the recognition

is not perfect and the number of words understood much fewer than the Kurzweil machine, for persons like the blind who cannot see the screen, the voice command option makes the computer much more user accessible. Similar voice command systems have subsequently been created for other personal computers, and it is likely that they will gain greater accuracy and more general use than just understanding menu commands in the coming years.

## FOREIGN LANGUAGES

Accustomed to English and European languages made up of letters from the Roman alphabet, we normally do not think about the considerable difficulties inherent in word processing in other languages. Two different cases are worthy of consideration: Arabic and Chinese. Like English, Arabic is a language with letters that combine to form words. But the printed form of Arabic is continuous writing: somewhat like cursive handwriting, the letters flow into each other. In addition, the language is written and read from right to left, like Hebrew, not left to right, like English. Computer scientists developing word processors have had to take both features of the language into account. Writing from right to left is not troublesome if the whole document is in Arabic; the problem arises when words in a European language are intermixed with Arabic text. When the writer signals a shift in orientation, a word processor from NCR stores the next set of characters in reverse, until the user signals a return to Arabic. When the text is printed right to left, the reversed characters appear in proper left-to-right order for the reader.

Also troublesome is the flowing cursive script, with a lot of special rules for combining characters as *ligatures*—graphic characters that stand for two letters. The ligature in English—one character for two letters—is familiar only in the printing of character pairs like *fl* and *œ*. Since Arabic has many more ligatures, the software must be engineered to monitor the typist's character strokes and automatically combine characters to make ligatures. Formatting of letters, with proper spacing and ligatures, is not perfect, but the results of several commercial systems from IBM, NCR, and Xerox have been impressive (Becker).

## CHARACTER LANGUAGES

Chinese does not even spell out words; words have their own graphic characters, or ideograms. Japanese works essentially the same way. Chinese has more than 50,000 characters, and it is said that to read elementary Chinese, a student must be able to recognize about 3000. Typewriters and automated keyboarding systems have always had the problem of how to make thousands of separate characters available to the typist. One recent computer solution developed by a Canadian company called Multi-Corp uses a 10-key method to define the strokes of a character, much as children are taught in grade school. As the typist combines strokes to build a character from the roots up, the software is narrowing the possibilities. When the list gets small, the user is shown the character choices on the screen and picks the correct one. On average, the correct character will show up after 2.7 keyboard strokes are given, and a practiced user can type about 50 characters per minute (Hutheesing, "Call It a Strokeboard"). A similar method from a Microsoft division called Lexicus uses a digitizer pad on which the user actually drafts the characters in proper stroke order using a stylus. As the computer monitors the strokes being formed, it is using fuzzy logic to match the character with choices from a graphical database of more than 19,000 characters. With accuracy of about 85 percent, Lexicus expects to release its Chinese software for use with Windows 95 software in early 1996 (Hutheesing, "The Mother of Development").

**FIGURE 6-20** As the writer creates a Chinese character with a stylus, software from Lexicus matches the strokes to a known database of characters using pattern recognition and composes the Chinese script on the computer screen.

A third approach uses Apple Computer's already developed success with speech recognition to retrieve Chinese characters from a database. Mandarin Chinese is a tone-based language with about 1,200 sounds, and a user repeats them to the computer in the training phase. Early results suggest that Chinese word processing may work better without any keyboard and more accurately with speech recognition than Kurzweil's tests with dictated English. Some users claim that the voice recognition system can achieve an accuracy rate of about 95 percent and produce about 60 words a minute. Motorola plans to create clones of the Macintosh for the vast personal computer market in China that may be bundled with the voice recognition software (Hardy).

Compared to word processing with Roman alphabets, methods of processing Chinese characters seem time-consuming and cumbersome. The problems faced with character languages truly call for creative solutions in the design of hardware and software for automated text production. Computers are finally providing the basic features of word processing for communication with ideograms through a combination of text, graphics, and voice recognition—an accomplishment that has been frustrating for decades.

## ▶ Summary

Whatever one's perspective, the field of word processing today has changed the nature of producing written documents. In addition to keying, word processing allows easy editing, formatting, filing, and printing of texts. Various checks, including spelling and stylistic help, can be automatically applied to word-processed materials. In areas like desktop publishing and voice mail, word processing today has forged alliances with both sound and graphic components. The computer is expanding the universe of the printed word, begun by Gutenberg, into the realm of multimedia, the world of picture, sound, and voice. Print culture—in education, journalism, printing, and publishing—throughout the world has been changed forever by the machine.

## ▶ Key Terms

automatic formatting of tabular data (p. 137)

automatic hyphenation (p. 139)

automatic numbering of pages (p. 137)

automatic renumbering of footnotes (p. 137)

automatic speech recognition (ASR) (p. 150)

boilerplate (p. 135)

centering of text (p. 136)

computer concordance (p. 145)

dedicated word processor (p. 131)

electronic cut and paste (block move) (p. 135)

grammatical analysis (p. 144)

indexing (p. 141)

justifying of lines (p. 136)

kerning (p. 148)

label maker (p. 137)

mail-merge (p. 131)

Musical Instrument Digital Interface (MIDI) (p. 149

networking (p. 145)

numeric keypad (p. 132)

on-line commenting system (p. 145)

on-line thesaurus (p. 141)

page preview (p. 137)

parsing (p. 144)

pattern matching (p. 136)

proportional spacing (p. 139)

Qwerty keyboard (p. 132)

 ## Self-Test

### MULTIPLE-CHOICE

1. All of the following are standard features of word processors except
   a. word wrap
   b. automatic indexing
   c. electronic cut and paste
   d. search and replace

2. The basic features of all modern word processing software can be broken down into five different categories: text preparation, editing, formatting, printing, and
   a. spell checking
   b. block move
   c. document storage and retrieval
   d. text correction

3. Full-featured word processing programs today may offer all of the following features except
   a. automatic renumbering of footnotes
   b. concording of the words of the text
   c. page preview before printing
   d. label making

4. Computer screens that have graphic capabilities typically offer which of the following word processing features?
   a. changes of type font
   b. different type styles: boldface, underlined, shadowed, etc.
   c. a variety of type sizes
   d. all of the above

5. Assume that a person has typed the sentence "The kat had mixed colour in its hare." Which of the following scenarios would be least likely using a standard spell checking program?
   a. The program would note that *kat* is a candidate for change.
   b. The program might note that *colour* is a British spelling and suggest a change to *color*.
   c. The program would note the incorrect form of *hare* in the sentence and suggest changing it to *hair*.
   d. None is unlikely, because a good spelling checker would catch all of the problems.

6. Style checkers routinely look for all of the following possible errors except
   a. sophisticated grammatical problems, like subject-verb agreement
   b. sexist and racist language
   c. confusing word pairs, like *stationery/stationary*
   d. text statistics, such as sentence lengths

7. Which of the following were instrumental in making desktop publishing such an important area of text processing?
   a. laser printers

    b. bit-mapped computer screens

    c. software that made layout and makeup of pages containing both text and graphics easy to create

    d. all of the above

8. All of the following seem to offer promise for word processing with character languages like Chinese. Which seems to be least promising?

    a. voice recognition of speech

    b. large keyboards with many characters

    c. drafting characters on a digitizing pad

    d. constructing the strokes of characters on a keyboard

## TRUE/FALSE

9. **T  F**  IBM coined the term *word processing* to describe new software for writing introduced with the IBM PC in 1981.

10. **T  F**  Today typewriting courses have been transformed into keyboarding courses using general word processing on personal computers.

11. **T  F**  Spelling checkers are more common in today's word processors than automatic hyphenation programs.

12. **T  F**  Using a computer program to decipher disputed authorship is common today because the stylistic fingerprints to identify an author are well known.

13. **T  F**  One of the potential drawbacks of the democratization of the printing process made possible by desktop publishing is the omission of the peer review process, which serves to separate quality work from inferior work.

14. **T  F**  The multimedia possibilities of modern computers are greatly affecting habits of music composition.

15. **T  F**  To handle homonyms—two words that sound alike but are spelled differently—the Kurzweil Voice Writer uses a large dictionary and automated hyphenation.

16. **T  F**  The spread of computers in writing classes can be attributed primarily to the availability of word processing and multimedia applications.

## FILL-IN

17. The process of preparing a list of addresses separate from the text of a form letter and then merging them at the keyboard is called _____.

18. _____ is an acronym for a computer screen that shows word-processed text exactly as it will be printed later.

19. Computers can make _____ of literary texts—alphabetical indexes showing the location of words in a text and displaying them in context.

20. In recent years computerized studies of _____ have found their way into law courts in Britain and Australia, but have not been accepted in the United States.

21. Some desktop publishing software allows _____, the process of merging letters for a pleasant visual effect.

22. _____ software allows a person to send an electronic letter to a colleague along with a spoken version or a question about it.

23. The standard interface for digital music, called ____, accepts digital codes for musical notes produced by the computer and sent to a synthesizer, where they are realized as sound.

24. Compared to Western languages like English, problems in word processing in _____ involve the cursive, flowing nature of the script and the fact that the language is written and read from right to left.

## ▶ Experiential Exercises

1. Try to find an electric typewriter (or even better, a manual one), and use it for a while so that you can see the features of typewriting in the days before word processing. Look especially for aspects of word processing that were not available in standard typewriters. Note at least five differences. If you cannot find an older typewriter, try to interview someone who used one at work and has converted to word processing. See what this person thinks are the advantages and possible disadvantages of word processing, which has essentially driven traditional typewriting out of business.

2. Studies show that the Dvorak keyboard layout makes keyboarding easier to learn than the traditional Qwerty keyboard. Research the principles of the Dvorak plan, which is supposed to make typing more natural. Examine an illustration of the keyboard in Figure 6-1, and find out if you can order a Dvorak keyboard for personal computers. Are they more expensive? Why have they not been more widely adopted if they make learning keyboarding simpler?

3. If your college has some personal computers still in use that have screens that are not WYSIWYG, look at word-processed documents created on them. Examine how the formatting characters for italics or underlining look on the computer screen. Are there special characters that indicate such features in the text? Does the word processing program offer a page preview feature, so that the user can see what to expect before printing?

4. Talk to someone who does a lot of keyboarding. Does this person use a spelling checker or style checker? What sorts of problems can occur if one puts total faith in these aids and goes ahead with printing the final draft of a document without checking it over? Make a list of several common errors that can be missed by a spelling or grammar checker.

5. In the library, look for the ongoing multivolume edition of the *Papers of Thomas Jefferson* (Princeton University Press). Find the volume that includes the merged indexes to the first 20 volumes, a massive computer indexing project. Look up a topic like slavery or agriculture, which Jefferson discussed in many of his papers. How much time and energy are saved in using such a merged index to search for a frequently discussed topic, compared to using the single-volume indexes? Discuss whether the editors of the project could have considered creating such a massive index without computer assistance.

6. Choose a favorite author and search for a concordance to the person's works in the library. In addition to the people and works mentioned in this text, computer concordances have been produced for the Bible, *Beowulf,*

Shakespeare, Milton, William Butler Yeats, Matthew Arnold, George Bernard Shaw, Joseph Conrad, Dylan Thomas, Henry Fielding, and many others. Take some time to examine the layout of the concordance, so that you can get a feel for how it may be useful for literary study.

7. The legal controversy over the validity of computer techniques for determining authorship has really heated up in Britain in the last few years. Research the current status of the controversy there, and ask a law librarian (if you can) to see whether American courts are now admitting such evidence.

8. Find out in what ways your institution uses desktop publishing. A good place to start would be the publications or printing office. Is it used by departments or professors to publish scholarly journals?

9. Newer personal computers are increasingly coming with built-in sound capabilities. One promising area is voice and speech recognition. The user can speak to the computer and get it to carry out a series of commands. If computers like these are not available on your campus, visit a local computer store to get a demonstration. How successful are the machines in understanding your voice, and how expensive are they compared to keyboard and mouse-driven machines? Do their current users or salespeople expect the next generation of machines to be voice-controlled as a standard feature?

## ▶ Critical Thinking Exercises

1. Did you learn keyboarding in school? Do you think it should be a mandatory requirement for high school graduation? Develop arguments on both sides of the issue.

2. Attack or defend the proposition that desktop publishing will lead to an increase in the quality of locally produced scholarly journals.

3. The freedom offered by word processing to experiment with type styles and graphics has opened up new opportunities for student creativity in writing classes. Discuss how word processing can allow you to write more creatively.

**ANSWERS TO SELF-TEST**

*Multiple-Choice*: 1. b;   2. c;   3. b;   4. d;   5. c;   6. a;   7. d;
8. b
*True/False*: 9. F;   10. T;   11. T;   12. F;   13. T;   14. T;   15. F;
16. F
*Fill-in*: 17. mail-merge;   18. WYSIWYG;   19. concordances;   20. authorship;   21. kerning;   22. voice mail;   23. MIDI;   24. Arabic

# CHAPTER 7

# Electronic Spreadsheets

▶ ## LEARNING OUTCOMES

*After completing this chapter, you should be able to:*

1. *List the essential features of all spreadsheets.*

2. *Construct a spreadsheet, including cells for values, formulas, and functions.*

3. *Define the what-if scenario and describe its uses.*

4. *Explain the natural connection between spreadsheet data and its graphic presentation.*

5. *Describe some general-purpose uses of spreadsheets, as well as specialized uses such as tax preparation and financial management.*

▶ ## COMPUTERS IN CONTEXT

*In 1978 Dan Bricklin, a graduate student at the Harvard Business School, tired of all the repetitive arithmetic calculations in his long accounting assignments. With his background as an undergraduate at MIT, Bricklin knew that the computer, especially adept at mathematical operations, could help him with these tasks. His choices were to record all his results from a hand calculator or to use the university mainframe computer, inconvenient for the changing daily assignments of his classwork. With Robert Frankston, a friend from MIT, he devised the first electronic spreadsheet program in 1979, a microcomputer program that made the rows and columns of the ledger sheet electronic.*

*The program, called VisiCalc (for Visible Calculator), ran on the popular Apple II personal computers of the late 1970s, and helped to make them and the personal computer itself acceptable in the business market. According to many commentators, the spreadsheet started the software revolution that spurred the growth of the microcomputer market. Although word processing ideas are older, they were not originally designed, like the spreadsheet, specifically for the personal computer. Today spreadsheet users have found many uses for this popular application, and programs with a variety of spreadsheet features are available for all machines from many software companies. In this Computer Triangle partnership, a specific human need and personal computer hardware led to the creation of software with capabilities far beyond the authors' original intent.*

**FIGURE 7-1** (A) Dan Bricklin, at right, and his colleague Robert Frankston designed (B) VisiCalc, the first spreadsheet, with the row and column layout of the ledger sheet.

## Spreadsheet Essentials

**cell:** The intersection of a row and column in a spreadsheet.

A spreadsheet is easily recognized by its format and appearance. The generic spreadsheet consists of the grid or matrix of elements, called **cells,** typical of the paper ledger sheet but presented on the computer screen. The cells are arranged in horizontal rows and vertical columns, like the layout of an account book or a teacher's grade book. In the paper ledgers, people record information in words and numbers in the columns and rows, and store calculations in others. In computer terms, these sheets hold input of names, dates, and amounts (whether money or grades); record them in a sort of memory; and present the results of calculations based on the data as an output record. Users do the processing themselves, elsewhere—perhaps with a pocket calculator.

The electronic spreadsheet not only mirrors the paper version in appearance, but adds a new, powerful element. Besides input, memory, and output, it offers *processing* as well. The spreadsheet has an electronic calculator incorporated within itself. Some of its cells contain text and figures, while others hold calculations based on that information. Deciding what will be contained or calculated in a particular cell remains under the control of the user, as with the paper ledger. If a number changes in one cell, any calculations that depend on it are refigured automatically. This feature of spreadsheets makes them **dynamic.** Cells that contain **formulas** for calculations that depend on other data will change if the data change. These cells with formulas which continually monitor other data cells are the truly distinguishing feature of a spreadsheet.

**dynamic:** A term applied to spreadsheets to describe their changing whenever new values are introduced, since all relations embodied in the spreadsheet must be reassessed relative to the new data.

**formula:** A numerical or logical relation or function added to a cell that expresses a relationship between other cell values and changes its value if they do.

Suppose, for example, a teacher recorded the first of three test grades erroneously. Having discovered the error, she needs to correct it in the grade book and recalculate the student's average (the three test scores divided by 3). In a spreadsheet she only needs to enter the new grade in the cell for the first test. The other cell, for holding the numerical average, contains an arithmetic formula that specifies that the average is figured by adding the contents of the three test grade cells and dividing the result by 3. When the first test score is corrected, the average is automatically recalculated and displayed in its cell. The teacher can print the output of the current spreadsheet whenever she desires, in effect freezing values of the cells for printing.

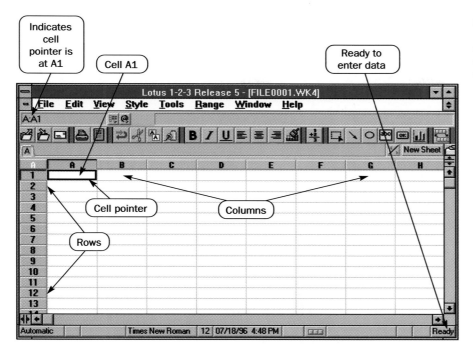

**FIGURE 7-2** A worksheets for Lotus 1-2-3 for Windows (Release 5) includes the basic elements of all spreadsheets: rows, columns, and cells.

## CONSTRUCTING A SPREADSHEET

Many everyday applications present themselves in a column-and-row format: itemized invoices, baseball standings, and even the Internal Revenue Service tax return. To understand the construction, workings, and usefulness of the spreadsheet with an example that hits everybody, let us examine the 1995 short IRS tax form, called the 1040EZ, shown in Figure 7-3. College students with simple income and deductions can use the short form to calculate their tax liability quickly, as soon as they receive their withholding statements from employers.

We shall use **Lotus 1-2-3 for Windows** Release5 (IBM Corp.), one of the most popular spreadsheet packages ever developed, to implement our own tax return in spreadsheet form on a computer running Windows 3.1. Lotus remains a dominant spreadsheet program for Intel machines with Borland's Quattro and Microsoft's Excel as popular alternatives; for the Macintosh, Microsoft's Excel is the favorite, with ClarisWorks (from Apple) probably the second choice. Because all current spreadsheets share many similarities, the 1-2-3 illustration will serve to introduce general spreadsheet principles.

At the top of the tax form are spaces for the taxpayer's name, address, and social security number. In the computer version, we open the package and get a blank **worksheet,** the term for a spreadsheet in process (see Figures 7-4 and 7-5). Initially empty in the middle, it has a set of numbered rows down the left side (1, 2, 3, and so on) and lettered columns across the top (A, B, C, D, E). Each cell in the worksheet (Figure 7-4) is directly identifiable by its row and column designation. We put our taxpayer's name, John Jones, in the first cell in the upper left-hand corner, the cell A1 (for column A, row 1) and use the next two rows in column A to store the address. We can widen the worksheet columns for a long field of information like the street address. For convenience, let us store the social security number in element A4, even though it appears on the right side of the tax form, and ignore the Presidential Election Campaign fund, not needed for the illustration.

**SOCIETY**

**Lotus 1-2-3:** One of the most popular spreadsheet programs, a successor to VisiCalc, the first spreadsheet.

**worksheet:** A term sometimes used for a spreadsheet.

**FIGURE 7-3** The 1040EZ tax form. Note that it can be viewed as a two-column document, one for instructions and the other for the monetary figures.

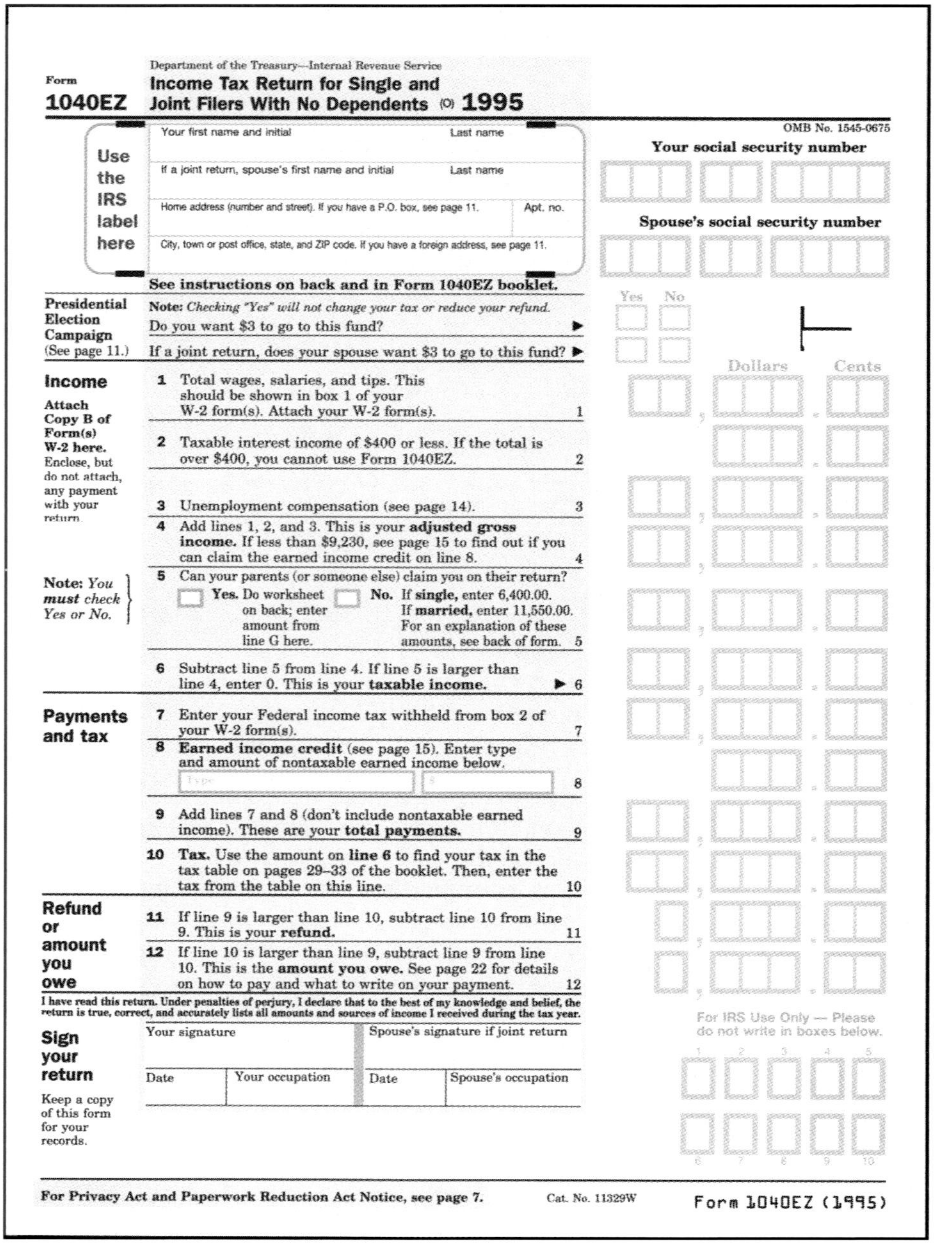

Form **1040EZ** Department of the Treasury—Internal Revenue Service
**Income Tax Return for Single and Joint Filers With No Dependents** (0) **1995**

OMB No. 1545-0675

Use the IRS label here

Your first name and initial | Last name

If a joint return, spouse's first name and initial | Last name

Home address (number and street). If you have a P.O. box, see page 11. | Apt. no.

City, town or post office, state, and ZIP code. If you have a foreign address, see page 11.

**See instructions on back and in Form 1040EZ booklet.**

**Your social security number**

**Spouse's social security number**

**Presidential Election Campaign** (See page 11.)
**Note:** *Checking "Yes" will not change your tax or reduce your refund.*
Do you want $3 to go to this fund? ▶ Yes No
If a joint return, does your spouse want $3 to go to this fund? ▶

Dollars Cents

**Income**
**Attach Copy B of Form(s) W-2 here.** Enclose, but do not attach, any payment with your return.

1 Total wages, salaries, and tips. This should be shown in box 1 of your W-2 form(s). Attach your W-2 form(s). 1

2 Taxable interest income of $400 or less. If the total is over $400, you cannot use Form 1040EZ. 2

3 Unemployment compensation (see page 14). 3

4 Add lines 1, 2, and 3. This is your **adjusted gross income.** If less than $9,230, see page 15 to find out if you can claim the earned income credit on line 8. 4

**Note:** *You must check Yes or No.*

5 Can your parents (or someone else) claim you on their return?
**Yes.** Do worksheet on back; enter amount from line G here.
**No.** If **single,** enter 6,400.00. If **married,** enter 11,550.00. For an explanation of these amounts, see back of form. 5

6 Subtract line 5 from line 4. If line 5 is larger than line 4, enter 0. This is your **taxable income.** ▶ 6

**Payments and tax**

7 Enter your Federal income tax withheld from box 2 of your W-2 form(s). 7

8 **Earned income credit** (see page 15). Enter type and amount of nontaxable earned income below. Type $ 8

9 Add lines 7 and 8 (don't include nontaxable earned income). These are your **total payments.** 9

10 **Tax.** Use the amount on **line 6** to find your tax in the tax table on pages 29–33 of the booklet. Then, enter the tax from the table on this line. 10

**Refund or amount you owe**

11 If line 9 is larger than line 10, subtract line 10 from line 9. This is your **refund.** 11

12 If line 10 is larger than line 9, subtract line 9 from line 10. This is the **amount you owe.** See page 22 for details on how to pay and what to write on your payment. 12

**I have read this return. Under penalties of perjury, I declare that to the best of my knowledge and belief, the return is true, correct, and accurately lists all amounts and sources of income I received during the tax year.**

**Sign your return**
Keep a copy of this form for your records.

Your signature | Spouse's signature if joint return
Date | Your occupation | Date | Spouse's occupation

For IRS Use Only — Please do not write in boxes below.
1 2 3 4 5
6 7 8 9 10

**For Privacy Act and Paperwork Reduction Act Notice, see page 7.** Cat. No. 11329W Form 1040EZ (1995)

**label:** Adding descriptive information to cells in a spreadsheet or to a graph based on a spreadsheet to make the results more readable and understandable.

**value:** The contents of a cell, perhaps a number or a formula.

**final formatting:** The final setup of the spreadsheet for printing or other form of presentation, including such characteristics as rounding numbers and adding currency signs.

The main body of the worksheet contains twelve lines of information in two columns: categories of monetary information and the numerical values themselves. Before we begin to enter them, let us add **labels** for each column, calling them Category and Amount. Leaving space for readability, we type these labels side by side in cells A6 and B6. Then we begin filling in the actual tax return in cells A7 and B7. Column A lists the categories of financial information and Column B lists the actual figures. In column B, rows 7 and 8 contain income information copied from John Jones' W-2 withholding form ($16,000) and interest statements ($360). Since Jones is employed, unemployment compensation is zero. These numbers, the data themselves, are called **values** in common spreadsheet terminology. (Dollar signs are omitted now but can be added later, in the **final formatting** of the spreadsheet.)

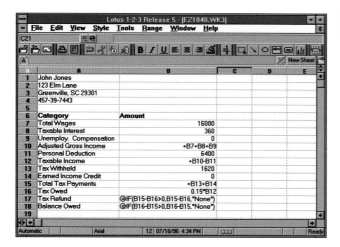

**FIGURE 7-4** Starting to prepare the tax return as a spreadsheet. Note that different cells contain text, numbers, and formulas.

## FORMULAS

Calculating the adjusted gross income introduces the first place for a calculation formula, which is to be the sum of the first three figures. After adding the name of the category in cell A10, we need to add the previous three amounts for cell B10. Instead of doing the sum directly, we record the addition formula in B10 as +B7+B8+B9. Putting a plus sign before a cell address in B10 signals to Lotus 1-2-3 that this new cell is one to be used for calculation. The program would take B7 inserted in cell B10 without the plus sign to be a label, like total wages. With the formula, we are specifying where the spreadsheet calculator is to get the three amounts for the sum, rather than the values themselves.

What happens is quite logical and straightforward. The computer gets the monetary figures from B7, B8, and B9, adds them in its processor, and stores the information immediately in cell B10 (16,000 + 360 + 0 = 16,360, shown in Figure 7-5). Of course, if either number is mistyped, the calculated sum will be incorrect. But this coding problem would be a problem on a paper ledger sheet as well. Computers can do many useful things for users, but they need correct data to do accurate work. As always, all three elements of the Computer Triangle must work together to get proper results.

The formula gives the spreadsheet its processing powers and sets it apart from the ledger sheet concept. Whereas Lotus 1-2-3 introduces nu-

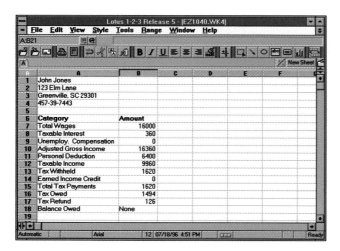

**FIGURE 7-5** With the information about yearly wages and interest amounts filled in, the rest of the financial column is calculated according to the formulas in Figure 7-4.

merical formulas with the plus sign, other popular spreadsheets signify formulas in other ways. For example, programs like Microsoft Works and ClarisWorks (Apple) use an equal sign for formulas. The equivalent of the Lotus formula for adjusted gross income in these packages would be =B7+B8+B9. With the initial equal sign, the programs recognize that what follows calls for an addition. B7 is an address containing a numeric value that needs to be added to the values in addresses B8 and B9.

Assuming that John Jones does not qualify as his parents' dependent, his personal exemption (line 11) was $6400 for 1995. The next row calls for another formula, to figure the total taxable income, or the amount of the adjusted gross income minus the exemption on line 11. Spreadsheet users get into the habit of thinking in terms of cells and formulas for the calculation of values, rather than the figures themselves. We introduce the formula +B10–B11 into row 12, column B, and the computer does the subtraction for us (16,360 – 6400 = 9960). The spreadsheet has calculated in line 12 the amount of taxable income on which tax was owed in 1995.

Line 13 lists the amount of tax withheld by Jones' employer (1620), which precedes the figuring of his actual tax on line 15. Jones made enough money in 1995 that his earned income credit is zero (line 14); thus the formula in line 15 of total tax payments yields the amount of tax withheld in line 13 (1620). Although most taxpayers look up their tax in a table, our program can calculate it directly. The percentage of tax owed in 1995 by single people with incomes under $19,000 was 15 percent of taxable income. In cell B16 we insert the tax calculation formula, 15 percent of cell B12: 0.15*B12. The symbol for multiplication in computers is the asterisk (*), to avoid confusion between the times sign and the letter $x$. The computer retrieves 9960 from B12 and multiplies it by 15 percent; the result (1494) goes into cell B16. In dollar terms, John Jones owes the IRS $1,494.00 in income tax for 1995.

## FUNCTIONS

**function:** A predefined relation built into the spreadsheet program that can be used as a formula for such purposes as averaging numbers or finding the maximum value in a group of cells.

If more tax has been withheld during the year than he owes, Jones is due a refund; otherwise, he owes the difference to the government. These two possibilities are covered by the last two lines of the 1040EZ form (lines 17 and 18 on the worksheet). We need to consider both cases separately. The software allows us to do comparisons between elements of the worksheet, with different outcomes determined by the results. Such comparisons utilize built-in **functions.** The user can incorporate if/then/else comparisons, important building blocks of structured program design (see Chapter 5), into the worksheet, specifying different outcomes for the comparison. For the refund case (line 17), we can structure a sentence that describes the situation as follows: If the amount of tax owed is less than the amount of tax withheld, then calculate the taxpayer's refund; else, put "None" in the refund slot.

Lotus 1-2-3 offers this sort of comparison as an IF function, introduced in the appropriate cell according to the following general definition: @IF(condition, true, false). The @ signals the program that a function will follow, and the true and false fields tell what to do for each of the possibilities of the comparison specified in the condition field. Given that B15 contains the total amount withheld and B16 the tax owed, the comparison for B17 is written in function notation as follows: @IF(B15–B16>0, B15–B16,"None"). The English interpretation of the function is straightforward. If the difference between tax withheld (B15) and tax owed (B16) is positive (>0), then the difference itself is put in cell B17 (the true alternative); else, the word *None* is put there (the false case). With such comparisons, spreadsheets can carry out multiple operations in one step. The program does the subtraction, then compares the result to 0, and finally chooses which of the two alternatives to put in cell B17. In this case, Jones gets a refund of $126, since (1620 − 1494 = 126) is greater than zero (see Figure 7-5).

A reverse situation pertains in line B18, for balance owed. If the difference between the tax owed and the amount withheld is positive, then the balance due should be calculated in this cell; else, the word *None* should be put there. In Lotus notation, we need @IF(B16−B15>0, B16−B15, "None") in cell B18. After the subtraction and comparison to zero, the appropriate action is taken. In this case, the subtraction (1494 − 1620 = −126) is not positive, and the false alternative is carried out: *None* is put in cell B18. The final worksheet (Figure 7-5) shows the refund on line 17 and no tax owed on line 18.

A little reflection reveals that the comparisons for these two lines could be worded differently and the true/false cases adjusted accordingly. For instance, the following functional test for balance owed is equivalent to the one first discussed: @IF(B15−B16>0,"None",B16−B15). Turning around the subtraction requires reversing the alternatives. Since there are several ways of developing conditional comparisons, the user must think carefully about the test to be made and the possible options before proceeding.

## RANGES

Most spreadsheet programs offer a large selection of other functions in addition to numerical comparison. The common SUM function @SUM (B7..B9) could have been used in row 9, for adjusted gross income, instead of the addition formula. Signifying several row or column elements is called specifying a **range**—in this case, from cell B7 to cell B9. Lotus 1-2-3 recognizes the function immediately, because it begins with the telltale @ sign. But we must remember that another spreadsheet package may signify its functions and formulas with a different notation. For instance, some programs use the colon to separate the first and last cells of a range (B7:B9 here).

**range:** A set of adjacent row or column cells treated as a unit, for example, to be placed in a function to get a sum of cell values in a column. Specifying a range of cells eliminates the need to list all of them individually.

The power of the SUM function with a stated range of cells becomes more obvious if 100 values must be added up rather than just 2. Writing an addition formula for 100 numbers is cumbersome. Specifying the range of cell addresses by listing the first and last only in the SUM function is preferable. All the values between these extreme addresses are automatically added by the function. Because summing a range of values is very common, Lotus 1-2-3 for Windows permits the user to click the SUM icon on the Smart Icon Palette (the 1+2=3 icon near the right) and add up the numbers automatically. The program examines the numeric data in the adjoining rows or columns and places the cell addresses automatically into the function argument inside the parentheses. Simultaneously its sums the numbers for the user in the current cell. Using the icon shortcut means the user does not have to type the range within the SUM function. Other typical spreadsheet functions include averaging numbers, sorting alphabetically for text data, and trigonometric functions for scientific and mathematical data. As spreadsheet applications have matured, the number and variety of operations they can carry out as functions have been greatly expanded.

## MACROS

With the evolution of spreadsheet software have come new capabilities, especially for people who readily think through problems in programming terms. Most spreadsheets allow users to develop their own functions for special needs through the use of **macros.** These macro operations are small programs stored within the spreadsheet and accessed by name, like the functions IF and SUM provided by the software developer. Using the

**macro:** In a spreadsheet, a programmer-designed function individually developed for a special need. Like functions provided with the spreadsheet program, macro operations are small programs stored within the spreadsheet itself and accessed by name.

**FIGURE 7-6** The tax return spreadsheet nicely formatted with dollars and cents for the numbers in the second column and colors added for emphasis.

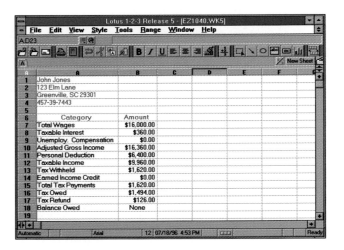

IF and SUM macros provided by the designer, individual users can create customized macros for their own needs.

For instance, suppose Marie Sanchez prices articles for a retail store. She needs a function for discounting that prints sale price tags based on the regular price minus the discount percentage, which varies from time to time. She creates within an unused section of her spreadsheet a small program called DISCT to calculate and print the discount price tag. Activating the macro requires two figures, the retail price and the discount rate. In the main portion of the spreadsheet, she calls up her macro by its name, DISCT, and adds within parentheses the two values required for its operation, such as 19.95 and .20. From the cell where the macro DISCT is inserted, the program retrieves the macro, figures the discount, and prints a price tag reflecting a 20 percent reduction on a $19.95 item. The ability to create macro functions adds additional personal programming capacity to the already powerful general calculation facilities of spreadsheet software.

### FORMATTING THE OUTPUT

**output presentation format:** Another term for final formatting and deciding how to present the completed spreadsheet.

**attribute:** The label, value, formula, or function stored in a cell. Displaying a spreadsheet in attribute format is useful for double-checking relationships among cells.

The spreadsheet version of the 1040EZ tax return is now complete. Perhaps John Jones wants a printed copy to show to his accountant. All that remains is setting up the **output presentation format** for the values and calculated figures as money, in dollars and cents. Then the finished, polished version can be saved on diskette or sent to a printer. Format options for numerical data common in spreadsheet software include rounded whole numbers, others with a certain number of decimal places, monetary amounts, and percentages. Jones can print not only the final version of the tax return with values (Figure 7-6), but a copy showing the **attributes**—a skeleton that displays all the labels, values, formulas, and functions (Figure 7-4). An attribute copy is useful for error checking if something seems out of order. All of the presentation features of the finished tax spreadsheet in Figure 7-6, including the colors, the currency choice, and the centering of the names in columns A and B, as well as the attribute formats, are available in Lotus 1-2-3 for Windows as options under the Style menu at the top. Spreadsheet programs today provide a full array of choices for printing out the data encoded in a worksheet.

## ▶ Uses for a Spreadsheet

Some rows of the tax spreadsheet contain text materials, and others hold numbers needed by arithmetic rules, so that at the end the program can calculate either a refund or the amount of tax owed. The formulas and functions of the worksheet take on meaning when the values of income, interest, exemptions, and tax withheld are entered. Because the spreadsheet embodies the relationship of all these values in determining tax liability, it can be used for *time-saving recalculation* if the data change. Suppose Jones forgets to include an interest amount of $30 on line 8. As soon as he changes this value from $360 to $390, the program automatically recalculates all the subsequent figures and comes up with a lowered refund of $121.50 (see Figure 7-7). All the cell relationships on the tax return remain active. Changing the interest figure has a ripple effect through the subsequent lines, adjusting everything along the way. The electronic spreadsheet eliminates the need for the user to refigure anything when the initial relationships have been properly set up. This feature of remaining dynamic, and thus changing with new data, constitutes the spreadsheet's greatest power.

## ELECTRONIC CUT AND PASTE

Jones can also use the completed worksheet for planning next year's schedule for withholding tax. First he makes a copy of the current cell settings and formulas in column C, to be used for next year, with the electronic cut and paste feature of the program. Of the several hundred possible columns available in the software, currently only columns A and B have been used. Using a mouse or cursor key to highlight the cells of col-

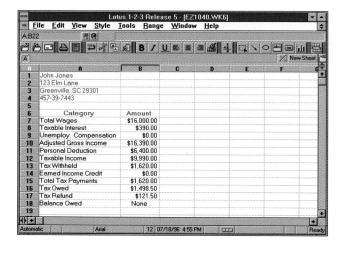

**FIGURE 7-7** The tax return including the revised interest payment of $390. Note that all of the subsequent relationships are recalculated by the spreadsheet as soon as the interest figure is changed.

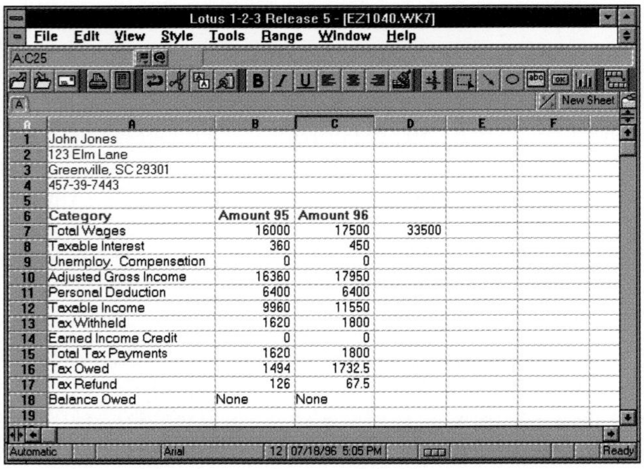

**FIGURE 7-8** The use of a spreadsheet for what-if scenarios. The spreadsheet relationships for 1995 have been copied into a third column for 1996170, and new figures have been included for tax planning.

umn B, he does a cut and paste, or block move, and moves the material to column C.

But electronic cut and paste in spreadsheets differs significantly in one important way from the parallel word processing feature. In word processing, the copied text is reproduced exactly in its new location in the document. In the spreadsheet, only the numerical values are copied exactly in the new column. The formulas and functions in column B, such as rows 10, 12, 15, 17, and 18, reference other cells in column B. As the software copies these formulas and functions into column C, *it automatically replaces references to B cells with the equivalent C cells.* Whereas B10 contains the formula +B7+B8+B9, cell C10 now reads +C7+C8+C9. The software carefully preserves the relationships for another column of cell data. The dynamic relationships between money figures for the current year have been moved over to another column, for the next year. Since Jones has copied the same values for income, interest, withholding, and so on, to column C, of course, the two columns at present contain the same figures.

Before proceeding, Jones can adjust the labels in cells B6 and C6 to Amount 95 and Amount 96, to distinguish them clearly from each other (Figure 7-8). He can also use column D to sum up rows of data in the same way that he has been doing with columns. For instance, putting the formula "+B7+C7" in cell D7 will sum up the total income for two years ($33,500). The spreadsheet allows the user total flexibility in what information to calculate where.

### WHAT-IF SCENARIOS

**what-if scenario:** Using a spreadsheet as a prediction device by making changes to data in some cells to see what impact they have on the overall spreadsheet.

In column C Jones can now estimate his income and interest for the coming year, to see how the current amount of withholding will affect his total tax liability. Testing different possibilities by changing figures within a worksheet is called a **what-if scenario,** a powerful simulation application of the spreadsheet. The name connotes the kind of question that can be asked with a completed worksheet. With expected income increases for the next year, Jones may wonder what will happen if he leaves the amount of withholding alone. Assuming the same rate of tax, he can simulate next year's situation before making the withholding decision. He types his new estimated income (17,500) and interest values (450) into cells C7 and C8, and the software refigures all the other C rows accordingly.

The spreadsheet estimates the tax for 1996 to be $1732.50. Jones may want to increase the withholding so that he will owe less tax on April 15 of the following year, or even get a refund. For instance, Figure 7-8 shows that increasing withholding to 1800 will still yield a small refund of $67.50. Using the spreadsheet to test a what-if scenario for insight, Jones can play around with estimated values to come up with an acceptable strategy for tax planning. Applying the what-if scenario to next year's estimated figures in column C makes the spreadsheet a powerful aid to Jones' future financial planning. Meanwhile, his original column B, for the present year, is intact.

## GRAPHIC OPTIONS

Programs like Lotus 1-2-3 have been described as integrated packages, because they bundle several kinds of applications software together into one product. Although Lotus 1-2-3's major strength has always been its spreadsheet, it does offer features for constructing databases and graphing data. Often a pictorial representation of data is easier and clearer to understand than columns of figures. Even spreadsheets not as integrated as Lotus 1-2-3 usually provide the ability to graph the data from the worksheet.

In our example, Jones may want to illustrate his income growth for the two years, now in columns B and C, as a line or bar graph or pie chart. Using either the mouse or cursor keys, he highlights the two figures in row 7 and picks the graphing option of his choice. The program then enters its graphics mode and creates the graph, with a scale of values along the side. Jones can label the axes, add a title, and print the graph, just as he did earlier on the worksheet.

In more complex spreadsheets, users can create overlapping bar charts or make a series of pie charts to show trends over several years or categories. Spreadsheet programs that run on machines using the GUI (Macintosh, OS/2, Microsoft Windows, Unix workstations) provide considerable choice and versatility in graph presentation, including color output to a screen or printer.

## TYPICAL USES

Planning activities that have been widely adapted to the spreadsheet include budgeting and proposal drafting. For instance, the owner of a small business may encode the costs of materials, labor, and overhead for a con-

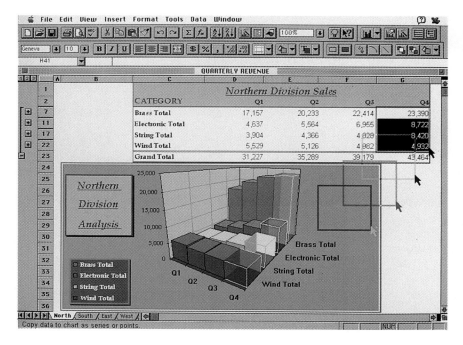

**FIGURE 7-9** This Excel spreadsheet (Microsoft) for Macintosh has been graphed as a colorful stacked bar graph.

tract bid into a spreadsheet and let the software figure the bottom line on profit or loss. Then figures can be readjusted to make an attractive proposal. Perhaps the owner can find materials at a lower price from another vendor and decrease his costs accordingly. Or he can decide whether to lower the profit margin to get a lower bid, or leave it alone and hope for a greater profit from the job. Playing around with the figures and what-if scenarios when all the data relationships have been captured and encoded in the spreadsheet has generally been the major attraction of this software. Changing values leads to automatic recalculation of other variables dependent on them.

## SPECIAL-PURPOSE SPREADSHEETS

The general usefulness of the spreadsheet concept has led to the development of special-purpose software in fields like tax planning and preparation and personal finance management. In the late 1980s, the first template programs appeared for doing taxes in Lotus 1-2-3. Designers mapped the look of the federal and some state income tax forms onto the popular spreadsheet software and worked out all the arithmetic relationships ahead of time. People owning Lotus 1-2-3 and already familiar with its use could buy the templates, load them into the general package, and then fill in their returns directly on screen. Some programs allowed completed returns to be printed out and sent to the IRS. Special-purpose software that is piggybacked onto already established applications software by a new set of developers is called **value-added software** (Badgett).

The bit-mapped graphic approach of the Macintosh and Windows computers has fostered the most comprehensive programs of this kind, called MacInTax and TurboTax (Intuit). MacInTax has received recognition for its excellence from magazines like *Byte* and *InfoWorld*. A standalone application not dependent on any other spreadsheet, MacInTax incorporates the federal short and long tax forms and all the complex

**value-added software:** Software in which additional customized features have been added to a base program, such as a tax preparation program in which a series of tax-form templates and formulas have been added to a basic spreadsheet.

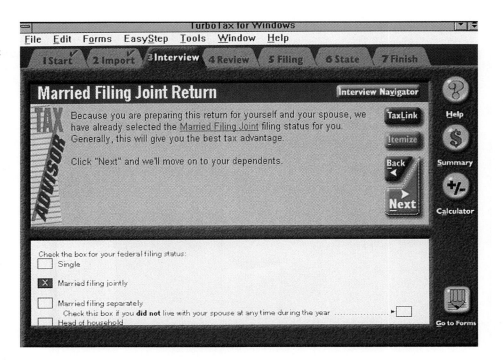

**FIGURE 7-10** Recent editions of TurboTax (Intuit) include tax advice, based on information the user has put into the program.

## TECHNOLOGICAL PERSPECTIVE

### Spreadsheet Applications in Science

Today the technology of the spreadsheet is widely understood and accepted in the worlds of business and personal computing. Once users understand how to map their information onto the format of rows and columns and then to express relationships among the data with formulas and functions, they can think of a variety of applications besides financial worksheets and teachers' grade books.

An article by Brian Hayes in *Scientific American* (October 1983) suggested several scientific phenomena that could be simulated with spreadsheets. The Game of Life, devised by John H. Conroy, simulates the growth and death of a colony of living cells in a grid pattern, according to a set of rules based on the eight possible neighbors each cell has. If there are two or three neighbors, the cell will survive into the next generation. With fewer, it will die of loneliness; with more, it will die of starvation and overcrowding. The spreadsheet grid pattern makes checking the status of neighboring cells easy (either 1 for a neighbor or 0 for none), so that several generations of grids can be readily calculated and stored. Spreadsheets with functions for generating random numbers can also test "percolation" processes, like the brewing of coffee and the spread of infectious diseases and forest fires.

More recently many college chemistry classes have adopted the spreadsheet for student experiments. Not only can calculations required for experiments be rapid and reliable, but students can create graphs effortlessly that reflect their data and experimental results (Edwards, McKay, and Sink). At the University of Arkansas students carry out experiments on a computer wired to record data automatically in the lab; the data are then already in the machine and ready for analysis with spreadsheet software. Experiments involve counting nuclear decay and study of acid/base titrations, a subject hard to demonstrate in an easily controlled environment. In the titration experiment, the computer notes the pH meter readings as the titrant material is added to the mixture manually. Titration curves for the collected data can then be graphed directly with the spreadsheet program and the relationships clearly seen (Durham).

Of course, spreadsheets are not designed specifically for these applications. Yet the built-in grid pattern, the ability to program individual cells, and the easy graphing capabilities facilitate even this sort of scientific activity in the spreadsheet.

---

schedules into one package, along with worksheets for users to list deductions by category and on-line help in filling out all the forms. MacInTax also offers a version for state and local tax preparation for every state having an income tax.

On the screen of the computer the user can open each of the MacInTax schedules in graphic form, just as they look in the printed versions. In true spreadsheet fashion, when figures are typed onto the appropriate lines, the program automatically adjusts other lines that are dependent on them. Sometimes these calculations take place on schedules that are not even opened up as windows on screen. For instance, the allowable medical deduction on Schedule A of the itemized 1040 long form must exceed a percentage of the adjusted gross income, calculated on the 1040 form itself. Only medical expenses above that amount are deductible (7.5 percent in 1995). As the user adds financial data to the 1040 form and arrives at the adjusted gross income, the program takes the percentage of the adjusted gross income and inserts it into Schedule A—before the user gets there.

Taxpayers can continue to tinker with deductions and various tax schedules until all their forms are finished and saved on disk. Even if income is forgotten until the last minute, the program refigures everything from there down, possibly involving several hundred calculations. What a saving of time and hassles over the manual method of filling out a return! Then with a laser printer, the saved files become handsome tax printouts that look like the government originals; only signatures are required before they are ready to send to the IRS. MacInTax is a big program that includes the tax forms, lots of on-line help, the spreadsheet calculation formulas, and options for printing once the figures are inserted. But at base it is a well-designed, special-purpose spreadsheet.

**FIGURE 7-11** A small sample of an Improv spreadsheet for Windows. The rows and columns are labeled by natural categories like optical goods arranged by sales year and region.

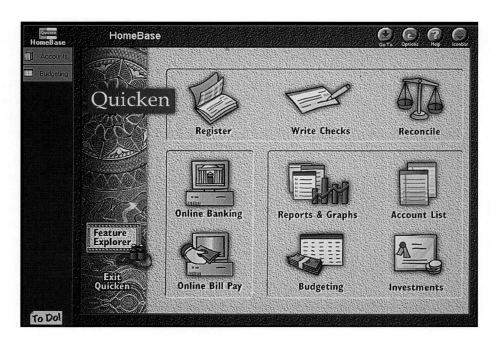

## FUTURE TRENDS

**HISTORY**

What is the future of the spreadsheet concept for the next few years? One answer was suggested by a Lotus product called Improv, which first appeared in 1990. Early reviewers received Improv as a major leap forward in what seemed a mature software application. Improv's main innovation released users from the constraint of thinking of cells in terms of rows and columns designated by letters and numbers (cells A3 and B7, for example). It allows users to define cells in a more natural way, with their own labels, just as they would if they were designing a table or grid on a piece of paper.

For instance, in the tax example, Jones could designate his rows directly, by their category names (removing column A completely), and redo his column labels as two years, 1995 and 1996. Then the correct cell to insert the income for 1995 would become Total Wages:95, and the equivalent for 1996, Total Wages:96. Users can think in English-language categories that make sense to them, rather than be tied to cell addresses like B7 and C7. Clearly, this is more like the way people organize data. Improv avoids the pitfall of getting lost in a large spreadsheet with many rows and columns, because the user just calls for information by named categories separated by a colon. Although this new way of structuring data was pioneering, the approach has not been widely adopted by other vendors; and the program has not been a runaway success.

More suggestive of the way that spreadsheet applications seem to be heading is the growing importance of personal financial software, especially the highly successful example of Quicken, a true "killer app" from Intuit with five million copies sold in its first decade. Quicken does all the things one might expect: write checks, balance the checkbook, give reminders about upcoming bills, set up a household budget, keep track of investments, draw charts or print reports to show how one's money is managed. Its check-writing application even has an "intelligent" mode that guesses the likely party to whom the check is to be addressed based on the first few letters that the user enters. Some enthusiastic users say that they decided to buy a personal computer because of this software alone, an argument that many people used to make because of word processing (Kantrowitz).

Like the rest of computing, this special-purpose spreadsheet application began adding a variety of on-line features to recent versions of the software in 1995. Quicken for Windows even offers Netscape so that users can access its World Wide Web site. More importantly, financial data for the Quicken program to manage is now available for the home user who has an account at a growing number of national banks, including American Express, Citibank, and First Chicago. Using their modems, home customers can see whether a check has cleared, download their checking and credit card statements, transfer funds among accounts, and have payments made automatically or by request. Many of the services of the local bank are at one's fingertips through the keyboard of the personal computer. As customers retrieve their records, they can be automatically sorted into the Quicken categories, such as medical or business expenses for later use in filing tax returns—a value-added feature not available from the local bank. One reviewer wryly commented that these extensions suggest that the era of on-line banking is near at hand, but even with color printers Quicken still cannot print cash at home (Manes).

**INTERNET**

Today the Internet is increasingly the link connecting all aspects of the Computer Triangle. The evolving on-line features of Quicken for home users suggest the broadening appeal of joining what was once a stand-alone application with the outer financial world through data communications. Personal computer users are moving to the center of the banking world via their modems and Quicken software.

**SOCIETY**

## ▶ Summary

As we have seen, the spreadsheet was developed for a practical need, the analysis of changing financial data. Many applications call for tabular arrangement of data, the row-and-column format; and the spreadsheet's ability to express relationships among cells by referring to addresses rather than to data values added generality and power to its features. Soon a lot of people saw that the "live" electronic cells fit a host of what-if activities in budgeting, planning, and simulation. Spreadsheets have been a runaway hit in personal computer software. Users who understand the basic elements of the active, computable cell find it easy to match applications to their own needs. Now considered standard software, spreadsheets and derivative software in the future perhaps will become more "user friendly" like Improv or more on-line like Quicken. Spreadsheet programs have a secure niche in the software market; people can expect continued improvements in their features and usability in the coming years.

## ▶ Key Terms

attribute (p. 164)

cell (p. 158)

dynamic (p. 158)

electronic spreadsheet (p. 157)

final formatting (p. 160)

formula (p. 158)

function (p. 162)

label (p. 160)

Lotus 1-2-3 (p. 159)

macro (p. 163)

output presentation format (p. 164)

range (p. 163)

value (p. 160)

value-added software (p. 168)

VisiCalc (p. 157)

what-if scenario (p. 166)

worksheet (p. 159)

 *Self-Test*

**MULTIPLE-CHOICE**

1. The first spreadsheet was developed to meet what need?
   a. calculating personal income taxes
   b. projecting budgets for corporate growth
   c. automating accounting homework assignments
   d. forecasting growth rates of inflation

2. Characteristic features of a spreadsheet include all of the following except
   a. defined titles for rows and columns
   b. horizontal rows and vertical columns of data
   c. active cells for data storage
   d. the ability to store relationships between numerical data

3. In terms of computer functions we have already identified, which one is not built into the old-style accounting ledger sheet but is included in a spreadsheet?
   a. input
   b. output
   c. storage
   d. processing

4. Which of the following everyday applications is appropriate for development on a spreadsheet?
   a. a teacher's grade book
   b. itemized business invoices
   c. baseball standings
   d. all of the above

5. Typical types of functions placed in cells of a spreadsheet include all of the following except
   a. averaging numbers
   b. indexing words by subject
   c. sorting text fields of data alphabetically
   d. calculating trigonometric functions for scientific and mathematical data

6. A spreadsheet displayed on the screen in attribute format will show
   a. labels
   b. formulas
   c. values
   d. all of the above

7. Which one of the following applications does not seem appropriate for a what-if scenario using a spreadsheet?
   a. flight training in graphic simulation
   b. proposal drafting for a contract job
   c. estimating taxes for the next year
   d. John Conway's simulation called the Game of Life

8. Which of the following features of new versions of Quicken represents an innovation compared to standard personal financial management software?
   a. automatic balancing of the checkbook
   b. help with budgeting
   c. on-line banking accounts
   d. portfolio analysis

## TRUE/FALSE

9. **T   F**   The original spreadsheet was developed by Dan Bricklin and his associates while he was in graduate school.

10. **T   F**   The practical success of VisiCalc is often credited with the wide acceptance of the **IBM PC** by the business community.

11. **T   F**   The term for a spreadsheet in process is a starter.

12. **T   F**   Grouping several row or column elements together in a function such as SUM is called specifying a range.

13. **T   F**   Electronic cut and paste in spreadsheets is identical in function to cut and paste in word processing.

14. **T   F**   What-if scenarios are a kind of simulation carried out with a spreadsheet.

15. **T   F**   Personal finance management programs are value-added, special-purpose spreadsheet software.

16. **T   F**   Many reviewers believe that the next generation of spreadsheet technology will resemble the Quicken software from Intuit.

## FILL-IN

17. The individual elements in the electronic grid or matrix of a spreadsheet are called its _____.

18. The data in spreadsheets, such as a set of text scores to be averaged, are called _____ in spreadsheet terminology.

19. Because of the _____ nature of a spreadsheet, when a number changes in one cell, any calculations that depend on it are refigured automatically in other cells.

20. The feature that operates on data values in cells and gives the spreadsheet its processing power is called a _____.

21. Some spreadsheets allow users to write their own customized functions, which are called _____.

22. _____ is probably the most popular spreadsheet package ever developed.

23. Using a spreadsheet for insight, to test a hypothesis with new data without messing up the original design, is called a _____.

24. Some tax preparation software provides add-on _____ with prepared formats and formulas, so users can do their taxes using Lotus 1-2-3.

## ▶ Experiential Exercises

1. Today the VisiCalc spreadsheet, developed by Dan Bricklin and his friends at Harvard and MIT, has been superseded by newer, fancier products. See what information you can find in the library about what happened to the VisiCalc product and its relationship to Lotus Corporation, the original producers of Lotus 1-2-3. Lotus was recently purchased by IBM Corporation.

2. Examine the features of spreadsheet programs available on your campus. Specifically, look up the variety of functions they offer, like SUM or AVERAGE, already programmed into the application. Talk to users to see which functions they often include in their spreadsheet formulas. Do they also write customized macros for frequently needed functions not provided by the software?

3. For people like business analysts and stockbrokers, the what-if scenario is one of the most important uses of the spreadsheet. Design a hypothetical scenario to allocate financial resources from different sources for financing a year at college. Assume that there are some stable savings for college, but that sources like summer jobs and government loans will vary from year to year. If you know the total costs, you can play with a mixture of known and variable funds to see what each must contribute to meet your financial needs. The point is to vary different funding categories according to an idea, such as "What if I could only make $2000 in the summer," and see how that variable will affect other financial sources. Try different scenarios, and report your results to your teacher (and perhaps your parents).

4. During the 1992 presidential campaign, Ross Perot made the "info-mercial" advertisement famous. Mr. Perot illustrated his points repeatedly with color charts of wages, employment trends, growth of government spending, and so on. A computer industry leader himself, Mr. Perot probably had the charts created with computer programs. Much commentary on his campaign discussed the usefulness of so many charts. Investigate some of the press accounts of the campaign. What was the consensus on the effectiveness of the charts?

5. Special-purpose software for tax preparation is based on the application of spreadsheet principles to the various lines of federal tax returns, like the 1040EZ form illustrated in the text. Go to a computer store and examine such a tax package. What other software features, such as word processing, graphics, or data communications, are built into the program? If you know anyone who uses a tax program to calculate and file a return, interview the person about what its best features are.

6. Investigate other kinds of special-purpose spreadsheets, including those for personal finances, budgeting, accounting, and investment in stocks and bonds. Some are for individuals and others for various professions, such as physicians and lawyers. Try to find and critique the features of at least one such program.

7. Look up one of the articles in the bibliography about spreadsheet uses in scientific experimentation. Consult your science department to see if anyone there is using a spreadsheet program for a research or educational application (not just for budgeting).

8. The Lotus program called Improv offers a rethinking of some of the basic concepts of the spreadsheet. To date, it has not been the great hit that Lotus 1-2-3 was when it came out. Trace the reception of Improv in computer magazines, and ask around on your campus to see if anyone is using it. Can you determine why it has not been as much of a success as its predecessor? Is there such an investment in materials prepared in original spreadsheet formats that people will not consider redoing their applications?

# ▶ Critical Thinking Exercises

1. Can you think of another idea, like the spreadsheet, that someone dreamed up to meet a practical need which turned out to have widespread application? It does not have to be in the computer field.

2. The appeal of the spreadsheet has been its general applicability to many problems. Think of at least three other applications that fit naturally into its row-and-column format, besides the teacher's grade book and the tax return.

3. Given the college financing scenario described in Experiential Exercise 3, think about the best ways to present the material graphically to your teacher or perhaps to a college loan officer. Charting options in most spreadsheets offer a wide range of possibilities, including line and bar graphs and pie charts. Which ones are most appropriate for making a case that you need more loan or scholarship money?

**ANSWERS TO SELF-TEST**

*Multiple-Choice*: 1. c;    2. a;    3. d;    4. d;    5. b;    6. d;    7. a;
8. c
*True/False*: 9. T;    10. F;    11. F;    12. T;    13. F;    14. T;    15. T;
16. T
*Fill-in*: 17. cells;    18. values;    19. dynamic;    20. formula;    21.
macros;    22. Lotus 1-2-3;    23. what-if scenario;    24. templates

# CHAPTER 8

# Databases

▶ **LEARNING OUTCOMES**

*After completing this chapter, you should be able to:*

1. *Use essential database concepts, including files, records, fields, and keys, to sort, search, and report information.*

2. *Construct a database application, including field definitions and encoding methods.*

3. *Use Boolean operations to search for information in a database.*

4. *Describe the three common types of database organization: relational, hierarchical, and networked.*

5. *Examine different database interfaces and judge their user friendliness.*

6. *Discuss the societal implications of amassing large private databases, and explain the importance of data integrity and security.*

▶ **COMPUTERS IN CONTEXT**

*During World War II, Dr. John Mauchly and J. Presper Eckert built one of the first computers, called ENIAC, in order to calculate rocket trajectories and artillery firing tables for the Army. After the war, they foresaw a host of nonmilitary applications for their machine, whose successor became the first commercial computer, UNIVAC I. Yet some forecasters in the early 1950s were not as prescient as Mauchly and Eckert; in fact, they predicted that about six mainframe scientific computers could handle the number of users and applications that would need them (*The Machine That Changed the World*, WGBH television series, 1992).*

*It was the growth of* data processing *in the 1950s that set off the explosion of early computing which has continued unabated to the present. After the appearance of UNIVAC I in 1951, business and government soon discovered that these early mainframe machines could store, process, update, retrieve, and print out their records of financial accounts, personnel files, tax information, and inventory records—to name only a few instances. These first programs often combined features of financial accounting and record filing, which we associate today with spreadsheets and database systems. Principles of database management—the filing, maintenance, retrieval, and reporting of information kept in data banks—are now well defined in the large field of computing called* information retrieval. *Today programs abound for personal computers that can handle a great variety of data types and situations.*

**FIGURE 8-1** Mauchly and Eckert with ENIAC, the computer designed in World War II for defense work that became the forerunner of UNIVAC I, the first commercial computer in 1951.

## ▶ Essential Features of Databases

All databases share common ideas. They are structured so that they can be sorted and searched for relevant information stored within them. To get a sense of database concepts, look at a few examples. A university keeps its transcript records in a large database. Included are each student's name; student number; addresses both at home and on campus; class standing and major field; and a list of current courses and courses already taken, with grades. Similarly, a department store has personnel records with employees' addresses; number of dependents for tax withholding; salaries; and applicable benefit plans. The Internal Revenue Service has similar files, with addresses; social security numbers; wages and salaries reported on W-2 forms; tax filing status (single or joint); number of dependents; and medical and charitable expenses. In libraries, the card catalog records information about each book: author, title, subject, publisher, copyright date, and call number. Social scientists doing public opinion surveys often collect data in categories like age, sex, race, political party, geographical location, and income.

### FILES, RECORDS, AND FIELDS

All these applications share common database ideas. Every **record** needs one main identifying **field,** called the **key,** to which associated information is attached. The college transcript probably uses the student number as the key. Otherwise, confusion can arise with common last names, like Smith and Lopez: in any large group, several Betty Smiths and Jose Lopezs may be present. Associated with the student number field are various other fields, identified by the category of information they contain: last name, first name and middle initial, street address, city, state, ZIP code, campus address, college class, departmental major, completed courses and grades, and current courses. Other fields may also warrant inclusion in the student's record: parents' names and addresses, status in or out of state, or campus honors. Each institution defines its fields to fit its own needs.

Building the data **file** of student information means creating a record for each person, accessed by a key, within which there are a number of fields of information. Files contain records, which contain fields. Each field contains data stored as characters of information, which is typically

**record:** A collection of related fields comprising one item in a data file, such as a complete book record in an on-line catalog.

**field:** A basic unit of information contained in a record, such as a name or street address in a mailing list created as a database.

**key:** The main identifying field in a data record to which associated information is attached, such as a student number for college records.

**file:** A collection of records in a database related to each other.

**FIGURE 8-2** Like student records, payroll information in a company is stored in a database file, composed of records and fields.

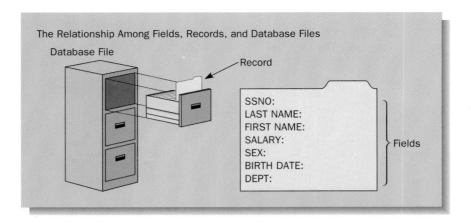

**database:** A collection of related files stored electronically that can be edited, joined, sorted, and searched.

either textual or numerical. A large **database** contains a number of data files, organized according to these principles.

For example, a data file of books in a library usually is keyed to the field containing the call number, which is unique for every record. Some other fields are the obvious ones taken from the traditional catalog card: author's last name, first name, book title, publisher, place of publication, date of publication, and subject headings (there may be several subfields in this category). If this data file is a part of a larger database for an automated circulation system, there may also be a separate data file that includes fields for status (checked out or in), due date if appropriate, location among several libraries, and number of copies. A common key, the book's call number, will probably link these two files in the database. In a similar way, the personnel database in a department store will have fields for names and addresses, along with deductions for dependents, benefits, and wage or salary data.

## SORTS

Organizing information into databases does not differ in concept from putting it on index cards and storing the cards in filing cabinets. But a com-

**FIGURE 8-3** Students access the on-line book catalog at colleges and schools using personal computers on a library network. The catalog itself is a large database.

puterized database allows greater flexibility in management of the content than a card-based file. People usually develop databases for **sorting, searching,** and **reporting** information. A software system designed to carry out these functions, which allows users to control and access information, is called a **database management system (DBMS).** The books in a library database may be sorted according to alphabetical order (of the authors' last names) or by call number, normally either the Dewey decimal system or the Library of Congress classification. Going through a card catalog, merged alphabetically by author, title, and subject, to sort all the cards by call number would be a very time-consuming and tedious process by hand.

Yet re-sorting the computer database of library materials is easy with database management software. The user instructs the program to sort the information in the field for call number in numerical order (for the Dewey decimal system) or alphabetical order (for the Library of Congress classification). Fast-sorting algorithms process the call numbers in that field, and the rest of the information about each book tags along. The program orders the library books into a list sorted by call number, which can be scanned on screen or printed out, along with any other information about the book desired by the user, such as author or title. This sorted list can be saved as a new index file.

Note that both files contain exactly the same information, but each has been ordered differently. Whenever a book's record is processed for sorting in one field, all of its information comes trailing along. The complete bibliographical record for each book is reordered into a new data file, but not destroyed in the original. Rearranging index cards in a file cabinet would destroy their original order. Compared to the process of copying the cards before sorting, which would be slow, boring, and prone to error, re-sorting and renaming copies of data files is a standard computer database operation.

**sorting:** Arranging records in a file according to a specified sequence, such as alphabetically or numerically, from lowest to highest.

**searching:** The process of setting up a search request and retrieving information in a database that fulfills the request, a standard feature of all database software.

**reporting:** The process of printing or displaying information contained in a database, often the last step in database management.

**database management system (DBMS):** Software used to create, maintain, retrieve, and produce reports about information kept in databases.

## SEARCHES

It is in searching that the advantages of the computerized database over the index card file become even more apparent. As part of a genealogical project, suppose you want to retrieve all books by people named Brown or Smith that were published in New York before 1850. First you go to the part of the file where books by authors named Brown are kept. Next you check each record for publication in New York prior to 1850 and record the results. Then you repeat the process for Smith. With database software, the search involves looking for information in several fields but can be set up just once, as follows:

Author: Brown or Smith

Place of publication: New York

Date of publication: before 1850

The program then goes through the segmenting of the database for you, according to a series of decisions that we can diagram in a flowchart as a series of yes-no questions in decision boxes (see Figure 8-4). The computer looks at each bibliographical record, one at a time, and applies the questions to it. Initially the author field is tested for Brown or Smith, then for New York, and finally for a date before 1850. Whenever one of the questions comes up negative, the record is skipped. Only records that pass all the tests are recorded and printed as answers to the search query. Meanwhile, nothing in the original database is destroyed or even moved around. What might take 30 or more minutes in a large university catalog can be accomplished in the computer catalog in a few seconds, before the manual search can even

**FIGURE 8-4** A flowchart illustrates the database decision process involved in searching for books by authors named Brown or Smith and published in New York before 1850.

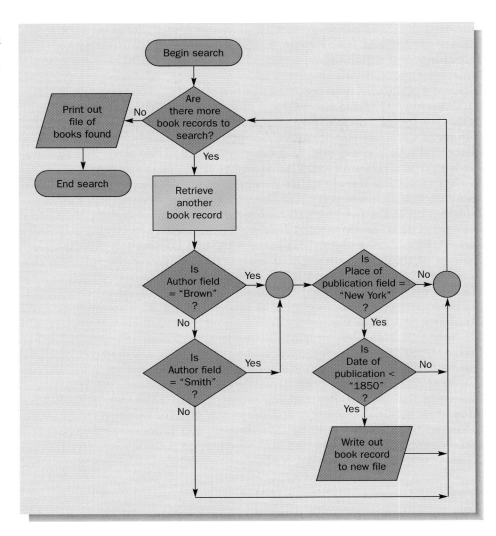

get started. No matter how many fields need to be examined, the program automatically segments the database for optimal searching.

Sorts and searches in the other applications already discussed are readily apparent. A college may want to find all the sophomores majoring in journalism who have a high grade-point average for consideration for a departmental award. Or the IRS may need to find single taxpayers with incomes over $100,000, and charity contributions of more than $20,000, for auditing. A company may search its personnel records for the names and addresses of employees with children, to write to them about a new day-care benefit package. And the social scientist can re-sort and query her survey data according to geographical, gender, and racial categories.

## ▶ Building a Database

Before database users can do sorts and searches with their files, they face important decisions about the structure of the database that will determine its effectiveness. Data definition and encoding methods are keys to future ease of use of the information contained in the database.

### DEFINING A DATABASE

A person designing a database, no matter what the application, must carefully consider the fields of information which will be associated together as each record, before any records are encoded. Some records may contain text, like names and addresses, while others may contain numerical information, like library call numbers, dates, or salary figures. Sometimes codes are used for certain fields (M and F for sex; I or O for in-state or out-of-state); these fields need be only one character long—a saving over spelled-out forms like *male* and *female*. Other fields, like the name and street address, need to be longer, and accept information in either structured form (such as last name, first name, and middle initial) or free form (which allows insertion of names in any order). Some databases of periodical articles, like the ERIC files of educational research, even have a long free-form field that contains an abstract of each entry. Such fields may be several hundred characters long, and contain both character and numerical information. All these details about the number and type of data fields in each record make up the **data definition** of the file.

A DBMS is a general-purpose package that handles encoding of data, sorting, searching, and reporting of the results. One of the most popular, user-friendly DBMS programs for Windows personal computers is Paradox 7 (from Borland), which is capable of holding up to 2 billion records of 400 characters each, with appropriate memory hardware. Most personal computer users will never have databases that exceed these limits. To illustrate the process of defining and using a database, let us create a small catalog of a college student's music library in Paradox 7. Because all database software programs share similarities, Paradox 7 will serve to introduce a variety of general database principles.

Before encoding individual records, we must first decide on the kinds of information that we want to store in the file, for possible use later, and then define the data fields for them. In addition to a unique item number for each record, tape, or compact disk, we will want to include the name of the artist or group, the title, the kind of music, the format (record, tape, CD), the cost of the item, the dates of recording and purchase, and the store where it was bought.

Paradox 7 is a Windows 95 program controlled with icons and pull-down menus, which include options such as *File, Edit, View, Table,* and *Record.* All these commands are actions that can be used with any Paradox database. To define the music data file, called a **table** in Paradox, one chooses New/Table under the *File* menubar and then inserts the name of the file, called MUSICLIB, in the Create Table window which pops up on the screen. The program then opens up a new window and asks the user to create all the data fields of the new table. This process is called the data definition step. The user then must specify a name for each field, give its type (alphanumeric characters, numbers, currency, or dates), decide on a width for the character fields, and mark all key fields with an asterisk. A **key field** is one that later may be searched for specific values. At this point, the machine is asking for the characteristics of the data fields, not the actual information for any of the recordings.

Assume that the following recordings are representative of the collection:

The Carpenters, *The Singles 1969–73*

Boston Pops, *Pops in Space*

Beatles, *Yellow Submarine*

Paul Simon, *Graceland*

Hootie and the Blowfish, *Cracked Rear View*

To capture the kinds of information wanted for these recordings will require nine fields: Recording number, Artist, Title, Type, Format, Recording date, Purchase date, Cost, and Source. Designing the data field definitions in Paradox 7 is fairly straightforward:

**data definition:** The process of deciding on the number and characteristics of all the data fields in each record in the early stages of developing a database.

**table:** Another name for a flat file, an arrangement of data into rows and columns, in relational database design.

**key field:** A main field that can be used to create an index for fast, random-access retrieval of records.

| STRUCTURE | FIELD NAME | TYPE | SIZE | KEY |
|:---:|:---|:---:|:---:|:---:|
| 1 | Rec_no | S | | * |
| 2 | Artist | A | 25 | * |
| 3 | Title | A | 30 | * |
| 4 | Type | A | 2 | * |
| 5 | Format | A | 1 | * |
| 6 | Rec_date | S | | * |
| 7 | Purc_date | S | | * |
| 8 | Cost | $ | | * |
| 9 | Source | A | 20 | * |

**alphanumeric:** Data represented in both alphabetical and numeric form. For instance, in the address 367 Main Street, all characters are alphanumeric, whether numbers or letters.

After the name of each field, the user specifies whether the data will be character, numeric, or monetary; as the cursor is moved, a message window prompts the user about what information is needed (Fig. 8-5). All fields are given an asterisk (key fields) so they can later be searched for specific information. The first field, Rec_no (for Recording number), is labeled a numeric integer field (denoted by *S* for a short integer), whereas the Artist field is **alphanumeric.** The letter *A*, for alphanumeric data, refers to material that is stored as characters and can be sorted alphabetically. As defined, the Artist field will hold up to 25 characters of information, which can include numbers and punctuation. If 25 characters is not enough for a group's name, the user has two choices: to widen the field or abbreviate the name. The same applies to the Title field, defined initially as character data of up to 30 characters. Some graphics-based packages (Microsoft Works for Macintosh, ClarisWorks) even allow users to define the field size for dragging the mouse to the desired width. Quality database software also allows for redefinition of fields at a later time if the field definitions are not sufficient.

Fields 4 and 5 allow the user to save space by using abbreviations for the type of music and the format (record, tape, or compact disk). Type of music means rock, soul, rap, vocal, country, mood, classical, and so on. For these two fields, using a short coding scheme of one or two symbols rather than full words conserves both storage space in memory and typing

**FIGURE 8-5** Defining the fields of information for a small music library in Paradox 7 for Windows 95.

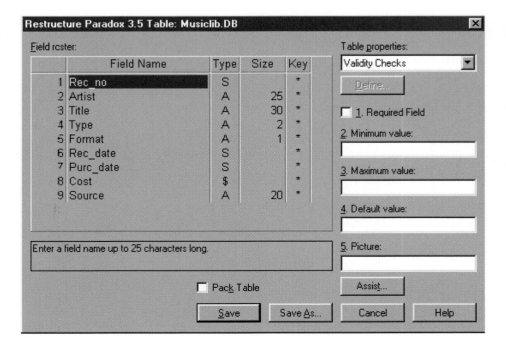

**Database Doomsday on January 1, 2000?**

Although the two-figure designation of years in a student's personal music library will not cause any serious problem when the year is encoded as 00, many important databases are in for serious problems because they record all year dates in two figures. As the century rolls around, computer clocks will pass from 12-31-99 to 01-01-00. Programs like databases in which sorting and searching depend on numerical comparisons will think that the year is 1900 again and make all kinds of erroneous calculations. For instance, bank statements will sort checks chronologically with those dated in the new year before those from 1999. It is even possible that the computer will think that a deposit made in late 1999 will have earned almost 100 years of interest! In this case, the human element in the Computer Triangle will be at risk because of hardware and software components.

The problem is caused by the common practice of storing dates in computers as six-figure numbers, which allows for only two digits for the year. When 99 turns over to 00, the computer will mistakenly assume that the cycle has begun all over. In this arithmetic 99 + 1 = 00 but 00 < 99. Using only two digits for the year means not having to type or store the others, since they have always been 1 and 9 during the computer age. Programming languages like COBOL define a year as a two-digit field.

Computer errors of this kind have already cropped up in databases for people who live to be a hundred. In 1992 a 104-year-old woman in Minnesota was notified that she was eligible for kindergarten since her database records showed that she was born in 88—assumed to be 1988, not 1888. Similarly a man who turned 101 got an insurance bill with a tripled premium because the program thought he was now a high-risk youthful driver of one-year-old. A Computer Risks Forum on the Internet regularly posts such glitches and discusses what to do at the turn of the century.

For modern systems the simple solution is to require that the year field of a date be four characters long, which will solve the problem until 10,000 A.D.! The biggest headaches are likely to occur in older computer programs that have been around for decades and are still used, the so-called dusty deck problem, for programs that go back to the punch card era. Some financial software at banks or insurance companies still in use today has its origins that long ago, even though their modern versions have been patched many times with new features and interfaces to users. Such huge legacy systems have been around so long that no one can remember how the original code was developed, and changing the date format may have other unforeseen consequences that cannot be apparent until the work has been started and thoroughly tested. Just as the turn of the calendar in the year 1000 was viewed with alarm in the Middle Ages because it might be the end of the world, so the turn of this computer millennium will cause disruption unless programmers get busy finding all of the program consequences of two-character dates in important systems and set about correcting them. As the Risk's Forum reminds its readers, it is not too soon to start (Hayes).

strokes in encoding the data. It makes no difference to the software whether the formats are encoded as character data (such as R, T, and C for records, tapes, and CDs) or numeric data (such as 1, 2, and 3). Probably one-letter abbreviations are better, because they are easier to remember when adding newly acquired recordings later. After some thought, we decide to use two characters for types of music, to avoid confusion with one-letter codes like C, which could stand for country or classical music; CO and CL are clearer, self-evident, and unambiguous.

The remaining fields follow readily. Dates of recording and purchase (Rec_date and Purc_date) will be two-digit numbers (89, 91, and so on) rather than full years. Paradox 7's designation of a date (the D field type) requires a full definition of month, day, and year—more detail than we need. We also do not need four digits for the year, even as we approach a change in century; 01 can be understood as 2001 as clearly as 89 is 1989 (there were no recordings in 1901). Because the Cost field is labeled as currency data, the program expects the data to be encoded in dollars and cents. The store where the recording was purchased (Source) is a character field, like Artist, of 20 characters in length.

We are now finished with the data definition and are ready to record this structure permanently. We have carefully considered the kinds of information about each recording that we want to keep for possible sorting and searching, and have worked to define a clear, unambiguous way of capturing it in a minimum number of characters, and thus keystrokes. Clicking the mouse on Done stores the permanent definition for the

MUSICLIB table. If we decide later to add other fields, Paradox 7 allows us to expand the record to accommodate them through its Restructure option under *Table* on the Main menubar.

## ENCODING DATA INTO THE DATABASE

**data entry:** The process of encoding data into fields to create database records.

We are now ready to begin typing in the actual information about our recordings, according to the field definitions we have made. **Data entry**, a standard function of all database software, is a choice accessible by two methods in Paradox 7: from Edit Data under *Table* menu or with the Edit Data icon (the pencil on the blank form) among the icon tools. Choosing either with the mouse opens a blank window for the newly defined MUSICLIB table. All the field names are displayed horizontally (though they may not all be seen at once on the screen), and are ready for information to be inserted using the keyboard and the cursor keys. The full entries for the first two recordings are displayed vertically here:

| | |
|---|---|
| Rec_no | 20 |
| Artist | The Carpenters |
| Title | The Singles 1969–73 |
| Type | VO |
| Format | T |
| Rec_date | 73 |
| Purc_date | 89 |
| Cost | 8.99 |
| Source | Record World |
| | |
| Rec_no | 21 |
| Artist | Boston Pops |
| Title | Pops in Space |
| Type | CL |
| Format | C |
| Rec_date | 80 |
| Purc_date | 91 |
| Cost | 16.99 |
| Source | Music Stax |

The input pattern is clear. The abbreviations are VO for Vocal, CL for Classical, T for Tape, and C for CD. The program presents the field names laid out horizontally on the input screen, so that data entry is simple and convenient. After every completed entry, the Enter key stores it and brings up another blank line for the next recording. If the input information is not typed according to the data definition (for instance, if a format is entered as CD, 2 characters rather than 1), the program will not accept it and will notify the user to correct it.

## SORTING THE FILE

Now that the database is in computer form, Paradox 7 becomes the tool for sorting and searching it for retrieval of information. A variety of ways to arrange and subdivide it are available. Perhaps the owner wants to sort the recordings in order of their date of production, with the newest ones at the top of the list. This is done in Paradox 7 by using the Sort option in the *Table* menu. First the program asks for a name for the new table to be created by the sorting process—here, MUSSORT1. Sorting in Paradox 7 creates a new table and leaves the original MUSICLIB table intact and unchanged. In the window that defines the MUSSORT1 table, the user chooses the field of information in the MUSICLIB file to be sorted—here the Rec_date field—and moves it to the Sort box by clicking the arrow. (see Figure 8-6).

The standard software sorting option is **ascending order,** which means that the Rec_date numerical field will be ordered from earlier to later years. Since an ordering with later dates listed first is wanted, the user must choose the **descending sort** option, overruling the default. Mouse clicks on two buttons will change the sorting order and activate the sort: Sort direction and OK. The new MUSSORT1 table is created, with the first entry being the one that was recorded last (see Figure 8-7). Paradox 7 allows the user to display the reordered list on the screen, edit the file further, or send it to an output device to get a printed copy.

One can even do **multiple-field sorting,** such as sorting items by recording date, and for instances of the same date, alphabetically by the name of the artist. In effect, this calls for two sorts, **primary** and **secondary,** one after the other. This process is very easy to specify in the Paradox 7 Sort window. The primary sort field, Rec_date, is moved to the Sort order window and set (first field, descending numerical order), and the secondary field, Artist, is then moved into the Sort order window below it. The program first reorders the index to the records by date, on the Rec_date field, and then sorts the resulting index alphabetically, in the Artist field, for dates that are the same. As a result, the two entries for 1980 will appear in alphabetical order, before any of the entries for earlier years. Incidentally, computers treat **alphabetical sorting** as sorting in ascending order, from A to Z, according to the ordered binary character codes for the letters (see Chapter 4). Typically database packages allow sorting according to any ordering scheme (ascending or descending, alphabetical or numerical), in several fields (primary, secondary, tertiary), according to the user's choice.

## SEARCHING FOR SPECIFIC RECORDS

Even more flexible and powerful are the searching, or information retrieval, possibilities of a database package like Paradox 7. Using the

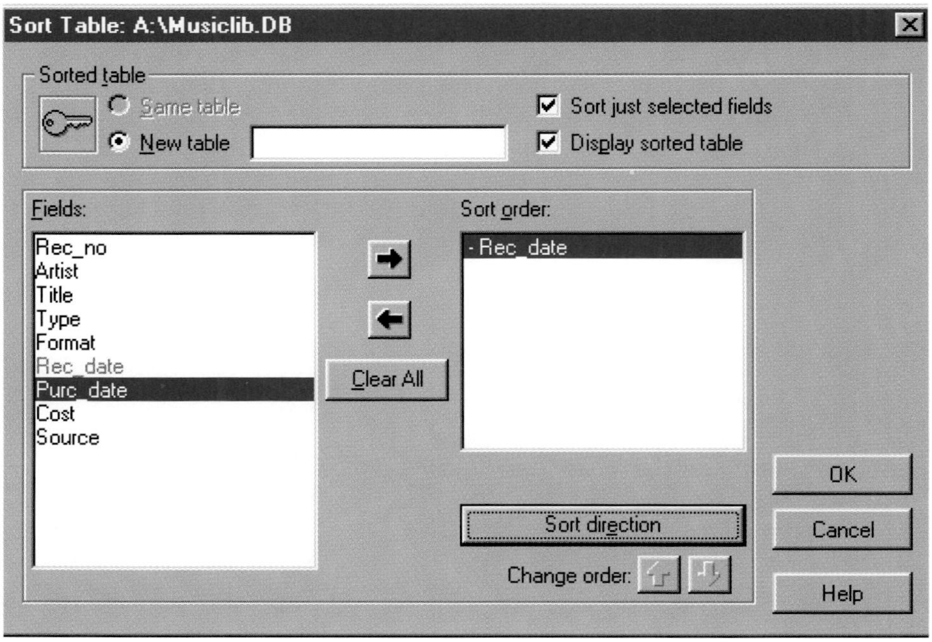

**ascending order:** Arrangement of data from lowest to highest in sequence.

**descending sort:** Arrangement of sorted data from highest to lowest in sequence.

**multiple-field sorting:** Sorting on two or more fields of information, one primary and the others secondary. For instance, in a mailing list database, a person may sort addresses by states, and then within states by ZIP code.

**primary sort:** The first field to be sorted in a database sorting operation.

**secondary sort:** A field in a database used for additional sorting after records have been arranged by the primary sorting operation on another field.

**alphabetical sorting:** Sorting records in a database in alphabetical order.

**FIGURE 8-6** Paradox 7 lists the fields of the music database for the user to set sorting options.

**FIGURE 8-7** Paradox 7 creates a new table called MUSSORT containing the results of sorting music in order of most recent recording date.

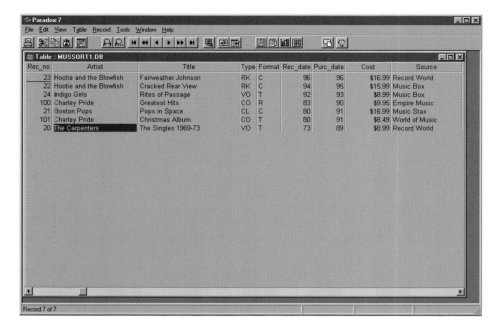

MUSICLIB table, we can find all country music titles, or just those performed by a particular artist or group, or recorded in a certain year or span of years. In effect, we can search in single or multiple fields, depending on what we want to know. For instance, suppose we want to find all the recordings in the library by Charley Pride. After the user chooses a new query under the *File* menu, the program requests first the name of the table to be searched. Given the name of the MUSICLIB file, Paradox 7 displays horizontally the list of fields created in the Data Entry process. We type Charley Pride in the Artist field and indicate all the fields we want to be displayed on the output screen. Thus a user can decide to see only the Artist and Title information, denoted with a check mark in the field, or all information for each Pride recording, by checking all the fields. When the display options have been set, choosing Run Query under the *Query* menu starts the search and retrieval process. Figure 8-8 displays both the search request for Charley Pride and the output in a Paradox Answer window, with three other fields checked: Rec_no, Title, and Rec_date. Of course, this window can also be printed or stored in a separate computer data file on disk.

Sometimes queries can get even more complicated than the example given earlier, of books by Smith or Jones published in New York before 1850. For instance, suppose the user wants to see only those country items recorded by Charley Pride in the period 1980–1985, but purchased in either 1989 or 1990. In this case, three fields of information need to be

**FIGURE 8-8** Results of a search in Paradox 7 for the recordings of Charley Pride. At the top the search for Pride in the Artist field is shown; below it, the results are shown with three additional fields of information, which have been checked in the search request: Rec_no, Title, and Rec_date.

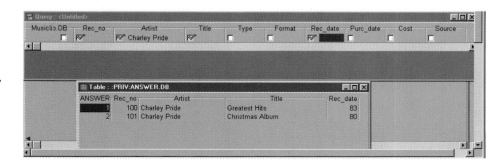

## TECHNOLOGICAL PERSPECTIVE

### Boolean Queries in the Arts and Sciences

People who use standard database software should become familiar with Boolean operators, named for the Irish mathematician George Boole, who first used them. **AND** (or **intersection**) and **OR** (or **union**) are often combined with a third operator, **NOT** (or **complement**) to carry out useful partitions of materials in databases. Commercial databases offering bibliographical services, like Lockheed DIALOG and on-line book catalogs and CD-ROM indexes to periodicals at university libraries, allow users to combine Boolean operations with the terms they are searching to narrow their searches. Lockheed DIALOG, for example, contains over 100 databases, most of them bibliographies like *Chemical Abstracts,* the Modern Language Association bibliography of modern literature, and the ERIC files of educational research. All of them can be queried for authors, titles, and content terms using Boolean operators.

Similarly, a university library catalog stored in a computer database may contain 2 or 3 million books. A student may be writing a paper on Alfred Tennyson and hypnotism. Her request "Author = Tennyson" will find all books for which Tennyson is the author's last name. If the student puts in "Subject = Tennyson," she will get references to all books about people named Tennyson. Limiting the search to "Tennyson, Alfred" in the query is the proper strategy, but even this can often elicit more than 100 references in a large library.

However, a request for "Tennyson, Alfred, and hypnotism" will separate out most references before they are shown on screen, and chances are good that the books identified will be the ones the student will find most relevant. The AND operator identifies only those books classified as being about *both* Alfred Tennyson *and* hypnotism. Out of 100 books about Tennyson and 300 about hypnotism, probably only a few are about both those subjects. The AND operator causes these titles to be "intersected" for display at the terminal. If the results are not satisfactory, the problem may lie more with improper subject classification of the Tennyson or hypnotism books than with the query submitted by the student.

Suppose the subject query is "Tennyson, Alfred, or hypnotism." Because the OR operation is inclusive, the student will be inundated with about 400 titles: all those about *either* subject, Tennyson or hypnotism. Of course, only a few of them will be relevant to the student's needs. The union operation is most useful in an early exploratory search, to get a sense of what is in a collection. If only a few titles show up, the wide net of the OR operation has found them. If the results are too many, then the user can begin to refine the query with AND and NOT, and focus the search on what is wanted.

NOT subdivides a category into those items that are and are *not* what is specified. For instance, an author search for "Tennyson not Alfred" will find books by other authors with that last name. Only the Tennyson authors who are not Alfred will be retrieved. Similarly, the query "Hypnotism not Freudian" will find titles about non-Freudian hypnosis. Understanding the use of Boolean operations, users of database systems—whether a software package like Paradox 7, a commercial bibliographic service like DIALOG, or an on-line catalog system in a library—can structure their requests to widen or narrow their search fields to zero in on what they want.

**AND (intersection):** A fundamental logical operator that retains only the elements that two sets of data have in common.

**OR (union):** A fundamental logical operator that combines all the elements of two sets of data into one larger set.

**NOT (complement):** A fundamental logical operator that retains only those elements of a set that are not specified. For instance, the NOT of Blue in the American flag is Red and White.

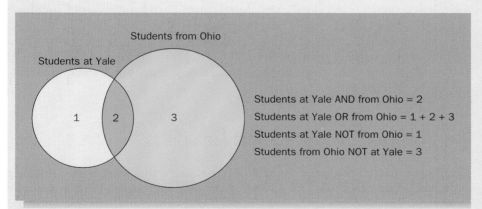

Students at Yale AND from Ohio = 2
Students at Yale OR from Ohio = 1 + 2 + 3
Students at Yale NOT from Ohio = 1
Students from Ohio NOT at Yale = 3

**FIGURE 8-9** A Venn diagram is often used to illustrate Boolean operations.

searched: Artist, Rec_date, and Purc_date. In the second and third fields, the values to be matched are not a simple choice (like Charley Pride as Artist). The year of the recording date can be any of the numbers 80–85, whereas the date of purchase must be either 89 or 90. We can paraphrase this search request in a structured English formula, as follows: "Retrieve all records with Artist equal to Charley Pride and Rec_date greater than 79

**Boolean operation:** One of the three logical operations AND, OR, and NOT, first used by George Boole, fundamental to doing searching in databases.

**numerical comparison operation:** A fundamental database operation, also found in programming languages, that compares two quantities for a relationship such as "less than" or "equal to."

**query by example (QBE):** A fill-in-the-blanks approach to building a database search, requiring a user to fill out a query form on the screen.

and less than 86 and Purc_date equal to 89 or 90." Here we combine for the first time the **Boolean operations** AND and OR and two operations of **numerical comparison,** *less than* ($<$) and *greater than* ($>$).

All these operations are needed for this search request in Paradox 7. After the *Ask* command has brought up the search screen, the user types the following terms in the three affected fields:

| Artist | Rec_date | Purc_date |
|---|---|---|
| Charley Pride | >79, <86 | 89 or 90 |

This search specification method is called **query by example (QBE),** a method in which a blank set of fields is filled in by the user with the data that are sought.

The search finds only one record that meets all the criteria:

| | |
|---|---|
| Rec_no | 100 |
| Artist | Charley Pride |
| Title | Greatest Hits |
| Type | CO |
| Format | R |
| Rec_date | 83 |
| Purc_date | 90 |
| Cost | 9.95 |
| Source | Empire Music |

It is displayed horizontally by field on the view screen, and can be saved or printed. Even more fields can be queried in one request, but searches are usually no more complex than this illustration. The key to creating such a request is thinking through it carefully, so that the requirements for each field can be easily and consistently encoded into the software query.

Compared to some other database packages, the rules in Paradox 7 for search requests are relatively simple to formulate. Full-featured database packages for personal computers, like Paradox 7, are very flexible in carrying out the basic elements of database management: data definition, data entry, sorting, searching, and reporting. They should be able to carry out fast and efficient sorts and searches, have a large capacity for data storage, and be easy and straightforward to use.

## ▶ Database Organization and Interfaces

Computer scientists who design databases are concerned with choosing appropriate database models and creating user interfaces. Decisions made in these areas will affect the ease and efficiency with which the intended audience of the software will be able to create and query database files with the program.

### DATABASE MODELS

Computer programmers who design database software and systems have done much research about the best ways to organize materials to maximize their efficiency in storage, sorting, and searching. Currently three models of database organization dominate the field: relational, hierarchical, and networked. Although nonspecialists do not need to know all the details, having some acquaintance with these models may help users to choose wisely if they need to select a database system. Most popular and well known today is the **relational,** or **tabular, model,** conceived in 1969 by Dr. Edgar F. Codd at IBM. Much commercial database software—like Paradox 7 or dBase IV (Borland)—is built on this idea, as are 4th Dimension (ACIUS) and FoxPro (Microsoft).

In the relational model, the fields of information for a record library would be organized within the computer as a series of tables in rows and columns. The software holds the relationships between the tables and manipulates them as needed for sorting and retrieval of data. In our Paradox 7 example, the MUSICLIB file was initially built as one table of nine fields. Resembling a spreadsheet, this one-table model is called a **flat file,** with columns for the fields and rows for each individual data record, containing the information about a single recording.

Large-scale database applications usually contain multiple tables of different, but related, information. We might have made three tables for the nine fields of music data—one for information about the recording; a second organized by kinds of music; and another for sales information, organized according to the store where a recording was purchased. The three tables might look like Figure 8-10.

Table 1 is related to Table 2 by having the artist field in common, and to Table 3 through its item number. The software would know that Table 1 connects the information found in Tables 2 and 3. The design of the relational model of multiple tables can be relatively simple and straightforward for the user; yet it owes its power to the relations that are defined between the tables. Because the basic structures of the model are flat-file tables of simple rows and columns, database software using this model is quite efficient and easy to design.

These characteristics do not apply as well to the other models. The **hierarchical model** works on the principle of the **family tree.** Computer scientists speak of grandparents, parents, and children in the tree structure when they talk about hierarchical systems. A sample tree, shown in Figure 8-11, for vocal recordings illustrates the idea. Branches of this structure represent recordings of vocalists. Parallel sections would branch off for other kinds of music, like rock or classical.

Although the structure is easy to understand, tracing down through the tree for queries that do not naturally fit the hierarchy can be time-consum-

**relational (tabular) model:** A design used in database systems in which relationships are created between one or more flat files or tables based on the idea that each pair of tables has a field in common.

**flat file:** A simple form of database consisting of one table of rows (records) and columns (fields) of data.

**hierarchical model:** A method for storing data in a database that looks like a family tree with one root and a number of branches or subdivisions.

**family tree:** A model for organizing a database in a hierarchical arrangement, with parent and children nodes.

**FIGURE 8-10** The music library presented as a relational database with three tables containing different fields of the information.

| TABLE 1 | | |
|---|---|---|
| **ITEM NUMBER** | **ARTIST** | **TITLE** |
| 20 | The Carpenters | The Singles 1969–73 |
| 21 | Boston Pops | Pops in Space |

| TABLE 2 | | | |
|---|---|---|---|
| **TYPE** | **FORMAT** | **ARTIST** | **RECORDING DATE** |
| VO | T | The Carpenters | 73 |
| CL | C | Boston Pops | 80 |

| TABLE 3 | | | |
|---|---|---|---|
| **STORE** | **ITEM NUMBER** | **PURCHASE DATE** | **COST** |
| Music Stax | 21 | 91 | 16.99 |
| Record World | 20 | 89 | 8.99 |

**FIGURE 8-11** A portion of the music library database arranged in a hierarchical tree structure diagram.

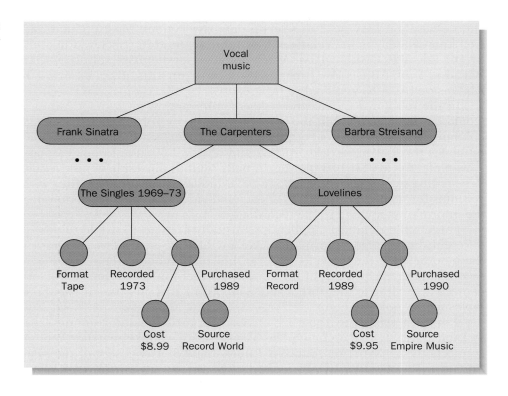

ing. For instance, a search for all the recordings made in 1993 would mean moving down through the tree to the bottom of each item, to examine its recording date. The hierarchical structure is especially appropriate for data naturally arranged in this order, such as the organization chart of a corporation or the biological classification of species. Otherwise, the user is better off with another model.

The **networked model** is more flexible in retrieval but more complicated for the designers who construct the programs. A network is a set of **nodes** of data and a great number of **links** between them. A simplified network for the student's music library might look like Figure 8-12. Note that every data field is connected to every other item with which it is associated. For example, all vocal recordings point to the Vocal node in the network. The computer program keeps up with all these links and traces through them in the retrieval process. Because it does not have the built-in hierarchy of the family tree model, anything related to anything else can be retrieved directly through the linking process. A network organization is also larger and more complicated than the tables of the relational model, since it must keep a record of all associated fields for every single node.

**networked model:** A database design for storing information by linking all records that are related with a list of pointers.

**node:** A record or field in a networked database with a series of links connecting it to all other associated nodes.

**link:** A pointer between nodes in a networked database signifying that they are related in some way.

### OBJECT-ORIENTED DATABASES

HyperCard, the popular hypertext multimedia environment for Macintosh, is organized according to the principles of a networked database. But it is a special kind of networked database, called **object-oriented.** Sound files, pictures, text, and graphics are associated with each other in individual windows. When a particular window is opened, the computer program knows where to find all the multimedia files belonging to it, because they are all linked together by the networked structure.

**object-oriented database:** A networked database that can link a variety of data objects like text, graphics, photos, video, and sound and associate them with an object, such as a "card" window in HyperCard.

Users access the information in a HyperCard application by means of objects: cards, windows, buttons. They may point with the mouse to a button on the current card to reveal a previously hidden text field on the screen, play a sound file associated with the current card, or move to another window. They can navigate among cards and fields, cycling through the data files to carry out sorts or searches, or assemble multimedia information about a topic—animation, sound, CD-ROM images, or videotape stored on videodisk. The HyperCard environment keeps up with all the networked links between these multiple types of data and activates them as the user clicks on buttons or windows. Although HyperCard provides a rich object-oriented programming environment not typical of most database software, it owes much of its flexibility to the networked organization of pointers and links that is built into it.

## DATABASE INTERFACES

In the example of a student's music library, we had to build the search requests in the way the software dictated. In computer terms, we were using the **software interface** to create search requests before releasing the program to find the records we wanted: for instance, all recordings by Charley Pride. The Paradox 7 program presented the various fields in the file on screen, and we typed Charley Pride in the artist field. Other database packages based on the GUI present the query in a window that is structured differently from the window containing the database information itself. After the user constructs the search query, the program closes the query window and displays the search output in the main database window. As noted earlier, filling in the blanks with the information desired from a particular field is called query by example, and is the most common access method for database searching.

Complex queries, such as the one requesting Charley Pride recordings made in 1980–1985 but bought in 1989 or 1990, require additional Boolean and numerical operations. For relational databases like Paradox 7, the internal search criteria for this query, not normally seen by the user, are based on **structured query language (SQL),** a database search standard recognized by the American National Standards Institute. This standard determines how software designers create the query definition. Most database users never need to learn SQL. Programmers create their software interfaces to make it easy for users to put search requests in the appropriate fields; then the program formulates the query according to SQL criteria. If the experienced user wants to type queries in SQL, a full-featured database package like Paradox 7 also allows this option.

**software interface:** A term that describes the way a database user communicates with the software, such as querying by example or using a natural language search strategy.

**structured query language (SQL):** A technical database search standard recognized by the American National Standards Institute and used by software designers to create their internal computer search criteria. Sometimes ordinary users build search requests in SQL, but most modern database software hides it from the user.

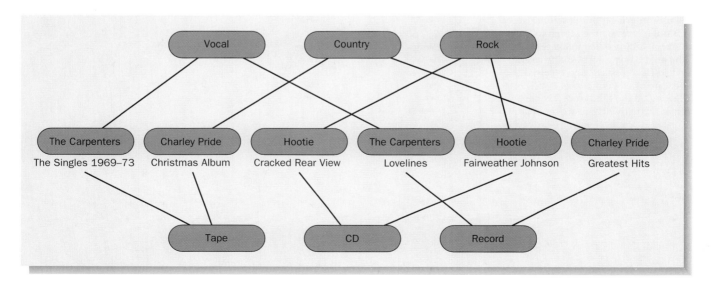

**FIGURE 8-12** The music library depicted as a networked database in diagram form.

## NATURAL LANGUAGE INTERFACES

**natural language interface:** A search strategy that allows querying a database directly in English, although the way the request is formulated is fairly restricted.

Some DBMS packages are now appearing that accept search requests typed directly in English, although the way the request is formulated is fairly restricted. This sort of **natural language interface** is especially appealing to new database users and those with little technological experience. The software must convert the English sentence to standard database query form before carrying out the search. The process involves some grammatical analysis and vocabulary searching to decipher the parts of the sentence that are needed to build the search request.

To get a sense of the possibilities, let us look at the way the Intelligent Assistant—the natural language component of a popular Windows database package called Q&A (Symantec)—allows users to develop their requests in English sentences. The Intelligent Assistant recognizes about 400 words, including verbs like *show, look up, sort,* and *print* and nouns like *list* and *report,* appropriate to many queries, as well as all the names of the user's data fields and records. In addition, the user can teach the Assistant new terms. Richard H. Shaw (*PC Magazine* 1990) devised a sample query to show how much the Assistant really "knows": "Show me a report of last year's sales for the Northeast division, sorted by salesperson and transaction date." The Assistant would "understand" four of the words (*show, report, sales,* and *division*) but would need to be taught about *last year's* and *Northeast.*

On the other hand, the request "Show me a list of all parts made for Dovers, Burgansts, Entices, Fendhis, and Alles between 1988 and 1994" can be automatically analyzed and the report produced on screen. Each of the five company names is understood because it appears in the field of customers. *Show* and *list* are in the prepared dictionary; *parts* is a field of information in the database; and the software knows what to do with "between 1988 and 1994," since the numbers are dates. To be really "intelligent" the program would have to do more linguistic analysis than it currently can, but the size of the program would be much greater, and the speed of the search would probably be slowed considerably.

Natural language interfaces are more a pioneering than a standard feature, but the success of programs like Q&A and the large amount of current research into information retrieval using ordinary English-language

**FIGURE 8-13** ClarisWorks 2.1 (Apple) illustrates querying a data base by example on a Macintosh, with its graphical user interface. In this case the user fills out a form on the screen to find all records of people named Smith who are testing a software program (called Beta-Testers) and received the software after 1 June 1994 (> 6-1-94). Clicking on the Find from Visible button at the left will activate the search.

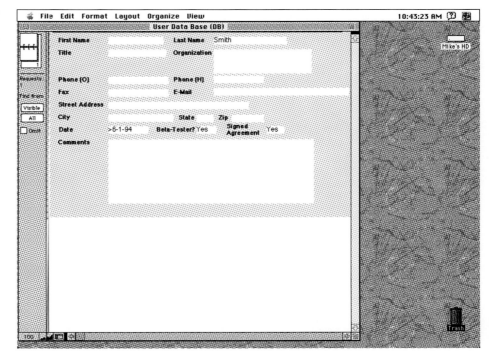

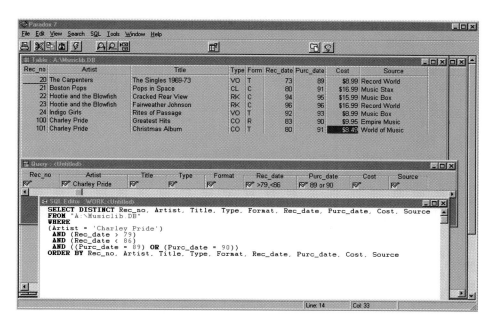

**FIGURE 8-14** Paradox 7 allows users optionally to encode their search queries in the SQL language. This illustration shows what a search request for recordings by Charlie Pride recorded between 1980 and 1985 (>79, <86) and purchased in either 1989 or 1990 looks like in normal Paradox form and in SQL.

queries suggest that such programs offer much promise for the future. Database software with natural language input represents a growing shift in priorities among elements of the Computer Triangle. Compared to the more complicated interfaces of a few years ago, convenience for new users, an aspect of concern for the human element, is assuming more attention in database software design today.

## ► Social Issues Surrounding Large Databases

Large-scale database applications have potential negative consequences not only for the owners of the information but also for the general public. Whereas issues like data integrity and security are professional concerns,

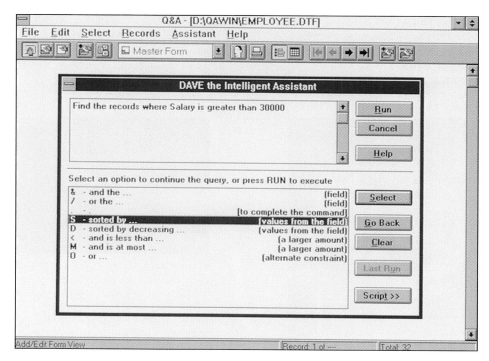

**FIGURE 8-15** Setting up a query in English to Q&A for Windows (Symantec), with its Intelligent Assistant called Dave. The user chooses among several options in the lower window about how to do the search.

the invasion of privacy for individuals affects databases created in the private sector, just as it does public, governmental databases. All of these concerns address the interconnections of people, hardware, and software embodied in the Computer Triangle.

## INTEGRITY AND SECURITY

When an organization has a large investment in the information held within its database, such as the reservations system of an airline, it must be concerned with questions of data integrity and data security. **Data integrity** refers to being sure that the information contained in the database is accurate and timely. Today thousands of travel agents throughout the world have access to airline reservations systems through terminals on their desks, and the types and kinds of fares change almost daily. When a customer calls for information about a route or a fare, the information must be up to date and correct. Lacking these characteristics, the airline company would soon find itself losing business; data integrity is critical to the maintenance of its business.

Airline executives are responsible for making decisions about fares and routes based on market research about travel patterns and competition, and then for seeing that the updated information is encoded correctly and monitored. Their computer staffs have full access to the fields and records of the database. Management can change the fare bases of particular flights between very competitive cities daily, if desired. The staff can even restructure the field definitions of the base—for example, to introduce a new fare category for senior citizens traveling together during off-peak seasons. They are in charge of maintaining the integrity of the database, where accuracy and timeliness mean money.

On the other hand, travel agents cannot change major characteristics of the database. They can search the complete file for particular flights, routes, times, and fares, and make reservations for customers on particular flights. The database program then assigns a seat to the traveler and changes the number of available seats. But agents cannot change flight times or fares. Their access to the database is limited to specific functions. The program has to have fail-safe procedures to prevent two agents from booking the same seat for two customers at the same time. It also needs **consistency checks** built into it, to catch erroneous data encoded by mistake. For example, if an agent tries to reserve a flight for February 29 in a non-leap year, the program should not allow the transaction. Obviously, companies like airlines and hotel chains, with major investments in the information contained in databases, have a large stake in maintaining data integrity.

**data integrity:** The need to ensure that information contained in a database is accurate and timely—that is, free of corruption by input or programming errors.

SOCIETY

**consistency check:** A software protection scheme added to a database management system to monitor data integrity. For instance, one should not be able to reserve flights for nonexistent dates like February 30.

**FIGURE 8-16** Clerks using an on-line airline reservations system can query the master database of flights and reserve seats, but they cannot make major changes to the database, such as changing fares.

**FIGURE 8-17** As soon as the ATM accepts this person's card, it will request the personal password of the customer, often called a PIN number (personal identification number).

Allied issues are **data protection** or **security.** Databases of bank records accessible from ATMs must be protected from unauthorized access by persons who have no business with them. Some sort of **password system** is used to gain access to the system. Customers insert their ATM cards and are then asked for their secret password codes, usually four numerical digits. If the code is correctly entered, the person can get the current balance and even deposit or withdraw money. If the password is incorrect, the system often gives the user a few more tries to log in. After several false starts, the machine usually keeps the card, for the user may have stolen it.

Another common strategy is the **log** of transactions, or **audit trail.** Any time a user accesses the database, the computer automatically logs the person's account number, the date, and the transaction. The record can be examined later if there has been a problem with the transaction. The receipt printed by an ATM at the close of the session is the customer's record of the transaction; the information is also logged electronically for the bank's permanent record.

## THE PRIVATE DATABASE EXPLOSION

A major societal hazard of the computer age is the vast amount of information about private citizens held in governmental and commercial databases. A complex society like the United States cannot maintain its current standard of living without the existence of much information. The mail-order catalog business is held together by toll-free numbers and clerks who enter orders into database programs, which produce the sales invoice; keep a record for inventory; allow management to monitor sales trends; and develop mailing lists of customers for future mailings. Files can be sorted by customer preferences for certain types of merchandise and then assembled as mailing labels sorted by ZIP code. These save on postage, since the postal service offers reduced rates for presorted mail.

Catalog retailers routinely sell their mailing lists to other companies, and buyers often receive new information from companies they have never bought from. State driver's license records are often sold to marketers and political parties. Much current marketing research, based in computers, is geared toward segmentation of the consumer population into interest and preference groups. These valuable databases are then sold to businesses or public interest groups for direct mail appeals. Credit rating bureaus hold very valuable information about the spending habits and creditworthiness of most families in the United States. Although the Fair Credit Reporting Act of 1970 allows a citizen access to his or her credit rating for purposes of correcting errors in it, many people are not aware of this protection. Yet department stores, banks, and lending institutions routinely examine these databases in judging credit applications, and spot checks indicate there are many errors in the files.

Even **Caller ID** services have come under attack for their uses in gathering personal data from customers. Phone companies sell the benefits for private users primarily as allowing people to see the numbers of obscene or harassing callers. Yet critics say that some people need to keep their anonymity: people who call AIDS hot lines, callers with crime reports on police tip lines, probation officers calling their clients (Johnson). Only in 1996 were telephone customers in California, the last in the nation, able to purchase Caller ID telephones, which allow the receiver of a call to see the name and phone number of the caller. Privacy activists in California were able to stall the service for years, even though people calling 800 and 900 numbers throughout the United States have been monitored since 1989.

The push to allow Caller ID services by phone companies has always been supported by private businesses. Phone companies make money from

**data protection (data security):** A term referring to strategies for protecting databases against illegal access or modification, such as needing a password to access a database.

**password system:** A software strategy of using a unique, normally secret, code to identify users before granting them access to a computer system or database for multiple users.

**log (audit trail):** A record kept automatically by a computer system of all users, times logged on, and transactions for record keeping and security purposes, especially with distributed access to large databases.

**SOCIETY**

**Caller ID:** A telephone service that allows a user with a phone equipped with a digital screen to see the number, and sometimes the name, of the caller. In a commercial setting this service often triggers a computer database to display other information about the caller.

Caller ID services, and businesses gather free marketing information from callers. Evan Hendricks, editor of the newsletter *Privacy Times*, sees the important issue as economic: "The main agenda here is to turn your phone number into a Social Security number, so that when you call a Caller ID-equipped business, your number is connected to a database and your profile comes up on a computer screen." People are giving up their privacy to aid telemarketers. With a phone number, the computer can look up the name and address of the party and build mailing lists, which are then sold for $30 per 1000 names.

Supporters of Caller ID say that the system has its own protections for privacy. Though many are not aware of it, customers can request phone companies to block the release of their numbers to those with equipment to read them. Or they can dial *67 before the remaining numbers of any single call, and that transmission cannot be identified by name and number at the other end of the line. As noted earlier, privacy issues always become complicated with technology. Yet in this case involving a combination of telephones and computers, the technology itself has evolved some safeguards for those who want to deactivate the service (Kaplan).

## NEW MARKETS FOR DATABASES

Two of the largest credit bureaus, TRW and Equifax, have recently begun expanding their list of services available for a fee to other businesses. Equifax offers lawyers a locator service, to find missing witnesses, debtors, heirs to an estate, shareholders, and so on. The information about the whereabouts of customers is updated daily, on the basis of credit card sales. TRW can provide marketers with selective lists of affluent customers making over $100,000 a year or lists of credit card holders with outstanding debt. Direct mail solicitation has also become a potent fund-raising tool in political campaigns. Records of attendance in political party functions like primaries provide opportunities to get names and addresses of interested citizens, who can later be contacted for financial help or other forms of participation in campaigns.

**SOCIETY**

---

### SOCIAL PERSPECTIVE

**Data Banks and the Right to Privacy**

The journalist Robert S. Boyd (Knight-Ridder) has studied the collection of personal information in the private sector. He noted in July 1990:

> Every time you use a credit card to make a purchase, telephone an 800 or 900 number, order from a catalog, buy or rent a car, reserve a hotel room or airline ticket, visit a doctor or go to the hospital, apply for insurance, take out a mortgage, seek a loan—in effect, engage in almost any transaction—you give over information about yourself.

> The data swept up at a grocery checkout counter—your choice of toothpaste, breakfast cereal, deodorant, contraceptives, whether you smoke cigarettes or drink beer—may seem petty.

> But it is worth millions of dollars to stores and manufacturers. And its value soars when it is linked to the names

of specific individuals, along with their lifestyles, shopping preferences and ability to pay.

As with government data banks that contain information about individuals, striking a balance between the needs of businesses to know about their customers and the individual's right to privacy becomes even more difficult with the power of database technology. Federal law has traditionally been more concerned with protecting the rights of citizens from government interference than with regulating data gathered in the private sector. Although the White House cosponsored a conference on privacy with the Consumer's League in June 1990, and Congress has had hearings about proliferating business databases, no significant legislation which curtails the gathering and distribution of private information by the credit industry and business seems imminent.

Even the American public is of two minds about privacy and data banks. A Louis Harris poll conducted for

Equifax, and reported by Robert Wallich in *Scientific American* in June 1991, revealed inconsistent opinions. Seventy-nine percent of those sampled thought that privacy was a fundamental right and were concerned about threats to it. But almost the same number (78 percent) would be upset if denied credit because of a credit report, and 54 percent approved the exchange of health information among insurers about previous medical claims before deciding to issue a new policy to a customer. Clearly, technology allows possibilities for market research based on sophisticated analyses of publicly collected data not possible a few years ago. Yet legitimate questions of data security, accuracy, and access remain at present unresolved in the minds of both the American people and their leaders.

**FIGURE 8-18 A&B** Two graphs published in *Privacy Journal* of opinion surveys in Canada and the United States in 1993 concerning the perceived threats to personal privacy of public and private databanks. Questions in the (A) Canadian survey suggest the issues involved in the privacy question; (B) the Louis Harris poll shows that U.S. citizens are increasingly concerned with the invasion of privacy.

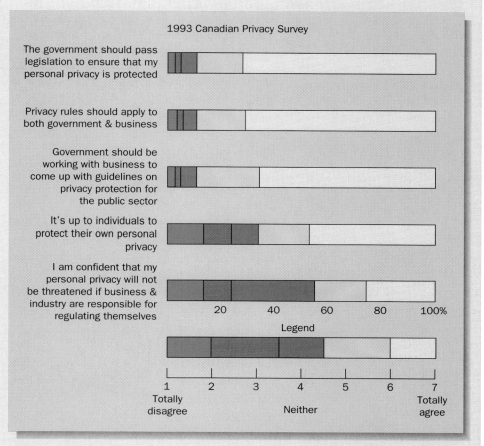

A

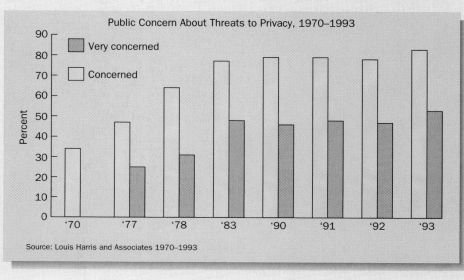

B

## ▶ Summary

Today database software may be the largest single category of computer programs with so many different uses and applications. The organization of information into records and fields that can be retrieved, sorted, searched, and printed opens up possibilities for expanded market research and very sophisticated segmented mailing lists not available even a few years ago. For example, an ordinary list of suburban names and addresses can become the basis for a powerful information source when it is merged with economic data from census files and sold to retailers. Standard models for database construction—relational, hierarchical, or networked—and different types of user interfaces offer different advantages, which users should understand before choosing software for their own needs. Given current trends, database applications will continue to expand in the private sector, where they are not as well regulated as those in the government sector. Consequently, issues like data integrity and security and concern for the privacy of individuals will continue to be major topics of discussion in the coming years.

## ▶ Key Terms

alphabetical sorting (p. 185)

alphanumeric (p. 182)

AND (intersection) (p. 187)

ascending order (p. 185)

Boolean operation (p. 188)

consistency check (p. 194)

Caller ID (p. 195)

database (p. 178)

database management system
 (DBMS) (p. 179)

data definition (p. 181)

data entry (p. 184)

data integrity (p. 194)

data processing (p. 176)

data protection (data security) (p. 195)

descending sort (p. 185)

family tree (p. 189)

field (p. 177)

file (p. 177)

flat file (p. 189)

hierarchical model (p. 189)

information retrieval (p. 176)

key (p. 177)

key field (p. 181)

link (p. 190)

log (audit trail) (p. 195)

multiple-field sorting (p. 185)

natural language interface (p. 192)

networked model (p. 190)

node (p. 190)

NOT (complement) (p. 187)

numerical comparison operation
 (p. 188)

object-oriented database (p. 190)

OR (union) (p. 187)

password system (p. 195)

primary sort (p. 185)

query by example (QBE) (p. 188)

record (p. 177)

relational (tabular) model (p. 189)

reporting (p. 179)

searching (p. 179)

secondary sort (p. 185)

software interface (p. 191)

sorting (p. 179)

structured query language (SQL)
 (p. 191)

table (p. 181)

## ▶ Self-Test

### MULTIPLE-CHOICE

1. Order the following database elements in proper sequence:
   a. files contain records that contain fields

b. records contain files that contain fields

c. fields contain records that contain characters

d. files contain fields that contain characters

2. All of the following are appropriate uses for a database package except

a. alphabetizing the names of members of a large civic club

b. finding students who scored more than 1300 points on the SAT

c. developing a computer file on potsherds collected on an archaeological dig

d. typing the draft of a large code of laws for revision

3. Which of the following is not a standard feature of database software?

a. data definition

b. data encoding

c. data sorting

d. data initiation

4. Which of the following is not a Boolean operation?

a. less than

b. OR

c. complement

d. intersection

5. Which of the following queries using Boolean logic will find all sophomores from out of state who are majoring in journalism or education?

a. students not in science or humanities and classified as sophomores

b. students not from this state and classified as sophomores or majors in journalism and education

c. journalism and education majors and sophomores not from this state

d. journalism or education majors not from this state and classified as sophomores

6. Which database model is both the most flexible for retrieval and the most complicated to design?

a. hierarchical

b. networked

c. relational

d. tabular

7. Which of the following interfaces is the most difficult to learn for building database queries?

a. QBE

b. natural language

c. SQL

d. flat query

8. All of the following are methods of database security except

a. passwords

b. logs of transactions

c. audit trails

d. security clearances

**TRUE/FALSE**

9. **T F** The growth of database software in the 1950s set off the explosion of computing which has continued to the present.

10. **T F** Normally a record contains one main identifying key field, to which associated information in other fields is attached.

11. **T F** Alphanumeric data refers to material that is stored in a database in character format and can be sorted alphabetically.

12. **T  F**   Binary field sorting, such as sorting music first by recording date and then alphabetically by the name of the artist, calls for two sorts, primary and secondary, one after the other.

13. **T  F**   Much database software for personal computers is built on the hierarchical model.

14. **T  F**   A flat file database is actually a one-table relational database.

15. **T  F**   Most ordinary database users never need to learn SQL, even though their database software is based on it.

16. **T  F**   Data integrity refers to being sure that the information contained in the database is free from outside tampering.

## FILL-IN

17. _____ can be defined as the filing, maintenance, retrieval, and reporting of information kept in data banks.

18. The process of deciding on the number and characteristics of all the data fields in each record is called the _____ stage of building a database.

19. In the search specification method called _____, a user fills in a blank set of fields with data that is being sought.

20. In the _____ database model, data are stored in a format resembling a table.

21. Pointers and links characteristic of a _____ database organization give HyperCard much of its flexibility in multimedia.

22. Database software that accepts search requests typed into the system directly in English is said to have a _____ interface.

23. Unlike airline reservations clerks, airline executives are responsible for maintenance of the _____ of the database, where accuracy and timeliness mean money.

24. In recent opinion polls a great majority of Americans thought that _____ was a fundamental right and were concerned about threats to it.

## ▶ Experiential Exercises

1. Investigate some of the databases regularly kept by your college or university. In a large institution, you may find that a department has its own database of information about its majors, alumni, or even prospective students. Find out about these files, their size, the uses for which they are kept, and what software is used to keep them current. Who has access to the information they contain?

2. To clarify the relationships between data files, records, fields, and keys, consult the card catalog or on-line catalog of books in your institution's library. You may need to get help from the library staff. What is the key field of each record, and how many fields make up each record? What is the size of the whole file in terms of records? Work out how many fields of information there are in the total catalog.

3. Using an on-line catalog of books, see if it is possible to do a search for all the books in the library that were written by people named Brown or Smith and were published in New York before 1850. Again, you may want to seek assistance from the library staff. What fields of information must be queried in the book record? What would a Boolean query for this search look like if it were written out in plain English?

4. Investigate a popular database management software package used on your campus or by a small company. Try to make a small file of records, such as the personal music library illustrated in this chapter. What database model is the software based on? What method is used to request a search, such as QBE in Paradox 7? Does the software seem to have easy-to-use features?

5. In order to appreciate the issues of data integrity and security, consult a DBMS manager in a large organization like a bank or department store, or perhaps the data processing department of your institution. Ask this person about controls on access and checks on the reliability of data in the files. Who is authorized to make changes to the information in the files? How important are integrity and security in the overall scheme of database maintenance?

6. Investigate whether public records in your state or province, such as driver's license records or voter lists, are sold to the public. Who can buy this information? What does it cost? Has there ever been any discussion in the press or legislature of the pros and cons of these sales? If so, what arguments were given to defend or criticize the practice?

## ▶ Critical Thinking Exercises

1. Try to invent different hypothetical situations that would naturally fit each of the three common database models: relational, hierarchical, and networked. Illustrate your examples with typical entries for each database.

2. Your major field of interest probably has many possible uses for a database. Think over the kinds of data that would be collected, and propose the kinds of searches and reports that might be generated. What model would be appropriate for this application? Would software such as that examined in question 4 above be suitable and convenient to use? Has someone in your field already created such a database?

3. Catalog sales companies that take phone orders usually have a Caller ID service, so that they can see your phone number when the call is answered. Typing this information into the computer, the clerk is shown your order history and profile, including your name, address, and credit card number. Discuss in a report whether this use of a Caller ID service represents an invasion of privacy or allows the company to provide faster, more reliable service keyed to your buying habits.

4. On balance, privately held data banks of information on consumer habits and lifestyles, including income, are more helpful than harmful. Discuss.

**ANSWERS TO SELF-TEST**

*Multiple-Choice*: 1. a;    2. d;    3. d;    4. a;    5. d;    6. b;    7. c;    8. d

*True/False*: 9. F;    10. T;    11. T;    12. F;    13. F;    14. T;    15. T;    16. F

*Fill-in*: 17. database management;    18. data definition;    19. query by example;    20. relational;    21. networked;    22. natural language;    23. data integrity;    24. privacy

# CHAPTER 9

# Computer Graphics and Videos

▶ **LEARNING OUTCOMES**

*After completing this chapter, you should be able to:*

1. *Describe the integral combination of hardware and software that makes computer graphics possible.*

2. *Explain the fundamentals of storing graphics information in binary notation in computers and presenting it on monitors and printers.*

3. *Describe the many kinds of graphics applications software, their characteristics, and their uses.*

4. *Discuss technologies on the frontiers of computer graphics, including ray tracing, graphics in the movies, fractal geometry, and virtual reality.*

▶ **COMPUTERS IN CONTEXT**

*In the early 1960s no one had imagined using a computer to play video games or show colorful images or movies on a computer screen. It was the era of the first large mainframes with input on punch cards and output on noisy line printers, all in uppercase. At MIT the experimental Whirlwind computer, built with Defense Department funds for military research, included the first CRT capable of displaying graphic images. From the Whirlwind evolved the TX-2 computer, which had a **light pen** to let the user draw on the new graphic display screens, offering a new frontier for human computer interaction.*

*Ivan Sutherland, an MIT graduate student, recognized the enormous potential for interactive graphics with this equipment and created the first such program for his dissertation research, called Sketchpad. He invokes the liberating spirit of* Alice in Wonderland *in an address on graphic possibilities in 1965: "A display connected to a digital computer gives us a chance to gain familiarity with concepts not realizable in the physical world. It is a looking glass into a mathematical wonderland" (quoted on the University of Virginia User Interface Group WWW site in 1996). Sitting at the CRT terminal, Sutherland could create and manipulate graphic shapes with the light pen, drawing upon previously stored graphic primitive elements like boxes and circles. With the light pen, he could rotate, resize, copy, and delete these shapes in real time on the screen, the first interactive computer graphics. Thus was born the first CAD software as a dissertation project, and Sutherland became the father of computer graphics (Bissell).*

*For the personal computer user, computer graphics has now come of age. Today almost all computers offer the GUI, and the mouse is a favored input device for graphic production. Images in an almost infinite number of colors and shades of gray can be produced on computer screens, and with increasingly flexible color printing processes.*

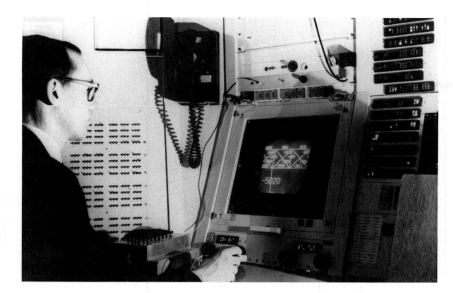

**FIGURE 9-1** In a snapshot from the early 1960s, Ivan Sutherland is working with his Sketchpad program, the first graphics software, on a primitive computer terminal at MIT.

**M**ore than spreadsheets or databases, which are mainly software applications, the technology of computer graphics requires an understanding of both hardware and software. The production of pictures and colors on a computer screen, or a hard copy display device like a printer, blends computer software and hardware in a harmonious whole. In order to examine modern computer graphics, one must appreciate the combination of hardware and software that makes them work.

## ▶ The Hardware Dimension

In order to create a graphic image on a screen, a computer must convert information, stored internally as binary data, into a stream of data for display as a pictorial image. In principle, there are two ways that graphics images are produced on a computer screen. Older graphic hardware used vector strategies, whereas most modern graphics hardware is of the raster type.

### VECTOR GRAPHICS

The earliest graphics terminals employed **vector graphics.** An electron beam moves over the screen and draws a line of glowing phosphors, which are excited by the electrical signal hitting them on the inside of the tube. Essentially, these monitors work like the familiar oscilloscope (Lewell). The computer stores a set of character-plotting commands in a **buffer memory** before they are transmitted to the screen. The commands may instruct the beam to begin at one point and move to another, producing the linear image in the process. Because the phosphor glow decays rapidly, the buffer has to refresh the image often to avoid flicker—hence its name, **refresh buffer.**

### RASTER GRAPHICS

In the 1970s **raster graphics,** based on the technology of television, became the cheaper and better alternative. Similar to a television tube, a

**light pen:** A handheld input stylus that uses a photocell to transmit signals to a computer screen, first used in CAD applications.

**vector graphics:** The earliest type of computer graphics, in which a set of character-plotting commands activate the phosphors of a computer display with an electron beam.

**buffer memory:** A temporary storage area where the computer stores a set of character-plotting commands in vector graphics before they are transmitted to the screen.

**refresh buffer:** In vector graphics, hardware that renews a phosphor-coated display screen with an electron beam to maintain information that would otherwise flicker.

**raster graphics:** A common method of presenting computer graphic images on a CRT, based on the technology of television, that uses an electron beam to excite phosphor dots (pixels) inside the CRT screen and make them glow.

**FIGURE 9-2** In vector graphics, coordinate points and plotting commands are sent from the computer to the screen, where the graphic image is drawn. The screen must be refreshed 30 to 60 times a second.

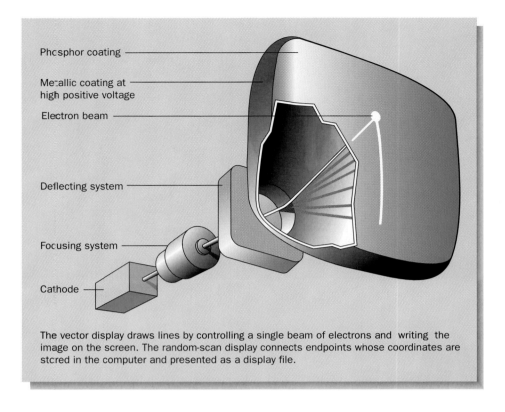

Phosphor coating

Metallic coating at high positive voltage

Electron beam

Deflecting system

Focusing system

Cathode

The vector display draws lines by controlling a single beam of electrons and writing the image on the screen. The random-scan display connects endpoints whose coordinates are stored in the computer and presented as a display file.

raster computer monitor consists of a large number of phosphor dots on the inside of the tube, which glow when hit by an electron beam. The dots are called pixels, an abbreviation of picture elements. Think of the screen as a set of rows and columns—a matrix composed of dots that can be turned on and off by a set of binary choices. The number of pixels on a computer screen is called its resolution; the higher the resolution, the sharper and more detailed the images that can be displayed on the screen.

An inexpensive personal computer monitor today has several hundred rows of pixels with even more columns in each row. Color monitors for both low-end Windows and Macintosh computers have 640 × 480 pixels (307,200). A more advanced graphics workstation has considerably more—probably at least 1000 rows and 1000 columns, for a total of more than 1 million pixels.

The image is displayed on a **raster** made up of horizontal rows of pixels. By continually cycling through the raster lines at a rate of 30 times a second, the hardware displays the image on the screen. In effect, each

**raster:** A term for the horizontal lines of pixels on a TV or CRT screen, refreshed at a rate of 30 times a second to display an image on the screen.

**FIGURE 9-3** The basic elements of raster graphics display. The graphics processor in the computer sends the image, pixel by pixel, to the frame buffer, where it is stored. From there the sweeper picks the image up and refreshes the screen about 30 times a second.

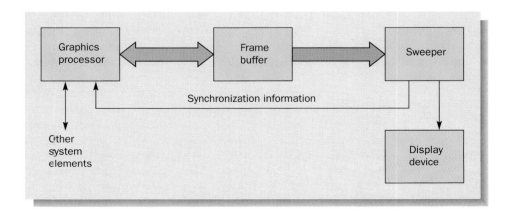

Graphics processor

Frame buffer

Sweeper

Synchronization information

Other system elements

Display device

**FIGURE 9-4** Creating a picture in a stadium section out of individual colored cards is analogous to creating a graphic image by displaying or printing a set of colored pixels.

pixel on the screen is shown 30 times per second to avoid flicker (Foley and van Dam). A raster graphics display system includes a **frame buffer,** which contains a record of every pixel on the screen, called a bit map. Accessing the frame buffer are the **graphics processor** and the **sweeper,** which updates the display screen (Bennett). The screen itself, where the graphic image is projected, is basically a television tube.

In computers like Macintosh and Window models, which are bit-mapped machines, all the displays are in reality a set of graphic images. Changing fonts in a word processor from Old English Gothic to a stylish modern italic is just a problem of replacing one picture of the letter font by its equivalent in another font. Similarly, drawing a line in a graphics program means that the software follows the direction of movement of the mouse on the table and darkens the equivalent line on the screen.

## PRINTER GRAPHICS

Printing a bit-mapped image is very similar in concept to displaying a set of pixels on the screen. Early dot-matrix printers created their images, however, not from bit maps, but from precoded dot patterns for letters and numbers. The computer sent the printer a signal to print a capital B, and the output device retrieved the B pattern and printed it. These printers could not produce a large variety of graphics characters besides those on the typewriter keyboard.

Bit-mapped dot-matrix printers and ink-jet printers, on the other hand, print all the pixels on the screen. Since printed images are just dumpings of the pixels in the frame buffer, the printer handles poetic text or a child's crude drawing in the same way. Whereas bit-mapped printers of the dot-matrix type offer low resolution, laser printers, also bit-mapped, have much finer quality and resolution—typically 300 to 600 dots per inch.

## GRAPHICS PLOTTERS

Plotters come in both vector and bit-mapped varieties. Large or small **flatbed plotters,** used in complex engineering drawings, work on the vector principle. The computer sends to the plotter instructions about where to start drawing a line, how long it is to be, and where to stop or turn in another direction. The drawing pen moves according to these instructions over the plotter paper, leaving the drawn image behind. Plotters may be equipped with several colored pens for complex and pleasing effects. The bit-mapped approach is embodied in **electrostatic plotters,** which print

**frame buffer:** In raster graphics, a special area of RAM that holds the pixel contents of a computer screen.

**graphics processor:** Part of a raster graphics display system that prepares pixel information for the frame buffer.

**sweeper:** An element of a raster graphics system that takes information from the frame buffer and updates the display screen.

**FIGURE 9-5** A desktop plotter can produce fine quality color printing of computer graphic files.

**flatbed plotter:** An output device that works on the vector principle. It accepts instructions from a computer about where to draw a line, how long it is to be, and where to stop or turn in another direction and moves its drawing pen accordingly.

**electrostatic plotter:** A plotter that uses electricity to transfer bit-mapped images to paper by printing raster pixels line by line, much as they are produced on a bit-mapped printer.

**fax machine:** A machine that scans documents and transmits them to either computers or other fax machines over a phone line.

**SOCIETY**

**digitizing scanner:** A hardware device that converts color or black-and-white images on paper to pixel images so that they may be processed by a computer.

**FIGURE 9-6** A fax copy is not usually a fine quality digitized image of the original, but it is easy to read and inexpensive to send.

the raster pixels line by line, much as they are produced on a bit-mapped printer (Demel and Miller). The process, however, often uses flimsy, shiny paper that does not hold up well to indefinite storage.

## FAX MACHINES

One of the most popular high-tech devices of the 1980s, now taken for granted, is the **fax machine,** a name suggestive of the facsimile process. Not only did Chinese students alert the world instantly by fax to the horrors of the Tiananmen Square massacre in 1989, but office workers regularly send lunch orders for hamburgers and fries by fax to the local diner around the corner.

A kind of special-purpose computer, a fax machine includes circuitry for three computer functions: an input digitizer, to convert the page into a bit-mapped image; a modem, to send the rasterized bit patterns over the phone lines to the receiving fax; and an electrostatic output printer, to display the bit-mapped image by printing it a line at a time. Fax scanning technology resembles that of commercial **digitizing scanners;** both convert materials shown in black on white paper to dots before transmitting them to another device, such as an internal computer memory, a diskette, or a phone line. The roll of thin, shiny paper in many fax machines is like that used in other electrostatic printing devices, but newer fax machines

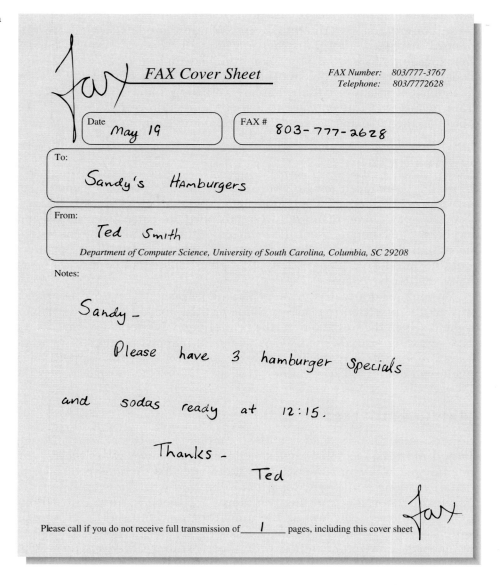

produce the image on plain paper. Both the input and output processes of fax machines utilize concepts of standard bit-mapped computer graphics.

## EARLY MONOCHROME AND COLOR SCREENS

A computer providing bit-mapped graphics must have stored inside its frame buffer the information that specifies how each of the several hundred thousand pixels will appear on the screen or hard copy output device. If the screen is monochrome, it can display only two colors, normally black and white or two shades of green or amber. In computer terms, each pixel is either turned on or off—the familiar binary choice—either white on a black background or reversed video with black on white. Color monitors, like TV screens, are equipped with an RGB (red-green-blue) video board. Although red, yellow, and blue are usually called the primary colors, red, green, and blue are the **additive primary colors** from which color television and color computer graphics are composed. Mixtures of these three electron signals, sent to a pixel on a TV screen, produce all the different shades and hues of color television (Lewell). A computer with an RGB video board attached to a monochrome screen yields eight gradations of shading from white to black, the so-called **gray scale.**

**additive primary colors:** The three colors, red, green, and blue, of which color computer graphics and color television are composed. Color monitors are equipped with an RGB (red-green-blue) video board to produce their colorful images.

**gray scale:** A term applied to the gradations of shadings from white to black that result from attaching an RGB video board to a monochrome screen.

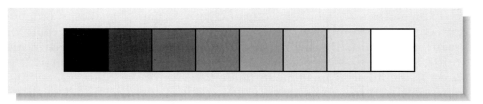

**FIGURE 9-7** A simple monochrome screen can produce eight shades from white to black, called gray scale.

Early personal computers used three bits of information on their video boards to store the recipe for what gray-scale shade or color was displayed on the screen. For instance, if all three bits were 0s, the pixel assigned to that byte would show up as black, whereas all 1s would be white. A total of eight gradations, from white to black, were possible (remember that three bits allow eight combinations of 0s and 1s). For color monitors there were eight hues, depending on which combination of eight bits was sent to the screen. The possible mixtures of red, green, and blue electron beams were as follows (Lewell):

| Red | Green | Blue | Result |
| --- | --- | --- | --- |
| on (binary 1) | off (binary 0) | off | red |
| off | on | off | green |
| off | off | on | blue |
| on | off | on | magenta |
| off | on | on | cyan |
| on | on | off | yellow |
| on | on | on | white |
| off | off | off | black |

According to this chart, a yellow pixel would be set from the raster information code 110. Anyone who remembers the early video games, like Pac-Man, will be familiar with these eight basic colors.

## MODERN COLOR SCREENS

In recent years, the standard for high-quality color reproduction on video boards has evolved into an 8-bit and a 24-bit code. The 8-bit code, which

**FIGURE 9-8** The popular early video game called PacMan offered eight-color graphics. Compared to a 1990s video arcade game, the look of PacMan seems simple and crude.

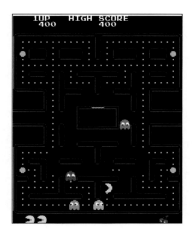

can conveniently be stored in 1 byte of computer memory, yields a total of 256 possible color combinations, since mathematically 256 is $2^8$. High-resolution color monitors with the 24-bit code combine three sets of 8-bit codes for each of the red, green, and blue signals. In practical terms, this means that the electron beam can be tuned to 256 shades of red and mixed with the same number of shades for the other colors.

Paint stores offer a huge palette of creatively named shades of red, but not nearly 256! Combining these 256 red possibilities with 256 each for green and blue allows the combined electron signal to produce, in all, 16,777,216 colors (256 × 256 × 256) on a high-quality color monitor. It is hard for the mind to imagine 16 million shades of the color palette, and impossible to think up descriptive names for even a hundredth of them! The richness of colors and shadings available on these screens is beyond the greatest dreams of the Impressionist painters, known for their brilliant experiments with color and light.

## COLOR PRINTING

Only in the last few years has the technology of electrostatic and laser printing allowed color production, and it still remains more expensive than black-and-white output. Color computer monitors mix the three primary additive colors (red, green, and blue) to create the light source that we see as the color on the screen. But color printers must mix materials on paper to reflect the desired color to the human eye. Thus they use the three **subtractive primary colors,** magenta, cyan, and yellow, which are each defined by the absence of one of the RGB colors.

One creates these subtractive primaries by cutting out one of the additive primaries from the light that is reflected to the eye off the white page. Yet one can create blue by combining the two subtractive primaries that

**subtractive primary colors:** The three primary colors, magenta, cyan, and yellow, defined by the absence of one of the RGB colors, created by eliminating that color from light reflected from a white page. These colors form the basis of color laser printing.

**FIGURE 9-9** An 8-bit code to create colors allows the creation of 256 different shades.

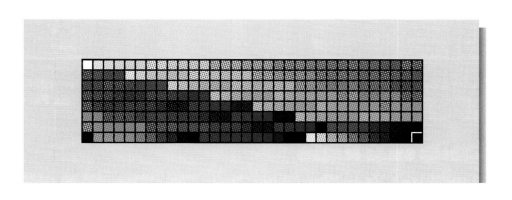

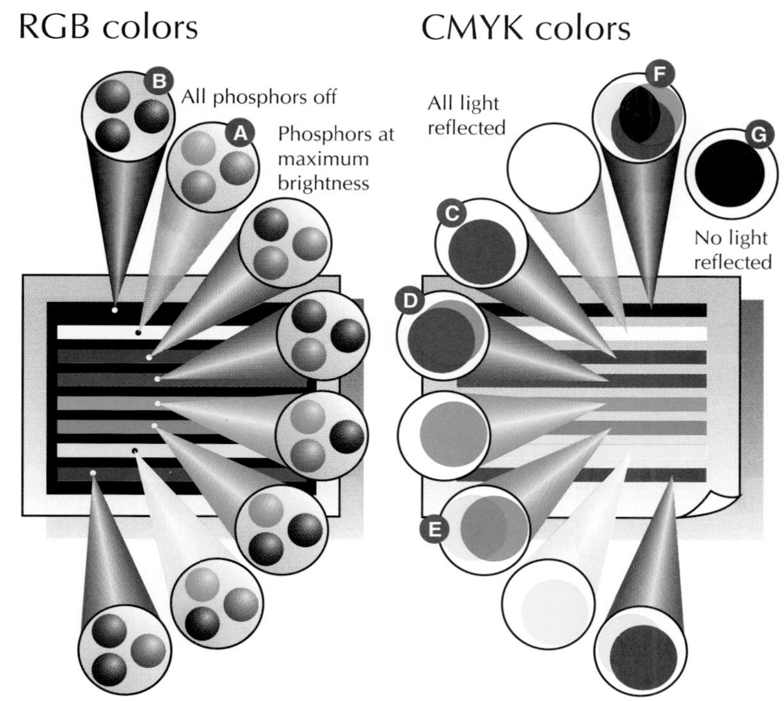

# RGB colors

# CMYK colors

**FIGURE 9-10** Creating different colors by the additive process, used on an RGB color screen, versus the subtractive process, found in the four-color process (CMYK) of color printers.

B — All phosphors off

A — Phosphors at maximum brightness

All light reflected

F

G

No light reflected

C

D

E

The light-based RGB model (above left), used with monitors, is additive. Monitor phosphors are red, green, or blue. When all three colors are illuminated at maximum brightness in a given section of the screen, you perceive a white pixel (A); when all three are turned off, you see a black pixel (B). Between those extremes, any color can be shown by varying the percentage of red, green, and blue that combine to create each pixel.

CMYK, a primary model for the printed page, is subtractive—light is absorbed, or subtracted, by cyan magenta, and yellow ink. In process-color printing (above right) layers of translucent inks are used, each subtracting certain colors of light.

Colors that are not absorbed pass through to the paper below, which reflects all colors. For example, magenta ink looks magenta because it allows magenta light to pass through but absorbs all other colors (C). Blue, composed of magenta and cyan ink, lets only those two colors of light through (D). Green, composed of yellow and cyan ink, lets only those colors through (E).

In theory, 100 percent each of cyan, magenta, and yellow produce black—all colors of light are subtracted, none reflected. In practice, however, cyan, magenta, and yellow inks are not pure, and when layered they create a muddy color (F). Printers add a dedicated black ink to achieve pure black (G).

contain it, magenta and cyan, in equal amounts. Blue is reflected to the eye, and the red and green elements inherent in magenta and cyan are absorbed. For black one needs equal amounts of all three primaries; but most printers get a truer black by providing it as a separate primary, called K in printing. The result is a printer process denoted by the initials CMYK (cyan, magenta, yellow, black), universally referred to as the **four-color process** in the printing industry. The four-color printing standard preceded the development of computers, and color printers have adopted its principles.

Color printers usually can produce seven primary colors (omitting white). More expensive models use a process called **dithering** to offer a wider spectrum of color. With dithering, a spot of color on the page is composed of a square matrix of tiny pixels (remember that laser printers produce 300 to 600 dots per inch), often 8 by 8. Adjusting the number of different-colored dots within the tiny matrix of eight allows for many

**four-color process:** The printing process used in color printing with laser printers, as well as in color book and magazine production. It is sometimes denoted by the initials CMYK (cyan, magenta, yellow, black), standing for the three subtractive colors, plus black, that are blended to create colored materials in print.

**dithering:** A process used in some color printers and graphics software to adjust the number of dots of different colors within a matrix of eight pixels to produce many shades.

**FIGURE 9-11** Two versions of this digitized photo of an autumn scene are displayed. In the second one the colors have been dithered, and the appearance is grainier. The dithering process is illustrated in the detailed sections, in which the pixels are magnified four times. One can see how the pixel colors have been spread out in the dithered version in both the wheelchair and the green background.

Original

Original 4:1 Blow-Up

Dithered

Dithered 4:1 Blow-Up

shades. Dithering risks the loss of sharp resolution, because the larger color unit is, in fact, a matrix of many color elements. All these processes of laying down several colors together are technically complicated, and the result is higher prices for color printers. The field is rapidly expanding, and one can expect quality to rise as prices fall from competition (Alford).

## ▶ The Software Component

From its early development, illustrated by the Logo programming language, graphics software has evolved in many areas to produce fancy effects in video games and realistic digital images. Presentation graphics and computer-aided design represent only two modern applications based on graphics software.

### GRAPHICS PROGRAMMING

SOCIETY

Computer programming languages have long allowed their users to give the machine commands to create simple graphics on the screen. In fact, the Logo language, developed by Seymour Papert to interest young children in the logic of computers, emphasizes the use of graphics programming to move a turtle around on screen or to move a robot turtle around on the floor of the classroom. Children are able to create a square with a series of repeated ordered steps, right out of structured program design, as follows:

```
TO SQUARE              To make a square
    REPEAT 4           Repeat the following 4 times
        FORWARD 100    Move forward 100 units
        RIGHT 90       Turn right 90 degrees
    END                Loop back to repeat
                       (Papert 1980, 59)
```

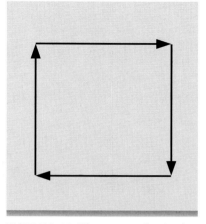

**FIGURE 9-12** The output of a simple Logo program to draw a square with 100 units on a side.

Children enjoy experimenting with different dimensions and angles and seeing the results immediately, either on the computer screen or as the turtle robot moves around the room. They are learning through doing graphics programming, which Papert calls "turtle geometry." Other high-level languages incorporate a variety of much more complicated graphics manipulation routines.

## VIDEO GAMES

Most youngsters are introduced to graphics software through **video games,** either on their own computer or television set or in the video arcade. With its simple maze and limited colors and actions, PacMan seems old-fashioned by today's standards. Video arcade addicts today get many opportunities for fast action, and a lot more detailed figures and animation in many more colors, than those of a generation ago. The graphics programs behind these games have to contend with many possible actions by a player using a joystick or action glove, and must react with an almost immediate response on screen. Movement of the joystick triggers a moving response by the figures on the screen. The resulting fast-paced action game represents probably the most popular example in the public mind of complex **computer animation.**

**video game:** One of the most popular and most widely recognized computer graphic applications, available in video arcades and home entertainment software.

**computer animation:** The creation and display of computer graphic images in rapid sequence to produce the effect of animation, exemplified in arcade video games.

## GRAPHICS SOFTWARE

Applications programs explicitly designed to allow users to develop their own graphics fall into two categories, called paint and draw programs. MacPaint, the first popular graphics package introduced on the original Macintosh, gave its name to the **paint software** category. Picking from a set of graphics tools with the mouse, the MacPaint designer could create freehand images on the screen or use the prepared shapes, shadings, and

**paint software:** Graphics programs that allow users to handle prepared shapes or do freehand sketching and manipulate their creations at the pixel level.

---

### EVOLUTIONARY PERSPECTIVE

#### CD-ROM Games: The Challenge of Myst

Today's visually rich video games come in a variety of forms: arcade games in shopping malls, to Sega and Nintendo cartridges, and the newest format, CD-ROM versions for home computers with large storage capacity for graphics, video, and animation. It is now estimated that 10 million personal computers are equipped with CD-ROM drives. Myst (Broderbund), the most popular CD-ROM game, was created by two brothers, Rand and Robyn Miller, working on Macintoshes, and had sold more than two million copies by early 1996. With its stunning graphic representations of a deserted island, Myst requires more mental problem-solving abilities than skill with a joystick to understand what is going on. The viewer is deposited on the island and caught up in a mystery to explain what happened to all of the people. The narrative line is gradually teased out of the multimedia effects, which include digitized video clips and computer animations in surreal locales.

Myst rewrote the success formula for CD-ROM games from shoot-em-up action and race sequences to a complex logic puzzle set in a graphical framework of dazzling beauty and mystery. The promised sequel, eagerly awaited by its fans, is now being produced with state-of-the-art Silicon Graphics workstations on a huge budget, and the company has grown from 9 to 20 employees.

Whether the sequel created by a large software team of artists and computer animators will be able to hold the narrative interest with the same satisfying effects as the first effort created on a small budget by the two brothers remains to be seen (Guttman).

**FIGURE 9-13** This foggy landscape of Myst suggests the haunting mystery of the most popular video game ever created.

**draw program:** A graphics program that provides commands to create regular shapes like rectangles as objects that can be resized or moved around without affecting other objects.

**object-oriented graphics software:** Draw programs that treat graphic constructions as objects suitable for repositioning and resizing as a unit.

type fonts to create boxes, circles, or fancy lettering. In magnified form, every pixel on the screen could be addressed with the mouse and set to black or left blank, which is the background color, white. Modern paint programs offer a full-color palette with similar features on a high-quality color monitor. Creative artists especially find the total access to and control over a variety of easy-to-use, flexible drawing tools to be attractive features of paint programs.

Also offering graphics tools, **draw programs** additionally focus on the created images as objects. They are thus called **object-oriented graphics software.** This means that a person may draw a small rectangular object on screen to represent a room in a house floor plan. Later the designer can pick up the room "object," enlarge or shrink it proportionally, rotate it, or stretch out one of its sides. What started as a paint-created image becomes encapsulated as a draw object and can be manipulated as a whole. The look each object has when created is carried along as it is modified. The ability to have many objects on the screen capable of being moved around

A

B

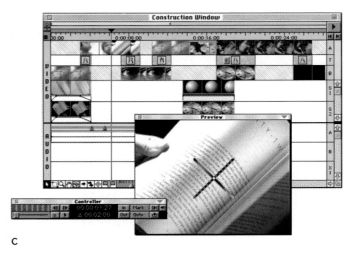

C

**FIGURE 9-14** Adobe Systems offers a full array of graphic imaging and manipulation software: (A) PageMaker for desktop publishing; (B) Illustrator, a graphics program that can produce commercial artistic effects; and (C) Premiere, which allows tracks of audio and video to be laid out on the same time line and edited together.

## EVOLUTIONARY PERSPECTIVE

### Moving from Graphics to the Internet

Adobe Systems is an industry pioneer in merging of graphics and multimedia capabilities into a suite of interrelated graphics software packages. Adobe got its start as creators of **PostScript,** the standard computer software to get a printer to understand a complex document with graphics and different fonts that led to the proliferation of laser printing and the desktop computing industry. Adobe today is known for several essential programs needed in any computer graphics shop: Photoshop, Illustrator, Premiere, and Acrobat. With Photoshop, a user can import a graphic image or digitized photograph created in any format to edit and store it in another format, whereas Illustrator is a full-featured graphics manipulation package, including color gradients and hundreds of PostScript fonts. One needs Premiere for creating and editing digitized video movies and videotape on the computer.

Three recent Adobe moves suggest the direction in which graphics software is moving in the Internet age. In 1994 the company bought Aldus, the producers of the popular desktop publishing software called PageMaker, and integrated it into its line of compatible software. Graphics created with other Adobe products integrate easily into PageMaker files.

Its format called Acrobat is intended to provide a standard for transmitting all kinds of electronic documents, a successor for PostScript appropriate for distribution on the Internet. The Acrobat format is very powerful since its colorful documents, which can be stored or printed, do not depend on the hardware where they are created or ultimately displayed (Young).

Acrobat has not been as universally accepted as HTML, the most favored format for World Wide Web documents. In response, Adobe created PageMill, a program that allows users to create Web documents without knowing HTML (Pitta). Recent agreements with corporate partners like IBM, Apple, and Netscape, the maker of the most popular browser software for the Web, can give Acrobat a strong base of users that they hope will further solidify their format as a new standard like their original PostScript definition for printer graphics. Like the rest of the computer community, the company that has led in desktop publishing and supported all forms of multimedia wants to have an important stake in the wired world of the Internet (Chao).

**PostScript:** A software standard created by Adobe Systems for describing a printed document containing a variety of fonts and graphics.

as units is a very attractive feature of draw programs to professionals like architectural designers.

## INTEGRATED GRAPHICS CAPABILITIES

Today many different software applications incorporate graphics capabilities among their features. We have already noted the importance of graphical elements in desktop publishing (Chapter 6) and spreadsheets (Chapter 7). Typically an object-oriented draw feature is included in a program designed primarily for another purpose. Spreadsheets can present their numerical data in an array of graph formats (bar graphs, pie charts, scatter plots, and so on). Desktop publishing software is actually a hybrid of a word processor and a draw program. The user can import both graphic images and text prepared elsewhere, and move them around or resize them in the layout of the printed page.

Today much word processing software allows graphic objects to be dropped into a text document, but its subsequent modification is usually not as flexible as it would be in a purely draw environment. Hypermedia applications created with systems like ToolBook and HyperCard favor multimedia over early hypertext software, which only allowed text materials to be linked. These newer programs derive much of their appeal from the inclusion of digitized photographs or author-created pictorial images. In all these cases, the addition of graphics to other kinds of applications software enhances the power and appeal of the final output.

## PRESENTATION GRAPHICS

Special-purpose software packages intended for making slides or giving animated presentations are heavily graphics-intensive and are usually classified as **presentation graphics** applications. The two dimensions of the

**presentation graphics:** Software that produces graphic representations of information, often used for presentations at meetings.

### Equipping the Multimedia Studio

Multimedia computer presentations are becoming widely used for education, training, and entertainment. Although normally heavy in graphics content, they often combine a variety of media—text, sound, graphics, digitized photographs, and video—in one digital package, such as a CD-ROM.

Suppose a person wants to set up a multimedia studio to produce such resources on a workstation or personal computer platform. What kinds of software and hardware would be required? First, the user would need a very fast Intel processor, like a Pentium; a higher-end Macintosh, such as the AV models, specifically designed for audiovisual applications or perhaps a graphics workstation from Silicon Graphics. At least 32MB of RAM memory is advisable. If the computer does not come equipped with one, the user would also need a **digitizer board** for video capture and perhaps another for audio input. A flatbed scanner would be essential for digitizing still images and photos.

Among software packages, two kinds are essential: a package for enhancing digitized images (like Photoshop from Adobe) and authoring software to allow the user to put all these digital resources together in a lesson or presentation. Authoring tools for multimedia run the gamut, from those that are simple to use for linking different media types (MediaLink from InterEd) to ones of medium complexity and more visual effects (Authorware from Macromedia) to the high-end professional standard, called Director (from Macromedia).

The most popular multimedia publishing project to date, a CD-ROM journey across Australia called *From Alice to Ocean* (Addison-Wesley and Against All Odds Productions) was produced in 1992 by a team of multimedia specialists using Director. Some industry observers think the project cost the publishers and Apple Computer, one of the sponsors, more than $1 million. Even experienced multimedia authors acknowledge that learning to use all the power of Director may take several months (Fisher). Nevertheless, the person desiring to get started in multimedia production can equip a reasonable studio with the hardware and software tools needed for just several thousand dollars. Like so many other fields in the computer age, multimedia development is becoming a cottage industry in schools, homes, and businesses across the continent.

**digitizer board:** A circuit board for a computer that accepts video input and digitizes it so that it may be seen on the computer screen.

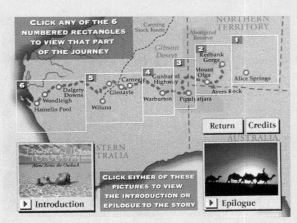

**FIGURE 9-15** *From Alice to Ocean* was one of the first popular CD-ROM multimedia products. Essentially an enhanced computer version of the book by the same title, this multimedia "book" includes video and sound, as well as magnificent digitized photography.

---

computer screen lend themselves to two-dimensional images and can even simulate three-dimensional (3-D) effects. Using the object orientation of draw packages, a user can easily create a two-dimensional image, such as a rectangle, and then choose a tool from the software to add a shadow behind it, for a 3-D effect. If the rectangle needs to be moved around on the screen, all characteristics of the object, including its shadow, go along with it (Yager). Many of these packages, the most popular of which is Microsoft PowerPoint, are designed to save images and play them back on the computer screen, like a series of color slides. Others allow the user to show them in rapid sequence, as in animation. Computer animation of this type resembles flipping through a series of cards to create the illusion of motion—an idea Walt Disney pioneered with Mickey Mouse cartoons and perfected in full-length animated movies like *Snow White* and *Cinderella*.

## DIGITIZED VIDEO

**digitized video:** A process in which a hardware circuit board on a computer accepts input from a TV or VCR and converts the images to digital format at a rate of between 15 and 30 frames a second, capturing full-motion video for the computer screen.

**full-motion video:** A term applied to video movies that can be edited and shown on a computer after they are digitized.

Newer video techniques go beyond animation in the capture and playing of **digitized video.** Common software approaches, such as QuickTime for Macintosh and Windows and Video for Windows, are becoming current standards in the fast-moving field of multimedia production. All are heavily memory-intensive, but allow users to create their own **full-motion videos** at their desktop computers.

First a hardware board installed on the computer accepts input from an analog TV signal, a VCR, or a minicam recorder and converts the images to digital format at a rate typically between 15 and 30 frames a second. Then the software uses complicated schemes for compressing the great number of images for storage on disk or in internal RAM, from which they can later be retrieved and displayed on a graphics computer screen. Since live television is distributed at 30 frames a second, the closer the digitized video approaches that figure, the more like television it seems to the viewer, presented directly on the computer screen.

## COMPUTER-AIDED DESIGN (CAD)

With its roots in Ivan Sutherland's Sketchpad, CAD software for computer-aided design and its related processes, **computer-aided engineering (CAE)** and **computer-aided manufacturing (CAM),** integrate the graphics of engineering drafting into the whole manufacturing process. Today's powerful personal computer models with high-resolution monitors now provide the processing speeds and large memories to run fine 3-D CAD software. Only a few years ago, CAD capabilities suitable for engineering and architectural applications could be handled only by the more expensive scientific workstations.

CAD truly represents **interactive computer graphics**, the ability to reposition a three-dimensional drawing with the mouse and to see the results immediately on the screen. Behind every CAD system is software for the heavy-duty mathematical calculations involved in creating and moving a 3-D object around on the screen at the same speed as the designer moves the mouse. The geometric transformation involved in adding 3-D shadowing to a rectangle, described on page 214, suggests in simple form the sort of mathematical calculation integral to CAD graphics.

To examine CAD in more detail, let us consider the usual **graphics primitives** available in a two-dimensional application. Included among these tools are point markers, various types of lines (connected, dotted, dashed, and so on), arcs and curves, and circles and various closed poly-

**MULTIMEDIA**

**computer-aided engineering (CAE):** The use of an integrated series of computer processes to design, test, and manufacture products, usually starting with computer-aided design (CAD).

**computer-aided manufacturing (CAM):** The use of a computer system to automate parts of a manufacturing process, such as producing machine parts directly on robotic lathes that receive their instructions from a CAD system. The abbreviation CAD/CAM applies to such integrated computer processes.

**interactive computer graphics:** A term applied to software and hardware systems that allow complicated graphics repositioning to be carried out in real time, such as in fine CAD systems.

**graphics primitives:** A set of graphic drawing elements like point markers, various types of lines, arcs and curves, circles, and closed polygons, included in software for CAD.

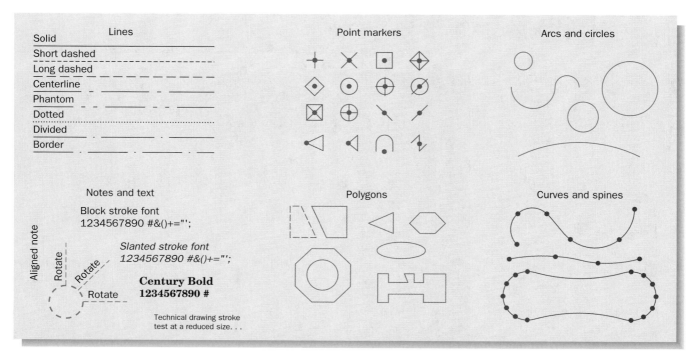

**FIGURE 9-16** A selection of the many drawing tools offered by typical CAD software. The user picks them with the mouse and creates a design on the screen.

gons, as well as some fonts for lettering (Pfortmiller). Suppose you were an architect designing a small tool shed. First you might lay out a simple floor plan for one room as an object and create the front view containing the door as another object. Linking them with the mouse and adding a three-dimensional effect with side walls, perhaps with windows, you have the 3-D rendering on the screen. Then you can rotate the image to see what the shed would look like from the side or the back or the bottom.

## REAL-TIME CAD EFFECTS

Preceding all these moves, the CAD software has stored a lot of geometric information in the data attributes of the shed, a complex object made up of simpler objects like the floor and the front view. Included in the computer description for each simple object are three elements: the $x$-$y$ coordinates, which determine its position of the screen; its attributes, such as style or color; and the connectivity relationships, which show how the pieces fit together (Foley and van Dam). As you move the shed around for different perspectives, the program must recalculate all the geometrical relationships before it creates the pixel representation on the screen. The cal-

**FIGURE 9-17** Auto CAD, the popular computer-aided design software from Auto Desk, has many uses: (A) from the design of complicated machinery like a sextant to (B) the architectural layout of a room, complete with furnishings and perspective.

A

B

culations become even more extensive if the shed is created in color, since multiple signals are sent to each pixel for color representation.

From the user's perspective, the computer is required to handle a huge amount of calculation and redrawing in real time. The term *real time* refers to all kinds of computer processes, not just interactive graphics, in which to the observer the output seems to be generated essentially at the same moment the input signal is given, with little or no delay. For instance, in a hospital intensive care unit, computers monitor heart patients' pulse rates and notify the nurse's station in real time when someone's pulse is dangerously low.

SOCIETY

The integration of CAD into the engineering process is revolutionizing the production of machine parts. Here CAD meets CAM in the realm of CAE. An engineer sets out to design and manufacture a replacement part for a broken joint in a large machine. He uses his CAD program to sketch out the part and stores the image. In an integrated CAE system, the measurements and characteristics of the part can be captured, tested mathematically for stress analysis, and incorporated into the instructions for turning out the finished joint on a robotic machine lathe.

This process includes the three elements of the Computer Triangle in all phases of the operation, from the original idea to the finished product. With such a CAD/CAM system, companies do not need to keep on hand a huge inventory of spare parts. When one is needed, it is created on demand. Warehouse costs are reduced, without loss of time in replacing broken machine parts when they are needed. The computer component is crucial to the success of the integrated manufacturing task.

## ▶ Frontiers in Advanced Computer Graphics

As CAD/CAM software matures and multimedia software spreads in advertising and education, new graphics challenges are constantly being faced. The ideal of the totally believable "realistic image" is leading to exciting new technologies in graphics computing.

### RAY TRACING AND RADIOSITY

How does the computer create the increasingly realistic still images one sees on high-resolution computer screens, with color shading, shadows, and reflected light? Two common software strategies are called ray tracing and ra-

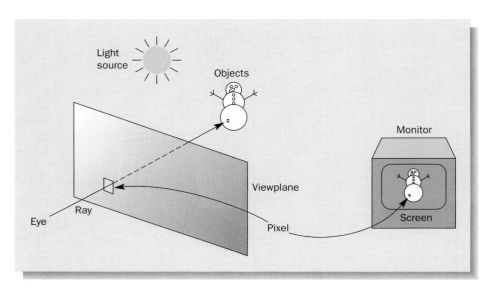

**FIGURE 9-18** In ray tracing, the scene is viewed from the location of the eye. If light is reflected from a part of an object to the eye, the ray tracing software will display it on the screen. Light that strikes behind the snowman will not be registered on the screen.

**FIGURE 9-19** Realistic reflections and shadows are added to the graphic images of these globes by ray-tracing software.

**ray tracing:** An enhancement technique for computer graphics that simulates the effect of reflected light rays in a three-dimensional scene on a two-dimensional computer screen.

diosity. **Ray tracing** simulates the effect of light rays in a three-dimensional scene presented in the two-dimensional space of the computer screen. From the viewpoint of their eyes, observers see the 3-D scene presented in the distance through the rectangular viewplane of the screen (Glassner). When light rays strike an object in real life, some are absorbed, others are refracted, and some are reflected into the eye and interpreted as an image.

Ray tracing works backwards from reality—from eye to object to light source. The computer program calculates which light rays will be reflected into the eye versus those that are absorbed or refracted in other directions, away from the eye. It figures out which parts of an object are not seen by the eye, because they are located outside the viewplane, and from that perspective are hidden surfaces (Sørensen). To do ray tracing requires massive computer computation, but today's scientific workstations and power-packed high-end personal computers can now do a creditable job of

A

B

**FIGURE 9-20** Two examples of photo-realism: (A) the desk scene includes extensive ray tracing for reflective and transparent surfaces, and (B) the cathedral is enhanced with radiosity, to suggest the effect of indirect light coming in the windows and reflected off the pillars.

creating a ray-traced image, called a **rendering**—a task that was formerly possible only with supercomputers (Yares).

Sometimes ray-traced images, which are, after all, only simulations, appear to have a hard edge—to be sharper than reality. The problem occurs because this method cannot handle textured environments with diffusely reflecting surfaces, like painted walls or carpets. In reality, such surfaces reflect light in all directions with equal intensity. The effects of simulated diffusion can be handled with software techniques borrowed from the engineering of heat transfer. In effect, the program adds shading information to the surfaces in the scene. Objects that are partially illuminated by diffuse light are enhanced by these **radiosity** methods (Wallace and Fujii). Ray tracing methods combined with radiosity can produce stunning high-resolution still computer images that approach **photo-realism,** which means they look real enough to be photographs (Yares). Today's discussions of photo-realism apply more to still images than to animation or video.

**rendering:** A general term for creating a ray-traced image.

**radiosity:** A software technique to simulate the effects of light diffusion and add shading to objects in computer graphic images that seem sharper than reality.

**photo-realism:** A term used to describe the increasingly realistic creations of computer graphics made possible by techniques like ray tracing.

## GRAPHICS IN MOVIES

The cover of *IEEE Computer* in August 1979 showed a frame of a computer animation created by Art Durinski of Information International, Inc., that simulated Luke Skywalker's famous X-wing fighter in the *Star Wars* films. "Entertainment and technology are ready for each other," forecast John Whitney, Jr., one of the founders of the Motion Picture Project at Information International (*IEEE Computer*, 5). But Whitney acknowledged that there was much to learn to match Hollywood's sophisticated special effects.

**HISTORY**

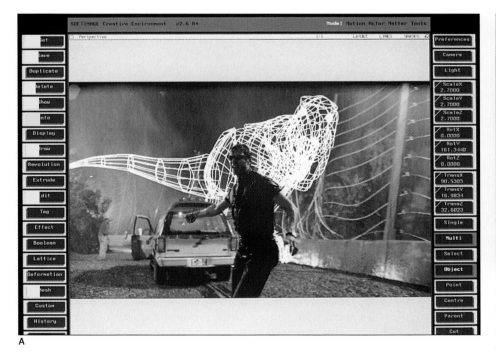

A

B

**FIGURE 9-21** (A) Its most spectacular result to date is surely the frighteningly believable, computer-generated dinosaurs combined with live actors in *Jurassic Park*. (B) George Lucas, the man behind *Star Wars*, was impressed with a computer simulation of Luke Skywalker's X-wing fighter, created by the Motion Picture Project and printed on the cover of *IEEE Computer*. As a result, he started his own computer animation studio.

**FIGURE 9-22** The photo-realistic *Toy Story*, whose main toy characters were a cowboy named Woody and an astronaut named Buzz, filled its full length of 77 minutes with computer animation, compared to 6 minutes in *Jurassic Park*.

George Lucas, the creator of *Star Wars*, was favorably enough impressed with the X-wing simulation to begin a major computer graphics effort for moviemaking in the early 1980s. Early efforts of this group, who developed their own hardware and software, included scenes for *Return of the Jedi*, the last *Star Wars* film, and a sequence called the Genesis Demo for *Star Trek II*. Meanwhile, the Motion Picture Project was using a Cray XMP supercomputer to produce 40 minutes of event simulation for *The Last Starfighter* (Sørensen). In recent years, computer graphics for scene simulation and other special effects in films have benefited from more powerful hardware at cheaper prices and improved algorithms. Effects in movies, like the liquid-metal man in *Terminator II* and the large cast of realistic and frightening dinosaurs in *Jurassic Park*, both from George Lucas's company, Industrial Light and Magic, have very successfully relied on computer-created full-motion video sequences combining actors and machine-produced images. The result has been several blockbuster box-office successes.

*Toy Story*, the most impressive computer achievement in movies to date, came out in late 1995 from Pixar, a spin-off company from Lucasfilm owned by Steve Jobs, one of the original founders of Apple. It is a full 77-minute film released by Disney but produced entirely on computers by animators working with computer graphics staff. There were no cels to paint and animate as in traditional Disney cartoon features, only images on color monitors. The film, widely acclaimed for its believable effects, features a cast of toys that come to life, and even the human characters, like the boy who owns the toys, are rendered images (Sragow). The computer task took four years to complete; on a weekly basis the maximum output was 3.5 minutes of animation. Sometimes one frame of animation took up to 20 hours to render. Each of the characters is modeled in 3-D with thousands of digital strings somewhat like those that marionettes have. That the main character, a cowboy toy called Woody, has more than 200 strings to make his facial movements suggests the magnitude of the job. In addition sets and locales were created with computer-assisted design technology (Braddock). The critical and financial success of *Toy Story* almost guarantees more spectacular computer productions as full-length movie features.

## FRACTALS

**fractal geometry:** A field of mathematics pioneered by Benoit Mandelbrot that involves the study of a set of infinitely recursive mathematical functions which seem to mirror natural phenomena like leaf and cloud formation.

One of the most fascinating developments in the graphics of movie and video effects comes from **fractal geometry,** an active research field in

**FIGURE 9-23** (A) Fern leaf patterns generated by fractal geometric functions. (B) The version of Monet's "Water-lilies pool—Harmony in Green" (1899) created by computers using fractal geometry gives a sense of the possibilities for artistic effect, compared to the (C) original painting.

mathematics pioneered by Benoit Mandelbrot of IBM. Mandelbrot studied a set of infinitely recursive mathematical functions, whose behavior can best be seen on a graphics terminal. These geometrical forms are described as mathematically self-similar, with fractional dimensions (hence the name *fractals;* see Mandelbrot). A repeated series of calculations of such functions creates infinitely regressive versions of the related geometric shape, rendering them in more and more detail as the individual units of measure get smaller. The results are bumpy, convoluted shapes that share important similarities with a variety of structures in nature: mountain ranges and irregular coastlines, leaf patterns in ferns, snowflakes, and cloud formations (*The Puzzle Master*).

Research continues on the relationship between these mathematical formulas and processes in nature, especially in botany. The fractal concept of self-similarity provides leads to understanding complex botanical features, like the growth of leaf patterns. It suggests that there exists a recur-

**HISTORY**

**FIGURE 9-24** Lucasfilm created this early simulated scene called *Point Reyes,* depicting a coastal landscape in California, in 1984. Most of the natural scenery is generated from fractals and foreshadowed the use of fractal landscapes in later movies.

**HISTORY**

sive mechanism in the natural development process which creates the leaves (Prusinkiewicz and Lindenmayer).

With computers, fractal graphics software can be used to create images that model natural phenomena. As long ago as 1980, Loren Carpenter impressed computer graphics experts with a film simulation of flight over a fractal mountain range, in which the detail got progressively refined as the camera appeared to approach the mountain and fly over it (Clark). One of the most complex early single frames of computer graphic art, called *Point Reyes* (a locale on the Pacific Coast near San Francisco), was created by artists at Lucasfilm in 1984. It included layers of fractal images of mountains, lakes, and rocks, which produced a successful simulated impression of reality (Sørensen). More an experiment than a commercial success, this image showed the viability of fractal geometry for creating realistic effects with fine graphics output.

**FIGURE 9-25** This frame of computer-enhanced graphics imagery from advertising illustrates morphing: the blending of one picture into another. Here the front of the car is turning into a tiger.

## VIRTUAL REALITY

The next stage in the continuing evolution of graphics appears to be **virtual reality (VR),** the ultimate fantasy of the video game enthusiast. Also known as **artificial reality, cyberspace,** and **tele-presence,** virtual reality combines the visual aspects of interactive computer graphics with the viewer's response to what he or she is seeing. It represents a superb current example of the Computer Triangle, a coordinated effort of hardware, software, and the participant. The effect is to put viewers wearing special goggles or helmets in the middle of a scene and let them move around in it at their own pace and even change it. As they turn their heads left, the scene changes to display within the 3-D stereoscopic goggles whatever is in that direction. Sensors within the helmet monitor eye or body movement and change the scene to create a wraparound effect. More than pictures, virtual reality immerses the viewer in a place, in which he or she may then roam around. Often, with a **data glove** or other device, the viewer can effect change in the simulated scene.

For example, at the University of North Carolina, a viewer can walk through parts of a simulated body, looking for tumors and getting ready to zap them with radiation. The application allows physicians to hunt for cancers and plan to focus their radiation beams on them for the best advantage. At NASA's Ames Research Center in California, researchers seem to fly over the ravines and cliffs of the Martian landscape, put together from Viking spaceship photos, to develop new ways of using the data that come back from planetary probes. Handicapped people wearing virtual reality goggles can play racquetball with seemingly real opponents by moving their data gloves to hit the "virtual" ball. They then hear a taped sound of the ball's impact with the racquet. The sense of reality is very believable, for as Randal Walser, head of the Cyberspace Project in Sausalito, California, says, give a few cues to the brain, such as the taped sound, and it will fill in the blanks (Stewart). Of course, virtual reality video arcades are already open in many cities.

Virtual reality combines computers, video, image processing, graphics, and sensor technologies to give the user 360 degrees of movement and the ability to interact with the environment. Many systems run in experimental situations, but from Ames Research Center have come the DataGlove, the DataSuit, and the EyePhone. The DataSuit expands the sensor capacities of the DataGlove to the whole body, and the EyePhone is a kind of 3-D stereoscopic headset. None of these products is inexpensive, with prices for the DataGlove and EyePhone in the thousands of dollars. Nevertheless,

**virtual reality (VR):** An environment created by computer technology that combines visual, auditory, and tactile interaction to create the illusion of realistic objects and sensory experiences for the user. Also called **artificial reality, cyberspace,** and **tele-presence.**

**data glove:** A glove filled with sensors to detect body movement and effect change in the simulated world of VR.

SOCIETY

**FIGURE 9-26** A virtual reality racquetball game. A handicapped person in a wheelchair could play this game against the live opponent by moving the red racquet and actually hearing the ball contact.

## EVOLUTIONARY PERSPECTIVE

### The Future of Virtual Reality

Today's critics of virtual reality comment that the media hype does not match the limitations of current systems. Their remarks echo the critics of computer graphics in the movies a decade ago. In addition to small screens with limited resolution, problems with "perceptual delay" between the movement of the viewer and the changed view in the headset sometimes give people motion sickness. Most systems cannot yet match the refresh speed of interactive computer graphics for television, 24 to 30 frames per second. All these problems require computer power available only on expensive processors (Arthur).

Yet commercial developers already are selling a variety of VR systems in the range of $400 to $1,000 for the home game market. They use either an enhanced pair of eyeglasses, which cut down on motion sickness, or the typical **head-mounted display goggles,** now called **HMDs.** They work with personal computers and TV game sets. People find VR for flight simulation using an HMD much more realistic than using a computer and a joystick (Rogers).

Apple Computer has introduced a type of VR with its QuickTime VR extension for digitized video to run on its computer screens and keep memory requirements down to a minimum. Given a set of still pictures depicting a 360-degree panorama or showing close-ups of an object or locale at different distances, QuickTime VR software merges the shots into a continuous whole, filling in the gaps and eliminating overlappings for a unified effect. The result can be a QuickTime movie to pan around the Grand Canyon or zoom in to catch a detail of Michelangelo's "David." Using a mouse or joystick, the viewer can look left or right, up or down. Virtual world applications include tours of homes or close-up views of famous sites more than games for the home market, but developers are just beginning to use the technology ("A Short Cut into Virtual Reality").

Virtual reality represents an expanded graphic technology in its infancy. We cannot foresee whether our lives in future will be similar to the virtual worlds envisioned by William Gibson, who coined the term *cyberspace* in *Neuromancer* (1984). In Gibson's science fiction novel, thousands took part daily in "consensual hallucination," though the stimulus was electrodes rather than a headset. We can already forecast applications of virtual reality in the handling of hazardous or radioactive materials, in medicine, and in simulated travel to faraway places, as well as in video games. Yet even virtual reality enthusiasts like Jaron Lanier, who makes the DataGlove, do not want to trade in real life for the most complex simulation. "The physical world is infinitely subtle. . . . A virtual Maui will never be as good as even the grungiest parts of the real Hoboken" (quoted in Stewart 45). Computers may simulate reality but will not replace it.

---

**head-mounted display (HMD):**   A term for a set of 3-D goggles equipped with CRTs inside for use in virtual reality games or other ap-

**FIGURE 9-27** As the user moves the data glove, the hand movements are sensed and displayed on the computer screen in real time.

as with all previous computer technology, the costs are bound to come down as ease of use and breadth of application to a wide variety of fields open up the field through competition (Leonard).

## ▶ Summary

Graphics effects have added immeasurably to the pleasures and capabilities of the computer for the average user, the TV and movie buff, the engineering designer, and the medical researcher. Combining the technology of the television screen, software for the mathematics of geometry, and the speeds of modern computer processors yields quite remarkable visual effects, both still and animated, in computer graphics. New techniques like ray tracing, radiosity, and virtual reality are making refinements to graphic imaging that move it closer to reality every day. Moving the computer from a keyboard-centered to a picture-based technology continues to open new possibilities that we have only begun to explore and exploit. As Marshall McLuhan taught us a generation ago in his book about this video-centered age (*Understanding Media* 1965), people respond to pictures more easily and more immediately than to the written word. An ancient Chinese proverb is true: a picture *is* worth a thousand words (Foley and van Dam).

## ▶ Key Terms

additive primary colors (p. 207)
buffer memory (p. 203)

computer-aided engineering (CAE)
(p. 215)

computer-aided manufacturing (CAM) (p. 215)

computer animation (p. 211)

data glove (p. 223)

digitized video (p. 214)

digitizer board (p. 214)

digitizing scanner (p. 206)

dithering (p. 209)

draw program (p. 212)

electrostatic plotter (p. 205)

fax machine (p. 206)

flatbed plotter (p. 205)

four-color process (p. 209)

fractal geometry (p. 220)

frame buffer (p. 205)

full-motion video (p. 214)

graphics primitives (p. 215)

graphics processor (p. 205)

gray scale (p. 207)

head-mounted display (HMD) (p. 224)

interactive computer graphics (p. 215)

light pen (p. 202)

object-oriented graphics software (p. 212)

paint software (p. 211)

photo-realism (p. 219)

PostScript (p. 213)

presentation graphics (p. 213)

radiosity (p. 219)

raster (p. 204)

raster graphics (p. 203)

ray tracing (p. 218)

refresh buffer (p. 203)

rendering (p. 219)

subtractive primary colors (p. 208)

sweeper (p. 205)

vector graphics (p. 203)

video game (p. 211)

virtual reality (VR); artificial reality, cyberspace, tele-presence (p. 223)

 *Self-Test*

## MULTIPLE-CHOICE

1. All of the following elements are associated with raster graphics except
   a. pixels
   b. screen resolution
   c. a bit map of the screen
   d. a vector processor

2. Dot-matrix and ink-jet printers designed on the bit-mapped principle could be expected to print which of the following types of images?
   a. small fonts for footnotes
   b. graphic designs done by students with painting software
   c. large headline fonts in exotic typefaces
   d. all of the above

3. Which of the following is not an essential element of fax technology?
   a. an input digitizer for images
   b. a laptop computer
   c. a modem connected to the phone lines
   d. an electrostatic output printer

4. In computer color graphics, which of the following is not an additive primary color?
   a. blue
   b. red
   c. yellow
   d. green

5. Using an eight-bit code to send a color signal to an RGB color monitor yields how many total possible color combinations?
   a. 8
   b. $8 \times 8 \times 8 = 512$
   c. $2^8 = 256$
   d. $3 \times 8 = 24$

6. All of the following represent software applications of computer graphics except
   a. the Logo computer language
   b. raster graphics
   c. paint and draw programs
   d. video games

7. Characteristic presentation graphics effects include
   a. two-dimensional and 3-D effects
   b. animation
   c. slide shows
   d. all of the above

8. To set up a multimedia studio, a user would need all of the following except
   a. a digitizer board
   b. a machine to press CDs
   c. multimedia authoring software
   d. a flatbed scanner

## TRUE/FALSE

9. **T   F**   Compared to spreadsheets or databases, which are mainly software applications, understanding how computer graphics works requires consideration of both the hardware and software components.

10. **T   F**   Today it is not uncommon for high-resolution monitors to have about 100,000 pixels on the screen.

11. **T   F**   Both the input and output parts of fax machines utilize concepts of bit-mapped graphics.

12. **T   F**   On a monochrome screen, signals from a computer with an RGB video board show up as three gradations of shading from white to black, which is called gray scale.

13. **T   F**   Because color printers mix materials on paper that will reflect the desired color to the human eye, they use the three primary subtractive colors: magenta, cyan, and yellow.

14. **T   F**   The ability to move objects around on the screen as units is a very attractive feature of paint programs to professionals like architects.

15. **T   F**   Practical research with fractals involves the relationship between these mathematical formulas and processes in nature, especially in botany.

16. **T   F**   Even with ray tracing and radiosity methods, photo-realism is still beyond the possibilities of computer production.

## FILL-IN

17. Since the 1970s the cheaper and better alternative to vector graphics has been _____, based on the technology of television.

18. The phosphor dots on the inside of a TV tube or CRT, which glow when hit by an electron beam, are called _____.

19. A computer with an _____ can send out a color signal to a monitor.

20. Color printers use a process called CMYK (cyan, magenta, yellow, black) that is universally referred to as the _____ in the printing industry.

21. _____ was innovative in its use of computer animation to create a full-length feature film, including all character movements and locales.

22. Behind every _____ system is software for heavy-duty mathematical calculations to create and move 3-D objects around on the screen as the designer moves the mouse.

23. Current scientific workstations and high-end personal computers can create a ray-traced image, called a _____, that was formerly possible only with supercomputers.

24. Also called cyberspace, _____ combines the visual aspects of interactive computer graphics with an ability to suggest a person's moving around in a simulated environment.

## ▶ Experiential Exercises

1. Trace the career of Ivan Sutherland after he created Sketchpad and left MIT. See if you can find out what projects he is working on now.

2. Research the raster principle that is the basis of television and modern graphics-based monitors. Pay attention to the similarities that are allowing graphics computer monitors to show video today.

3. Examine the characteristics of the computer monitors that are available in your college laboratories. What kind of graphics do they support? Are they color or black and white? How many pixels do the monitors have on their screens (a question about graphic resolution)? You may have to get advice from the hardware staff of the computer center or the computer science department.

4. Also investigate printing possibilities on the campus, including plotters and various kinds of printers. How many of these hardware devices are graphics-based in their technology? Do not assume that all printing devices do graphics well. Are any color printers available? If so, arrange for a demonstration.

5. Research the difference in computer technology between presentation of colors using the additive primary colors (red, green, and blue) and the subtractive primary colors (magenta, cyan, and yellow). Why are the additive colors used in computer monitors and the subtractive ones in color printing? Note also how the mixture of the additive colors creates the subtractive ones as well as black and white. Why do some color printers use a fourth primary color to create black?

6. Compare the quality of the graphics presentation in a home video game from Nintendo or Sega and games offered in video arcades. Also look at some examples of the new generation of video games being distributed on CD-ROM disks to be played on modern personal computers. Why would graphics quality be better in CD-ROM or arcade games? Investigate the role of computer memories, video boards, and processors in the presentation of animated graphics.

7. Try to find graphics applications packages on your campus of both the paint and draw varieties. Compare the ways they create images, as well as their differences. Why do two standards exist, rather than just one? Which method seems easier to use and is more flexible? What types of users prefer one type of application over the other?

8. The movie *Toy Story*, which came out in 1995, used more computer-generated images than any previous movie, and the results were stunning and highly successful at the box office. Many newspapers and magazines carried stories about the importance of graphics production in the movie. Look up some of this material in the library, and prepare a report on the role of computer-generated images in the movie and how they were created.

9. Today the study of fractals is interdisciplinary. Are there professors at your institution interested in fractal geometry? Are they faculty members in mathematics or computer science, or in the biological and other natural sciences? Are any in the visual arts or video production? If you cannot find any interest in fractals among the faculty, look up some of the books that show images created from fractal geometry, especially those that seem to mirror plant growth and geological formations.

10. Try to visit a virtual reality video arcade to get a feel for the integration of graphics with the other senses.

 ## Critical Thinking Exercises

1. With the increasing proliferation of computers and software for creating multimedia, discuss the premise that the college term paper of the near future will be a multimedia presentation authored and displayed on a computer.

2. Is there a culture of young people more addicted to virtual reality games than to real life? Would such a habit be healthy? Try to imagine applications in which virtual reality will be beneficial besides those in entertainment. Do you believe that virtual reality will be accepted in the coming generation as the next frontier for computer exploration? Why or why not?

3. With the success of total computer animation in Disney's *Toy Story*, the days of the traditional cel-animated feature film like *Pocohontas* are numbered. Discuss.

**ANSWERS TO SELF-TEST**

*Multiple-Choice*: 1. d;    2. d;    3. b;    4. c;    5. c;    6. b;    7. d;
8. b
*True/False*: 9. T;    10. F;    11. T;    12. F;    13. T;    14. F;    15. T;
16. F
*Fill-in*: 17. raster graphics;    18. pixels;    19. RGB video board;    20.
four-color process;    21. *Toy Story*;    22. CAD;    23. rendering;    24.
virtual reality

# CHAPTER 10

# Networks, Communications, and the Internet

▶ **LEARNING OUTCOMES**

*After completing this chapter, you should be able to:*

1. *Explain the technical connection between computers and modern telecommunications equipment.*

2. *Describe the following standard network applications, including their features and main uses: local area networks, electronic mail, bulletin board systems, and wide area networks.*

3. *Describe the major aspects of the Internet and its wide diversity of application.*

4. *Explain the effects of telecommuting on the work environment.*

5. *Discuss the hacker culture and its diverse relationships to society.*

6. *Discuss the free speech issues raised by widespread networking.*

▶ **COMPUTERS IN CONTEXT**

*The few people in the room at UCLA on November 21, 1969, could not have foreseen that they were starting a revolution called the Internet in creating the first computer network to send a message to the Stanford Research Institute several hundred miles away. Unlike Morse with the telegraph, no one who was there can even remember what the first e-mail message was; unlike the Wright brothers and the airplane, no pictures were taken to record the event. What mattered was that the connection of two mainframe computers via a phone line worked. Thus was born the Internet, arguably the most important development in computing today.*

*At the height of the Cold War, the federal government saw the potential of using the public telephone system to transmit data and messages between research sites—military, university, and commercial—to share technical information and spur cooperation. In the middle 1960s, a group of computer scientists at the Advanced Research Projects Agency (ARPA) of the U. S. Department of Defense began to consider whether computer sites could be connected for communication. With contract help from Bolt Beranek and Newman Inc., ARPA funded research and construction of devices to allow computers with different operating systems to encode, send, and decode information between machines through the national phone network. The first sites on the **ARPANET**, the grandfather of today's Internet, were UCLA, Stanford, UC Santa Barbara, and the University of Utah; by 1971 there were about two dozen nodes, including Harvard and MIT; and by 1981, more than 200 (Kantrowitz and Rogers).*

**FIGURE 10-1** Three of the graduate students who worked on the original Internet project at UCLA—Jon Postel, Steve Crocker, and Vinton Cerf (left to right)—tried to illustrate its design with zucchini and tin cans at the twenty-fifth anniversary in 1994.

*The Internet is today the largest network of interconnected computers in the world. Since 1969, the network's capacity and number of sites have continued to grow as the mission and the technical power of the network have broadened, so that today the Internet has connections on all continents. It has long since expanded beyond the top level of research communities, and now embraces almost all higher education institutions, large businesses and organizations, and millions of home users in this country, with an estimated 30 million users in 1994. Many envision an evolving successor to the Internet, which Vice President Albert Gore has called the* **Information Superhighway**—*a network perhaps as important for America's technological future as the interstate highway system was for an earlier era. Gore envisions the network linking all secondary and primary schools in the next few years; and Vinton Cerf, a graduate student at UCLA in 1969 and now president of the nonprofit Internet Society, foresees 100 million American users by the end of the decade, in addition to millions of users overseas (Radin).*

**Information Superhighway:** A common term for the growth of infrastructure involving the Internet and the spread of high-speed data network services throughout the United States.

Clearly computers are now integral parts of the communications systems of the modern world. A variety of networks, in addition to the Internet, integrating communications and computers fill a large and diverse category of applications in all phases of computing. Before considering the many forms of networking, it is worthwhile for us to look at the main technical issues involved with data communications and networking computers.

## ▶ Technical Issues in Data Communications

In common with graphics, as compared to other standard computer applications, computer networking requires understanding of technical issues of both hardware and software. Data generated on computers must be capable of being transmitted without error over a communications channel, such as a phone line. Normally, this sort of transmission is different from internal data transmission within the computer itself.

### DIGITAL (PARALLEL) TRANSMISSION

In the simplest sense, the field of data communications links the computer and the telephone or telecommunications system. For most of their history, computers have been digital in nature, and telephone communications have been analog. It is important to understand the difference. As discussed in Chapter 4, information in computers is stored and manipulated in binary digital form, so that numbers, letters, and punctuation marks are all represented as a series of binary digits. Similarly, graphic images and sounds are coded in machines as binary maps of pixels and digital numbers representing samples of the sound frequencies.

Within the computer itself, the information must be transferred around from the keyboard to the memory chips to the processor and the screen by a physical electrical connection called a data bus. Bus architecture transfers information as groups of digital signals. Early personal computers were built with 8-bit buses; today's machines have either 16-, 32-, or 64-bit buses. An 8-bit bus, for example, can transfer the Extended ASCII

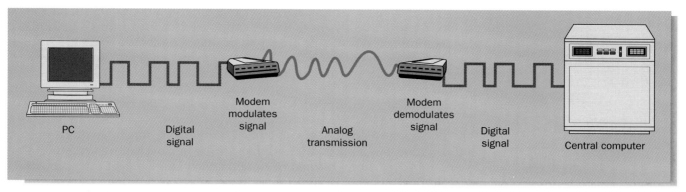

**FIGURE 10-2**  The modem takes digital information from a computer and puts it out onto the phone lines as an analog signal. The modem at the receiving end accepts the signal and converts it back to digital form for the central computer. This diagram might fit a student at home contacting his college's mainframe, from which Gopher is accessed.

code for capital A (the 8 binary digits 10100001) all at one time from storage as one byte of computer memory to the processor. This feature of sending a bundled set of bits over a bus all at the same time is called **parallel transmission** of data. More modern, wider bus architectures can transfer more than one character to an expanded processor (either 16 or 32 bits in length) in the same unit of time. As processor and bus configurations have widened, computer speeds have increased concomitantly.

### ANALOG (SERIAL) TRANSMISSION

On the other hand, telephone transmission of data has traditionally been carried out by a **serial process.** That means that a telephone message is sent out as a continuous series of **analog signals** through the system. A computer data file sent over an analog telephone line must be converted from digital data to analog signals. Thus transmitting capital A as a byte of computer data over an analog phone line requires the sending of eight signals in series—one for each of the eight bits.

 The standard device that is used to connect a personal computer with the telephone system is a modem (the name is an acronym for *modulation/demodulation*). Its job is to transfer the information being moved around in computer buses in parallel fashion to serial form (modulation), so that one binary digit at a time can be released to the phone line. Before sending the data as a stream of serial bits, the modem dials the phone number at the other end. After the connection is established at the receiving end of the communication, another modem accepts the serial data from the phone line and transforms them back into parallel form, suitable for bus distribution throughout the receiving computer (demodulation).

### BAUD RATE

The measure of transmission speed of a modem is called its **baud rate,** which is stated in **bits per second** (abbreviated **bps**). Early modems offered rates of 300 bps, but today the choices are usually 14,400 or 28,800 bits per second. The newer machines are thus many times faster at data transmission than the first modems! At 14,400 baud, a modem should be able to transfer 1800 ASCII characters per second, given that each character is 8 bits in length. In practice, the rate of character transfer is somewhat slower because an extra bit for error detection, called a **parity bit,** may be added to each byte. Thus the baud rate of a modem, expressed in

**parallel transmission:** Method of transmitting data within a computer in which a bundled set of bits is sent over a data bus all at the same time.

**serial process:** The transmission of data in a communications channel like a phone line one bit at a time.

**analog signal:** A signal often transmitted over telephone lines in the form of electronic waves.

**baud rate:** A measure of the speed at which data are transmitted over communications lines by a modem, expressed as bits per second.

**bits per second (bps):** The measure expressing the transmission speed of a modem; usually, but not always, synonymous with its baud rate.

**parity bits:** Single bits attached to each byte to check that data are being transmitted correctly through a communications channel.

**FIGURE 10-3** Modems today come in a variety of sizes and shapes: external desktop models, internal circuit boards, and small PCMCIA cards, like a credit card, suitable for insertion in a laptop computer.

bps, often transfers somewhat fewer meaningful bits of data. Baud rate is not necessarily equivalent to the effective rate of bps transmission for data.

Assuming a typed page of text holds about 2800 characters (35 lines of 80 characters), a common 14,400-baud modem can send a full page of text over the lines in less than two seconds (2800 divided by 1800). Clearly it would not take long for a boss to send an employee a memo with a personal computer equipped with a modern modem, even if one were in California and the other in New York. The memo could even be sent as a fax document using today's popular fax modems, machines that prepare information, whether text or graphics, in fax format before sending it to a remote fax machine. Instead of sending each character of a text in ASCII format, fax modems transmit a digitized image of a page—a series of pixels—that can be reconstituted at the receiving fax machine.

## COMMUNICATIONS SOFTWARE

Normally a user of a modem has **communications software** to ease the process of making the connection to another computer or of setting up a document in fax format. Such software, which normally comes with a modem when it is purchased, works directly with the modem hardware for efficient data communications. It usually can store lists of phone numbers, automatically dial the phone numbers to open communication, and then handle distribution of packets of data both coming into and going out of the computer.

Sending a file out is called **uploading** it; retrieving a file from elsewhere is called **downloading.** For example, if a person downloads a file from an on-line bulletin board, communications software on the personal computer makes it easy to open a file and store the data there for later retrieval locally. The user now has a stored personal copy of something retrieved at long distance. The downloaded document is a new copy, and can be edited or printed after the connection with its distant source has been closed.

Personal computer users of the Internet may have their own commercial accounts with a local Internet provider to be able to access the World Wide Web, or they may become members of national information utilities like CompuServe or America Online to gain access. In either case, they will use communications software to connect to their Internet host before being able to log onto the Web and move around among its myriad sites using their browser software. First they must log onto an Internet site before surfing the Web or using other Internet services, described in more detail later in the chapter.

## NETWORKS

A group of computers connected together in a **network** can communicate with each other directly through a physical link. Today computers in many classrooms and offices are networked so they can share resources, such as a laser printer, or send electronic mail to each other. If these workstations are in relatively close proximity to each other, within a room or a building, they are usually set up in a **local area network (LAN).** LANs may interconnect a great variety of hardware devices, such as personal computers, terminals to mainframes, printers, and fax machines (Rhodes). Typically they span an area no more than a few kilometers in diameter and are owned by a single organization (Tanenbaum). Perhaps as many as 10 office workers may share two laser printers. Any of them may route a document to one of the laser printers when it is ready for printing without disrupting the routine of the other workers. Software on the laser printers

**communications software:** A program that enables a computer to be connected to other computers or that allows a document to be set up in fax format.

**uploading:** Transferring files to a central computer on a network from a remote machine such as a personal computer.

**downloading:** Transferring files from a host computer on a network to remote machines, typically microcomputers.

**network:** A group of computers or other devices, like printers, connected to form a system that can communicate with each other directly through a physical link.

**local area network (LAN):** A system of networked computers and other hardware, like printers, that are in relatively close proximity to one another.

"queues up" multiple jobs in the order in which they arrive, and prints them one after the other.

Computer labs in colleges and universities are often networked as LANs, to allow all the students in a room to share the same software. A **site license** is paid for multiple-user access to the shared package. One copy of the software is usually kept on a large hard disk drive on the network, and downloaded to individual computers as needed.

## LAN SOFTWARE

Often a LAN is run by a special host computer, called a **file server,** containing a big hard disk. The network supervisor assigns to each user a log-in name, a password, and an account on the network. Individuals can gain access to the network from any workstation using a standard log-on procedure; unauthorized users without valid passwords are denied access by the software. Users can store their files in personal accounts on the server, and protect them from use by others by denying access to anyone but the owner. File servers thus provide a considerable measure of security for shared hardware and software, as well as for personal data files. Users can log on at any station with a log-in name and password, and all the equipment and shared software on the network are available for their use.

LANs often have software that allows electronic mail (e-mail) between users. A user may write notes or transmit files to other authorized users by forwarding the materials to their e-mail addresses, normally identified by their log-in names. When users log into the network, the mail software notifies them if they have new mail awaiting their perusal. E-mail can be read on the screen, saved as a permanent file, printed, or deleted, as appropriate. Voice mail systems are similar, except that the mail is a digitized recording of a message. Voice mail can only be heard or stored; it does not exist as a typed text file.

## TYPES OF NETWORK TRANSMISSION

Individual computers in LANs are joined to each other by a wired connection, which may be of several kinds: twisted-pair wire, coaxial cable, or fiber optic cable. Each has its characteristic advantages and liabilities. The oldest kind of cable is **twisted-pair,** which is common copper phone wire. The chief advantage of twisted-pair wire is price. It is cheapest to install but works best with a small number of hardware devices in a relatively confined area. Having more than 25 or 30 units on a network, for example, often leads to serious degradation of service with ordinary twisted-pair connections.

**Coaxial cable,** used to distribute network programs in the early days of television, is also a metallic wire connection. A broader-band communication channel than twisted-pair, it is capable of sending many more signals per unit of distance, with less degradation of the signal than twisted-pair (300 to 500 million bps versus probably 16 million for twisted-pair). Coaxial cable is more expensive to install than twisted-pair wire. Nevertheless, recent advances in twisted-pair connections are now supporting communication at the same rate as coaxial cable. Designers expect that it will be even faster in the near future.

**Fiber optic cable** is currently the fastest, most modern type of cable, and the least susceptible to signal degradation, but it comes at a higher cost of installation. Fiber optic cable is made of glass fibers, and the transmitted signals are pulses of light rather than electronic waves. Thus the transmission of data, whether phone calls or computer information, is no longer analog electronics but digital pulses of light. Compared to coaxial

**site license:** A fee paid to a software company to allow multiple users at a site to access or copy a piece of software.

**file server:** A term applied to both a host computer and its special software that makes programs and data available to individual workstations on a network.

**FIGURE 10-4** Students in this laboratory are connected by a LAN to the printers, which they share. They can probably also send electronic mail to each other.

**twisted-pair wire:** Two copper wires twisted together, often used for home telephone lines and for computer connections in a LAN.

**coaxial cable:** A common metallic cable used for hardwired communications channels because it can carry large amounts of data.

**fiber optic cable:** A modern communications channel using light impulses traveling through clear glass fibers to transmit data safely at very high speeds.

**FIGURE 10-5** The common kinds of network connections: twisted-pair, coaxial cable, and fiber optic cable.

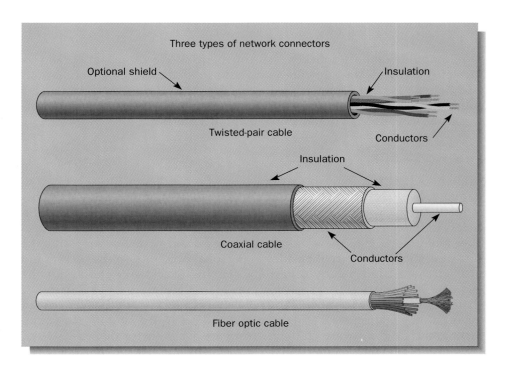

Three types of network connectors

Optional shield

Insulation

Twisted-pair cable

Conductors

Insulation

Coaxial cable

Conductors

Fiber optic cable

**FIGURE 10-6** Each of threadlike fiber optic cables glowing here are capable of sending massive amounts of digital information as pulses of light.

cable, fiber optic cable can carry two or three times as much data (at least 1 billion bps versus 300 to 500 million for coaxial cable). Unlike the analog signals of metallic cable, fiber optic networks are not subject to static and cannot be easily tapped by electronic snoopers, because their signal is not electronic. This characteristic may be worth consideration if activity on the LAN requires heavy security. Familiar today in some national long-distance phone systems, fiber optic cable is currently least used for LANs, but is increasingly attractive for large systems requiring the distribution of very large quantities of data (Bryce).

## ▶ Network Applications

Details about cable connections and modems with parity bits are technical hardware issues. Once they are settled, various software possibilities open up. Ways to configure networks for local and long-distance access are many, each with its characteristic advantages.

### CAMPUS BACKBONES

Additional important decisions are involved if an organization wants to connect several LANs beyond an office or classroom setting for e-mail or Inte_net access. For example, suppose that computer science, engineering, business, English, and journalism have their own separate LANs, often made up of different, incompatible configurations of computers. They may want to set up a campus network to allow students to leave messages for each other on different LANs. The departments may interconnect through a campus **backbone** of complex data transmission protocols, which accept data from one LAN, convert them to a standard format, and transmit them via coaxial or fiber optic cable to another LAN, where they are converted to the appropriate file format for that LAN network. Maybe the main campus computer center will be the central conduit; methods of access may

**backbone:** A term applied to a high-speed communications channel that links several LANs or computer installations in an institution like a college.

**FIGURE 10-7** The campus backbone at MIT links more than 10,000 computers, mainly with fiber optic connections.

vary widely, from direct connections to access through modems and phone lines.

## WIDE AREA NETWORKS

As soon as local network connections are in place, the campus will want to hook up to the Internet and join its backbone to the worldwide network. This moves it beyond the domain of LANs into the much more complex area of **wide area networks (WANs).** Unlike LANs, WANs may span several continents, and are normally owned by a variety of organizations. Although early WANs transferred data at slower rates than LANs, current research on the growth and improvement of the Internet is seeking speeds that will make all sites in this country accessible by WANs as quickly as by any LAN.

In this wider ballpark, a letter file produced by a student on an Intel computer can be sent to the campus mainframe and then released to the Internet, to be sent to a friend attending a college halfway across the country. Along the way it will pass through a variety of relays, called **bridges** or **gateways,** of interconnected systems, perhaps consisting of mainframes from companies like IBM or Control Data, or of Unix workstations from

**wide area network (WAN):** A geographically dispersed communications network, with many owners, linking computers for the purpose of communicating with each other, such as a national network for airline reservations.

**bridge (gateway):** A hardware interface for interconnecting similar computer networks.

**FIGURE 10-8** This map illustrates the Internet traffic load in the United States in late 1994. The lighter the lines, the greater the number of bytes carried by the network; white lines represent a trillion bytes of Internet activity.

Digital Equipment or Sun Microsystems. All these individual computer systems have their own internal operating systems, and yet they allow files not meant for them to pass through to the next node, until the letter gets to the college or university the friend is attending. There the local computer accepts the message and transfers it to the mailbox of the intended receiver. When the friend logs onto the network the next day, mail software on the computer will notify her that she has an e-mail message (Tanenbaum).

The complicated **network protocols** that allow different computers with dissimilar internal workings to receive and transmit Internet messages transparently have been developing for the last 25 years and have gradually evolved into a set of international standards. Software is now available that connects all sorts of computers to the Internet. As the technical aspects of data transmission have improved and international standards have been accepted, Internet sites and connections to it have sprung up throughout the world. Ironically, even places formerly behind the Iron Curtain have joined the worldwide Internet system, although its origins in **ARPANET** were part of the Cold War defense strategy.

**network protocol:** A set of technical specifications that allow different computers to receive and transmit Internet messages through their interconnected communication channels.

**ARPANET:** The grandfather of the Internet, founded in the 1960s by the Advanced Research Projects Agency of the U.S. Defense Department to network selected universities and defense research contractors.

## ▶ The World of the Internet

Usually when we have referred to the Internet, the context has been the World Wide Web or use of the network for cross-country electronic mail. These are only two of the many services that the Internet supports between its thousands of nodes throughout the world. Because of its widespread application, the Internet is the most important buzzword in computing today. Yet we must remember that the Internet itself is just a collection of interconnected computers, hardware of different makes and models, networked with high-speed communications channels and capable of sharing data in many forms. Software knits these many hardware components together for many worthwhile applications.

### ORIGINAL INTERNET SERVICES

The first users of the Internet, scientists and engineers using primarily Unix computers, developed its earliest applications, including electronic mail and the ability to transfer computer-readable files of information. These technical people created the first protocols, which were not very user friendly, by the standards of modern software like Web browsers. One well-known standard called **FTP** (which stands for **file transfer protocol**) allows a user on one computer to log onto a remote machine and retrieve a file at long distance. For instance, one can read about a piece of free software available from some university, then log onto the site and download it to the host computer. Many local computer bulletin boards and Internet sites provide archives of freeware and shareware for retrieval using FTP software.

**FTP (file transfer protocol):** A common Internet standard which supports transfer of files over the network.

**Telnet** software, the reverse of FTP, lets a user at one computer log on to another machine, often in a remote location, and work on that computer via the Internet connection. If the person does not have an account on that machine, Telnet allows logon as an anonymous user, who can browse around in the files there and perhaps decide to download some archival software via FTP. Lots of libraries around the country support Telnet, so that remote users can examine the catalog of books and even carry out Boolean searches on titles or authors from afar. Of course, one cannot normally retrieve the books or articles directly because they are un-

**Telnet:** An Internet protocol that permits a user to log onto a remote computer on the Net and work on it at long distance.

der copyright and are not usually in computer-readable form. Some scientists use Telnet to connect to a regional supercomputer center and run programs there on their data, which are uploaded from their home site. With FTP and Telnet, Internet users can reach out to computer services not available on their personal or campus computer system (McKeown and Watson).

Many popular electronic mail packages exist for use on the Internet, most associated with different host computer hardware. E-mail is normally quicker and cheaper than regular postal services, called **snail mail** by computer insiders. In the UNIX community, programs called Mailx, Pine, and Elm have been used for many years. Compared with a variety of alternatives like Eudora, popular on Macintoshes and Intel systems, these earlier programs are not as easy for the novice to use. Many other convenient commercial mail systems also are available for Intel and Mac personal computers. All e-mail systems provide the same basic functions: the ability to receive and send messages via the local server, the possibility to read or print them from the screen, forwarding and copying of messages to be relayed to others, and an e-mail address list of frequent correspondents. The host server retains a person's account and receives e-mail for later inspection by the user.

**snail mail:** Computer jargon for surface mail, which is normally slower than electronic mail.

A concept called **netiquette** refers to accepted manners on e-mail. Because it is very easy to forward e-mail correspondence, one should consider that more people may see a letter than just the original recipient. One should be prudent in forwarding lots of mail to others, which just fills up everyone's disk storage on the server. Some people think that people who compose all of their e-mail in upper case are shouting (Ackermann). **Smileys** are popular ways to express emotion via e-mail using a series of keystrokes. Figure 10-9 illustrates a wide variety of smiley conventions.

**netiquette:** A term for acceptable manners on electronic mail.

During the years that the Internet has been developing, thousands of **USENET** newsgroups have been formed on every sort of topic. Subscribers to these on-line discussion groups—sometimes open to everyone, sometimes requiring a registration—can post queries for others to answer or respond in written form to some topic of discussion. A person who has been thinking of buying a color printer may ask for opinions from others on best features and brands; a hardware newsgroup may have hundreds of

**smiley:** A set of keystrokes that can be included in e-mail to express emotion in a kind of graphical shorthand.

**USENET:** A general term for the thousands of user discussion groups on the Internet devoted to many subjects, including some that are strictly for adults.

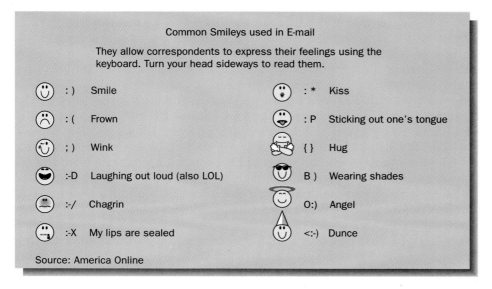

Common Smileys used in E-mail

They allow correspondents to express their feelings using the keyboard. Turn your head sideways to read them.

| : ) | Smile | | : * | Kiss |
| : ( | Frown | | : P | Sticking out one's tongue |
| ; ) | Wink | | { } | Hug |
| :-D | Laughing out loud (also LOL) | | B ) | Wearing shades |
| :-/ | Chagrin | | O:) | Angel |
| :-X | My lips are sealed | | <:-) | Dunce |

Source: America Online

**FIGURE 10-9** Common Smileys used in e-mail allow correspondents to express their feelings using the keyboard. Turn your head sideways to read them.

entries on color printing. Many USENET groups are set up in professional fields of inquiry, and their readers will be notified of upcoming conferences, calls for professional papers, and even job openings.

## CLIENT/SERVER APPLICATIONS

**Gopher:** A popular text-based worldwide document search and retrieval protocol developed for the Internet.

**Gopher,** a public information bulletin board service begun at the University of Minnesota in the late 1980s, is named for the mascot of Minnesota sports teams. The name also suggests the process of burrowing through a series of available files for relevant, useful, or entertaining information that is added to Gopher sites all over the world. Gopher contains only text-based information, such as college phone books, movie reviews of recent Hollywood productions, and a growing list of on-line books in computer-readable form, like the texts of Shakespeare's plays. Having accessed the information through a series of Gopher menus, a user can either read it on the screen or download it to a personal computer.

Gopher became the first popular Internet application outside the scientific community because it is easy to use and contains a great variety of free information available for Internet users. It showed the possibilities of Internet for a mass audience and laid the foundations for the World Wide Web. Like Gopher, the Web is a **client/server** application. This means that at the home site of the Web or Gopher server is running software that accepts network requests for information. The client, who is probably far distant from the server, has software that can contact the server and ask for information to be sent over the Internet to this computer. Gopher software and Web browsers act in similar ways. The Web can be seen as a subsequent development of the Gopher idea with a GUI interface, and the documents distributed on the Web can contain text, sound, pictures, graphics, and even video clips.

**client/server:** A computer environment in which applications on a file server are sent out to client machines as needed. The client machine can access and display information sent out from the server.

## ADVANTAGES OF THE WEB

The phenomenal growth and popularity of the Internet in the last few years can be ascribed primarily to the World Wide Web. In fact, in 1995 traffic on the Web surpassed electronic mail as the most used Internet function for the first time. In 1989 the European Laboratory for Particle Physics (CERN) in Geneva created the Web to allow physicists to study a variety of documents—the web of interconnections between them—by jumping from one to another with a mouse. At first browser software like Lynx was text-based, linking only hypertext documents. Most Web software innovation has been done in North America: originally at the National Center for Supercomputer Applications (NCSA) at the University of Illinois, where the first important GUI browser software called Mosaic was created in 1993, and most recently at Netscape Communications, where Marc Andreessen and many of his programmer friends from Illinois moved to found a commercial company in 1994 (McKeown and Watson).

HISTORY

**Web page:** The name for a document formatted to contain information for distribution on the World Wide Web. It may contain hypertext links to other pages and various multimedia resources.

**HTML (Hypertext Markup Language):** The standard formatting language for creating World Wide Web pages with text, graphics, and other media.

A Web document, called a **Web page,** usually contains a number of hot link points to other Web pages. Clicking on a hot link will open the referenced Web page on the user's screen. The formatting language called **HTML (Hypertext Markup Language)** creates this form of hypertext as a series of embedded codes in the text of a Web page. HTML, which many people find easy to learn, currently supports Web pages containing all types of media formats, and the results are colorful and interesting. All of the media are easily accessible through the graphical user interface of browser software.

A link in a Web page may point to a document that is located elsewhere on the Internet, and the browser will retrieve it for display. In effect, a web of pages is connected by referring to each other at various Internet addresses, whether they are local or long distance, from the original Web page site, called the **home page.** People who have created home pages often include links to their favorite Web sites, which can be literally anywhere in the world. Readers of their home pages can jump to these sites with the click of the mouse. There they may find a wealth of information: photos, tables, a set of nested pages of information, even sounds and small animations.

Browsers are primarily intended to allow Internet users to find and display Web pages, but as time has passed the browsers have incorporated all of the other Internet services within their functions: FTP, Telnet, e-mail, and Gopher access. For instance, much free software can be downloaded from many archives on the Web using the FTP protocol, which is activated by a click of the mouse in one's browser package. The Web has made the Internet accessible to the ordinary computer user. When Mosaic came out in 1993, the New York Times called it "the killer application of the Internet" that would revolutionize the Net much as spreadsheets changed the face of planning (McKeown and Watson, 26). By 1995 Dr. Larry Smarr, head of NCSA, was forecasting that by the year 2000 about a billion people would have personal computers, compared to about 200 million in 1995, all with Web access (McKeown and Watson, 26).

**home page:** A term for the opening Web document that one sees at a site, which may contain links to other pages.

**FIGURE 10-10** The student creators of the popular Yahoo search engine for the Web: Jerry Yang (left) and David Filo.

## WEB INDEXES

The popularity of Web browsers continues to spur innovative additions and plug-in software modules for these packages that provide more spectacular effects in Web documents. First the user needs to be aware of the several indexing services offered on the Web. There is so much information on a myriad of topics on the Web that one usually starts with one of these **search engines.** One called InfoSeek is included in the Netscape browser, but others like Lycos and Alta Vista can be accessed with the package. A popular index called Yahoo was created by two students at Stanford, David Filo and Jerry Yang. It resembles the telephone yellow pages by suggesting Web sites in categories that may meet the user's request (Tanaka and Hannah). Another powerful Web site called SavvySearch at Colorado State plugs the user's request into several search engines and displays the results of all of them ("Welcome to the Web!").

**search engine:** Any of the many indexing programs created for searching for information on World Wide Web pages, usually based on Boolean search strategies.

Not all search engines work the same way or produce the same results. Often it is worthwhile looking at several indexes for a hard-to-find subject. Many look at important content words on the home pages and give a prediction factor about how successful the site will be for the query. Sometimes the results are quite surprising. For instance, a graduate student named Pamela kept "getting hits on her home page," jargon for those logging on, by people looking for information about Pamela Anderson, the sultry star of *Baywatch*. In order to discourage these unwanted and no doubt disappointed voyeurs, Pamela added the following line, "If you are looking for Pamela Anderson, you've got the wrong babe." Unfortunately this sentence with both *Anderson* and *babe* made the search engines find her page more frequently, and she got even more hits and e-mail from strangers throughout the world, thinking she was the TV star. In fact, her home page was more popular than her university's.

## PLUG-INS FOR WEB BROWSERS

**Java:** A programming language now being used to create small, self-contained applications, called applets, suitable for being distributed on the World Wide Web and run on the client machine.

Innovative plug-in software modules that appear almost every month add functionality and power to Web browsers, especially Netscape. **Java,** from James Gosling at Sun Microsystems, is a whole programming environment, a new computer language that allows creation of "applets," little programs that can be added to Web pages for live animation, interactive computer games, and changing ticker tape displays as a Web document is being viewed. When one looks at a Web page with an embedded Java program, the Internet is distributing this software and running it in real time, as it comes up on the client's computer. Users do not have the software resident on their machines beforehand, and it makes no difference what their machine hardware is. Traditional problems of compatibility between computers disappear, since Java creates its own "virtual machine" within the network software. Java applications are encrypted so that they are immune to viruses and carry all of their requirements with them. All that users need to run them is the browser to download the page containing a Java applet.

Gosling set out to create in 1990 what became Java as a way to create an object-based programming environment that was small and crashproof, for he initially envisioned it for running small consumer appliances. Wedding his ideas to the Internet gives it great power and presence. Some people think that the Java model may predict a different future for computing: that the Internet will become the computer. Programs will be delivered over the Net rather than be controlled at the local machines. Companies like Microsoft that create large operating systems and big software packages may be especially vulnerable to the philosophy of Java. In fact, Bill Gates of Microsoft has said that "Java is there to overthrow what we've done" (quoted by Elmer-Dewitt, 59). Whether this paradigm repre-

**FIGURE 10-11** This Web page highlighting the circus history of Wisconsin includes a clever animated Java applet of the circus train at the bottom. When the applet is active, the train, full of circus animals, runs across the screen at increasing speeds, accompanied by the sound of the circus calliope.

sents the wave of the future or not, Java is already enlivening thousands of commercial Web pages with colorful action and animation.

The Internet is also becoming the realm of multimedia sound and video with add-ons like RealAudio, CU-SeeMe videoconferencing software from Cornell, and VRML (Virtual Reality Modeling Language) coding of files to simulate virtual reality on the Net. With both sound and video, the problem has always been the bandwidth capacity of the Internet for distribution of very large digital files so that the delay in playback of sound and video is not unpleasant or too jerky. RealAudio solves this problem by clever compression techniques to shrink audio files and play them as it is delivering them over the network.

Not an extension of HTML, VRML is its own hardware independent language that allows Web designers to tell the computer how to create 3-D virtual worlds. They can create their own small virtual spaces directly in the language, which could be navigated by users with relatively low-speed network connections (Flohr). A VRML file might permit users to move around in a virtual environment such as a concert hall before buying a ticket. Or in an electronic Web marketplace, one could pick up a product and examine it from all sides before deciding to buy it (Meyer 1995). The future of videoconferencing via the Internet, which previously had been an expensive application using telephone technology, is suggested by the CU-SeeMe technology. In sum, the multimedia possibilities of the Internet are only now becoming reality, and the future seems very bright, with speedier modems and other, faster modes of Internet delivery on the horizon (McConville, Magid, and Jones).

## PUBLIC INFORMATION UTILITIES

The private sector also offers a variety of commercial public-access information services for personal computer users or businesses that have grown up independently from the Internet until recently. Crucial to their success are **value-added networks (VANs).** Organizations like Telenet

**value-added network (VAN):** A communications channel leased from a telephone company to offer customers with modems access to network services through a local or toll-free number.

**FIGURE 10-12** In this set of screens from CU-SeeMe on a Windows95 computer, a man in Kansas is having a videoconference with several people in France.

**TABLE 10-1** *Services Typically Offered to Customers of an Information Utility*

Direct access to the World Wide Web and other Internet Services
News, weather, and sports, continually updated
Communications and e-mail with other members
Shopping in on-line catalogs, using a credit card
Stock quotes and business information
Travel services, including on-line reservations services
Consumer information, such as features from *Consumer Reports* and *American Health*
Education, including features for kids from *National Geographic* and *Weekly Reader*
Banking, offering on-line payment of bills without checks for a fee
Expert columns and forums covering a wide range of topics for the whole family: hobbies, foods, books, personal finance
Computers and software support, with electronic bulletin boards supported by leading companies
Reference material, such as encyclopedias and dictionaries on-line
Entertainment, including interactive games and simulations
Grocery shopping, available on-line in some communities

*(Compiled from CompuServe and Prodigy services)*

**information utility:** A term applied to a commercial network information service like CompuServe or Prodigy, which sells access to its wide variety of files and public forums.

**INTERNET**

and Tymnet lease lines from the big telecommunications companies and offer access to their services to people with modems through a local or toll-free telephone number (Rhodes).

Built on this access method, **information utilities** grew up as public-access database systems and bulletin boards. The most popular and widely used public information utilities today are CompuServe, Prodigy, and America Online. Microsoft even introduced its own on-line network with Windows 95, but its success has been questioned by some critics. As soon as the World Wide Web made the publicly developed Internet a popular alternative as an information source to the older commercial services, they were obliged to offer Web access to their subscribers or risk losing them to local Internet providers springing up all over the country. Consequently, all of the big three now have Web browsers built into their full menu of services.

These comprehensive on-line utilities offer thousands of users hundreds of services as well as public forums, e-mail, and Internet access. A subscriber pays a monthly connection fee for a password and sometimes a per-minute charge for additional connection time beyond the monthly allotment. In every reasonably large center, users dial a local VAN number for connection to the service. They then gain access to a wide variety of on-line features after logging on with their personal password, which is used for verification and billing.

On-line forums offer discussion of every conceivable topic, from politics, ecology, and advice on computer problems to information about health issues, travel tips, and *Consumer Reports* quality ratings. One issue of the CompuServe user's magazine offered a tour of the sorts of things one can get: an employment advertising network; a weekly annotated listing of network television offerings; on-line reference works listing the spellings of specialized vocabulary from computer, health, or business literature, which are often not found in spelling checkers; and advice on how to become proficient in the international language called Esperanto. In most cases, information can be downloaded to one's computer if a copy is wanted. More than a computer bulletin board, a service like CompuServe also provides users with an on-line airline guide, network shopping, an electronic encyclopedia, video games, and e-mail privileges to other

CompuServe members. For making reservations or shopping on-line, the user needs a credit card.

Consumers have a great choice of on-line services from the older information utilities, who have been in the marketplace longer than the World Wide Web or private access providers to the Internet. To lure customers, the utilities are rushing to offer additional features in addition to the Web while they keep their rates competitive with local services. Among their value-added services, they tout their on-line chat lines, somewhat more user friendly than USENET discussion groups, at the same time offering the USENET choices as well. They are signing up news magazines and newspapers, which can be searched by keyword.

Critics complain that much of the information available lacks depth or interest and that most people do not have the time to utilize all of this information glut. Some believe that the information bulletin boards segmented into popular topics with space for customers to leave their comments may be the most enduring features of the utilities. Today everyone is trying to offer opportunities for the public to move into the world of cyberspace. Whether the information utilities will just evolve into attractive, national access providers to the Internet with user-friendly interfaces remains an open question. Given the vast and exciting range of information possibilities being offered to anyone with a modem, the clear winner in the race to capture the public on-line market is the consumer—the people side of the Computer Triangle (Meyer 1994).

**SOCIETY**

---

## SOCIAL PERSPECTIVE

### Electronic Conferences

On a long-distance computer network, whether commercial or public domain, people can carry on extended conferences through the medium of e-mail. If the conference is **closed format,** the conference operator publishes the password for access to the forum only to those who are invited to participate. For example, a distinguished panel of scientists might be called together to discuss the latest ideas on global warming. Typically a set period of time, such as several days or a week, is set aside for the conference. Participants from around the world can add their contributions and respond to the remarks of others without leaving their personal computers. No matter what the time, the conference is open for reading and discussion. People in Europe can monitor the discussion and add material to it while American and Japanese members sleep. For these users, the conference is real time—that is, it is taking place in their current time frame—though colleagues elsewhere are not on-line. Lots of time and expense are saved because no travel is involved, and the conference itself is completed in several days, without jet lag. Similarly, a program committee for an international professional society can hold a closed conference via computer to plan its next meeting. Members can comment on abstracts submitted for presentation and decide on the final list of speakers through the medium of e-mail.

On a public bulletin board system, computer conferencing is typically more openly organized; any interested party can contribute to the **open forum.** The WELL, organized by the Whole Earth Catalog company, offers an open forum for a few dollars a month, and has running conferences on such topics as war and law, birth, death, work, the information age, and—the most popular of all—the Grateful Dead and their music. Each conference has a host whose job is to monitor the discussion and see that everyone has an opportunity to contribute. Organizers speak of the freedom of the discussion, the sense of community that it engenders, and the varied backgrounds of the participants. In a conference about issues of constitutional freedom in the information age were found a magazine editor, a college teacher, a retired Army colonel, a business executive from Pacific Bell, and even an official from the Congressional Office of Technology Assessment. Truly, the open nature of the public computer conference offers a sense of democracy and free exchange of ideas on-line for the cost of a few dollars and a personal computer equipped with a modem (Coate in Kelly).

---

**closed format:** A term applied to an electronic conference available only to those invited to participate.

**open forum:** A computer conference set up on a public bulletin board system that allows anyone who logs on to participate.

**FIGURE 10-13** CompuServe users are encouraged to explore its variety of services on-line, each highlighted with a colorful cartoon.

## ▶ Networks and Society

Often in the Computer Triangle, growth in hardware and software capabilities affects the way people live with computers. Now that the computer and the telecommunications industries have linked up the world, changes fostered by the network revolution have an impact not only on the nature of the workplace, but also on controversial issues like free speech and even espionage with computers.

### NETWORKING AND THE WORK ENVIRONMENT

As long ago as 1981, James Martin, an acknowledged authority on computer networking, wrote that "given the right telecommunications *almost any white-collar work* could be done at home" (Martin, 127). With networks, he envisioned secretaries doing their typing at home and sending it via e-mail to the office for printing. Groups preparing a joint proposal could conference together on the draft as it was being created. The master copy of the document itself would reside on an office computer, though the individual authors would not need to be there. Managers could spend some of their work time at home, keeping up with their business by phone and e-mail.

Indeed, the savings of time and energy involved in not commuting to the office every day represent an economic boon to both manager and company. With **telecommuting,** more time is spent on quality work and less on a long commute from the suburbs. For professional parents especially, this pattern of work at home, coordinated with the office through networked computing, offers an attractive alternative to quitting during

**telecommuting:** The use of personal computers and data communications at home to do work without being physically present at the office.

**FIGURE 10-14** This telecommuting worker has her computer and fax machine at home for communication with the office and other businesses, but she still has time to answer her child's questions.

the early years with young children. Offices can be smaller, because not so many employees are at work simultaneously.

## EFFECTS OF TELECOMMUTING

According to a 1990 report in *The Wall Street Journal*, more than 9 million Americans were telecommuters by 1990. Their work hours had become more fluid, and managers had less eyeball contact with them. Critics say that less time around the watercooler means loss of a sense of community in the workplace and cuts down on chance encounters that may lead to new ideas. On the other hand, telecommuting may be the only way to keep a valued worker who wants to stay home with the baby. One telecommuter found his "social contact around the watercooler" by keeping up with associates via e-mail on CompuServe.

SOCIETY

Some managers worry that work will not get done at home because of distractions like television, not available at the office. Yet studies show that telecommuters are frequently more compulsive about getting work done than office workers, often putting in long hours at a stretch not conceivable at the workplace. Most researchers into these changing work habits recommend that all workers spend some time each week at the office, and have a clearly defined boundary at home between professional work done there and the routines of ordinary life. Sometimes not being at the office can stand in the way of advancement. Even managers who encourage telecommuting acknowledge that it changes the work routine and calls for a clear understanding by all parties of the ground rules in order to succeed (Crossen). As in other Computer Triangle examples, the technology of the computer is changing the landscape of work in ways never envi-

**FIGURE 10-15** The Web site for Rackes Direct features classic design that fits its offerings of traditional women's fashions.

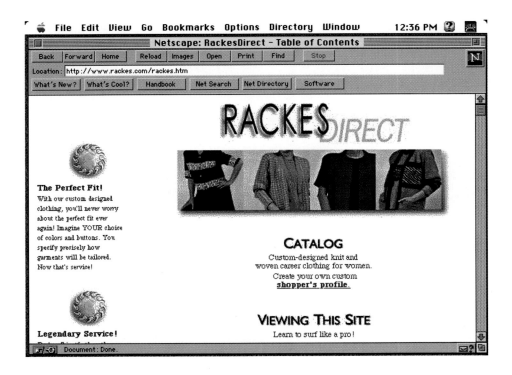

sioned in earlier times. Whether they are beneficial or not depends on how the participants adapt to the new work patterns.

## COMMERCE ON THE INTERNET

When millions of people began logging onto the World Wide Web every day, business saw a whole new market and rapidly moved on-line. Today Java applet inserts into Web pages bring animated ads to recent versions of browser software, and companies large and small are offering their wares in colorful digital catalogs on the Web. Most people have gotten their browser software for free, and someday advertisers may underwrite Web services as they do radio and television. Just as e-mail has created a whole new kind of correspondence with quick delivery and no stamps to buy, one may expect that on-line shopping can be just as lucrative for retailers as the shopping networks on cable television (Eisenberg).

Net surfers have done a lot of browsing among the many on-line bazaars, but not very much shopping. A November 1995, Nielson survey indicated that more than 37 million people had access to the Internet, and 18 million were using the Web. However, only 14 percent of those had actually ordered something on-line with a credit card ("Who's on the Web?"). An on-line women's custom-made clothing Web site called RackesDirect offers a case in point. Barbara Rackes owned a successful chain of retail clothing stores in the Southeast catering to women executives, and was chosen national small business retailer in 1994. In 1995 she decided to close all her stores and create a custom design clothing business on the Internet—a bold step into business in cyberspace.

In addition to its stylish catalog, the Web site asks customers to create a profile on-line, including information about preferred dress sizes and colors. Like her earlier businesses, her Web site quickly received recognition as a quality commercial Internet business after it opened in February 1996. As a result, in the first three months on-line, she had received a lot of publicity and more than 20,000 people logging onto her site, including many overseas visitors. People have sent in lots of fan mail and inquiries about the service; however, not as many of these Net surfers ordered the custom-designed clothing offered for sale as Rackes expected. Rackes suggests that her usual customers are not yet used to shopping on the Web.

Will all of the hype about Web business opportunities really pan out? Richard Clodfelter, who teaches a university course in Internet retailing, suggest three reasons why people are not buying from Web-based companies: fear of credit card fraud if one charges over the Web, the possibility of "cyber scams," and the inability to touch the merchandise. For pioneering retailers like Rackes, Clodfelter feels that when Web purchasing catches on her credibility as a quality Internet business will pay off in sales (Lofton). People also cannot touch the product with catalog sales, and millions order merchandise from companies like L. L. Bean every day and give out their credit card numbers on the phone with no worry about safety.

## INTERNET SECURITY

Security of personal information such as a credit card number remains a public concern, even though many experts say that shopping on the Internet is probably more safe than with a credit card and a toll-free number. A widely publicized 1995 case in which two graduate students at Berkeley easily broke the security features of an early version of the popular Netscape browser probably raised much of the public distrust (Zazueta). Compared to catalog shopping by phone, Douglas Barnes (who designs secure computer systems) still thinks that personal security fears on the Net are unwarranted: "Credit card information is given out to hundreds of thousands of low paid clerks all over the country every day—it would be hard to imagine a less secure approach" (Wiese).

Browser software is rapidly adding better **encryption software** to make Internet transactions secure from hackers. The most common approach involves **public key (PK) cryptography,** ingenious software solutions that use pairs of numerical "keys" to encode and decode private messages. A customer who uses PK software for Web shopping has two keys, one public and one private which get scrambled with an order. At the other end of the line, the company can use the public key to decode the message, but it never knows the private key. It can be sure that the message came from the originator, a kind of **digital signature.** If the company needs to send correspondence to the customer, it can use the person's public key for coding the message, and only that one person can decode it (Eisenberg).

**INTERNET**

**encryption software:** A category of computer programs to encode a document so that it cannot be read if it is intercepted by unauthorized users in a network transaction.

**public key (PK) cryptography:** A kind of software algorithm based on pairs of numerical keys, one public and one private, for encrypting e-mail and other network transactions.

**digital signature:** A term for a secure transaction code used to encode sensitive personal information sent over a network so that the decoder will know that it is unique to the sender.

## HACKER ETHICS

Everyone has heard stories of hackers, brilliant computer "nerds" who crack the passwords and log onto a Defense Department computer to read the secret missile codes. In fact, the movie *War Games* has such a teenage hero, who almost sets off the Third World War by interfering with defense radar systems. Not all hackers are addicted to long-distance computer safecracking; they can be described as technically competent computer whizzes for whom the challenge of some computer puzzle has become completely overwhelming. Steven Levy (1984) wrote a book about famous hackers who pioneered much of the personal computer revolution, including Steve Wozniak of Apple and Adam Osborne of the ill-fated machine of the same name. Levy identifies certain principles that motivate hackers, including the beliefs that computer access should be unlimited and total and that information should be free. Hackers praise decentralization of power, and distrust the authority of government and big corporations.

**SOCIETY**

**The Social Dimensions of Encryption Software**

The most widely known encryption software is called PGP (for Pretty Good Privacy), freeware written and distributed by Phil Zimmermann, a Colorado computer programmer, and based on PK ideas. Ironically since the federal government considers crytography methods as munitions, it has been hounding Zimmermann for giving PGP away on the Internet, since it can be downloaded in foreign countries. Zimmermann is accused of violating export laws in deliberately releasing his software on public Internet sites. The government, whose National Security Agency allegedly cannot crack the PGP code, contends that criminals and spies can use this software to hide their illegal dealings on the Net from snooping by authorized police and security authorities.

Meanwhile, the Electronic Frontiers Foundation, a public interest group concerned about censorship on the Internet, gave Zimmermann an award for his contribution to privacy for ordinary users. How the case against Zimmermann is resolved probably will not settle the cryptography wars, even though such techniques are key to privacy in e-mail and commercial transactions on the Internet (Levy 1995). As is often the case in computer issues, the technology raises difficult social issues. Software intended to protect the privacy of a citizen's digital information on networks may also work to hinder law enforcement in tracking criminals' records encrypted with the same software.

**FIGURE 10-16** Eventually the Federal government dropped its charges against Phil Zimmerman, the author of the popular PGP encryption software.

## HACKERS AND THE INTERNET

SOCIETY

HISTORY

Many hackers find their ultimate challenge in invading networks like the Internet. Looking for a way to unlock a forbidden treasure chest, they poke around in computer files that are supposed to be secure from snooping and leave a warning message. In fact, Robert Morris was trying to show the weak defenses of the Internet when he released the dangerous Internet worm in 1988 (see Chapter 5).

The case of the world's most notorious hacker, Kevin Mitnick, suggests one kind of mind that loves to break into computer networks. After being a teenage hacker in his youth, Mitnick was convicted of criminal activity for reading e-mail of Digital Equipment and MCI employees in the late 1980s and served a year in federal prison in 1989. Breaking probation in California in 1992, he went underground and resumed his compulsive

**FIGURE 10-17** (A) After his own computer files were invaded, computer security expert Tsutomo Shimomura in 1995 helped law enforcement agencies track down and arrest (B) Kevin Mitnick, the most famous hacker of all time, by monitoring his Internet activity.

A

B

hacking. His boldest stunt in late 1995 eventually led to his undoing. On Christmas Day he logged into the home computer of a leading computer security expert, Tsutomu Shimomura of the San Diego Supercomputer Center, and stole thousands of his data files. Over the next two months Shimomura never stopped tracking Mitnick, who continued his spree of breaking into computer networks and stealing files, including the credit card numbers of 20,000 people from Netcom in California.

When Mitnick chose The WELL, the popular Internet provider in Sausalito, California, to stash Shimomura's records in an inactive account, the Japanese security expert was onto his trail. Monitoring the hacker's every keystroke while he remained unnoticed via The WELL and later at Netcom in San Jose, Shimomura began to suspect that the target was Mitnick. Eventually he determined that the hacker was using a cellular phone through a Netcom dial-in center in Raleigh, North Carolina. Four days later Shimomura and the FBI were able to pinpoint the phone to Mitnick's apartment and carry out the arrest. When he saw Shimomura at the courtroom, Mitnick congratulated him with the greeting, "I respect your skills." Mitnick faces a possible sentence of 35 years in jail and $500,000 in fines (see two articles by Markoff).

Although he had all of the credit card numbers from California, Mitnick had never used them for illegal purchases. Analysts see several characteristics in his personality that account for his obsessive behavior: a reclusive personality with few ordinary successes in life, a desire for power to control networks and phone systems, a need to exhibit his technical prowess, and the hubris to believe that even the best could not catch him. Mitnick's career shows how technically clever he was and how obsessively powerful the attraction was to crack any code, a puzzle that had to be solved. Although there will always be hackers, not many are as devious, compulsive, or neurotic as Kevin Mitnick. Even so, his exploits suggest the fragile nature and vulnerability of the nation's computer networks (Hafner). According to Shimomura, there are two lessons to learn from this search: that society will not allow such behavior to go unpunished and that it must work even harder to beef up security protocols on computer networks ("Interview with the Cybersleuth").

SOCIETY

## ESPIONAGE ON THE NETWORK

Sometimes hacking is involved in international spying. A true story of espionage on the Internet involves the clever detective work of Clifford Stoll, an astronomer working at the Lawrence Berkeley Laboratory in California. When assigned to find a 75-cent discrepancy in the computer's accounting system, Stoll began a long, involved, technologically sophisticated search for a person called "Hunter." In fact, no one with that log-in name had a valid machine account; nor could Stoll explain someone's using the log-in of a former employee and dialing in from a modem. The search eventually led to a group of hackers in Hannover, Germany, who were tapping into American defense computers, downloading data, and selling them to the Soviets in East Germany. Using a Tymnet connection originating at Bremen University, these Cold War hackers acquired "superuser" privileges at Berkeley and then readily snooped in a variety of military computers all over the United States and overseas.

Stoll's most frustrating experience was getting the FBI and CIA to understand that he might be on to a military spy mission. They thought that a 75-cent error could not be important. He finally got the crooks to stay on line long enough to trace their foreign phone number by creating a large but fake military file that would appear important to spies. With the phone number known, Stoll was on the way to solving the case (Stoll). This fasci-

SOCIETY

HISTORY

**FIGURE 10-18** Clifford Stoll, an astronomer working at the Lawrence Berkeley Laboratory, found that what looked like a discrepancy of 75 cents in a computer billing account really was the tell-tale sign of computer theft of American defense information by German hackers.

## SOCIAL PERSPECTIVE

### Hacking and Free Speech

The Federal Computer Fraud and Abuse Act of 1986 that was used to prosecute Robert Morris has in recent years been turned loose on several hacker groups. Critics like science fiction novelist Bruce Sterling claim that business and government seem to have trouble distinguishing between young hackers and serious criminals on the Internet. In 1990 AT&T had a major crash in New York State caused by a fault in their own software, but for a time they suspected hacker saboteurs. This event led to charges against a number of young computer whizzes because they were readers of a hacker publication where a document about AT&T's 911 system had been published after it was downloaded from a network. Also arrested was Steve Jackson, a publisher of fantasy role-playing computer games in Austin, Texas, because the government thought he was publishing secrets for hacker invasion of other computer installations. His computers and valuable data files about his games and business were seized.

In response to these crackdowns, Mitch Kapor, founder of Lotus Development Corporation; Steve Wozniak, co-founder of Apple; John Gilmore of Sun Microsystems; and other computer professionals founded in 1990 the *Electronic Frontier Foundation (EFF)*, a civil liberties group for hackers. They contend that on-line computer bulletin board systems are protected by the free speech clause of the First Amendment to the Constitution. In a 1990 showcase Chicago trial about theft of the AT&T 911 document, the Federal Computer Fraud and Abuse Act ran up against another federal law from 1986, the Electronic Communications Privacy Act, an antibugging ordinance. The latter law calls for prior notice before surveillance over telecommunications. In complicated legal maneuvering the government's prosecution case against the hacker theft fell apart, and it seemed that the legal resources of EFF had spoken for free speech

among the hacker community (Sterling). Without EFF's financial help for legal defense and voluntary supporting testimony from computer professionals, the hacker defendant would probably have gone to jail ("Score One for the Hackers of America").

Yet important conflicting issues raised in the Chicago trial still remain unsettled. The trial did not affirm or invalidate the case for government snooping on hackers who may be snooping on public networks. Meanwhile, the EFF has established its own forum on the Internet, where conversation about free speech in cyberspace continues (Sterling). In March, 1993, a federal judge ruled that the Secret Service damaged Steve Jackson's business and awarded him $50,000 in damages (O'Conner). Surprisingly this trial received almost no coverage in national news media. Because the Chicago case was stopped, its basic question remains unresolved: is computer intrusion through a network criminal activity or an exercise in free speech in the information age?

**FIGURE 10-19** Steve Jackson, a producer of video games, had his files raided by the Secret Service because he was suspected of illegal distribution of stolen hacker documents. In 1993, he won a suit against the government in a case ignored by the news media.

nating story illustrates several morals: some hackers are out to do no good, and it is possible to navigate computer networks worldwide, accessing supposedly secure computer files without heavy password security. More than with single machines, computer security of networked computers and the files stored on them remains a continued concern of large organizations with sensitive files.

## FREE SPEECH VERSUS CENSORSHIP OF NETWORK INFORMATION

SOCIETY

Issues of free speech and free expression have spilled over from the largely underground world of hackers to the very public forum of Prodigy, the commercial information utility. In 1989 Prodigy shut down a debate between gays and religious fundamentalists and raised its fee structure for frequent users of e-mail, such as contributors to controversial forums. When some subscribers advocated a boycott of Prodigy advertisers, Prodigy banned their discussion (O'Connor). The company said that it would monitor submissions and exercise judgment if it found the debate too personal. When anti-Semitic notices began appearing, the company

## EVOLUTIONARY PERSPECTIVE

### The Information Superhighway

Thirty years ago, communications theorist Marshal McLuhan wrote about the global village being created by worldwide television and other mass media. Now worldwide networks like the Internet have made data transfer as easy and common as television by satellite. Indeed, network bulletin boards regularly post the leading-edge ideas of the computer age, long before they reach the academic journals or public press. They are truly on the cutting edge of the computer revolution. The High-Performance Computing Act, sponsored by then Senator Albert Gore and signed by President Bush in 1991, set the course for what Vice President Gore calls the Information Superhighway. Connected with fiber optic connections, the **National Research and Education Network (NREN)** will replace the Internet. It is intended to revolutionize the infrastructure of education, commerce, and communications throughout the United States and give it a competitive edge versus networks being developed by the Japanese and Germans. Supporters say industries, schools, and private homes will soon have access to data services like customized TV or long-distance medicine, only imagined today (Schwartz).

---

**National Research and Education Network (NREN):** The supernetwork funded by the U.S. government to upgrade the Internet in order to link industries, schools, and private homes across the nation via high-speed fiber optic connections.

---

again stepped in to ban comments "grossly repugnant to community standards" (Schwartz). In 1993 the service intervened a third time to shut down its bulletin board, called "Frank Discussion," because explicit sexual solicitations were becoming too frequent. Critics like Rory J. O'Connor, who distributes an on-line computer column to newspapers, sees a "Big Brother" mentality in these censorship actions from Prodigy's corporate owners at that time, IBM and Sears. The choice between free speech and community standards of decency, familiar in printed materials, has turned up on the computer network pathways.

On several occasions children have been lured away from home on network chat lines. In one case from America Online that ended happily, a fifteen-year-old boy disappeared from his Oregon home with a ticket and money sent to him from a seemingly older man in San Francisco. According to the man in phone calls to the boy's parents, they met on a gay and lesbian forum. However, when the parents began pressuring authorities and America Online, the boy turned up unharmed at the San Francisco airport; the older man turned out to be another teenager. A national center for missing children said in 1995 that about a dozen cases of on-line pedophiles soliciting underage children had been reported during the previous year (Peyser, Murr, and French).

Senator James Exon of Nebraska became so concerned with on-line pornography and other sexual practices on various network services that he introduced the most sweeping federal legislation ever proposed for network censorship. He wrote the legislation to protect children from explicit adult materials distributed on networks. Eventually it became a part of the Federal Telecommunications Act as the **Communications Decency Act,** which became law in 1996. The Exon proposal makes it a federal offense to allow indecent materials available to minors on a public computer network, and conviction can lead to as much as $100,000 in fines and a jail term. Commercial information utilities are liable if someone uploads a pornographic idea to one of their chat lines; they are supposed to be responsible for policing what goes out on their networks.

Net surfers who take pride in their on-line freedom of speech think the much freer Internet is impossible to control and police and fought the bill's passage. By May 1996, three federal judges were trying to decide if the broad strokes of the act represented a violation of the free speech guarantee of the First Amendment. Judge Stewart Dalzell asked a government witness how the Internet is any different from the printed media, where

**Communications Decency Act:** A 1996 federal law that makes it a crime to distribute sexually explicit materials over a computer network that might be seen by minors.

publication of a pornographic photo is not considered criminal activity: "What is it about this medium—he most democratic of mediums that the human mind has come up with yet—that makes it different from print in terms of the constitutional protection it should receive?" (Levy 1996, 80)

In the same week, a member of the conservative American Family Association who was unhappy that Playboy-type photos were available on CompuServe complained to the FBI. Yet CompuServe had placed explicit warnings on this network area and provided users with a software option for parents to block offending materials from access to their children. Eventually the FBI investigation was dropped, pending the court decision about the legality of the new law. The matter of how the new network culture is to be regulated is so controversial that the Supreme Court will probably be asked to render a final judgment on the Communications Decency Act (Levy 1996). In cases like this, the social side of the Computer Triangle is placed in a legal and cultural quandary pitting the freedom of unlimited access to information that computer networks provide against a concern for policing public morals. Often there are no easy answers.

**SOCIETY**

## ▶ Summary

Today, someone with a personal computer and a modem connection to the phone system can tap into a variety of resources available on-line: the Internet, bulletin boards, information utilities, e-mail, and even the office file server. Computer networks, both local and wide area, are already changing the face of office management through electronic conferencing and telecommuting. As more and more people move on-line, debates about free speech, hacker rights, censorship, and privacy enter the computer arena. Not surprisingly, these discussions resemble views expressed in other areas like the public press, where similar questions are regularly debated. No doubt societal standards about what is appropriate behavior on computer networks will continue to evolve as network services continue to expand over the digital superhighways of the future.

## ▶ Key Terms

analog signal (p. 231)

ARPANET (p. 236)

backbone (p. 234)

baud rate (p. 231)

bits per second (bps) (p. 231)

bridge (gateway) (p. 235)

client/server (p. 238)

closed format (p. 243)

coaxial cable (p. 233)

communications software (p. 232)

Communications Decency Act (p. 251)

digital signature (p. 247)

downloading (p. 232)

encryption software (p. 247)

fiber optic cable (p. 233)

file server (p. 233)

FTP (file transfer protocol) (p. 236)

Gopher (p. 238)

HTML (Hypertext Markup Language) (p. 238)

home page (p. 239)

Information Superhighway (p. 230)

information utility (p. 242)

Java (p. 240)

local area network (LAN) (p. 232)

National Research and Education Network (NREN) (p. 251)

netiquette (p. 237)

network (p. 232)

network protocol (p. 236)

open forum (p. 243)

parallel transmission (p. 231)

parity bits (p. 231)

public key (PK) cryptography (p. 247)

search engine (p. 239)

serial process (p. 231)

site license (p. 233)

smiley (p. 237)

snail mail (p. 237)

telecommuting (p. 245)

telnet (p. 236)

twisted-pair wire (p. 233)

uploading (p. 232)

USENET (p. 237)

value-added network (VAN) (p. 241)

Web page (p. 238)

wide area network (WAN) (p. 235)

 Self-Test

## MULTIPLE CHOICE

1. Inside the computer, information is transferred around among components by a physical electrical connection called a
   a. bus
   b. modem
   c. communication line
   d. parallel channel

2. All of the following are elements associated with the transmission of data over modems except
   a. baud rate
   b. fax possibilities
   c. site licenses
   d. bits per second

3. All of the following characteristics apply to LANs except
   a. sharing resources like laser printers
   b. networking that spans an entire state
   c. allowing e-mail between users
   d. buying site licenses for shared software

4. Which of the following is not used to connect LANs physically?
   a. satellite communications
   b. twisted-pair copper wire
   c. fiber optic cable
   d. coaxial cable

5. Which of the following is not an Internet service?
   a. Telnet
   b. Tymnet
   c. FTP
   d. Gopher

6. Which of the following constitutes an advantage of electronic conferencing?
   a. Worldwide participants can contribute on their own time schedule.
   b. Savings can be realized by eliminating long-distance travel.
   c. Organizers can monitor the discussion and see that everyone has an opportunity to contribute.
   d. all of the above

7. Which of the following is most often quoted as a disadvantage of telecommuting?
   a. Work hours must be more flexible.
   b. A sense of community around the watercooler is lost.
   c. Workers stay at home to raise children, yet remain employed.
   d. Changing work habits suggest that the work week will become a mix

of time each week at the office as well as time at home.

8. Probably the most disturbing thing that came out of the hacker rights trial in Chicago in 1990, about theft of the AT&T 911 document, was
   a. It did not convict a confirmed hacker thief.
   b. It led to the founding of the EFF, a civil libertarian group.
   c. A basic legal question remains unresolved: whether hacker activity is criminal or an exercise in free speech.
   d. Two federal laws—on computer fraud and privacy in electronic communications—were in conflict.

## TRUE/FALSE

9. **T  F**  The origins of the Internet can be traced to Cold War policy for using the telephone system to transmit computer data and messages between research sites—military, university, and commercial—to share technical information.

10. **T  F**  One main difference between computers and telephone systems is that the latter transmit data in parallel fashion, whereas the usual method of data transmission in computers is serial.

11. **T  F**  The Internet has always had a commercial component, the information utility like CompuServe or America Online.

12. **T  F**  The World Wide Web may be seen as the Internet killer app, for it set off the current popularity of the Net.

13. **T  F**  Most hackers are not brilliant computer nerds who crack passwords and log onto sensitive defense computers to read military secrets.

14. **T  F**  Computer leaders like Steve Wozniak and Mitch Kapor were instrumental in founding the EFF, a civil liberties group in favor of hacker rights.

15. **T  F**  If explicit graphic images of child pornography were distributed over its network, America Online, an information utility, would be liable for prosecution according to the Communications Decency Act of 1996.

16. **T  F**  Supporters of the Information Superhighway predict that industries, schools, and private homes will have access to data services like customized TV or long-distance medicine in the near future.

## FILL-IN

17. The field of data communications links the computer and the _____ system.

18. Normally, a computer data file sent out over a telephone line must be converted from digital data to _____ signals before transmission.

19. If a person retrieves a file from an on-line bulletin board like Gopher, the process of retrieving the file from elsewhere is called _____.

20. A group of computers connected together in a _____ can communicate with each other directly through a physical link.

21. Setting up a campus network to create Internet access for students working on different LANs involves interconnecting them through a _____ of complex data transmission protocols.

22. _____ like Telenet and Tymnet lease phone lines from large telecommunications companies and offer access to their services through toll-free telephone numbers; using this access method, information utilities have grown up to offer a variety of services to people with modems.

23. In recent years there has been considerable growth in _____, which means that workers can spend some of their work time at home, keeping up with their business by phone and e-mail.

24. The _____ has recently been used against the activities of several hacker groups, most notably in the case of a stolen AT&T 911 document.

## ▶ Experiential Exercises

1. Check to see if your institution is on the Internet. If it is, get an account and log onto a Gopher bulletin board or the World Wide Web. Take some time to familiarize yourself with the wide array of features available there. Try some activities, such as accessing the card catalog at a distant college library, and look up one of your professor's books. The best way to appreciate the Internet is to go exploring.

2. Research the history of the Information Superhighway (ARPANET, NSFNet, Internet, NREN). Focus on two interrelated aspects: the increasing technological capacity over the years and the politics of government funding as the on-line resources and user base broadened.

3. In an encyclopedia, look up analog devices, including some of the earliest computers. Clarify your understanding of how information is transmitted by an analog process like a wave in a typical phone line. Distinguish this process from the direct transmission of digital data using light pulses in fiber optic cable.

4. Investigate the difference between sending a letter to a friend by regular modem and fax modem. Understanding how these two devices work will highlight the distinction between text viewed as characters and as images.

5. Find out what kinds of LAN networks are available on your campus for student use. What software is offered on line there? What instructional uses are made of the networks? Check out the security precautions for assuring privacy of student data files.

6. To get a sense of the interconnections between sites on the Internet, find a network coordinator on the campus, perhaps at the computer center. Ask this person to show you the trail of an Internet message between your college and a distant site. What computers and their addresses were used as go-betweens? How long did the message take to travel between the two computers at each end of the line?

7. If possible, log on and compare the kinds of information available free on a local bulletin board, the World Wide Web, or Gopher to the kind of services offered by a commercial information utility, like Prodigy or CompuServe. If you do not have access to one of the utilities, you should be able to find descriptions of their features in the college library.

8. Try to interview a person who does some telecommuting as a part of his or her job. What does this person see as its main advantages? What are the principal drawbacks? Does the person's boss share these sentiments?

9. Check out Clifford Stoll's fascinating book *The Cuckoo's Egg* (1989), recounting the full, humorous, and even frustrating story of sniffing out the German Internet spies. Pay attention to the technological methods he devised to catch the spies at work. Follow the clues that led him to reject his logical assumption that the hacker invader was an American. What became of the hackers once they were caught?

## ▶ Critical Thinking Exercises

1. Bruce Sterling's book on the hacker culture and the government's case against it (*The Hacker Crackdown* 1992) is another wonderful piece of folklore about the computer age. What kind of people were the hackers who reprinted the AT&T document and distributed it on bulletin boards? Were they the nerds that popular culture wants us to believe all hackers are? Did their beliefs about freedom of access on networks fit the expected code of hackers? You might also investigate in the library how the government case against Steve Jackson, unresolved at the time Sterling's book was finished, was finally settled.

2. Sometimes politicians in Washington suggest that parts of the Internet should be sold off to the private sector. New businesses could then lease services to users. Many current Internet users see the possibility of selling a public resource, developed with tax money, as a threat to their free access to Internet capabilities. What precedents exist for privatizing public facilities? Is this a good idea?

**ANSWERS TO SELF-TEST**

*Multiple-Choice*: 1. a;   2. c;   3. b;   4. a;   5. b;   6. d;   7. b;
8. c

*True/False*: 9. T;   10. F;   11. F;   12. T;   13. T;   14. T;   15. T;
16. T

*Fill-in*: 17. telephone;   18. analog;   19. downloading;   20. network;
21. campus backbone;   22. value-added networks;   23. telecommuting;   24. Federal Computer Fraud and Abuse Act

# CHAPTER 11

# Artificial Intelligence

▶ ## LEARNING OUTCOMES

*After completing this chapter, you should be able to:*

1. *Define the essential issues of artificial intelligence by means of the Turing test and HAL in 2001.*

2. *Describe the main areas of productive research in artificial intelligence today, including natural language processing, expert systems, logic programs, robotics, and neural networks.*

3. *List and explain the significance of important milestones in the history of artificial intelligence, including CYC, SHRDLU, DENDRAL, and Deep Blue.*

4. *Define and explain concepts that have been important to the development of artificial intelligence, such as heuristics, world knowledge, parallel processing, and fuzzy logic.*

5. *Discuss the status of artificial intelligence today and its challenges for the future.*

▶ ## COMPUTERS IN CONTEXT

*In 1950 Alan Turing, one of the giants among the founders of computer science, addressed the subject of "Computing Machinery and Intelligence" in a provocative article in the psychology journal* Mind. *Turing had helped to build the Colossus computer in Britain to crack German military codes in the Second World War. And he had laid a theoretical foundation for computing with the concept of the Turing machine, providing a very powerful basis for a theory of computation. In his 1950 article, Turing wondered whether computers could ever be considered to "think" in the human sense. As we turn to the future of computing in artificial intelligence, we can look back for guidance to Turing's early idea of what constitutes intelligent machine behavior: the famous* Turing test.

*Alan Turing imagined a scenario in which there were three typing terminals, two on one side of a wall, connected to a third in a second room. In the room with two machines, one terminal would be operated by a person and the other by a computer. A human being in the other room would converse with both terminals and ask the two whatever he or she wanted. The questioner's objective would be to tell the difference between the human and machine answerers. According to Turing, if the machine's responses were as intelligible to the interrogator as the human respondent's, then we could say that computers can think. A sample of Turing's proposed dialogue gives a sense of the sort of queries between people and machine that the Turing test proposes:*

*Q: Please write me a sonnet on the subject of the Forth Bridge [a well-known British engineering achievement, a bridge over the Firth of Forth in Scotland].*

*A: Count me out on this one. I never could write poetry.*

*Q: Add 34957 to 70764.*

*A: (Pause about 30 seconds and then give as answer) 105621.*

*Q: Do you play chess?*

*A: Yes.*

*Q: I have K[ing] at my K1 and no other pieces. You have only K at K6 and R[ook] at R1. It is your move. What do you play?*

*A: (After a pause of 15 seconds) R-R8 mate.*

*In his brilliant book on minds and machines, Gödel, Escher, Bach (1979), Douglas Hofstadter quotes this dialogue and points out that the long delay in the addition problem is followed with the wrong answer. Both the delay and the error seem more characteristic of a person than a computer. On the other hand, computers today play a very respectable game of chess, probably the most famous game of logic. Note that the interrogator is unable to get the respondent to try to write poetry. Some computer programs do write poetry-like texts, but their products are not in danger of being confused with those of Emily Dickinson or Robert Frost.*

*Alan Turing believed that by the end of the century, "general educated opinion will have altered so much that one will be able to speak of machines thinking without expecting to be contradicted" (quoted by Hofstadter, 597). Much research in artificial intelligence is working on issues of language understanding, pattern recognition, and logical programming—all featured in Turing's imaginary dialogue. Yet only in limited domains can any computer envisioned today be considered close to meeting the full **Turing test**.*

**FIGURE 11-1** Alan Turing, one of the pioneers of modern computing, proposed the Turing test of artificial intelligence in 1950. In a paper still studied by researchers, Turing set out goals for an "intelligent" computer which have not yet been met by artificial intelligence applications.

**Turing test:** Alan Turing's 1950 description of a dialogue in which a person tries to guess which of two conversations is being conducted with a person and which with a computer. This test has become a standard model used to judge the "intellengence" of many AI applications.

**FIGURE 11-2** A diagram of the Turing test. The questioner asks for information from the human respondent and the computer. If the questioner cannot tell the computer responses from those of the person, according to Turing, we should say that the computer can think.

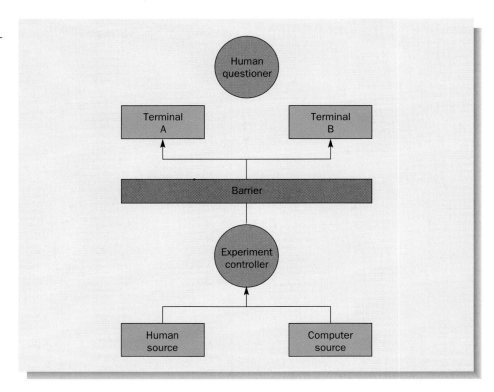

## Defining Artificial Intelligence

On the other hand, Arthur Clarke's fictional HAL 9000 computer, on board the spaceship in the movie *2001: A Space Odyssey* (screenplay with Stanley Kubrick, novel by Clarke alone, 1968) more than meets the Turing test of machine intelligence. HAL's name stands for Heuristically programmed ALgorithmic computer; but some wags at the time saw a joke on IBM, the world computing leader in the 1960s, since the name is only one letter shift off (Baer). HAL is not a robot in the usual science-fiction humanoid sense, but is wired into the controlling machinery of the spaceship, like a microprocessor in a microwave oven or a digital watch. There are two human crewmen on the space mission to Jupiter, but HAL is the only one who knows the true purpose of the mission. He readily carries on conversations with the crew and plays a mean game of chess while controlling the flight of the spaceship. He can see everything going on aboard the ship and even seems to have human emotions.

The main problem in the plot comes when HAL begins to act a bit erratic, and the two crewmen, Poole and Bowman, try to shut him off. HAL's only mission is "the fulfillment of his assigned program . . . more than an obsession . . . the only reason for his existence" (Clarke, 148). To protect himself and the mission, HAL sets Poole adrift in space and almost manages to trap Bowman before this last man aboard the spaceship finally pulls the plug. The point is that Clarke envisioned machines like HAL to be far more powerfully intelligent than Turing's machine by the second year of the next decade. HAL has vision, language, logic, and even a basic biological sense of survival. As we examine various levels of research in artificial intelligence today, we should keep HAL's capabilities in mind.

How does one define **artificial intelligence (AI)?** The term was coined by John MacCarthy in 1956 to apply to computer applications that prior to the machine's invention were considered uniquely human in nature, and there have been many definitions in the intervening years. One of the most quoted, Marvin Minsky's definition—"the science of making machines do things that would require intelligence if done by man"—avoids the question of whether the computer is working like the brain and is thus acting in a human way (quoted by Decker and Hirshfield, 315). As we noted in Chapter 1, the silicon basis of modern microprocessors differs from the organic nature of our biological brains. So long as it gets the same results as a person, the computer is acting, according to Minsky, with AI. It is irrelevant to ask questions about whether it is replacing the human being's unique status in the worlds of philosophy and theology.

Let us organize a survey of the various kinds of AI research that seem most productive today around HAL's characteristics: his capacity to understand human language, his logical faculties, his visual ability to see all the activities aboard the spaceship, and his robotic capacities to monitor and control all the processes of the space journey. In computer science, these areas are called *natural language processing, expert systems* and *logic programs*, like chess playing, *neural networks* for visual and image processing, and *robotics*. Each has its successes and special challenges.

**FIGURE 11-3** A computer named HAL shared the space mission to Jupiter in the movie *2001* with two astronauts, including Commander David Bowman, shown here communicating with the computer. HAL was at least as intelligent as the crew; in fact, his abilities would satisfy the Turing test of artificial intelligence.

**artificial intelligence (AI):** The branch of computer science concerned with understanding the nature of human intelligence, with the goal of simulating aspects of it with a computer.

## Natural Language Processing

We have already seen (in Chapter 6) that word processing today encompasses a variety of text-based applications, including indexing and concordances. These applications are classified as **text processing,** though the

**text processing:** A field concerned with text-based applications of computers, including indexing, hyphenation, and concordances.

programs have little knowledge of the natural languages with which they are dealing. For instance, if a person misspells *sky* as *sly* in the sentence "The sly is clear," a spelling checker will not flag it, for it is a legitimately spelled English word, even though the sentence makes no sense. AI programs in natural language processing aim to "understand" the sentence and catch such deviant sentences.

In the early days of computing in the 1950s and 1960s, the fast speed and large memory sizes of computers made them attractive for attempts at **automated machine translation.** In fact, the U.S. Defense Department put considerable research funds into a number of such projects, especially those meant to translate Russian materials at the height of the Cold War. The dictionaries of two languages—such as English and Russian—were encoded into the computer, along with their rules of grammar. The idea was to take a sentence in the source language, like English, and to analyze it grammatically for subject, verb, and other constructions. Then the program looked up the equivalent Russian words in the dictionary. All that was needed was to generate a grammatically correct Russian sentence using the words that had been retrieved from the dictionary.

A lot of experiments of this kind were tried, with few successful results. For example, the sentence "Fruit flies like green bananas" was interpreted to be about fruit that flew in the same manner as flying green bananas! Literally speaking, the sentence does mean that (or would if *fruit* were the subject); but the correct interpretation is about the eating preferences of a type of insect. People, however, have no difficulty developing the right interpretation, since neither fruit nor bananas fly under their own power.

## SYNTAX AND SEMANTICS

Grammatically the sentence "Fruit flies like green bananas" may make sense, but the first meaning is nonsense. AI analysis of language today not only looks at the grammatical relations of the words of the sentence—the **syntax** features—but also at the meaning components, called **semantics.** Modern computer grammars might try to make *fruit* the subject of the sentence, but the semantic parts of the program would reject that possibility, since flying is not an appropriate action for fruit. The grammar would then try the other, correct interpretation, with *fruit flies* as the subject. Semantics serves to find the correct syntactic analysis of the sentence.

An early program that many people thought was exhibiting artificial intelligence was developed by Joseph Weizenbaum at MIT in the mid-1960s. Weizenbaum called it **ELIZA,** for Eliza Doolittle of Bernard Shaw's *Pygmalion* and Lerner and Loewe's musical *My Fair Lady.* Like the original Eliza, the program acts as if it knows more than it does. It carries on an interactive conversation with the human speaker much as a psychoanalyst does with a patient. Although the program seems to follow the person's remarks with sympathetic understanding, in fact the responses are generated entirely from cues (or lack of them) in the human correspondent's remarks. For example, a reference to the person's mother leads ELIZA to query for more information about the correspondent's family.

ELIZA's first users were very impressed with its seeming intelligence; it seemed that ELIZA might be HAL's first cousin. However, Weizenbaum made clear in his explanation of the program that it never really "understands" anything about the subject's dialogue. In terms of natural language processing, ELIZA does little syntactic analysis and includes only rudimentary semantic information, such as the association of *mother* with *family.* The program carries out simple syntactic transformations (sentences with *I* become *you* with the same verb—"I'm depressed" to "you are depressed")

**HISTORY**

**automated machine translation:** A research field in linguistics and computer science that translates one human language into another with computers.

**syntax:** The field of linguistics concerned with the grammatical relations of words in a sentence.

**semantics:** The field of linguistic analysis concerned with the meaning component of language, still one of the greatest challenges of natural language processing with computers.

**ELIZA:** An early experimental computer program in AI that carried on a dialogue with a person. The computer appeared to understand what was being said but in fact was just filling blanks in formulaic conversation.

**HISTORY**

—and pattern matching for certain words like *mother.* Like the questions asking for more information, the parroting back of the person's dialogue accounts for ELIZA's reputation as a sympathetic listener. Although it appeared to many that computers were closing in on the Turing test, the ELIZA experiment was really a series of elaborate, clever tricks. Weizenbaum warned people not to be taken in by too optimistic predictions about intelligent machines. Much work remained in understanding how human language works before machines could converse intelligently with people (Weizenbaum).

## HEURISTICS, WORLD KNOWLEDGE, AND COMMON SENSE

One area in language analysis that needed further development was a series of heuristic rules to decipher what is going on in human language. **Heuristics** are ad hoc rules that can be applied in particular situations for automated understanding. People take for granted much information about the world around them, information called **world knowledge.** This kind of information must be specified exactly to the program, often as heuristics. As an example, in the 1960s a computer program was given the sentence "I saw the man in the park with a telescope" in order to see if it could sort out all the possible meanings. Am I in the park, or looking out a window through a telescope at a man in the park? Is the man standing in a park that contains a telescope? Or does the man have a telescope? In other words, the sentence is inherently ambiguous without any further context to clarify who is in the park and where both the observer and the telescope are.

Given this challenge, the computer was able to sort out all the possibilities; but it also noticed something that the people who constructed the sentence never thought of. It interpreted the sentence as being about an act of sawing. The program suggested this interpretation: I am sawing the man in two in the park that contains the telescope! The grammar works, but the meaning does not compute. No person had considered this reading, because people know that sawing people is not grammatically appropriate behavior, except in the very restricted arenas of magic acts and gruesome crimes. What the computer program lacked was the world knowledge people take for granted about the incompatibility of saws applied to human beings. It needed a heuristic to reject this interpretation unless it knew more about the circumstances of the sentence. Hardware and software, two elements of the Computer Triangle, in this instance were not smart enough to replace people, the third element. Modern natural language research with computers must incorporate all three elements of syntax, semantics, and heuristics if it is really going to "understand" human language.

The approach to world knowledge favored by Doug Lenat's **CYC** Project (taken from encyclopedia) is to fill the computer with enormous doses of common sense. Over the past decade CYC's language analysts have fed their computer programs more than a million concepts about human reality: that people must be awake to eat, that they usually can see other peoples' noses but not their hearts, that they cannot remember events that have not happened yet. Cutting a lump of peanut butter in two leaves one with two lumps of peanut butter, whereas cutting a table into two parts does not leave either part a table. Funded heavily with corporate research money, CYC is filled with world knowledge about causality, intention, contradiction, beliefs, and emotions and logical rules to allow the computer to make new and valid inferences about its facts (Lenat).

As research funds have become scarce because progress was slow, Lenat is now moving CYC's knowledge out of the research lab into com-

**heuristics:** Exploratory methods for problem solving that can be applied in particular situations for automated understanding, often consisting of rules of thumb or other ad hoc strategies.

**HISTORY**

**world knowledge:** Information that people take for granted that must be explicitly stated in computer programs, often as heuristic rules.

**CYC:** An well-known project to develop computer understanding of common sense knowledge of the real world, involving encoding millions of facts and relations between them, so that the machine can draw inferences automatically.

**FIGURE 11-4** A classic example of a problem with an early machine translation program to translate English into Russian. What is the main problem: syntax, semantics, heuristics, or world knowledge?

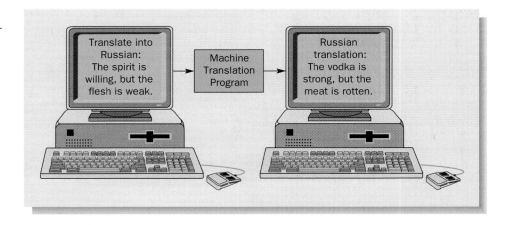

mercial applications in information retrieval and word processing. Asked to find photos of people at risk for cancer, CYC retrieved a picture of a girl on a beach, for it reasoned that people get lots of skin exposure to the sun there and may get skin cancer (Stipp). Earlier we noted that a spelling checker would not note the error if one typed *sly* for *sky*. Lenat gives a similar example for *Huckleberry Finn* with the sentence, "Huck thought it felt good to rest his bare toes on the warm rough wooden sock." Although socks and toes are statistically often found together, CYC would guess that the word should have been *dock*, presumably because people like to go barefoot by the river on sunny days (Lenat). Whether CYC's prototype applications will become full-blown systems remains for the future, but the project has shown some promise in real world understanding inferred from large bodies of encoded facts drawn from language materials.

## LANGUAGE UNDERSTANDING IN LIMITED DOMAINS

Another insight from recent natural language research is that language understanding is so complex that at present it can only be expected to work in **limited domains,** with a constrained vocabulary. When Doug Lenat began CYC ten years ago, he thought that his common sense computer would be able to handle much of human understanding. Now he understands that CYC needs to sacrifice completeness of inference in favor of what he calls "expressiveness and efficiency" in smaller practical applications (Lenat, 37).

The success of **SHRDLU,** developed by Terry Winograd at the MIT Artificial Intelligence Laboratory, illustrates results in a limited domain. Sometimes called **BLOCKS WORLD,** this program understands a model world made up of blocks of different shapes, sizes, and colors (see Figure 11-5 adapted from Winograd's *Understanding Natural Language*). It can be asked in English sentences to find and move the blocks around. It accepts verbal commands from a keyboard, analyzes them for both syntax and semantics, and instructs a robot to carry out the action. The program knows only a limited range of actions, such as *find* and *pick up,* and a small set of block objects, like cubes and pyramids. Yet within this domain it can "understand" most commands and carry out the desired actions. When it was completed, no other computer natural language systems had been so successful in accepting instructions and carrying them out according to the wishes of the human user. Ideas from SHRDLU have been adopted and modified for 20 years, but no general natural language query systems have yet been devised that can converse on any topic.

**HISTORY**

**limited domain:** A term that describes how various kinds of success in AI have been achieved in relatively small, constrained areas of application.

**SHRDLU (BLOCKS WORLD):** A pioneering natural language application designed by Terry Winograd, with features for understanding both the grammar and semantics of instructions for moving a set of blocks around on a plane surface.

# ▶ Expert Systems and Other Logic Systems

Both CYC and SHRDLU represent types of natural language expert systems, a popular AI concept based on knowledge gathered from people about how they make decisions. Bruce D'Ambrosio has defined an expert system as "an automated copy of human expertise" (D'Ambrosio, 282). The idea is that the computer models the behavior of the human expert in making decisions. For a particular application, an expert system must contain information about how people think about a problem (its **knowledge base:** facts and relations among them); how they use their knowledge to make decisions (the **inference engine:** methods of using relations for problem solving); and how to learn from experience and adapt to changing conditions.

SHRDLU knows how to recognize geometrical shapes, and holds information about their relative sizes and colors in its knowledge base. Having analyzed the user's linguistic request for a particular action, such as "Pick up a big red block," the computer program consults its knowledge base, finds the red blocks of whatever shape, compares their sizes, and then instructs the robot to pick up the largest red one. It infers that the request for a "big" block means that it must compare dimensions of size and choose the largest. A later request to find a taller block and put it in the box requires the program to learn from its previous experiences. It has to remember the earlier red block, find a taller one, and put it in the box. Having solved these problems, it can move the tall, blue block to the box.

**knowledge base:** In an expert system, facts and relations among them gleaned from human experts.

**inference engine:** In an expert system, the use of reasoning, based on using the knowledge encoded into the system, to solve problems.

## KNOWLEDGE BASES VERSUS DATABASES

A knowledge base is more complicated than a database, such as the one developed for a personal music library in Chapter 8. A traditional database contains facts, like record titles and dates of recording, which can be sorted and queried. The knowledge base about blocks also holds facts—sizes, shapes, and colors—but it encodes relationships among them which instruct the computer how to make inferences, as a person does. If a user asks for a big block, the system must know what facts must be sought and compared to determine the big block. Relationships that people take for granted, like world knowledge about when something is judged big, must be explicitly stated in the computer's knowledge base.

## PRACTICAL EXPERT SYSTEMS

Expert systems have been developed in a number of fields, including chemistry, medicine, finance, and investment. The first such system, called **DENDRAL,** was developed by a team of chemists and computer scientists at Stanford in the 1960s. It takes information about chemical compounds gleaned from analysis of their characteristics with a mass spectrograph and classifies them according to type. The inference engine in DENDRAL has encoded into it the rules for possible chemical bondings, of which there exist thousands of mathematical combinations. DENDRAL contains the sequence of logical processes used by expert chemists—its heuristics—to classify a compound. It follows them through in its automated fashion with its very large knowledge base of chemical information—more than a person can keep in memory—to carry out the identification of molecular structure.

**HISTORY**

**DENDRAL:** An early successful expert system for classifying chemical compounds based on their spectrographic characteristics and the rules that govern chemical bonding.

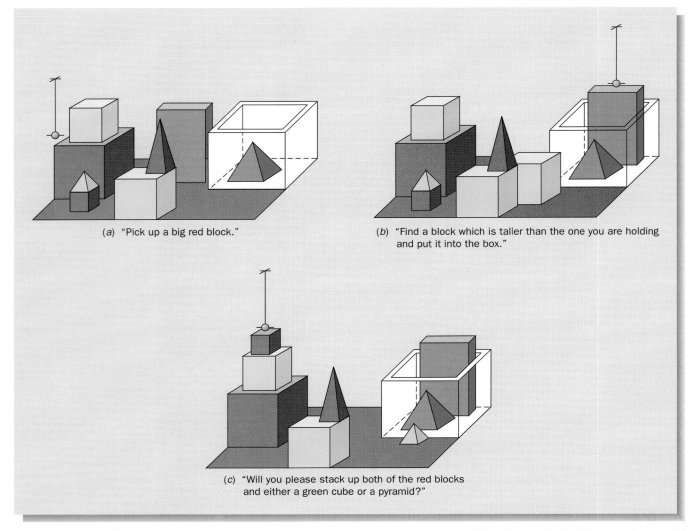

(a) "Pick up a big red block."

(b) "Find a block which is taller than the one you are holding and put it into the box."

(c) "Will you please stack up both of the red blocks and either a green cube or a pyramid?"

**FIGURE 11-5** By following the dialogue between the user and the **BLOCKS WORLD** program on the computer, you can see the results of the requests in the three illustrations. The robot that moves the blocks around is the vertical line with the ring at the end.

Pick up a big red block.
OK.
Grasp the pyramid.
I DON'T UNDERSTAND WHICH PYRAMID YOU MEAN.
Find a block which is taller than the one you are holding and put it into the box.
BY "IT," I ASSUME YOU MEAN THE BLOCK WHICH IS TALLER THAN THE ONE I AM HOLDING.
OK.

What does the box contain?
THE BLUE PYRAMID AND THE BLUE BLOCK.
What is the pyramid supported by?
THE BOX.
How many blocks are not in the box?
FOUR OF THEM.
Is at least one of them narrower than the one which I told you to pick up?
YES, THE RED CUBE.
Will you please stack up both of the red blocks and either a green cube or a pyramid?
OK.

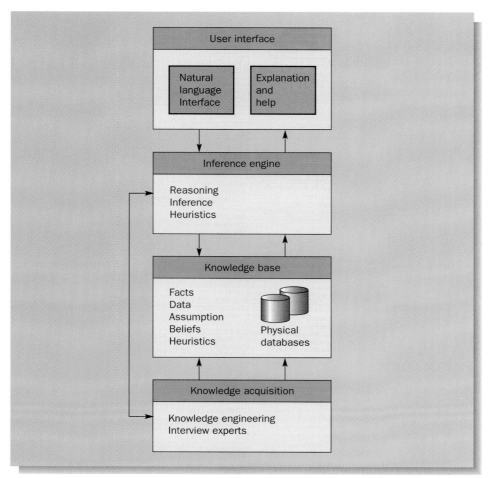

**FIGURE 11-6** The elements involved in a fully developed expert system. At the center of it are the knowledge base of information and the inference engine that queries it. Specialists called knowledge engineers interview experts in a field and try to capture information and relationships that can be encoded into the knowledge base and incorporated into the inference engine. The user of the system interacts with the program through an interface presented in natural language.

As an example of the rules applied by the **DENDRAL** inference engine, which models a chemist's reasoning, consider the following:

*If the spectrum for the molecule has two peaks at masses X1 and X2 such that*

    *a.* X1 + X2 = M + 28, and

    *b.* X1 − 28 is a high peak, and

    *c.* X2 − 28 is a high peak, and

    *d.* At least one of X1 or X2 is high,

*Then the molecule contains a ketone group.*

                      *(quoted in Harmon and King, 135)*

This sort of if/then condition, familiar from the discussion on programming, is called a **production rule** when it is used in an expert system. The knowledge base takes the spectrographic masses and applies a large number of such production rules in the process of analyzing the molecule. The designers of DENDRAL spent approximately 15 person-years developing the heuristics involved in the expert chemist's train of reasoning and eventually incorporated all of this "knowledge" into the program.

**production rule:** An if/then condition incorporated into the inference engine of an expert system.

**FIGURE 11-7** Engineers use computer expert systems to examine components and processes in an automobile engine and diagnose possible problems.

HISTORY

## FUZZY LOGIC

Approximate reasoning in expert systems involves the concept of fuzzy logic, a field pioneered by Professor Lotfi Zadeh at the University of California at Berkeley in the 1960s. Zadeh realized that pure propositional logic was too exact for many practical purposes. People use looser, vaguer comparative measures in making decisions. That is to say, reality exhibits shades of gray more often than black-and-white distinctions. Fuzzy logic allows computers to be programmed "to mimic the imprecise way humans make decisions" (Rogers and Hoshiai, 46).

To suggest the flavor of a fuzzy logic solution of a problem, consider computer-based document retrieval. Scholars in the humanities and social sciences complain that current computerized bibliographies require search requests that are too specific to match the more subjective nature of their requests. As a result, they are often disappointed with the results. With fuzzy logic, it should be possible to create a bibliographical query including subjective language such as a request for "a few important recent articles on euthanasia." Common retrieval systems in use today require requests to be exact, like "six articles written in 1992 or 1993 about euthanasia," and have no way to request "important" articles. Fuzzy logic researchers are also trying to find out how experts in a field know that a request for euthanasia would want to pick up articles cataloged under mercy killing, and probably even medical ethics about death and dying. They are working on information processing concepts for synonyms—how one verbal request implies another in a person's mind—as well as on what it means to want only "important recent articles."

Japanese manufacturers are producing the first rush of practical products incorporating fuzzy logic circuits in various appliances: washers, cameras, air conditioners. A Panasonic washer uses an optical sensor to tell how dirty the clothes are and adjusts the wash cycle and amount of detergent automatically. A new camera will adjust itself for changing light conditions, whereas the air conditioner will balance room temperature depending on the number of people in the room. In 1990 there were more than 2000 fuzzy logic patients in Japan, and several U.S. companies were getting

**Expert Systems in Medicine**

Several expert systems have been applied to the processes of diagnosis in medicine. **INTERNIST,** written at the University of Pittsburgh, is used in internal medicine. It holds a knowledge base of information about more than 500 diseases and 2900 symptoms associated with them. As the doctor encodes into the computer the characteristic symptoms of the patient, the program gradually narrows down the possible infections, in effect modeling the reasoning processes of the doctor. Although INTERNIST is very successful in disease identification, some clinical users get irritated at the extra time it spends assessing diseases that are, in fact, inappropriate. It is more exhaustive in looking at possibilities than are the more intuitive humans (Harmon and King).

   **MYCIN,** from Stanford, is aimed at identifying bacterial infections and suggesting treatment. The process is interactive between the doctor and the computer. Data about the patient, the infection, and its characteristics are input one at a time. By a series of production rules of the form "If this is true, then ask about these things next," MYCIN gradually zeroes in on the kind of bacterial infection under investigation. To illustrate, MYCIN is asking about a culture from a spinal tap (CSF) of a patient called SALLY; the answers are the physician's:

Has SALLY recently had symptoms of persistent headache or other abnormal neurologic symptoms (dizziness, lethargy, etc.)?

Yes

Has SALLY recently had objective evidence of abnormal neurologic signs (nuchal rigidity, coma, seizures, etc.) documented by physician observation or examination?

Yes

The CSF cultures will be considered to be associated with MENINGITIS.

(Quoted in Harmon and King, 17)

   In the phase of the program where treatment is suggested, the program asks about the susceptibility of the patient to allergic reactions associated with different drugs suitable for treating the infection. It then suggests drugs that minimize negative side effects for the patient. If the doctor wants to know the chain of logic that is leading the program to make its suggestions, MYCIN can be queried to explain its train of thought. Of course, the doctor can also reject MYCIN's suggestions at any time in the process. In tests against physicians, MYCIN's prescriptions were as good as, and in some cases better than, the human counterparts'.

   Similar to INTERNIST for internal medicine, MYCIN models the diagnostic process of the specialist in bacterial infections. Both systems took many hours to develop (MYCIN took about 50 person-years of effort), but deal with relatively limited domains within the field of medicine (Harmon and King). Despite these impressive successes, there seems little likelihood that one's family physician is soon going to be replaced by a computer program. As with natural language, the two nonhuman sides of the Computer Triangle cannot completely replace the human side.

---

**INTERNIST:** An expert system from the University of Pittsburgh for use in identifying infections in internal medicine, based on a knowledge base of information about more than 500 diseases and their symptoms.

**MYCIN:** An expert system designed at Stanford University to diagnose and suggest treatment for various kinds of bacterial infections.

interested in developing the idea for consumer goods. One Sears Kenmore refrigerator already includes fuzzy circuits for automatic defrosting. Buyers can expect fuzzy concepts to be included in a host of "smart" appliances (Rogers and Hoshiai). Fuzzy expert systems ideas have moved from theory to practical uses in appliances, and we can expect continued research in other, more human activities based in language, like document retrieval.

## GAME PLAYING

Natural language understanding and expert systems are only two subdivisions of the broad class of problems addressed by AI. Numerous successes in automated chess-playing programs illustrate the more mathematical capabilities of the "intelligent" machine. Although somewhat of a simplification, game-playing programs from tic-tac-toe to checkers, chess, and the Oriental game called Go depend on the computer's ability to examine a large number of possible moves in a short period of time and logically assess their probable success or failure. In computer tic-tac-toe, the machine reassesses the board after every move, calculates its best move of those re-

**A**

**B**

**FIGURE 11-8** (A) Professor Lotfi Zadeh of California at Berkeley formulated the concepts of fuzzy logic in the 1960s. (B) This cartoon takes the idea of incorporating fuzzy circuitry in "smart" appliances to an extreme.

**brute force:** Solving a problem like a chess move by using the computer's ability to examine a large number of possible moves quickly in order to assess each for its potential for success or failure.

**combinatorial explosion:** The greatly increasing number of possible alternative moves that must be examined in looking forward several moves in games like chess or Go to choose the best move.

**HISTORY**

**FIGURE 11-9** In the heralded chess match between Garry Kasparov and the Deep Blue computer in 1996, the pieces were moved for the computer by one of its IBM programmers.

maining, and chooses that one. The method of play may be called **brute force** combined with heuristics about what is best; all possibilities are tried before one strategy is adopted.

## COMPUTER CHESS

Chess programs are similar, but the number of possible moves that must be examined with forecasts about their successes in future moves grows in a **combinatorial explosion.** One recent computer chess program called Deep Thought could examine 720,000 moves per second and played a respectable game in 1989 with the Russian master, Garry Kasparov—but lost. Its successor, called Deep Blue, again challenged Kasparov in February 1996, and again most experts expected it to lose. Everyone was surprised when the computer won the opening match, the first victory ever by a machine against a grand champion. Eventually Kasparov's instinct and intuition beat the computer's hundreds of processors and analyses of millions of moves per second by a score of 4 to 2, including one win and two draws for the computer.

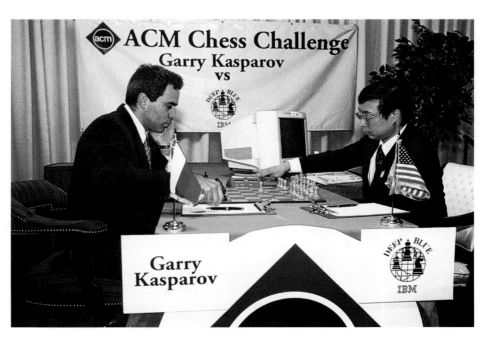

Deep Blue combined massive brute force analysis of moves and their consequences with a very selective process of assessment that led it to accept or reject some moves like a human champion. In fact, its knowledge base contained an extensive expert system of chess games to draw on for decision making. Even Kasparov was impressed with its performance, for he congratulated the IBM research team that programmed the computer heartily at the end of the week-long match: "For the first time I saw something approaching artificial intelligence" (quoted in Weber, 18 February 1996). Most experts were willing to agree that this match was a watershed. Deep Blue's combination of brute force and selectivity was not unlike the way a human champion thinks, though not in the same ratio. It would only be a matter of time before a computer would be the world chess champion (Weber, 19 February 1996).

The computer's ability to do mathematical combinatorics so quickly makes it possible to consider problems previously thought insolvable. Everyone has heard the old story that a million monkeys sitting in a room typing would eventually produce Shakespeare's works. With AI such a situation can be seriously contemplated, given the incredible speed and flexibility of modern computer processors and the size of their memories. Game-playing programs based in mathematics have produced increasing successes in AI since its earliest days.

## ▶ Robotics

In 1921 a Czech playwright named Karel Capek introduced the term *robot* into modern consciousness in his futuristic science fiction play, *R. U. R.* The term itself derives from the Czech word for labor or work, *robota*. The play's title refers to a company called Rossum's Universal Robots that made humanlike robots to do man's work. *R. U. R.* popularized the idea that robots looked and acted like humans, as they have so often been depicted in Hollywood movies. But the modern computerized **robotic machine** is usually far less glamorous. It may be an automated assembly-line vehicle delivering parts to workers or a riveting machine assembling metal

**robotic machine:** A robot typically engineered with sensors and a gripper arm to carry out an automated industrial process.

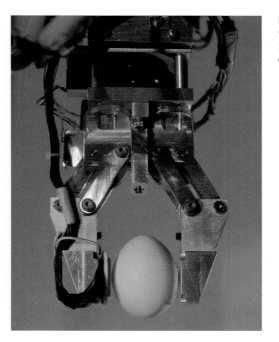

**FIGURE 11-10** A robot gripper arm in which the touch sensors are tuned finely enough to pick up an egg without breaking it.

**process control application:** A process in manufacturing often suitable for installation of robotic machines, such as automated welding on an assembly line.

**gripper:** A robotic arm capable of moving in three-dimensional space and picking up another object.

**visualization systems:** Robotic machines, such as some automated security systems, with television cameras and feedback mechanisms capable of analyzing a scene and carrying out an action based on what is seen.

**image analysis:** A research field in computer science concerned with developing technologies for automatic understanding of what a computer is seeing, such as identifying a target or an incoming enemy missile with a smart weapon.

**sensory feedback:** The ability of a robotic machine to receive sensory information as data and adjust its behavior accordingly, the highest level of achievement in today's robots.

sheets for automobile bodies. It is often used for **process control applications** in manufacturing.

## SENSORY ABILITIES

In many cases, robotic machines are engineered with abilities to sense and feel the outside world and interact with it. Like people, their *sensors* have perceptual facilities—to see, to touch, to hear—before they carry out other actions such as moving or grasping. Typically a robot has a **gripper** arm capable of moving in three-dimensional space and picking up another object (Feldman). It may be fitted to pick up a screw and bolt it to a metal frame or rivet two pieces of metal together. Sensitive robot grippers can pick up an egg without breaking it. Feedback built into the gripping process determines the proper tension to apply without harming the egg.

Robotic **visualization systems** include television cameras and feedback mechanisms to look at a scene, analyze it, and carry out some action based on what is seen. Automated security systems may have TV monitoring equipment that sets off an alarm when something moves into its field of vision. Recognizing what is being seen is a far more complex challenge, for, as scientist Thomas Binford reminds us, the retina of one eye contains about 100 million vision cells (Minsky). Much active scientific research in visualization and **image analysis** has implications for robotics of the future.

Machines with **sensory feedback** represent the highest level of robotic technology today. But the way robotic sensors work is not nearly as complicated as human sensation, as we have suggested above. Whereas about two-thirds of the brain is given over to tactile sensation picked up by 300 sensors per square inch of the human body, robotic sensors are limited to a specific job in order to have the data processing power to handle the sensory detail (Feldman). Whether this is "intelligence," like so much of AI, depends on one's definition. Certainly the "smart" appliances equipped with fuzzy logic circuits combine state-of-the-art ideas from one branch of artificial intelligence with engineered robotics. These little robots on chips are a giant step up from the automated riveting machine.

**FIGURE 11-11** A robot explorer called Dante II and created at Carnegie Mellon is being lowered into an active Alaskan volcano in 1994. Although several unexpected hitches stopped the experiments before their completion, the tests proved that a robotic device could navigate a hazardous terrain, like a volcano, on its own.

## ROBOTIC ADVANTAGES

In manufacturing, robots offer several advantages. They relieve workers of many tedious and dirty jobs. They can be used in hazardous environments: in radioactive areas, in space, or under the sea. The permanent orbiting space station proposed by NASA could not be built without the assistance of industrial robots for assembly of parts in outer space. Robots improve productivity by assuring a lower unit cost than manual workers doing the same job. Rate of output is predictable, and quality is consistent over many parts produced.

SOCIETY

Yet the cost of introducing industrial robots is high in the start-up phase. The machines are not only expensive but necessitate changes in the work environment. Manufacturers who can make the initial heavy financial investment in industrial robots reap their savings over the long haul. The increasing number of robots appearing in factories over the last decade has changed the jobs of the labor force working alongside them. Workers need new skills and better education for this new age of human-machine partnership in manufacturing: the Computer Triangle in action.

## ▶ Neural Networks

Artificial intelligence overlaps with neurophysiology and psychology in a field called **neural networks,** or **connectionism.** Neural networks are an attempt to model with computer processors the human brain's processes—learning, understanding, and remembering. Neuroscientists speak in terms of thousands of neurons that fire across synapses, making connections that become the behavioral patterns we call learning and remembering. They speak of long-term and short-term memory. Even so, today's brain scientists cannot say for sure exactly how the mind learns (Tazelaar).

**neural networks (connectionism):** A computer technique intended to model the human brain's processes in learning, understanding, and remembering.

## PARALLEL PROCESSING

To simulate with computer processors neurons and their connections requires linking more than one processor in a network configuration that allows **parallel processing.** Parallel computing leaves behind the older paradigm of sequential processing introduced into computing by von Neumann and discussed in Chapter 4. Instead of one operation following another in sequential order on one processor, input signals are sent out at once to several processors wired in parallel, and each sets to work on them simultaneously. If the processors need to share data, they are interconnected in the network. Analogously, we believe, a series of electrochemical signals are sent to the brain from the eye or the ear and are dispersed over a large neuron network in order to make sense of them.

**parallel processing:** A combination of multiple interconnected processors and software techniques that analyze input data simultaneously rather than serially; useful in neural networks.

Rather than "programming" a neural network of parallel processors, one first "teaches" it to give acceptable answers—the computer process analogous to human learning. In the training process, a person feeds known information into a neural network, assigns weights to the various processor connections, and then runs the network many times so that the output, the learned information, is satisfactorily correct. Given this learned response, the network is ready to take new data and recognize the same phenomenon when it is presented again (Obermeier and Barron). For example, neural networks have been used to understand speech sounds. The network of interconnected processors is fed a sound, such as a long A, multiple times until its weights stabilize throughout the network. When later sounds are input, the network should be able to pick out this

**FIGURE 11-12** A neural network designed to identify T as the first letter of a word. The processor for T is surrounded by its neighbor processor nodes for other letters. The words that are being examined are at the top, and the arrows represent signals they send to different processors as they are being analyzed.

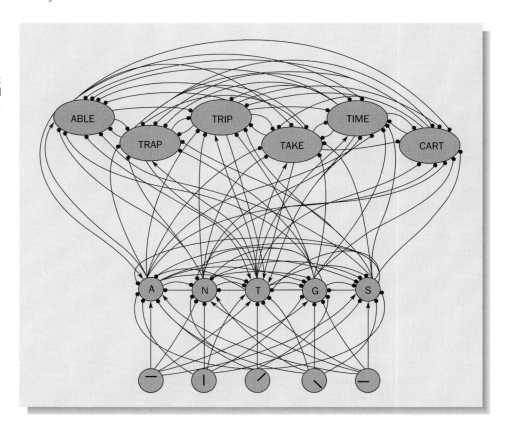

long vowel, even if it is mixed up with other sounds in a word like *day*. If the computer could learn all the sounds in English, it would be a full-fledged automated speech recognition system, but progress to date has not been that fast.

## APPLICATIONS OF NEURAL NETWORKS

Neural networks are not intended for the logical and computational processes of sequential computers, like balancing checkbooks or playing chess, but they can do a passable job at making good guesses or resolving conflicting data (Anderson). Areas for which they seem promising include pattern matching—whether of visual images, speech, or even handwriting—and sensor processing.

A successful neural network of the latter kind is called SNOOPE (System of Nuclear On-line Observation of Potential Explosives). SNOOPE scans pieces of luggage on conveyor belts at airports, looking for concealed plastic explosives. Its input signals are sensed from the radiation given off by the neutrons in the explosives. First tested in the Los Angeles and San Francisco airports, SNOOPE can scan up to 10 bags per minute and make a decision about which ones are suspect. The neutron analysis method does not damage film or magnetically recorded materials, like cassette tapes or diskettes. It is now being put into place in major metropolitan airports throughout the world.

Of perhaps more interest for psychologists are the pattern matching applications under study for visual image processing, continuous speech recognition, or reading handwriting, including Japanese characters (Obermeier and Barron). It should come as no surprise that much of this work includes the principles of **pattern matching** with fuzzy logic.

SOCIETY

**pattern matching:** The human ability to recognize underlying patterns of similarity in different contexts, such as handwriting styles and dialects, for which neural networks using fuzzy logic seem appropriate.

## EVOLUTIONARY PERSPECTIVE

### The Uses of Artificial Intelligence

The frontiers of AI and cognitive science merge the concerns of psychology, logic, linguistics, engineering, and computer science in focusing on aspects of intelligence—how we know what we know, how we think. At one end of the spectrum, Roger Schank, an acknowledged leader in the field of cognitive science, makes a distinction between the theoretical issues of the subject and the applied spinoffs, or workable systems: "When an AI idea is turned into a useful system, in some sense it isn't AI anymore. The construction of such a system requires all kinds of non-AI programming effort—to make the idea work in a real environment, on real computers, in some useful way. Such a system is made possible by the AI idea, but the program's merit comes from its functionality, not its heritage" (Schank and Hunter, 155). According to Schank, AI is concerned with the implications of being able to solve the problem of monkeys and Shakespeare seriously, not with whether the solution is implemented.

Indeed, the idea of mind as program takes on the importance of interpretive metaphor in AI. Sherry Turkle has noted in her examination of the computer culture that AI shares with psychoanalysis the opportunity to look at many old questions in the social sciences and humanities in new and exciting ways. Just as the concept of the unconscious in Freud restructured our understanding of personal and psychological phenomena in fundamental ways, so the concept of the program and computational processes may change the ways we view understanding. Edward Fredkin of MIT has gone so far as to say that "artificial intelligence is the next step in evolution" (quoted by Turkle, 242). Joseph Weizenbaum, an early AI pioneer with ELIZA, and later one of its most severe critics, has been bold to stress the metaphoric power of the "information processing view of the world": it constitutes an intellectual framework applicable to many new questions, and provides within itself the criteria for judging the adequacy of the proposed answers (Van Tassel).

---

Connectionism remains controversial within the AI community. Though a parallel computer processor may be 10,000 times faster than a neuron in the brain, the brain can do a pattern recognition job, like sound recognition, much faster than any current computer model. **Cognitive scientists,** interested in brain–computer analogues, attribute this human power to the brain's architecture. The brain appears to function in a highly parallel manner, with distributed processing. Individual neurons may seem relatively simple, but their strength comes from the massively parallel way that the brain's 10 billion neurons work together through their interconnections. Neural networks are an attempt to formalize this paradigm to understand certain kinds of intelligent phenomena (vision, language, speech). But critics are correct in cautioning researchers not to overstate the similarity between the brain and the connectionist models that exist today (Addanki in Shapiro et al.).

**cognitive scientist:** A scientist, perhaps trained in computer science, psychology, linguistics, neuroscience, or philosophy, interested in the study of brain/computer analogues.

## HAL RECONSIDERED

Artificial intelligence has not yet reached the stage of HAL's development, as envisioned by Arthur Clarke and Stanley Kubrick in 1968. A news service story distributed on January 12, 1992, noted that that day was HAL's birthday. As the fictional computer was dying, it revealed that it had become operational on that date, at a factory in Urbana, Illinois. "HAL is not ready to get turned on," said Bruce Walker about real-life computers in January 1992, although some of HAL's features, such as advanced language abilities, are being extensively worked on. At the time, Marvin Minsky, the AI pioneer who was an advisor for the film *2001,* stressed that "computers are very good at all sorts of specialized things that people have figured out how to program them for, but they don't have any common sense" (Arar and Strauss). This very human characteristic continues to be a source of lively AI research in projects like CYC. As the recent success of the computer program Deep Blue also attests, researchers are making real strides every year in matching HAL's ability to play championship chess.

## ▶ Summary

On multiple research fronts, computers are being trained to understand human language and speech and to think in the fuzzy terms we take for granted. Human expertise is the basis of expert systems in limited domains, and neural networks are learning to act somewhat like the way the brain seems to work. Industrial robots are sensing real-world phenomena and responding with productive work. AI has identified many of the issues that must be better addressed in coming years: better understanding of the semantics and heuristics of natural languages; incorporation of the world knowledge and common sense of a child; and extension of the domains of expert systems. In fact, there may still be time for AI researchers to meet the challenge of HAL's computer timetable, which will come due in 2001.

## ▶ Key Terms

artificial intelligence (AI) (p. 259)

automated machine translation (p. 260)

brute force (p. 268)

cognitive scientist (p. 273)

combinational explosion (p. 268)

CYC (p. 261)

DENDRAL (p. 263)

ELIZA (p. 260)

gripper (p. 270)

heuristics (p. 261)

image analysis (p. 270)

inference engine (p. 263)

INTERNIST (p. 267)

knowledge base (p. 263)

limited domain (p. 262)

MYCIN (p. 267)

neural networks (connectionism) (p. 271)

parallel processing (p. 271)

pattern matching (p. 271)

process control application (p. 270)

production rule (p. 265)

robotic machine (p. 269)

semantics (p. 260)

sensory feedback (p. 270)

SHRDLU (BLOCKS WORLD) (p. 262)

syntax (p. 260)

text processing (p. 259)

Turing test (p. 258)

visualization systems (p. 270)

world knowledge (p. 261)

## ▶ Self-Test

**MULTIPLE-CHOICE**

1. HAL in *2001* exhibited all of the following aspects of AI except
   a. vision
   b. language
   c. reproductive power
   d. logic

2. Which of the following is not recognized as a currently active area of research in AI?
   a. robotics
   b. natural language processing
   c. the Turing test
   d. expert systems

3. Computers will need which of the following if they are really going to "understand" human language?
   a. syntax
   b. heuristics
   c. semantics
   d. all of the above

4. Which of the following is not an essential component of modern expert systems?
   a. a grammatical parser
   b. a knowledge base
   c. an inference engine
   d. an ability to adapt to changing conditions

5. Which of the following is not a recognized expert system?
   a. CYC
   b. MYCIN
   c. ELIZA
   d. DENDRAL

6. Which of the following concepts is not associated with artificial intelligence in game playing?
   a. a selectivity function based on expert systems concepts
   b. natural language analysis
   c. the combinatorial explosion of possible moves
   d. brute force solutions

7. All of the following are robotic applications except
   a. chess playing
   b. process control
   c. image analysis
   d. visualization systems

8. Which of the following represents an advantage of using robotic techniques in the workplace?
   a. Robots can be used in hazardous environments.
   b. Robots can do work that is tedious for people.
   c. Robots lower unit costs compared to manual work for the same job.
   d. all of the above

## TRUE/FALSE

9. **T  F**   In several domains computers today can be considered close to meeting the full Turing test.

10. **T  F**   According to Marvin Minsky, AI is "the science of making machines do things that would require intelligence if done by man."

11. **T  F**   When ELIZA was completed, no other computer natural language system had been so successful in accepting instructions and carrying them out according to the wishes of the human user.

12. **T  F**   World knowledge, which people take for granted, must be explicitly stated in the knowledge base of an expert system.

13. **T  F**   An expert system like MYCIN takes many hours to develop but deals with a relatively limited domain of knowledge.

14. **T  F**   Machines with sensory feedback represent the highest level of robotic technology today.

15. **T  F**   Robotic sensors have all the human perceptual abilities—to see, to touch, to hear, to taste, to smell.

16. **T  F**   To simulate neurons and their connections requires linking

more than one computer processor in a network configuration so that they work together as an expert system.

## FILL-IN

17. According to the _____, if a computer's responses are as intelligible to a human interrogator as a person's responses in an interactive dialogue, then we should consider that computers can think.

18. _____ carries on an interactive dialogue with a person much as a psychoanalyst does with a patient, and with sympathetic remarks and requests for further clarification seems to exhibit intelligence.

19. Whereas a traditional database contains facts that can be sorted and queried, a _____ holds not only facts but relationships among them, which allows the computer to make inferences about them.

20. An if/then condition, familiar from structured programming, is called a _____ when it is used in an expert system.

21. Approximate reasoning in expert systems involves the concept of _____, which allows computers to simulate the imprecise way people make decisions.

22. Modern computerized _____ are more likely to be riveting machines assembling metal sheets for automobile bodies than machines with humanlike characteristics.

23. In _____, operations are farmed out to several parallel processors at once, and each processor works on them simultaneously.

24. _____ are adept at making good guesses or resolving conflicts among data in areas like pattern matching and sensor processing.

## ▶ Experiential Exercises

1. ELIZA and another AI computer program called PARRY, which simulates the responses of a paranoid person, appeared to early observers to be moving in the direction of meeting the Turing test. Hofstadter (pages 599–601) quotes a dialogue between the two programs to give a sense of their responses. Research these in enough detail to see how their "minds" worked (in the case of PARRY, its paranoid mind).

2. Research the similarities and differences between creating a knowledge base for an expert system and a typical database application. Why is it usually more difficult to design a knowledge base?

3. Investigate factories in your area to see how robotics have been introduced into the manufacturing process. What are the main uses of robotic machines: process control, automated transportation vehicles, visualization, or others? Are the robots programmable for different jobs or single-purpose machines?

4. Do some research on the social effects of robotics. When robots are installed in factories, are employees laid off or given jobs in other areas? Is retraining of workers required? Does management argue that productivity has gone up and costs have come down with robotics, even though the initial costs of conversion are high?

5. The chess match between Garry Kasparov and IBM's Deep Blue in February 1996 was widely covered in the news media and on the World Wide Web. Research some of the views that computer scientists and philosophers of creativity expressed about the implications of a computer beating a world champion chessmaster.

# ▶ Critical Thinking Exercises

1. In *Gödel, Escher, Bach* (pages 595–99), Douglas Hofstadter covers in detail the concept of intelligence in the Turing test and Alan Turing's answers to various objections expected against it. Discuss each of the objections to see if it has validity against the points of the Turing test. You may want to read Turing's original article in order to see a truly creative mind at work.

2. Consider the first two lines of Lewis Carroll's "Jabberwocky":

> *'Twas brillig and the slithy toves*
> *Did gyre and gimble in the wabe:*

What clues among the legitimate words in the sentence could help a computer decipher the parts of speech of the nonsense words? Which kind of knowledge—of English syntax or semantics—contributes most to correct interpretation of the questionable terms?

3. A famous machine translation program rendered the English phrase "Out of sight, out of mind" into Japanese as "Invisible, insane." Of the three program components, syntax, semantics, and heuristics, which was the weakest link in the program that produced this translation? Discuss.

4. Expert systems similar to MYCIN are being developed in fields like medicine, legal affairs, and stock investment. In the future, such computer programs may help to diagnose diseases, answer legal questions, and suggest financial investments. Will professionals in these fields try to stop the creation of such programs? If these expert systems are accepted by consumers, will they help to keep the costs of professional services down? Discuss.

5. Fuzzy logic concepts have been more popular in the development of appliances, like dryers and cameras, than in applications dependent on language materials, such as document retrieval. Consider the bibliographical query "I need several classic articles on education and accreditation." Analyze the "fuzzy" characteristics of the request, and discuss the criteria a computer retrieval system based on fuzzy logic would use to decide what information fulfills the requirements of the query.

6. Discuss the similarities between neural networks with parallel processing and the the human brain. How can neural networks made of inorganic materials like silicon be taught to act like the human mind? Does it matter that AI is not organic in nature?

## ANSWERS TO SELF-TEST

*Multiple-Choice*: 1. c;  2. c;  3. d;  4. a;  5. c;  6. b;  7. a;
8. d
*True/False*: 9. F;  10. T;  11. F;  12. T;  13. T;  14. T;  15. F;
16. F
*Fill-in*: 17. Turing test;  18. ELIZA;  19. knowledge base;  20. production rule;  21. fuzzy logic;  22. robots;  23. parallel processing;
24. neural networks

# CHAPTER 12

# Computers and the Future

▶ **LEARNING OUTCOMES**

*After completing this chapter, you should be able to:*

1. *Discuss the great possibilities for human good and the potential societal drawbacks of the Human Genome Project.*

2. *Describe impending technological advances in digital electronics—telephones, television, and computers—including applications for entertainment, education, and broadcasting.*

3. *Describe new hardware developments, including palmtop computers, network computers, and future microprocessors.*

4. *Describe new software trends, including (a) Windows NT and its rivals and (b) artificial intelligence, including intelligent agents and artificial life.*

5. *Discuss the role of people in the Computer Triangle in terms of (a) government support for high-tech industrial initiatives and (b) Alvin Toffler's futuristic view of societal change in the Information Age.*

▶ **COMPUTERS IN CONTEXT**

*The Human Genome Project, a cooperative international effort to crack the human genetic code, provides several important clues to the place of computers in society in the near future. The human genome contains 23 pairs of chromosomes. Scientists have been working to detect the patterns of the approximately 3 billion nucleotides or bases (adenine, guanine, cytosine, and thymine) that are strung out as gene sequences on the chromosomes. If specific gene patterns can be discovered that distinguish genetic disorders like cystic fibrosis or sickle cell anemia, gene therapy may be possible to reverse the process. A transposed base in a normal sequence may also indicate a tendency toward muscular dystrophy or heart disease (New Scientist). In 1989 it was estimated that the Human Genome Project would take 15 years and $3 billion in funding (Science News). By 1994 more than 200,000 gene sequences had been isolated, and the pace of identification was doubling the number of sequences in less than 2 years (Begley and Rogers). The Project is surely one of the most visible of the Federal Grand Challenge Problems discussed in Chapter 2.*

*To meet this biological challenge, scientists are turning to a variety of computer techniques to unscramble more of these gene sequences faster. Special computer chips, such as the Fast Data Finder developed at Cal Tech in cooperation with two high-tech companies, combine up to 10,000 processors working in parallel sequence to identify patterns much more quickly than people could ever do. Leroy Hood, of Cal Tech, says his computer workstation can search 27 million sequences in about 3 seconds against known ones stored in a computer database, called GEN-BANK. Earlier computerized methods took hours or even days (New Scientist).*

*Edward Uberbacher, of Oak Ridge, has put together a neural network program called GRAIL, which runs on personal computers. It uses artificial intelligence ideas to separate the gene codes from the other 95 percent of the base sequences which lie in between the genes. Uberbacher explains the principles of GRAIL with a comparison to written texts: "An analog is, if you looked at a page of an engineering text and a page of a romance novel, you could tell by looking at a few dozen random words which was which" (quoted in Roberts, 805). Specifically, the program trains the neural network—a set of parallel processors—with statistical data gleaned from analyzing 100 sequences at a time. With all neural networks, the training phase, in which the network "learns" what is important and what to ignore in the incoming sequences, is crucial to its success with later data. With GRAIL, the network gradually begins to separate genuine gene code sequences from the noncoding materials around them. Uberbacher claims that the program finds 90 percent of the genes correctly and very quickly. Like Fast Data Finder, GRAIL does not need the power of a supercomputer, common in early genome research, to do its work fast and accurately (Roberts).*

**B**oth these projects represent the growth of computational science, a promising future for scientific computing. Edward Uberbacher, described by Leslie Roberts as "a biophysicist-turned-computational-biologist," is himself typical of the new generation of natural scientists, who are incorporating computers as an integral part of their work. All three elements of the Computer Triangle—hardware in special chips for parallel processing; software with advanced AI techniques; and people with expertise in computing and the natural sciences—are crucial to the success of the Human Genome Project, certainly one of the most significant scientific challenges of our time. Indeed, the Project could not be carried out within the estimated 15 years of funding without intensive use of computing throughout the process. In fact, the project has been so successful that the

**FIGURE 12-1** In the Human Genome Project, scientists are using computers to crack the genetic code years faster than they could have done it by other methods.

**FIGURE 12-2** The GRAIL program first checks seven variables about a DNA sequence. It then feeds this information into a neural network to decipher a true gene sequence from long strings of DNA codes that hold no meaning.

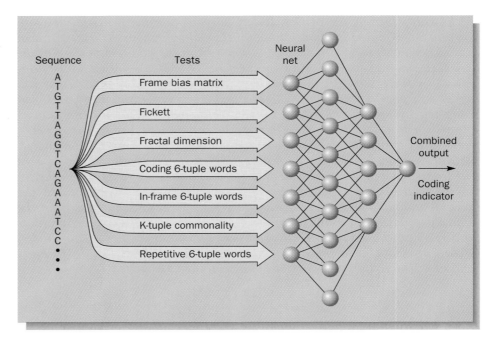

GEN-BANK computer database at the National Center for Biotechnology Information doubles in size every 21 months (Begley and Rogers).

SOCIETY

As a massively funded government research project in the sciences, the Genome Project has sometimes been compared to the Manhattan Project and the Apollo space program. And just as the Manhattan Project's product, the atomic bomb, begat a host of problems, including radioactive fallout and the nuclear arms race, so the Genome Project raises serious ethical questions. For example, if scientists use a computer to isolate the gene that causes Alzheimer's disease, can they copyright it and form a private company to market a cure? Does knowledge of gene functions encroach on personal privacy? What if an insurance company knows that a young person has a gene that shows a proclivity for heart disease as one ages and decides to deny life insurance coverage? Bioethics must be considered along with biotechnology, for none of these questions has an easy answer (Lee).

SOCIETY

In a similar way, the increasing discussion of the right to die in the United States results from the ability, through computer-controlled devices, to keep people alive when previously they would have just died. Technology may seem neutral, but its effects on people have never been and never will be. As we consider various futures for computing in the next decade, we must keep in mind the societal dimensions of technological change.

## ▶ *Computing in the* 1990s

Computational science, parallel processing, and neural networks are no longer frontier areas of computing in the sciences. As the Human Genome Project illustrates, they are becoming accepted methods even with scientific workstations and personal computers, which offer levels of processing power and speed for the home, the office, or the laboratory at prices unimagined even a decade ago. To predict exactly what the typical personal computer will be and how much it will cost in the year 2000 is impossible, but there are already indications of what its characteristic applications may be. Readers of computing magazines like *Byte*, *PCWorld*, and

*MacWorld* are constantly exposed not only to stories about the newest trends in computing, but to predictions about the future. Even the public press—newspapers and television—regularly carries stories introducing themes for computing in the future. It is worth noting that predictions about popular computing often hinge not on whether some new application or feature is technologically possible, but whether it will meet public acceptance and approval, and thus become a commercial success. Current buzzwords like *fiber optics* and *digital broadcasting* suggest one direction in which computing in the next decade seems to be going, one that is worth further investigation.

## THE ALL-DIGITAL WORLD OF ELECTRONICS

Since the first mainframe computers were introduced in the 1950s, the computer has been a digital device. Among the tools devised by humans, it has the most general application, because it works with the simplest system of symbolizing information, the binary codes implicit in its electronic basis. As we have seen, all sorts of human methods of communication can be stored and manipulated symbolically in the computer in digital form: language, mathematics, sound, pictures.

Other electronic media, such as telephone systems, television, and the recording industry, have been shifting over to digital storage and transmission of data for some time. The musical compact disk, available since 1983, is digitally recorded, and its cousin, the CD-ROM (compact disk read-only memory), have become popular for distributing large multimedia computer files in digital format. Fiber optic cable is rapidly replacing older twisted-pair and coaxial cable in the telephone and cable television industries. Whereas the two older types of wire carry signals in the analog form of sound waves, fiber optic cable carries digital signals in the form of light pulses. With the increasing speed of digital communications, pioneered by the Internet, enormous quantities of information can be exchanged across the country or the globe in what is essentially an instant.

A few years ago discussions about **high-definition television (HDTV)** centered on the Japanese idea of transmitting analog signals and the American preference for digital. A research development aimed at producing television monitors with more than twice the horizontal and vertical resolution of today's sets and CD-quality sound, HDTV also involves the computer industry. Experts acknowledge that these new sets will be virtual computers, filled with semiconductor chips that perform a host of functions (Frenkel). Commercial analog HDTV models are available in Japan with brilliant, crisp pictures but have had little success elsewhere since an American company, General Instrument, was able to create an equally impressive digital signal in 1990. Even the Japanese in 1994 acknowledged that the digital method would be the standard in the future (Powell and Itoi). Since television sets today process TV transmissions by an analog process, digital HDTV would require viewers to buy a new TV set.

Even with current analog sets, networks and cable companies are distributing their signals digitally, across the continent or to the home, via satellite or over fiber optic lines. What is to be gained by merging all electronic media into a common digital signal? Answers include **compatibility**—the ability to share resources all stored in a similar technology—and interactivity among different sources of information. A movie produced in digital format could be ordered with a small hand-held computer device, much like a common remote controller, and sent out from a regional center over cable and phone lines. The home controller/computer replaces the video store, and the movie is transmitted directly to an indi-

**high-definition television (HDTV):** The next generation of television with much higher picture quality, to be distributed digitally and capable of being integrated with computers to offer many services and information resources to the home.

**compatibility:** The ability to connect different computer systems or media so that they can work together.

**FIGURE 12-3** A computer graphics designer in Japan is using HDTV images to create a fashion catalog.

INTERNET

**bandwidth:** The capacity of a phone line or other communications channel for distributing data—voice, graphics, text, video—measured in bits per second.

**compression:** A software process of storing a digital file, such as a sound or a video, in a compressed form to save storage space or speed up its transmission time over a network.

vidual's house. The video game of the next generation will offer realistic graphics presented on the television screen, and levels of interactive play that today are available only in the virtual reality games at some arcades.

## DIGITAL BROADCASTING ON THE INTERNET

The rapid growth of the Internet is already suggesting possibilities for digital broadcasting only imagined five years ago. Technical hurdles are being addressed and improved almost on a monthly basis. These include the **bandwidth** of phone transmission, the **compression** of large multimedia files, and the instabilities of Internet packets of information. Bandwidth refers to the capacity of the phone lines and modems to transmit and receive large files of digital information for sound and movies fast enough to make the result acceptable to the receiver. Whereas the typical analog

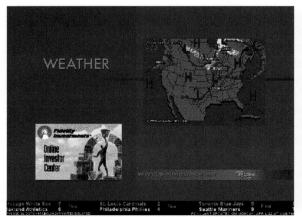
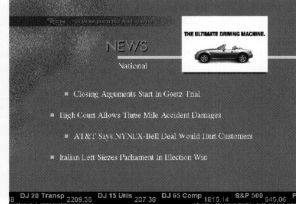

**FIGURE 12-4** Innovative screen saver software called PointCast represents "narrowcasting" over the Internet. Users can personally configure their computers to receive what they want: up-to-date news, weather, sports, and stock prices, all updated several times an hour. Different people in the same office can be getting different information from PointCast at the same time.

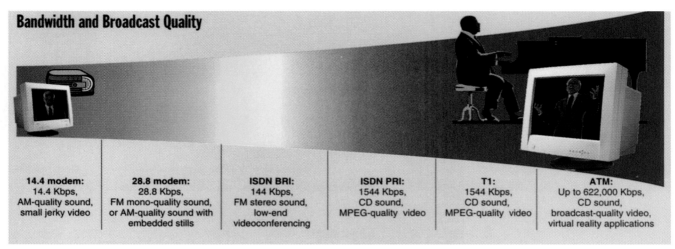

**Bandwidth and Broadcast Quality**

| 14.4 modem: | 28.8 modem: | ISDN BRI: | ISDN PRI: | T1: | ATM: |
|---|---|---|---|---|---|
| 14.4 Kbps, AM-quality sound, small jerky video | 28.8 Kbps, FM mono-quality sound, or AM-quality sound with embedded stills | 144 Kbps, FM stereo sound, low-end videoconferencing | 1544 Kbps, CD sound, MPEG-quality video | 1544 Kbps, CD sound, MPEG-quality video | Up to 622,000 Kbps, CD sound, broadcast-quality video, virtual reality applications |

**FIGURE 12-5** A comparative table on the quantities and types of information that can be carried by different modes of digital transmission.

phone lines and 28.8 baud modems are stretched to their limit with these media, several new international standards—ISDN, T-1, and ATM lines—are becoming more common, especially in business, and are dropping in price. In addition, cable modems can offer very fast access to the Internet through local cable outlets.

Meanwhile, the ability to optimize the bandwidth by data compression remains an active research area. Xing Technology's system called StreamWorks recently delivered a speech by Scott Cook, the head of Quicken, on the Net as reasonable quality sound in close to real time on a 14.4 baud modem, and other systems like RealAudio (Progressive Network) and InternetWave (VocalTec) offer other solutions. For video transmission the standard compression scheme is called **MPEG,** which allows portions of a digital image that do not change from frame to frame not to be stored. MPEG keeps a notation in the file that this segment of video is "ditto" from the previous frame. Currently one cannot be sure that an Internet packet of data will arrive in the same order as it was sent, and thus the decompression will lose detail. An Internet video conference or speech with missing frames would be more acceptable to the viewer than a movie or important technical information such as a close analysis of a medical problem. The emerging MPEG-2 format is geared to present broadcast quality, full-screen video, but bandwidth remains a problem.

**MPEG:** A standard format for encoding video files in a compressed form.

Another Internet broadcasting mode called **multicasting** is used to create the MBone (which stands for Multicasting Backbone). The MBone sends out its video and audio signal to many computers at the same time. To appreciate MBone concerts from its House of Blues in Los Angeles or shortwave from World Radio Network in London requires a T-1 line and heavy-duty Unix workstation. Yet by the year 2000 many people believe that the bandwidth-hungry MBone will be worldwide. In these pioneering days for digital Internet broadcasting one cannot know what bandwidths, transmission methods, and compression schemes will win out, but the future will clearly offer incredible broadcast possibilities in real time, given the pace of technical improvements since 1994.

**multicasting:** An Internet protocol for distributing the same digital files from one computer to multiple other computers at the same time.

Applications of Internet broadcasting are already springing up. Networks like ABC, NBC, and NPR have live radio newscasts on the Net.

**FIGURE 12-6** The creators of MBone—Steve Deering, Steve Casner, and Van Jacobson, shown from left to right—have been multicasting rock concerts on the Internet since 1994, as well as political speeches and medical conferences.

SOCIETY

Of the approximately half a million Web sites in mid-1996, how many might want to introduce broadcasting with a modest investment in software and a file server? Remote sports coverage is a natural application. A fan could hear a World Series game or an important college football matchup in real time at any Internet site, even overseas. College lectures, where the teacher is not moving around much, could be viewed on computer TV. Videoconferencing with software like CU-SeeMe (White Pine Software) can even be carried on 14.4 baud modems with acceptable reception. Eventually these broadband applications will clog the capacity of the Internet, with consequent degradation of service, and upgrading the network will be necessary for realizing the full potential of what is already possible (Dejesus).

## DIGITAL MULTIMEDIA

**edutainment:** A term to describe the use of interactive, visual, or multimedia strategies of video games to present educational materials on a computer.

In multimedia, many forecasters see a great growth in what is being called **edutainment:** the blending of educational materials with the interactive, highly visual delivery strategies of video games. Studies show that whereas people retain only about 10 percent of what they see and 20 percent of what they hear, they can remember about half of what they see and hear together, and even 80 percent of what they see, hear, and do. With these results, the educational advantages of multimedia presentation, like television or movies (sight and sound), are obvious, but even more so with interactive multimedia, with its component of interaction and response by the learner ("Teaching Minds to Fly with Discs and Mice").

For instance, a laboratory science lesson of the near future may not only show the student what happens in a chemical reaction, but may allow the user to choose among several options in completing the experiment. The student may even cause a dangerous explosion without injuring anyone in the multimedia simulation environment. The variety of programs already available in foreign languages and social sciences on CD-ROM technology suggests the interactive multimedia future, when the CD may be replaced with digital lessons on line.

## ECONOMIC DEVELOPMENT POSSIBILITIES

That business sees digital delivery as ripe for development in the consumer market is clearly shown in several strategic alliances completed in 1996. The economic attractions are obvious, with more than 92 million TVs in the United States and 25 million home computers already in place. The last few years have seen a number of mergers between phone, cable TV, and computer firms, in the anticipation of the digital future, especially with the growth of the Internet. The passage of the Telecommunications Act of 1996 opened up possibilities formerly prohibited by laws and regulations, some as old as 75 years. Although all of the implications of this mammoth bill will only be defined by many court rulings (for instance, the Communications Decency Act, discussed in Chapter 10), clearly the new law changes the telecommunications landscape by opening competition in home delivery of services between long-distance phone companies like AT&T and MCI, the Baby Bell regional phone companies, and the cable companies. Each segment can move into commercial turf formerly reserved for the other.

The law hopes that leveling the field will lead to lower prices and faster innovation. Critics worry that the reverse will take place: that a few big firms will come to concentrate and dominate the market (Weingarten).

HISTORY

FIGURE 12-7 Studies show that adding multimedia resources like sound and video to educational software should increase the amount of material retained by students.

**FIGURE 12-8** Will the field of digital interactivity be the Golden Egg? *Newsweek* featured its appeal and the possible economic bonanza on its cover in May, 1993.

**video telephony:** A long-distance telephone conversation with live video and sound.

**TABLE 12-1** *The U.S. Lead in the Information Age*

| TELEPHONES | U.S. | JAPAN | EUROPE |
|---|---|---|---|
| Lines per 100 people | 48.9 | 42.2 | 42.2 |
| Calls per person per month | 43.4 | 46.1 | 48.7 |
| Cellular telephones per 100 people | 2.6 | 1.2 | 1.2 |
| **TELEVISION** | | | |
| Households with cable (percent) | 55.4 | 13.3 | 14.5 |
| VCR related expenditures per household per year in dollars | 44.6 | 35.3 | 14.1 |
| **COMPUTERS** | | | |
| Personal computers per 100 people | 28.1 | 7.8 | 9.6 |
| Database production (percent of world) | 56.0 | 2.0 | 32.0 |

*Source: Consumer Federation of America*

This may be the case in three large mergers that took place within weeks of the passage of the law between pairs of Baby Bells (Bell Atlantic and Nynex in the East and SBC Communications and Pacific Telesis in the West) and a union of US West, another Baby Bell, and Continental Cablevision, the third largest cable company. Already big telecom players like AT&T and MCI are offering Internet access. Who will control Internet access and services—the computer industry, the telephone companies, or the cable systems—is yet to be sorted out, but it seems clear that something will happen. The number of big companies putting money into these projects virtually guarantees it.

Compared to what is currently offered by the Internet, services in the digital, interactive future will be greatly expanded. Fiber optics carrying 500 channels of digitally distributed television makes possible much more than present cable systems: interactive education at home; foreign-language broadcasts; Broadway plays or an old-favorite TV show on pay-for-view; and virtual-reality shopping. Interactive movies will let viewers choose alternative scenarios at critical points in the story. It is easy to foresee personal **video telephony,** true two-way communication of picture and sound between distant telephone numbers ("An Interactive Life").

## EVOLUTIONARY PERSPECTIVE

### Public Versus Private Interests in the Information Superhighway

If public money is spent on upgrading access to the Internet for public institutions like schools and libraries, what about the individual viewer? Customers will have to pay for the array of digital services offered. How many people will be willing to pay additional fees, probably double their current cable bills, for 500 or 1000 TV channels? Will they see the value for the extra expense? How many channels can a couch potato reasonably be expected to watch and interact with? Obviously, corporations are moving ahead rapidly with plans to develop equipment and offer services they believe the public is ready to purchase. Typical of this view is a remark by Arno A. Penzias, of AT&T Bell Laboratories: "The country needs an information supermarket, not an informa-

tion superhighway" (quoted in Stix, 106). This is the same commercial mind set that led to Prodigy and CompuServe a decade ago.

Already the United States has a preponderant lead in the use of television and personal computers, compared to Europe and Japan. Many believe that the multimedia digital frontier can spur the revival of the American electronics industry. Typical of those who view this frontier of merging digital media as an area of vast opportunity and uncertainty, Congressman Edward J. Markey has called it the Wild West of our time, since it offers lots of challenges, no fixed rules, and no clear jurisdictions of public versus private law (Stix). The next decade should give some indication of how it will shake down: what fortunes will be made, what ideas will catch on.

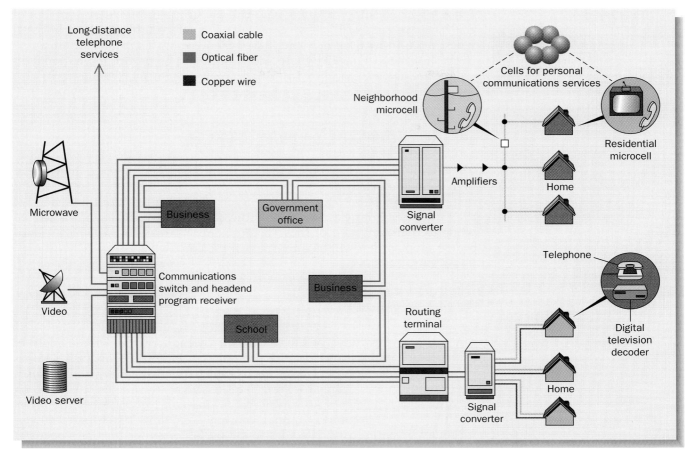

**FIGURE 12-9** Local communications are evolving along several lines to allow delivery of digital information along with traditional telephone and cable signals. Note the combination of different kinds of connections—fiber optic, coaxial, and twisted pair copper wire—within the system.

## INFRASTRUCTURE ISSUES

Currently AT&T phone lines can send about 3.4 gigabytes (billions of bytes) of information across the continent per second, which means they can handle more than three encyclopedias worth of text every second. These distribution speeds on an intercontinental basis require at each end of the line "on and off ramps," or "toll booths," to allow users to tap into the resources of digital interactivity. With deregulation after the new Telecommunications Act, a big turf war is brewing between the phone and cable companies about who will control access to the technology.

How can a digital signal be delivered to homes, many of which are presently connected to the phone lines with twisted-pair copper wire, and to cable systems with coaxial cable? Does the whole country need to be fiber optic on the local level—a rather expensive undertaking? Congressman Edward J. Markey of Massachusetts, former chairman of the House Subcommittee on Telecommunications and Finance, thinks so. He envisions a digital fiber infrastructure to lead the United States well into the next century. "The goal is not fiber to the home but information to the home" (quoted in Stix, 104). With declining federal revenues for all kinds of technology, costs for stringing fiber to homes will likely be left to consumers.

SOCIETY

A larger question remains: who will pay for continued development of the infrastructure of the Internet itself? The telecommunications bill provides for "universal service" but leaves vague what this means for advances in the Internet. Issues like these will continue to be part of the national dialogue about the expanding Information Superhighway (Weingarten).

## ▶ Revisiting the Computer Triangle

The computing revolution has always been composed of three interdependent elements: hardware, software, and the people who use computers. In fact, throughout the book we have referred to them as the three sides of the Computer Triangle. As we look toward the future, perhaps it is worthwhile to consider each of these components in turn, to see where trends are developing that will be important in the coming years.

## ▶ Hardware

Since the earliest days of the mainframe computer, and increasingly in these fast-changing times for the personal computer, the operative words in hardware development have always been *smaller*, *faster*, and *cheaper*. The rule of thumb seems to work like this: whatever a person bought six months or a year ago is now available at one-half to two-thirds the price, and the original amount of money can buy something much more powerful today. Eventually one decides to choose a computer for one's needs at the present, with the awareness that this choice is not for a lifetime. In a few years, an upgrade may not cost any more, but speed and processing power will be greatly enhanced.

Within the same range of machines—the Windows family, based on Intel chips; the Macintosh PowerPC family, based on Motorola/IBM chips; or the workstation market that supports Unix—the software that a person is accustomed to using will probably be supported on the new platform. Increasingly, processors are even more accommodating through emulation of other hardware. **Emulation** means that one processor can be programmed to act like a different one, so that applications that run on the older chip will still work on the new one in its emulation mode.

**emulation:** The imitation of one computer system by another, so that software created for the computer being imitated will run on the other without changing it.

**FIGURE 12-10** A prototype architecture for supplying a gigabyte's worth of information to the home is being tested by Time Warner in Orlando. It consists of a hybrid of fiber optic and coaxial methods and includes input channels for delivery of cable television, Internet, and telephone services, along with return channels for output of information from the home to the outside world.

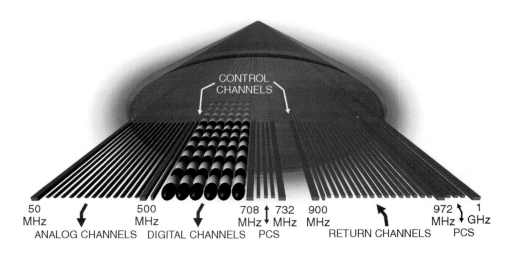

## PALMTOP COMPUTERS

Predictions about the next major wave of computer hardware are always risky, especially at the low end of the consumer market. A case in point: the highly touted **personal digital assistants (PDAs),** including the Apple Newton, the Sharp Zaurus, the Sony Magic Link, and numerous others with price tags of a few hundred dollars have never really caught on. Designed as **palmtop,** or **hand-held,** computers, they were intended to give a mobile society access to information and communication links for notes and memos on the run. According to the advertisements, everyone needs something to keep up with addresses and phone numbers, an electronic, digital organizer rather than a paper-based one. Given their early performance for the price, most people stuck with their paper-based daily organizers or inexpensive Sharp Wizards.

Unlike Sharp products, the Apple Newton has no keyboard but was designed to accept handwritten input, created with a stylus and deciphered by built-in cursive and graphics recognition software. Unfortunately the first pattern recognition algorithms in the software were notoriously inaccurate in understanding handwriting. Eventually software called Graffiti (Palm Computing) made this approach effective, for it requires that the user print characters in a fixed style. With about an hour of training, a person can learn to use its 36 characters (26 letters and 10 digits) and strokes for punctuation marks and foreign language accents, and the accuracy of recognition is very high. Another problem with early PDAs was their short battery life; since they were palmtop computers, they were not designed primarily for plug-in usage (Zilber, "Toy Story").

Meanwhile many hardware and software add-ons have been created for PDAs that give them more functionality than a daily organizer. For instance, the Sony Magic Link connects to SkyTel paging through a **wireless infrared communications** card and message systems like AT&T's PersonaLink services with a built-in modem for e-mail and fax capability. Included are versions of Quicken and America Online access software. New browser software called NetHopper (AllPen Software) for Newton allows this PDA to read Web pages in text mode, send e-mail, and store pages in memory so that they can be read later (Croal and Stone). Whether these enhanced PDA models will finally find a secure niche in the $500–600 market for electronic digital organizers remains to be proven.

## NETWORK COMPUTERS

The newest idea for the $500 market is the "WebBoy," the concept nickname of a stripped-down computer that allows users to access the Internet for Web surfing and e-mail but lacks many other functions that one expects in a laptop or desktop personal computer. Many hardware companies are promising to offer such **network computers (NCs or Web PCs)** by the end of 1996: Sun Microsystems, IBM, Oracle, Apple, and others. This development is not surprising, for it represents the convergence of computers, communications, and the consumer electronics (Zilber, "Prime-Time Player"). For instance, Larry Ellison, chairman of Oracle, the large software company, thinks that today's personal computer is too costly, too powerful, and too complicated for most users. What they want is not a full-fledged desktop machine, a "mini mainframe," but a network computer for a reasonable price that will let them communicate over the Internet, send e-mail, and download software. People like Ellison are suggesting that the arrival of the Internet for everyman represents a new **paradigm shift** away from the personal computer to an easier-to-use "**information appliance**" for everyday computer chores like word processing,

**FIGURE 12-11** The Sony Magic Link personal digital assistant has no keyboard and an attractive graphical presentation of its software options. The user makes choices with a stylus. Like other PDAs, it can handle communications through infrared wireless technology similar to a TV remote.

**palmtop (hand-held):** A small portable computer weighing one pound or less.

**personal digital assistant (PDA):** A new breed of palmtop computer designed to adapt to the user's style of working rather than requiring the person to follow the work pattern of the desktop computer.

**wireless infrared remote communications:** uses the "point and click" technology of the TV remote controller. It transfers files to another device.

**network computer (NC or Web PC):** A new type of stripped-down computer primarily designed to access the World Wide Web. It will allow users to gather information, write e-mail, and access software through downloading.

**paradigm shift:** A term for a major shift in thinking about an important subject. For instance, if the desktop model of personal computing were replaced with decentralized network computing based on the client/server model of the World Wide Web, computing would have undergone a paradigm shift.

**"information appliance":** Current jargon for a wide range of computer devices expected in the near future that will allow users to access information on the Internet with easy-to-use interfaces.

**FIGURE 12-12** One possible model for an American network computer is the Bandai NC, introduced to the Japanese consumer market in early 1996. It was developed with Apple Computer for Web access and video game playing with a controller shaped like a boomerang.

**LCD (liquid crystal display):** A liquid-filled display screen that creates images when electrically charged, used in watches, calculators, and portable computers.

SOCIETY          INTERNET

**FIGURE 12-13** Graffiti (Palm Computing) will recognize all of the common characters—letters, numbers, and punctuation marks—if the writer will use the correct stylus strokes with a PDA like the Apple Newton.

Net access, and video games that offers no more threat that an television set.

NCs are not palmtop machines but will look much like small desktop or laptop models. The Oracle prototype has a keyboard, a monochrome **LCD** flat screen, a built-in modem, and a mouse. To keep costs down, it lacks a hard or floppy disk drive, a CD-ROM drive, or a color screen. Eric Schmidt, involved in the creation of an NC for Sun Microsystems, argues that there is no need for a hard disk. The large files that a user will want are available on the Internet, and the browser software can download it when it is wanted. Sun's Java software fits this paradigm, since its applets are delivered over the Net and then turn the host computer into its virtual machine for their execution (Meyer).

As suggested in Chapter 10, such a vision of an Internet/NC future really represents a change from current desktop computing and its hardware and software. Proponents see more than the consumer market as customers for the network computer. Even the corporate world is a target for these Web PCs, for they could save money on administrative costs of keeping large PC networks running. Instead of costly upgrades for massive memory and greater processor speeds, businesses could buy smaller systems and download small applets from the Internet for doing traditional jobs like conventional spreadsheet analysis. Schools could afford to buy NCs to let students surf the Web for educational materials and correspond with overseas pen pals. According to industry analyst Michael Arrington, for schools "$500 is an important entry point, a price point that would allow them to buy computers en masse. It could move computers from the media lab onto the students' desktops" (quoted in Halfhill, "Inside the Web

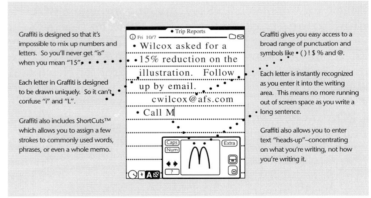

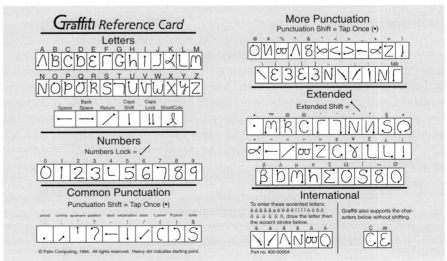

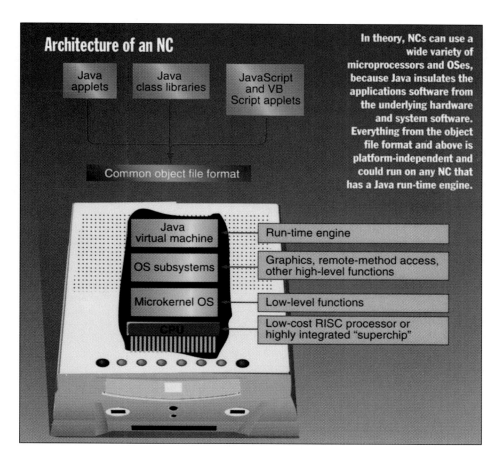

**Architecture of an NC**

Java applets

Java class libraries

JavaScript and VB Script applets

Common object file format

Java virtual machine — Run-time engine

OS subsystems — Graphics, remote-method access, other high-level functions

Microkernel OS — Low-level functions

CPU — Low-cost RISC processor or highly integrated "superchip"

In theory, NCs can use a wide variety of microprocessors and OSes, because Java insulates the applications software from the underlying hardware and system software. Everything from the object file format and above is platform-independent and could run on any NC that has a Java run-time engine.

**FIGURE 12-14** Early in 1996, *Byte* magazine presented this schematic plan for a network computer, based on current technology.

PC," 46). As noted earlier, one key to the success of this vision of the near future is speedy broadband access to and stability of the now global Internet.

## THE FUTURE OF PROCESSORS

Another key to the hardware future remains the processor that sits at the command center of the machine. Power Macs, Unix workstations, and even the Newton are based on modern **RISC** designs. The most advanced Intel chip, the P6, has also adopted RISC techniques, which is a departure from Intel's 486 and Pentium inheritance (Halfhill, "Intel's P6"). RISC chips maximize their power with a reduced number of machine instructions (hence the name **reduced instruction set computing**). They can deliver stunning performance in Unix scientific workstations at the higher-priced end of the desktop computer spectrum. Several Web computers that have been proposed will run on inexpensive RISC chips. The Power Macintosh is based on the PowerPC RISC chip architecture first developed as the IBM POWER chip set for RS/6000 workstations and manufactured by Motorola (Bortman). This RISC design gets great power at cost savings and enhanced performance both for the massive number crunching needed in computer graphics and scientific computing and for greatly expanded features in the operating system (Thomas).

Every 18 months silicon microprocessors double in speed, though they are still made by the same lithographic layering process, (somewhat like baking a pizza) that has been used for years. Improvements in architecture design account for continued increased performance. One of these strategies is called **pipelining**, a process that means that the processor stages

**RISC (reduced instruction set computing) chip:** A microprocessor chip with fewer and simpler instructions capable of performing complex tasks by combining simple instructions and reducing processing time.

**pipelining:** A process to speed up the throughput of a microprocessor by staging different jobs to run concurrently rather than doing them in sequence.

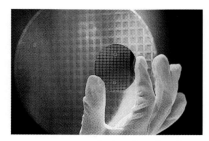

**FIGURE 12-15** The hand in the photo is holding the original Intel 4004 microprocessor wafer in front of a much larger modern Intel silicon wafer. Chips are created on these wafers by a lithographic manufacturing process and then cut out.

different jobs to run concurrently rather than doing them in sequence. The more stages that can be set in motion at the same time, the faster the processor performs. In 1995 one processor used deep pipelining and improved the effective speed of a 100 MHz computer to 300 MHz. We can expect that in the next century a 250 MHz machine with pipelining could carry out one billion instructions per second.

Another improvement involves placing a small memory called a **cache** directly on the chip. Instructions that the chip needs frequently are loaded permanently in the cache memory, so that the processor does not have to retrieve them from slower external memory chips. And **superscalar processing** resembles parallel processing on the chip, though it avoids the problem of communication among processes. With superscaling, the hardware automatically finds instructions that are launched at the same time (Patterson). The Intel P6, with 5.5 million transistors, incorporates all of these features to advantage—pipelining, superscalar architecture, and several caches on the chip—as do several of its competing chip designers (Nex-Gen, Cyrix, and AMD) (Halfhill, "Intel's P6"). Compared to the first microprocessors 25 years ago, today's chips are estimated to be 25,000 times better in speed and effective power. Continued tweaking of silicon chips should achieve even more impressive performances into the next century.

What if we reach the physical limits to improvement with the silicon chip? Already researchers have been testing other materials that would allow levels of miniaturization that can never be met by the lithographic manufacturing process. For instance, using ideas from quantum physics, scientists are exploring trapping electrons in quantum dots, a kind of molecular array, so that their movement can be monitored. Presence of an electron can be interpreted as a binary 1 and absence as binary 0, the basis of modern computing. Much of this work is very experimental, because at the quantum-mechanical level, movements may not be stable and may be hard to verify reliably.

Another approach, which has been contemplated for more than a decade, involves creation of circuits out of biological molecules. Organic circuits can then probably be synthesized with microorganisms rather than in factories. One possible molecule under consideration alters its shape in response to light, so that an optical circuit could be the basis of computing (Patterson). Leonard Adleman, a mathematician at the University of Southern California, in 1995 created a DNA-based computer that solved a challenging puzzle in mathematics much like the brain works, with massive parallel processing. With these biological approaches, the dichotomy that has always existed between organic nature and inorganic machine may finally break down within the next century (Levy).

**cache:** Another design strategy to improve processor performance by placing a small memory directly on a chip so that the processor has rapid access to frequently used instructions, which are stored there.

**superscalar processing:** A processor strategy similar to parallel processing on the chip that allows the hardware automatically to find instructions that are launched at the same time so that it can maximize their efficient use.

# ▶ *Software*

Analysts were surprised in 1991 with the agreement between Apple and IBM, hardware rivals in the 1980s, to cooperate in the development of the PowerPC chip and new computers with friendly GUIs like the Macintosh. Many saw this alliance aimed directly at the challenge of Microsoft, the most successful computer company of the 1990s, and its president, Bill Gates. Yet Microsoft makes software, not machinery.

## THE MICROSOFT EMPIRE

Microsoft tends to be considered as more than a large corporation with thousands of employees. Its popular image is always seen as embodying

the hard-driving personality of its founder, Bill Gates. Already the wealthiest man in America, with estimated assets of 15 billion dollars at 40 years of age in 1995, Gates got his start by licensing the DOS operating system to IBM for their first PC in the early 1980s (Levy, "Bill's New Vision"). Then Microsoft moved into software production, eventually offering a wide range of applications software for both Intel machines and Macintoshes, with such successes as Microsoft Works, Word, and Excel. Today the operating systems environments Windows 3.1 and Windows 95 are estimated to control more than 70 percent of the world's personal computers. Meanwhile, Microsoft Office, the current integrated package for such applications as word processing, spreadsheets, and electronic mail, is taking more than 85 percent of sales for applications software suites, according to market research (Halfhill, "Unix vs. Windows NT"). Microsoft is truly the gigantic presence in software.

The two-year period 1994–1996 was a roller-coaster ride for Microsoft. In 1994, the Justice Department finally slapped the company's hands as a result of complaints from applications software competitors, that control of the Windows operating system, along with its ongoing software development based on Windows, gave Microsoft essentially a monopoly. Yet a federal judge refused to accept the judgment and blasted the company's domination of computing as "a potential threat to this nation's economic well-being" (quoted by Levy, "Antitrust and Common Sense," 78). Yet Microsoft sales help the balance of trade, and this ruling remains unsettled on appeals. Summer 1995 heralded the arrival of Windows 95 and its subsequent enormous sale after the most heavily promoted advertising campaign in computer history. Windows 95 included software to log onto the new Microsoft Network, aimed at the market for public information utilities like Prodigy and America Online.

Just when everything seemed in place, Netscape, the World Wide Web, and Sun's Java hit the computing headlines; and Bill Gates and his company were again threatened. Internet browsers may replace information utilities, and Java applets may obviate the need for desktop computers to have large, complicated operation systems and a lot of applications software loaded directly on them. All of this functionality may be accessed over the Internet. At the start of 1995, Microsoft had only four employees working on its own browser software, while thousands of people were downloading Netscape every day and surfing the Net. As 1996 began, Microsoft had rebounded with 600 people to create its Internet Explorer, distributed free, but it did not yet have the features or audience of Netscape (Levy, "The Browser War").

In May 1996, a market survey indicated that the popular Netscape Navigator browser was preferred by 84 percent of Internet surfers. (Avalos). Could this new "killer app," from a company with 700 employees—and indeed a new view of what the future of computing would be—pose a threat to Microsoft, with its 19,000 workers? According to its president, Jim Barksdale, Netscape has a mission to save the Internet from Gates and Microsoft: "In the ultimate final analysis it will determine whether or not one person rules all software in the world" (quoted in Levy, "The Browser War," 48). This late push from a company with unlimited resources will make the competition with Netscape formidable (Levy, "The Browser War"). While the resolution of the "browser war" remains unsettled, the moral for popular computing software seems clear: nothing stays the same very long. Computer change comes faster and faster, and the future seems to be reinventing itself almost every year.

**FIGURE 12-16** Bill Gates, the head of Microsoft, is known as a tough business competitor and fervent evangelist for his products.

## WINDOWS NT AND ITS CHALLENGERS

One of the dominant operating systems of the coming years for large system installations seems likely to be the version of Windows called Windows NT. Windows NT is a full operating system designed to network together all kinds of computers and office equipment, like telephones, copiers, and fax machines. After several years as a system in trial, Windows NT is catching on, primarily because it is especially poised to take advantage of its edge with the very large installed base of Intel machines and the popular Microsoft Office software. And managers who make the decisions on purchases are comfortable with the financial clout of the Microsoft company that promises continued support and improvement of the operating system (Halfhill, "Unix vs. Windows NT").

## EVOLUTIONARY PERSPECTIVE

### Netscape Runs on "Internet Time"

No story in recent computing history has captured the imagination like the fantastic and furious success of the Internet's Netscape Navigator, certainly the hottest software of the 1990s. It all started with a group of highly creative programmers led by Marc Andreessen at the nonprofit National Center for Supercomputing Applications (NCSA) at Illinois, who released the first version of Mosaic, the first graphical browser, in January 1993. By early 1994 Mosaic was so popular that the former head of Silicon Graphics, Jim Clark, convinced Andreessen, aged 24, to found a company. They went back to Illinois and hired six of Andreessen's buddies to move to California and recreate the program in a fuller form for the commercial market. In effect, the brain trust from Mosaic redid the whole thing from scratch, only better, and released the first version of Netscape Navigator within eight months before the end of 1994 (Wolf).

In a phenomenal stock sale in summer 1995, the company went public; and Version 2.0 came out much improved in the fall of that year. By the spring of 1996, a third version of the software in **beta form** was being downloaded all over the world with new add-ons to give the software added value and capabilities. In Silicon Valley, the pace of change was so hectic that people now began to speak of "Internet time," where a new company must convince venture capitalists that it can create a product, gain a market presence, go public with a stock sale, or sell out to someone else—all in 18 months. According to David Hancock of Hitachi's portable computer division, "Speed is God. And time is the devil."

Microsoft, Netscape's greatest competitor, used to bring out updated versions of its software every 18 months or two years. Yet to catch Netscape, it released three versions of its Internet Explorer on the network between August of 1995 and May of 1996, most of them in beta versions, not fully tested. Web distribution is a new kind of market in which one copy of a product can be loaded on the Net and distributed worldwide; no need for huge factories and massive distribution mechanisms. Market share is the most important indicator of whether a product is successful. For workers in this high-tech, high-intensity industry, lots of stress and the chance for quick rewards are partners. Can this pace of change continue? Can big companies like Sun Microsystems, IBM, and Microsoft adapt to this style as a permanent mode of operation? These questions are still unanswered. Meanwhile, Andreessen and his cronies are instant millionaires, like their nemesis Bill Gates before them (Markoff).

**beta software:** A version of a software product released to the public for use and testing with no guarantee from the originators that the program is free of bugs.

FIGURE 12-17 In 1994 Jim Clark (right), former head of Silicon Graphics, convinced Marc Andreessen (left) and his student friends at the University of Illinois to come to California and found Netscape Communications. By the end of 1994 they had created the first version of the popular browser software, Netscape Navigator.

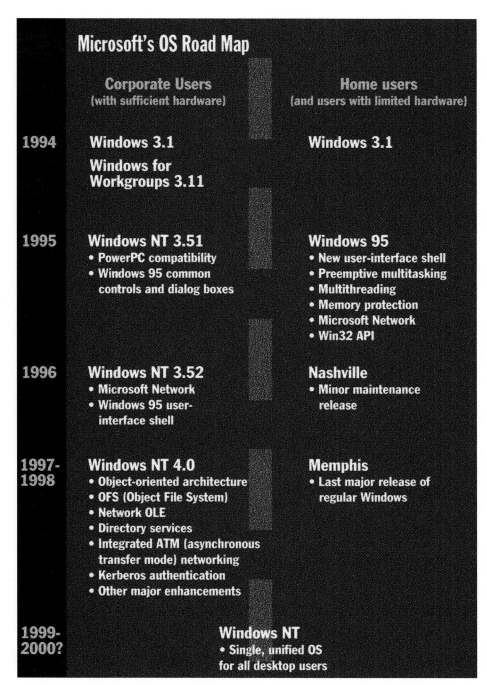

## Microsoft's OS Road Map

| | Corporate Users<br>(with sufficient hardware) | Home users<br>(and users with limited hardware) |
|---|---|---|
| **1994** | Windows 3.1<br><br>Windows for<br>Workgroups 3.11 | Windows 3.1 |
| **1995** | Windows NT 3.51<br>• PowerPC compatibility<br>• Windows 95 common<br>  controls and dialog boxes | Windows 95<br>• New user-interface shell<br>• Preemptive multitasking<br>• Multithreading<br>• Memory protection<br>• Microsoft Network<br>• Win32 API |
| **1996** | Windows NT 3.52<br>• Microsoft Network<br>• Windows 95 user-<br>  interface shell | Nashville<br>• Minor maintenance<br>  release |
| **1997-<br>1998** | Windows NT 4.0<br>• Object-oriented architecture<br>• OFS (Object File System)<br>• Network OLE<br>• Directory services<br>• Integrated ATM (asynchronous<br>  transfer mode) networking<br>• Kerberos authentication<br>• Other major enhancements | Memphis<br>• Last major release of<br>  regular Windows |
| **1999-<br>2000?** | Windows NT<br>• Single, unified OS<br>for all desktop users | |

**FIGURE 12-18** The introduction of Windows 95 was the first in a series of ongoing evolutionary upgrades in Microsoft operating systems leading to the predominance of Windows NT by the turn of the century.

No longer just for Intel processors, Microsoft is attempting with NT to be the dominant player in computing that IBM once was; but its base is in operating system software, not hardware. Yet critics point out that competing operating systems work better for particular applications—especially Unix for networking of workstations and distributed computing, and Macintosh, with its GUI more fully integrated into the operating system itself than Windows 95 (Udell). The Unix community has heavy strength in the workstation market and a lot of powerful corporate hardware supporters, like Sun Microsystems. Apple is already working on a total upgrade of its desktop operating system, called Copland and expected in 1997; and Sun has made great strides in the emerging World Wide Web with the success of Java. Even though Java is a programming language, people perceive Sun's commitment to Unix as setting an Internet standard. It also seems that Unix will be the preferred operating system for the new $500 network computers (Halfhill, "Unix vs. Windows NT").

Thus new or improved operating systems of several competing companies and technologies will, no doubt, be the focus of the next several years of computer evolution. Some forecasters believe that the marketing power of the Microsoft software giant will hold the key to acceptance of Windows NT. Today different systems coexist and compete successfully for customer acceptance, and the future will probably be much the same. If the past is any guide, all systems that win popular approval will offer more flexibility and user-friendliness with both current and future software applications and networking features, as prices continue to moderate through competition.

## INTELLIGENT AGENTS

SOCIETY

**intelligent agent:** Experimental AI software designed to sift through masses of information available in the future world of cyberspace to suggest topics of interest or importance for an individual.

Suppose multimedia workstations make available to the user the equivalent of three encyclopedias worth of information every second, the current speed of AT&Ts transmission of digital data. How can the ordinary user cope with the information overload that this delivery of an almost infinite choice of materials will offer? Are people really ready to channel-hop through 500 or 1000 TV channels or surf through 50,000 home pages on the Web? The solution may be **intelligent agents,** a kind of AI software that will sift through the masses of information and winnow out what will be of interest or importance to an individual.

The newspaper industry seems particularly interested in this approach, since it recognizes the threat to print culture posed by the digital media future. Knight-Ridder, Gannett, Hearst, and Times Mirror have worked with the MIT Media Laboratory to develop agents that have been called "the software version of the television character Max Headroom" (Stix, 107). As a person browses through an on-line version of a paper, the agent will monitor the behavior and keep up with the reader's preferences. It will develop a user profile of interests and needs, then go off seeking related information that needs to be retrieved—in effect sifting through enormous files of information to produce a personalized newspaper. Similarly, Max Headroom was noted for browsing through huge information data banks to retrieve facts to entertain his viewers. Meanwhile, the agents will help the editors to see what their readers want and to make this sort of story available. At present, editors spend a lot of time trying to decide what will sell; with the agent, they will be given much more data with which to make those decisions. Modern newspapers are already digital, up to the point of printing on paper; and many are going on-line with Web versions. Intelligent agents will help readers cope with the increasing glut of information. (Stix).

The powerful AI idea of intelligent agents applies to more than finding relevant information within massive resources in digital databases, using TV or computer monitors. Its basic premise is not new: the computer monitors a person's behavior and develops a user profile of some behavior, which can then be acted on by the machine. Perhaps the person asks for aid from the computer database. For instance, some systems already exist to query computers built into cars about how to find an address. Sensors along the road tell the computer where the car is located, and the software works out the appropriate route to the destination. Many predict that it is

**FIGURE 12-19** Roger Fidler was one of the Knight-Ridder pioneer group proposing an electronic newspaper with intelligent agents to customize it for individual readers.

only a matter of years before such systems will also drive the car there, guided by the sensors along the highway. In observing the speed limits and sensing other vehicles along the road, the automated car may be safer than many drivers.

Even the clothes dryer with a fuzzy logic chip to check the moisture content of clothes in order to stop the process before they are too dry can be viewed as a kind of "intelligent agent." The appliance contains canned software in preprogrammed chips—one example of a special-purpose computer built into a machine that exhibits limited intelligence for a specific set of jobs. Handwriting analysis software like Graffiti for a personal digital assistant like Newton also represents this trend. The pattern recognition involved in this process has always been a skill easier for people than computers. A cognitive function, pattern recognition is a kind of intelligence. Every year more complicated software solutions are being hardwired into specialized chips. We can expect many more intelligent assistants in the next computer generation, for a wide variety of specialized tasks.

## ARTIFICIAL LIFE

Not all researchers in artificial intelligence believe that the analytical approach of starting with central intelligence and working out to the senses represents the best approach to AI. People like Rodney Brooks at MIT examine simple organic creatures like insects, and posit much simpler systems at work there than a complex AI rule-based system on a large parallel or supercomputer system. A roach that runs when you turn on the light in the kitchen does not have great intelligence, but its adaptation to the situation and its action in running away are impressive behaviors. Scholars working in the area called **artificial life** study the simple adaptive and robust control systems of insects and reproduce them in robotic **insectoids** (Beer, Chiel, and Sterling).

For instance, Brooks uses a design philosophy called **subsumption architecture** to create a set of interconnected simple processors that can each carry out basic behaviors. So that it can move across the floor and avoid obstacles, a Brooks insectoid is equipped with detectors to sense objects and instructions to move around or over them. According to subsumption architecture, complex behavior is composed of a combination of simple actions; it does not need to presuppose an overarching intelligence concerned with how the obstacle got there. Robotic insectoids with names like Attila and Hannibal are very adept in moving across the floor by combining a lot of simple instructions to move their limbs separately.

**artificial life:** A field of AI research that studies the adaptive control systems of insects and reproduces them in robotic insectoids.

**insectoids:** The robotic insects designed by researchers who investigate insect control systems to create artificial life.

**subsumption architecture:** A design philosophy espoused by some artificial life researchers to create a set of interconnected simple processors that can each carry out basic behaviors, modeling complex behavior with a combination of simple actions.

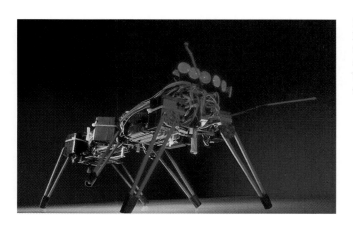

**FIGURE 12-20** The robotic insectoid called Genghis, created by Rodney Brooks of MIT, a proponent of minimalist artificial intelligence. Like real insects, the robot can maneuver around obstacles by moving its limbs in a walking motion with a set of interconnected processors, each of which is relatively simple in design.

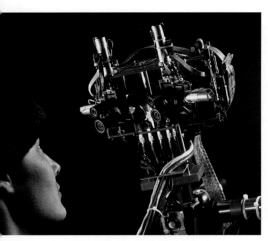

**FIGURE 12-21** Rodney Brooks and his research team are now applying their AI ideas to build their first humanoid robot, named Cog. Cog is supposed to learn from its experiences in moving around the physical world and modify its behavior accordingly.

Brooks suggests that these simple creatures of artificial life may be the models for robotic machines to navigate the unfamiliar terrain of other planets. Although the insectoid's simple processors exhibit considerable successful behavior, Brooks does not claim that the system "knows" anything. Perhaps it is enough for a robot to behave in ways that allow it to survive or do a small job and not worry about a grander controlling intelligence (Wallich). Brooks's latest project is a humanoid robot called Cog, which is intended to mimic the behavior of a two-year-old child, with sensory systems for touch, sight, and hearing. As with the insectoids, Cog's intelligence will be based on its sense experience from the real world around it, not some symbolic overall intelligence model. Brooks launched his five-year project on Cog at a party in 1992 for the birth of HAL, the robot in *2001* (see Chapter 11): "I realized there was no HAL on the horizon. That was very sad. It got me to thinking, what would it take to make a Hal?" (quoted in Stipp, 222). Brooks believes that much of higher human cognition has evolved from ancient sensory and motor systems so that he will build his intelligent robot from the bottom up. In Brooks's view of robot evolution, Cog will eventually learn from its experience and even do some interesting things not predicted by rule-based systems. No matter whether Cog beats Hal to 2001, this school of minimalist AI researchers poses serious questions about the basic theoretical foundations of other branches of AI, such as expert systems and natural language processing.

## ▶ People and Computers

Terms for the 1990s like *interactivity, Web PCs,* and *Windows NT* address new trends in hardware and software design. How will these and other computing ideas affect people in the next decade? Emerging developments in politics and economics suggest some of the answers.

### COMPUTERS AND NATIONAL POLICY

Chapter 3 contrasts the United States' and Japan's policies regarding governmental support for private business. But recent American administrations have been more willing to foster high-tech development as a national priority than formerly. The boundary between public and private business in high technology has been blurring, as has been true in Japan for years. The Bush administration supported the Grand Challenge problems in scientific computing, including the NREN extension of Internet; and the Clinton-Gore administration campaigned on public support for the growth of private enterprise in cutting-edge technologies. In 1993, Clinton and Gore pledged to "restore America's economic leadership" by helping industry in three ways: with research funds; with technology transfer of ideas to small business; and with governmental support of antipollution and energy-saving policies (quoted in Levinson, 42).

The Clinton initiatives seem much less ambitious than Japan's have been. Federal policy is shifting from military to civilian research, especially in computer networks and cleaner-running automobiles. Nevertheless, in these days of budget deficits, the amounts of money allocated to these technologies will be modest and probably will never reach Japanese proportions. The lesson of unpredictable technological innovation has struck home in America, too. Who would have believed a few years ago that both IBM, the world's computer leader, and its corporate rival, Apple Computer, would soon be in financial trouble? In 1990 it appeared that Japanese HDTV, based on analog signals, would sweep the

**SOCIETY**

## EVOLUTIONARY PERSPECTIVE

### The Case of the Japanese Fifth Generation

The Fifth Generation computer project in Japan offers a cautionary tale for American high-tech initiatives. In the early 1980s the Japanese government began massive financial support of industry for the development of practical "Knowledge Information Processing Systems"—computers based on artificial intelligence that were not just information-processing machines. This initiative to create intelligent machines, which would be pioneered throughout the world by Japanese industry, became known as the **Fifth Generation project,** its name denoting another generation in the evolution of computers (Feigenbaum and McCorduck). The first four **computer generations** were characterized by hardware innovations as follows:

1. the first commercial vacuum-tube machines, like UNIVAC I (1951)

2. transistorized computers, like the IBM 650 (late 1950s)

3. integrated circuit mainframes, like the IBM 360 (1960s)

4. personal computers based on the microprocessor, which became the standard in the 1970s and 1980s

With their world lead in robotics production, and the appearance of the first appliances incorporating fuzzy logic circuits, some of the Japanese AI research efforts began to pay off in practical systems in the early 1990s. Yet in 1992, the project was officially declared dead, without success in creating computers with such grand goals as learning to speak like humans. Much pure research was carried out, but the dream of Japanese dominance of the AI industry never materialized.

Why was the Fifth Generation canceled? The 10-year project could not keep up with the fast pace of change in computing. Even the Japanese Ministry of International Trade and Industry (MITI), which funded the project, could not predict which computing technologies would be significant in the future. During the decade of the project, the unexpected development of inexpensive general-purpose scientific workstations and massively parallel systems far beyond the power of Fifth Generation designs effectively killed the project's economic potential before it was completed. Training a large number of qualified Japanese computer scientists represents a longer-term benefit of the project, more than the creation of many significant products. At the end of the project in 1992, the Japanese willingly offered all their technology free to anyone in the world who wanted it (Pollack).

**Fifth Generation project:** A 10-year research project funded by the Japanese government to develop a new class of intelligent computers, discontinued in 1992 without achieving the results it had anticipated.

**computer generation:** A term for a series of computers that are based on the same hardware technology. For instance, personal computers belong to the fourth generation of computers, the age of microprocessors.

world. But when an American company called General Instrument, not supported by government funds, introduced a digital prototype, the analog model was doomed. According to Joseph Farrell, a Berkeley economist, "HDTV is a success story for the nonconsensus approach to technology policy" (quoted in Levinson, 43). The lessons for the future seem clear: national policy in high-tech industry does not break down easily into a dichotomy between free markets and government intervention (Levinson).

## ALVIN TOFFLER AND FUTURISM

That development and control of high technology is more complex than centralized industrial policy and governmental funding programs may suggest would not surprise Alvin Toffler. With *Future Shock* (1970) and *The Third Wave* (1980), Toffler became the best-known futurist in the United States today, if not in the world. In the years just before the personal computer explosion, *Future Shock* forecast the increasing rate of the spiral of change that has accompanied the Information Age. In fact, *The Third Wave* defined the characteristics of the Information Age, the third major wave in the history of technology. The First Wave, the Agricultural Age, lasted from the dawn of recorded time to the Industrial Revolution. This Second Wave began at the end of the eighteenth century, and lasted about 200 years.

**SOCIETY**

Given the increasing speed of change Toffler predicted that the Third Wave will last only into the beginning of the twenty-first century.

Toffler's book, called *Powershift* (1990), tries to define the character of emerging trends for the next century. His vision, abstracted in an essay in *Newsweek* in 1990, offers much more than a cybernetic picture of the future, with electronic houses and robotic automobiles. Toffler sees the changing nature of power, especially economic, as tied to information, which is collected from a myriad of sources, stored in computers, and instantly transmitted worldwide through communications technology. Credit and cash cards, paid for in advance, will become the floating electronic currency of the world, managed by computer and more fluid than the monetary regulation provided by central banks. Toffler speaks of money becoming "informationalized." All purchases are double payments: one pays for the good or service, and the second gives information about the purchaser. For instance, ordering from a catalog mail order house with a credit card requires the customer to pass on to the company much personal information, which ends up in a database that is useful for market research on the lifestyles of buyers. Toffler raises important questions about whether this "interest-free information loan" is an invasion of privacy, or in fact has any value until it is collected and processed. In effect, society lacks laws and economic rules to apply to new questions about the control of information.

Toffler speaks of the modern world economy as "super-symbolic"; those organizations that are able to harness it will be the leaders of the next generation. Able to amass and use information quickly, they will tend not to be big bureaucratic governments and corporations but small, fam-

**FIGURE 12-22** Alvin Toffler in *Powershift* has arresting insights and thought-provoking comments about the future. These two cartoons, based on the book, emphasize the centrality of information in today's world. In the first, a new system for making money that depends on instant communication and dissemination of information has "torn the belly out of some industrial giants." The second represents double payments by consumers: first with money and second with information about themselves that is worth money to the sellers.

ily-style units that work in niche markets. Big organizations (IBM, automakers, the federal government) will find it hard to adapt quickly, and will want to hold on to the status quo. With spreadsheets and on-line Internet databases, small firms will not require a large class of middle managers to handle their information needs. They will contract directly with large concerns to offer their services. For example, today's computer or automobile may have parts made in four countries and be assembled in a fifth. Within the organization of one of these **fam-firms,** groups of specialists will develop: from the information librarians who seek out new ideas on the Web, to the software team, to the marketers, to the security people who protect the intellectual properties being exploited by the firm.

Governments will find it as difficult as large corporations to hold a national consensus. Interest groups of every kind will have data banks on the concerns of members and politicians, and will be able to mobilize support for their agendas. Mass media will empower small splinter groups through exposure to the global Internet. International corporations will stretch over national boundaries and will be difficult to regulate on a national basis. Toffler says that high-tech democratic societies have become "de-massified," and warns of possible reactionary forces developing as backlashes to the spiral of uncertainty and change.

**fam-firm:** A term used by Alvin Toffler for a small contracting company of the future made up of information specialists and lacking a large class of middle managers to handle information needs.

## A CALL FOR FREEDOM

Amid these baffling tendencies toward decentralization, Toffler's solution is more freedom of expression. Keeping open the channels of information will become a top priority in industry and politics. Choking off the free flow of ideas will doom the chances of a company or society to advance. Sounding like Internet surfers and civil libertarians who are attacking the Communications Decency Act in court, Toffler identifies new alliances to help civilization remain in control of information:

> *The fight for free expression, once the province of intellectuals, thus becomes the concern of all who favor economic advance. Like adequate education, freedom of expression is a precondition for economic competitiveness. This is the basis for an unusual political coalition of the future—bringing together two groups often opposed since the Industrial Revolution: intellectuals, scientists, artists and civil libertarians on one hand, advanced managers and even shareholders and capitalists on the other. Such a coalition is the best guarantee of both intellectual and economic advance as companies and countries alike speed into the Powershift Era. (Toffler in* Newsweek, *92)*

Some computer professionals and world politicians seem to agree. In a wide-ranging roundtable discussion to celebrate the 15th anniversary of *Byte* magazine in 1990, soon after the breakup of communism, one of the dominant themes was the freedom of the computer age. Jerry Pournelle, a leading *Byte* columnist, commented that the Chinese did not know how to shut down the fax system that reported the Tiananmen massacre and quoted Arthur Koestler in 1946: "The necessary and sufficient condition for the end of totalitarianism is the free exchange of ideas. Well, you can't operate without it." His colleague, Mike Malloy, agreed: "You can't put the genie back in the bottle" (both quoted in "Byte's 15th Anniversary Summit," 366).

In a speech after the Israeli-PLO accord in February 1994, Israeli Foreign Minister Shimon Peres struck a similar Tofflerian theme with a warning to dictators in the Arab world: "What brought down the Soviet Union was not a political party or a military coup but the winds of information. And that is happening everywhere" (quoted in Lewis). The freedom that unfettered information unleashes for its users is seen as very powerful and liberating. Certainly computers and communications collect and spread information around the world today in quantities unknown in any previous age.

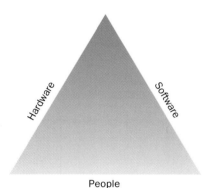

## ▶ The Computer Triangle: A Closing Note

In many cases the computer has already been liberating for individuals. Handicapped persons are able to control their lives and manage their environments with computerized devices. Students in poor inner-city schools are learning to read with individualized multimedia learning packages and interactive tutorial help from their teachers, like their suburban counterparts. Lonely senior citizens are accessing computer news groups and e-mail to reach out from their homes to others around the country. Scientists are using computers to create "designer drugs" and prosthetic devices, to make life healthier and safer for millions. Consultants in the emerging democracies of Eastern Europe are using computer spreadsheets and databases to teach democratic ways in elections and business, and tapping the Internet to get advice from the West. It is widely believed that the computer is a facilitator of democratic growth in these countries.

On the other hand, in the nineteenth century, the historian Lord Acton made the famous remark that "All power tends to corrupt, and absolute power corrupts absolutely." The computer is certainly the most empowering technology that society has today, not just in the military sense of smart weapons. Governments and businesses collect information on everyone, some of it considered private. The positive or negative use of this information depends on the safeguards of the law and the actions of those who control access to it. Surely awareness of the possibilities for abuse of computer power, and a commitment to use this tool for positive human good, should be one of the main goals of computer literacy today.

Twenty years ago, Stanley Rothman and Charles Mosmann, in an early computer literacy text (1976), pointed out that the freedom to act as an individual has been available to only a small minority of people throughout history. In fact, it is very expensive—dependent on education, information, and the power to move freely in the world. They reasoned that a world of individual freedom seemed feasible only in a human society improved by the power of technology that is utilized for the common good. Given the increasing presence of computers in daily life, the power of computing viewed in this perspective need not become the corrupting power that Lord Acton's axiom foretells. Whatever the hardware and software innovations of the coming years turn out to be, we can reasonably predict that they will continue to broaden the scope of computer application for everyone. As individuals and as a society, people need to be committed to seeing that the computer remains a positive, liberating force for growth and change in the future that lies before us. That constitutes the enduring challenge of the Computer Triangle.

 Key Terms

artificial life (p. 297)

bandwidth (p. 282)

beta software (p. 294)

cache (p. 292)

compatibility (p. 281)

compression (p. 282)

computer generation (p. 299)

edutainment (p. 284)

emulation (p. 288)

fam-firm (p. 301)

Fifth Generation project (p. 299)

high-definition television (HDTV) (p. 281)

"information appliance" (p. 289)

insectoid (p. 297)

intelligent agent (p. 296)

LCD (liquid crystal display) (p. 290)

MPEG (p. 283)

multicasting (p. 283)

network computer (NC or Web PC) (p. 289)

palmtop (hand-held) (p. 289)

paradigm shift (p. 289)

personal digital assistant (PDA) (p. 289)

pipelining (p. 291)

RISC (reduced instruction set computing) chip (p. 291)

subsumption architecture (p. 297)

superscalar processing (p. 292)

video telephony (p. 286)

wireless infrared remote communications (p. 289)


▶ Self-Test

## MULTIPLE-CHOICE

1. The Human Genome Project, one of the most visible of the Federal Grand Challenge Problems, combines ideas from all of the following computer research areas except
   a. computational science
   b. artificial life
   c. parallel processing
   d. neural networks

2. Which of the following is not already a digital medium for the storage and transmission of information?
   a. network television
   b. CDs for music
   c. CD-ROM video games
   d. fiber optic telephone lines

3. Which of the following is an advantage of merging all electronic media into a common digital signal?
   a. compatibility among kinds of information
   b. the ability to share resources stored in a similar technology
   c. possible interactivity among different types of information
   d. all of the above

4. All of the following technical hurdles to broadcasting over the Internet are under active research except
   a. instabilities of Internet information packets
   b. bandwidth for file transmission
   c. rechargable batteries
   d. compression schemes for multimedia

5. The new generation of network computers represents the convergence of which of the following?
   a. consumer electronics
   b. communications
   c. computers
   d. all of the above

6. Which of the following operating systems can be expected to compete favorably with Windows NT in the next generation of large computer systems?
   a. Intel P6
   b. Unix
   c. MS-DOS
   d. hardtware products of the IBM/Apple alliance

7. Which of the following is an instance of an intelligent agent built into a computer?
   a. fuzzy logic in appliances
   b. handwriting analysis software
   c. user profiling for document retrieval
   d. all of the above

8. Which of the following statements does not characterize the Fifth Generation computer project?
   a. The Japanese are world leaders in robotics.
   b. Fifth Generation computers were massively parallel microprocessors.
   c. Some of the fruits of the project led to fuzzy logic in appliances.
   d. Project leaders could not predict computing changes during the 1980s.

## TRUE/FALSE

9. **T  F**  Just as the Manhattan Project led to problems of radioactive fallout and the nuclear arms race, the Human Genome Project is already causing serious political problems.

10. **T  F**  Compared to what is currently offered by information utilities, the possible services to be offered in the digital, interactive future can be greatly expanded.

11. **T  F**  It is expected that the next few years will see a turf war between phone and cable companies about who will control access to the technology of digital information transmission.

12. **T  F**  Perhaps the most innovative feature of the Apple Newton is that it understands voice-activated input by means of its built-in audio recognition software.

13. **T  F**  The IBM/Apple alliance produced a computer that merged the processing power of an IBM machine with the popular GUI of the Macintosh.

14. **T  F**  The predominance of Microsoft in the computer world of the early 1990s can be attributed to its lead in the production of computer hardware based on Intel chips.

15. **T  F**  Researchers specializing in artificial life study the simple adaptive control systems of insects and reproduce them in robotic insects.

16. **T  F**  Alvin Toffler sees information as the key to the changing nature of economic power in today's world.

### FILL-IN

17. _____, now expected to be available to consumers before the year 2000, is expected to deliver its TV signal in a digital format.

18. _____ is a recently coined term to describe the blending of multimedia educational materials with the interactive, highly visual delivery strategies of video games.

19. New computer chips are often expected to provide _____ of older processors—that is, applications created for an older chip will still work on the new one, which is programmed to act like the old one.

20. ____ microprocessors maximize their power with a reduced number of machine instructions, and are currently used to deliver high performance in scientific workstations and even NCs.

21. More than Windows 3.1 or Windows 95, _____ is a new, full operating system developed by Microsoft to network together all kinds of computers and office equipment, like telephones, copiers, and fax machines.

22. _____ in software are under development to sift through the enormous quantities of digital information that will be available in the future and pick out information of interest or importance for individuals.

23. According to the principles of _____ in AI, complex behavior is composed of a combination of simple actions that can be re-created with a set of interconnected simple processors to carry out basic behaviors.

24. Small, flexible companies made up of groups of specialists, including information librarians, software designers, and people with marketing skill, are called _____.

## ▶ Experiential Exercises

1. Investigate the phenomenon of electronic books available these days on CD-ROM. What is to be gained by having a Dickens novel in this form? Would you rather read the book on the computer or in bound form?

2. Research the characteristics that distinguish broadcasting on the Internet. How well does it work? What new software possibilities have been created to take advantage of this new technology?

3. Monitor the "warfare" forecast in the computer magazines between Netscape Navigator and Microsoft Internet Explorer. Which side seems to be winning out? Can both worlds coexist side by side and prosper from each other's innovations?

4. Research AI arguments for and against artificial life, to see how some of its assumptions call into question basic tenets of traditional artificial intelligence. Scientists are moving artificial life up from insectoids to more useful creatures. What are some of the proposed uses for these creatures?

5. Study the several technological initiatives of the Clinton-Gore administration, such as NREN and the plan to build a super-efficient car with defense materials—to have the government work with the private sector in sponsoring technological progress. What seem to be the main advantages and objections to the plan? Do the arguments break down along conservative-liberal lines, or do they tend to blur those distinctions? Where is computing in these discussions?

6. In *Powershift,* Alvin Toffler suggests that small, lean companies that can adapt quickly will be better able to prosper in the future than large bureaucracies, like governments and big corporations. Research his arguments, and discuss what he might think of government support for corporate development in high-tech industries. Note especially Toffler's point about the centrality of information for growth before you dismiss the idea that he would be against government support for the Internet.

## ► Critical Thinking Exercises

1. Given the increasing rate of integration of the computer industry, cable TV, and telephone and communications companies, the scope of the digital revolution is beginning to take shape. Describe a trend that seems to be gaining acceptance with the public and leading to economic success for some industry or company. Is the success due more to technological innovation or to a strategic alliance of companies with convergent interests?

2. Discuss the implications of Arno Penzias's metaphorical remark (quoted in the text) that "the country needs an information supermarket, not an information superhighway."

3. How does the technology of PDAs, like Apple's Newton, make it more than a notepad, like the Sharp Wizard? Is it worth the cost? Will a hand-held controller of digital television containing an "intelligent agent" be some sort of PDA?

4. Defend or refute the contention that the Information Age, based on computers, will foster freedom rather than lead to accumulation of power by a few large organizations.

**ANSWERS TO SELF-TEST**

*Multiple-Choice*: 1. b;   2. a;   3. d;   4. c;   5. d;   6. b;   7. d;
8. b
*True/False*: 9. F;   10. T;   11. T;   12. F;   13. F;   14. F;   15. T;
16. T
*Fill-in*: 17. high-definition television;   18. edutainment;   19. emulation;   20. RISC;   21. Windows NT;   22. intelligent agents;   23. subsumption architecture;   24. fam-firms

# Glossary

**additive primary colors:** The three colors, red, green, and blue, of which color computer graphics and color television are composed. Color monitors are equipped with an RGB (red-green-blue) video board to produce their colorful images.

**algorithm:** A predetermined series of instructions for carrying out a task in a finite number of steps.

**alphabetical sorting:** Sorting records in a database in alphabetical order.

**alphanumeric:** Data represented in both alphabetical and numeric form. For instance, in the address 367 Main Street, all characters are alphanumeric, whether numbers or letters.

**analog signal:** A signal often transmitted over telephone lines in the form of electronic waves.

**analog/digital input:** Hardware that senses a physical measurement, like the directional movement of a mouse, and converts it to digital data for input to the computer.

**AND (intersection):** A fundamental logical operator that retains only the elements that two sets of data have in common.

**applications software:** A program for a personal computer designed to carry out a common user need, such as word processing or a spreadsheet program.

**arithmetic function:** One of the arithmetic operations—addition, subtraction, multiplication, or division—included in most programming languages.

**arithmetic/logic unit:** The processor unit in the CPU that performs arithmetic and comparison operations.

**ARPANET:** The grandfather of the Internet, founded in the 1960s by the Advanced Research Projects Agency of the U.S. Defense Department to network selected universities and defense research contractors.

**artificial intelligence (AI):** The branch of computer science concerned with understanding the nature of human intelligence, with the goal of simulating aspects of it with a computer.

**artificial life:** A field of AI research that studies the adaptive control systems of insects and reproduces them in robotic insectoids.

**ascending order:** Arrangement of data from lowest to highest in sequence.

**ASCII (American Standard Code for Information Interchange):** The most common character code used for microcomputers and data communications. Standard ASCII consists of seven bits per character; Extended ASCII of eight bits.

**assembler:** A program that translates assembly language code to binary machine language before it is run by a computer.

**assembly language:** A computer language of symbolic instructions and addresses that convert into binary machine language codes on a one-to-one basis.

**attribute:** The label, value, formula, or function stored in a cell. Displaying a spreadsheet in attribute format is useful for double-checking relationships among cells.

**automated machine translation:** A research field in linguistics and computer science that translates one human language into another with computers.

**automated teller machine (ATM):** An interactive input/output device for banking where customers gain access to the machine by means of a PIN (personal identification number). Normally they can then make deposits, withdraw money, and get other information about their accounts.

**automatic formatting of tabular data:** A feature of full-featured word processors that lines up monetary figures under the decimal point, useful for producing tables of figures.

**automatic hyphenation:** A feature of some word processors that can be set to let the program automatically divide words at the end of a line according to the rules of hyphenation of the language or suggest a division and wait for user confirmation.

**automatic numbering of pages:** A standard word processing feature of numbering pages at the top or bottom as the text is being keyed.

**automatic renumbering of footnotes:** A convenient word processing feature that renumbers when a revision has been made and footnotes have been added or deleted.

**automatic speech recognition (ASR):** A lively research area in speech processing to recognize a person's voice and respond to voice commands or type out what has been said.

**backbone:** A term applied to a high-speed communications channel that links several LANs or computer installations in an institution like a college.

**bandwidth:** The capacity of a phone line or other communications channel for distributing data— voice, graphics, text, video—measured in bits per second.

**BASIC:** A high-level programming language originally designed at Dartmouth for teaching students to program and later regularly distributed with early microcomputers.

**baud rate:** A measure of the speed at which data are transmitted over communications lines by a modem, expressed as bits per second.

**beta software:** A version of a software product released to the public for use and testing with no guarantee from the originators that the program is free of bugs.

**binary coding:** A system for representing information in a computer with two states of electromagnetic phenomena, which can be denoted by the binary digits 1 and 0.

**binary integer:** A whole number, either positive or negative, composed of binary digits 0 and 1 representing powers of 2.

**bit:** An abbreviation for *binary digit*, which can be either 0 or 1.

**bit map:** A record of every pixel on a computer screen, contained in the frame buffer of a raster graphics display system. A graphic image kept in a bitmap format of pixels can be displayed on a screen or printed by modern printers.

**bit-mapped:** A term used to describe images composed of patterns of dots and displayed on graphics computer screens.

**bits per second (bps):** The measure expressing the transmission speed of a modem; usually, but not always, synonymous with its baud rate.

**boilerplate:** A block of standard text, such as formulaic parts of a legal document like a will, that are saved and inserted in many documents with a word processor.

**bomb:** A crash of a computer system caused by a virus, which may cause a hard disk or diskette to be erased or permanently damaged.

**Boolean operation:** One of the three logical operations AND, OR, and NOT, first used by George Boole, fundamental to doing searching in databases.

**Braille printer:** A printer that produces Braille output for blind people.

**bridge (gateway):** A hardware interface for interconnecting similar computer networks.

**browser software:** A computer program like Netscape Navigator which allows users to log onto remote sites on the Internet and retrieve information stored as World Wide Web documents.

**brute force:** Solving a problem like a chess move by using the computer's ability to examine a large number of possible moves quickly in order to assess

each for its potential for success or failure.

**buffer memory:** A temporary storage area where the computer stores a set of character-plotting commands in vector graphics before they are transmitted to the screen.

**bug:** A term for a program error, usually in software, that causes it to crash or malfunction.

**bulletin board:** A dial-up computer network site typically offering news and programs that may be downloaded to one's computer.

**byte:** A unit of memory in the computer consisting of eight consecutive bits, often used to store one character of data or information.

**C:** A high-level programming language popular with technical programmers because of its many features, including some assembly language functions.

**cache:** Another design strategy to improve processor performance by placing a small memory directly on a chip so that the processor has rapid access to frequently used instructions, which are stored there.

**Caller ID:** A telephone service that allows a user with a phone equipped with a digital screen to see the number, and sometimes the name, of a caller. In a commercial setting this service often triggers a computer database to display other information about the caller.

**campus backbone:** A set of data transmission protocols that translates data from a LAN to a standard format and sends them to another LAN.

**cassette tape:** An older form of serial memory, common in early personal

computers. Inexpensive and portable, it holds a large amount of data for its size.

**cathode ray tube (CRT) or visual display terminal (VDT):** The most common type of computer screen or monitor.

**CD-ROM:** A compact disk on which large volumes of information are stored digitally and accessed by laser beam.

**CD-ROM drive:** Hardware that can access digital data stored on a compact disk by reading it with a laser beam.

**cell:** The intersection of a row and column in a spreadsheet.

**centering of text:** A cumbersome practice in typewriting that is standard with word processing.

**central processing unit (CPU):** The core of a microcomputer system. It contains both the arithmetic/logic unit and the control unit.

**chin switch:** A hardware device that allows people who cannot move a mouse with their hands to move the cursor on a computer screen by moving their chins.

**client/server:** A computer environment in which applications on a file server are sent out to client machines as needed. The client machine can access and display information sent out from the server.

**closed format:** A term applied to an electronic conference available only to those invited to participate.

**coaxial cable:** A common metallic cable used for hardwired communications channels because it can carry large amounts of data.

**COBOL:** A older but still very powerful and popular high-level programming

language designed for business data processing.

**cognitive scientist:** A scientist, perhaps trained in computer science, psychology, linguistics, neuroscience, or philosophy, interested in the study of brain/computer analogues.

**cold type:** Setting type and producing pages on computer screens. The resulting computer typesetting files can be printed by laser and xerographic processes. Older Linotype methods set what was called "hot type."

**combinatorial explosion:** The greatly increasing number of possible alternative moves that must be examined in looking forward several moves in games like chess or Go to choose the best move.

**communications software:** A program that enables a computer to be connected to other computers or that allows a document to be set up in fax format.

**compact disk (CD):** A common mass storage medium based on the same technology as audio CDs, suitable for storing large amounts of fixed data like encyclopedias or video games.

**compatibility:** The ability to connect different computer systems or media so that they can work together.

**compiler:** Software that translates a program written in a high-level language into lower-level language instructions. As an additional benefit, it searches along the way for grammar errors in the program.

**compression:** A software process of storing a digital file, such as a sound or a video, in a compressed form to save storage space or speed up its transmission time over a network.

**computational science:** A partnership between computer science and the laboratory sciences. It combines the computer's ability to do massive amounts of mathematical calculations quickly and to represent the results as graphic images to solve problems in the physical and biological sciences.

**computer:** An electrical machine system capable of accepting data in symbolic form and processing it. The results are normally produced as output in some form.

**computer animation:** The creation and display of computer graphic images in rapid sequence to produce the effect of animation, exemplified in arcade video games.

**computer architecture:** A term to describe the design and layout of the electronic components of a computer system.

**computer concordance:** The use of computers to make indexes of words within their context for classic literary texts, the first literary application of computers, begun in the 1950s.

**computer conferencing:** Multiple users commenting on an issue of common interest via electronic mail. Individual members of can monitor what others are adding to the conference and contribute over a set period of time.

**Computer Decency Act (1995):** A federal law that makes it a crime to distribute sexually explicit materials over a computer network that might be seen by minors.

**Computer Fraud and Abuse Act (1986):** A U.S. federal law that makes accessing a federal computer without authorization and causing damage greater than $1000 a felony; aimed at hacker invasions of public computers.

**computer generation:** A term for a series of computers that are based on the same hardware technology. For instance, personal computers belong to the fourth generation of computers, the age of microprocessors.

**computer graphics:** The methods and techniques for creating and displaying pictures or images on computer screens or other output devices like printers or plotters.

**computer matching:** The controversial practice of merging records collected by different government databases to find suspected criminals, such as people who have reneged on alimony.

**computer monitoring:** Employing a computer system to monitor the vital signs of critically ill patients automatically and to display the results on a computer screen at the nurses' station.

**computer phobia:** A feeling of unease and helplessness around computers sometimes felt by people unfamiliar with them. Taking a computer literacy course should help to relieve this condition.

**computer screen:** A device, also called a monitor, similar to a television screen for displaying the output of a computer.

**computer video game:** Video games designed for use on personal computers, combining graphics and sound effects.

**computer virus:** Software that invades operating systems or application programs through contact with corrupted files. It may seriously damage computer files if not eradicated.

**computer-aided engineering (CAE):** The use of an integrated series of computer processes to design, test, and manufacture products, usually starting with computer-aided design (CAD).

**computer-aided manufacturing (CAM):** The use of a computer system to automate parts of a manufacturing process, such as producing machine parts directly on robotic lathes that receive their instructions from a CAD system. The abbreviation CAD/CAM applies to such integrated computer processes.

**computer-assisted design (CAD):** Using computer graphics software to aid the process of design, especially in architecture or engineering.

**computer-assisted instruction (CAI):** The use of computers in some form for instruction, such as drill-and-practice in foreign languages.

**computerized axial tomography (CAT or CT scanner):** Using a CAT or CT scanner to combine x-rays with computer graphic imagery techniques to offer fine quality images for medical diagnosis of conditions like brain tumor.

**consistency check:** A software protection scheme added to a database management system to monitor data integrity. For instance, one should not be able to reserve flights for nonexistent dates like February 30.

**control function:** One of the five elements of any computer system, handled in hardware by the CPU.

**control program (operating system):** An internal computer program designed to connect the user to the machine and monitor all activity within the machine, also called an operating system.

**copy protection:** A software strategy employed by program developers to make it difficult to copy software illegally.

**core memory:** An older kind of random-access memory (RAM) device that held its magnetic charge even when the power was off. RAM memory chips replaced core memory because core was more expensive to produce, larger in size, and slower to access.

**Crime Control Act of 1973:** U.S. federal law that allows citizens access to criminal records about them that may be in error in order to correct them.

**cursor:** A small blinking arrow, vertical line, or underline on a computer screen to indicate where the next input will be displayed.

**cybernetics:** The study of how control mechanisms work, both in the nervous system of animals and in automation for machines.

**CYC:** A well-known project to develop computer understanding of commonsense knowledge of the real world, involving encoding millions of facts and relations between them, so that the machine can draw inferences automatically.

**data:** A general term for numbers, letters, and other symbols processed by a computer to produce information.

**data bus:** An electrical path to transfer data and instructions back and forth between internal memory devices and the processor.

**data communications:** Transferring data or information between computer-related devices such as electronic mail.

**data definition:** The process of deciding on the number and characteristics of all the data fields in each record in the early stages of developing a database.

**data entry:** The process of encoding data into fields to create database records.

**data glove:** A glove filled with sensors to detect body movement and effect change in the simulated world of VR.

**data integrity:** The need to insure that information contained in a database is accurate and timely—that is, free of corruption by input or programming errors.

**data processing:** A general term that stands for all the logical, arithmetic, and input/output operations that can be performed on data by a computer.

**data protection (data security):** A term referring to strategies for protecting databases against illegal access or modification, such as needing a password to access a database.

**database:** A collection of related files stored electronically that can be edited, joined, sorted, and searched.

**database management system (DBMS):** Software used to create, maintain, retrieve, and produce reports about information kept in databases.

**debugging:** The process of correcting errors in a computer program, often helped by error diagnostics from the compiler.

**decision box (branch):** One of the fundamental building blocks of flowcharting, offering a choice between alternative directions to continue, analogous to selection in structured programming.

**dedicated word processor:** A specialized computer typewriter designed only for word processing.

**DENDRAL:** An early successful expert system for classifying chemical compounds based on their spectrographic characteristics and the rules that govern chemical bonding.

**descending sort:** Arrangement of sorted data from highest to lowest in sequence.

**desktop:** The background of a computer screen with a GUI on which icons and windows appear.

**desktop publishing:** Using software to do page design and computer typesetting with laser printers for publications such as newsletters and magazines.

**digital (numeric) data:** A term that applies to forms of data that can be expressed in numeric terms and thus can be readily processed by digital computers.

**digital signature:** A term for a secure transaction code used to encode sensitive personal information sent over a network so that the decoder will know that it is unique to the sender.

**digital television:** The transmission of television signals in a digital form. Current television is sent out as analog signals, but future television is probably going to be digitally distributed, much like electronic mail and other forms of data communication today.

**digitized:** A term for information that has been converted into binary digits for computer processing.

**digitized video:** A process in which a hardware circuit board on a computer accepts input from a TV or VCR and converts the images to digital format at a rate of between 15 and 30 frames a second, capturing full-motion video for the computer screen.

**digitizer board:** A circuit board for a computer that accepts video input and digitizes it so that it may be seen on the computer screen.

**digitizing scanner:** A hardware device that converts color or black-and-white images on paper to pixel images so that they may be processed by a computer.

**disk drive:** The most common form of secondary storage hardware device. A drive can read programs and data stored on diskettes or hard disks and transfer them to internal memory.

**diskette:** The most common form of secondary storage—small, inexpensive, and portable—which records data as magnetized bits that are read by a disk drive.

**distance learning:** The delivery of educational course materials offsite, formerly through videotape and closed-circuit television, now often carried out with shared content resources on the Internet.

**dithering:** A process used in some color printers and graphics software to adjust the number of dots of different colors within a matrix of eight pixels to produce many shades.

**DOS:** An abbreviation for Disk Operating System, the popular operating system developed by Microsoft and found on IBM-compatible computers.

**dot-matrix printer:** An impact printer that prints characters on paper as a series of dots based on grid pattern designs.

**downloading:** Transferring files from a host computer on a network to remote machines, typically microcomputers.

**downsizing:** A term for the shrinking size of modern corporations and the subsequent loss of jobs, including many middle managers.

**draw program:** A graphics program that provides commands to create regular shapes—like rectangles—as objects that can be resized or moved around without affecting other objects.

**drill-and-practice educational software:** Instructional computer programs that drill students on materials for mastery, such as foreign language grammar exercises.

**dynamic:** A term applied to spreadsheets to describe their changing whenever new values are introduced, since all relations embodied in the spreadsheet must be reassessed relative to the new data.

**EBCDIC (Extended Binary Coded Decimal Interchange Code):** A standard character code using 8 bits per character devised for IBM mainframes in the 1960s but less frequently used today than ASCII.

**edutainment:** A term to describe the use of interactive, visual, or multimedia strategies of video games to present educational materials on a computer.

**electronic cut and paste (block move):** A standard word processing feature that allows selecting a letter, word, or section of text; deleting it from its current location; and moving it somewhere else in the current or another document.

**electronic mail:** Application that enables users to electronically send and receive messages to colleagues using data communications technology with computers.

**electronic prosthetics:** Computerized devices developed to replace or bypass missing or inoperative body parts.

**electrostatic plotter:** A plotter that uses electricity to transfer bit-mapped images to paper by printing raster pixels line by line, much as they are produced on a bit-mapped printer.

**ELIZA:** An early experimental computer program in AI that carried on a dialogue with a person. The computer appeared to understand what was being said but in fact was just filling blanks in formulaic conversation.

**emulation:** The imitation of one computer system by another, so that software created for the computer being imitated will run on the other without changing it.

**encryption software:** A category of computer programs to encode a document so that it cannot be read if it is intercepted by unauthorized users in a network transaction.

**ergonomics:** The study of how to adapt machines and working conditions to people to minimize health risks.

**even parity:** Indicates that the total number of 1s in the unit of transmitted information must be even.

**executive (monitor) program:** Other terms for an operating system.

**expert system:** A category of computer software in artificial intelligence designed to model the behavior of human experts in some field and frequently coded in a logic programming language.

**Fair Credit Reporting Act of 1970:** U.S. federal law allowing people to inspect their credit records so that they may challenge erroneous information included in the computer files.

**fam-firm:** A term used by Alvin Toffler for a small contracting company of the future made up of information specialists and lacking a large class of middle managers to handle information needs.

**family tree:** A model for organizing a database in a hierarchical arrangement, with parent and children nodes.

**fax machine:** A machine that scans documents and transmits them to either computers or other fax machines over a phone line.

**Federal Privacy Act of 1974:** U.S. law enacted after Watergate invasions of privacy that limits the kinds of information the federal government can gather on private citizens to that which is "relevant and necessary."

**fiber optic cable:** A modern communications channel using light impulses traveling through clear glass fibers to transmit data safely at very high speeds.

**fiber optics:** Transmitting computer information or telephone signals in a digital form in cables made of glass fibers.

**field:** A basic unit of information contained in a record, such as a name or street address in a mailing list created as a database.

**Fifth Generation project:** A 10-year research project funded by the Japanese government to develop a new class of intelligent computers, discontinued in 1992 without achieving the results it had anticipated.

**file:** A collection of records in a database related to each other.

**file management:** Software for storing simple files, such as mailing lists for a small company, in which one file is accessed at a time.

**file server:** A term applied to both a host computer and its special software that makes programs and data available to individual workstations on a network.

**final formatting:** The final setup of the spreadsheet for printing or other form of presentation, including such characteristics as rounding numbers and adding currency signs.

**flat file:** A simple form of database consisting of one table of rows (records) and columns (fields) of data.

**flatbed plotter:** An output device that works on the vector principle. It accepts instructions from a computer about where to draw a line, how long it is to be, and where to stop or turn in another direction and moves its drawing pen accordingly.

**flatbed scanner:** An input device to digitize photographs and drawings as a set of dots, called pixels, so that they can be processed by computers.

**floppy disk drive:** A hardware device that can read data inserted into it from diskettes or write information out onto diskettes. Early diskettes were flexible plastic and called "floppy." Most diskettes today are no longer floppy, but the term stuck for the disk drive that reads them, as opposed to a hard disk drive.

**flowchart (flow diagram):** A graphic representation of an algorithm, often used in the design phase of programming to work out the logical flow of a program.

**formula:** A numerical or logical relation or function added to a cell that expresses a relationship between other cell values and changes its value if they do.

**FORTRAN:** The oldest high-level programming language, designed in the 1950s primarily for mathematical and scientific applications.

**four-color process:** The printing process used in color printing with laser printers, as well as in color book and magazine production. It is sometimes denoted by the initials CMYK (cyan, magenta, yellow, black), standing for the three subtractive colors, plus black, that are blended to create colored materials in print.

**fractal geometry:** A field of mathematics pioneered by Benoit Mandelbrot that involves the study of a set of infinitely recursive mathematical functions which seem to mirror natural phenomena like leaf and cloud formation.

**frame buffer:** In raster graphics, a special area of RAM that holds the pixel contents of a computer screen.

**Freedom of Information Act of 1970:** U.S. law that guarantees citizens the right to see information collected about them by federal agencies like the IRS.

**freeware:** Software often made available free of charge on electronic bulletin boards and through user groups.

**front-end system:** "User friendly" software developed to stand between the user and a complicated operating system. Examples include Microsoft Windows for DOS and X Windows for Unix.

**FTP (file transfer protocol):** A common Internet standard which supports transfer of files over the network.

**full-motion video:** A term applied to video movies that can be edited and shown on a computer after they are digitized.

**function:** A predefined relation built into the spreadsheet program that can be used as a formula for such purposes as averaging numbers or finding the maximum value in a group of cells.

**function keys:** Shortcut keys on the keyboard that are set up to send commands to the operating system, especially in MS-DOS systems.

**fuzzy logic:** A field of artificial intelligence in which computers analyze logical relationships that are more or less true, as contrasted to ordinary logic, where relations are more crisp.

**general-purpose computer:** A computer suitable for being programmed for a wide variety of tasks or applications.

**gigabyte (GB):** A measure of main memory or auxiliary storage size, comprising one billion storage positions.

**gigaflop (GFLOP):** A billion floating point (mathematical) instructions per second, a measure of the speed and power of current supercomputers, which could carry out this many operations in one second.

**Gopher:** A popular text-based worldwide document search and retrieval protocol developed for the Internet.

**grammatical analysis:** An area of linguistic application of computers in which the machine is programmed to parse sentences, an area of research that needs improvement before it will be widely used in practical applications.

**graphical user interface (GUI):** A computer interface, commonly accessed with a pointing device like a mouse, that uses pictures, graphic symbols, windows, and menus to represent commands, choices, and actions.

**graphical workstation:** A computer designed specifically to carry out complicated graphics speedily and efficiently.

**graphics package:** Software for drawing, charting, and presenting graphics and illustrations.

**graphics primitives:** A set of graphic drawing elements like point markers, various types of lines, arcs and curves, circles, and closed polygons, included in software for CAD.

**graphics processor:** Part of a raster graphics display system that prepares pixel information for the frame buffer.

**gray scale:** A term applied to the gradations of shadings from white to black that result from attaching an RGB video board to a monochrome screen.

**gripper:** A robotic arm capable of moving in three-dimensional space and picking up another object.

**hacker:** A computer user addicted to long-distance computing with data communications software, sometimes illegally tapping into government or industry computer systems.

**hard copy:** Output printed on paper.

**hard disk drive:** A storage device that can store hundreds of millions of characters or more.

**hardware:** Any computer machinery that performs information-processing functions.

**head-mounted display (HMD):** A term for a set of 3-D goggles equipped with CRTs inside for use in virtual reality games or other applications.

**head pointer:** A hardware device for handicapped people who cannot use a mouse with their hands to select an object on a computer screen by head movement.

**heuristics:** Exploratory methods for problem solving that can be applied in particular situations for automated understanding, often consisting of rules of thumb or other ad hoc strategies.

**hierarchical model:** A method for storing data in a database that looks like a family tree with one root and a number of branches or subdivisions.

**high-definition television (HDTV):** The next generation of television with much higher picture quality, probably distributed digitally and capable of being integrated with computers to offer many services and information resources to the home.

**high-level language:** A programming language that is more like English than it is like assembly language and thus easier to use in writing programs. Compiler and interpreter languages are all high-level languages.

**home page:** A term used for the opening screen of a Web application, which typically will contain text and graphics. It is accessed through its own address over the Internet.

**HTML (Hypertext Markup Language):** The standard formatting language for creating World Wide Web pages with text, graphics, and other media.

**human-computer (man-machine) interface:** Term coined to refer to the points of connection and interaction between people and computer systems. Problems caused by human input of bad data to computers represent a breakdown at the interface point between people and the system.

**hypertext:** A computer application that integrates at least one other medium with text, such as sound or graphics.

**IBM-compatible:** A computer based on Intel microprocessors that uses the MS-DOS operating system. The first popular Intel/DOS machine was the IBM Personal Computer (Intel 8088 processor).

**icon:** A picture on a computer screen with a graphical user interface that represents a physical object, such as a file folder, a program, or a trash can.

**if/then/else condition:** A branching condition in both pseudocode and structured programming.

**image analysis:** A research field in computer science concerned with developing technologies for automatic understanding of what a computer is seeing, such as identifying a target or an incoming enemy missile with a smart weapon.

**impact printer:** A printer in which a keystroke actually hits the paper, like a typewriter, to produce hard copy.

**indexing:** A text processing application to index a text, which works best when the user is actively involved in the process.

**inference engine:** In an expert system, the use of reasoning, based on using the knowledge encoded into the system, to solve problems.

**"information appliance":** Current jargon for a wide range of computer devices expected in the near future that will allow users to access information on the Internet with easy-to-use interfaces.

**information retrieval:** A field of specialization in computer science that looks at systematic ways of storing and retrieving data, including consideration of database design and implementation.

**Information Superhighway:** A common term for the growth of infrastructure involving the Internet and the spread of high-speed data network services throughout the United States.

**information utility:** A term applied to a commercial

network information service like CompuServe or Prodigy that sells access to its wide variety of files and public forums.

**ink-jet printer:** An inexpensive nonimpact printer in which tiny dot patterns are sprayed onto paper to form characters.

**input:** The process of transferring data into a computer system for storage and processing.

**insectoids:** The robotic insects designed by researchers who investigate insect control systems to create artificial life.

**instruction decoder:** A part of the control unit of the CPU which receives machine language instructions, interprets them, and carries them out.

**integer:** Any positive or negative whole number, including zero.

**integrated package:** Multifunctional software that combines several applications under one consistent user interface. Different application programs in the package can share data with each other.

**intelligent agent:** Experimental AI software designed to sift through masses of information available in the future world of cyberspace to suggest topics of interest or importance for an individual.

**interactive computer graphics:** A term applied to software and hardware systems that allow complicated graphics repositioning to be carried out in real time, such as in fine CAD systems.

**interactive multimedia:** A multimedia production produced for access on a computer so that a user can

move around its resources in any order.

**internal clock speed:** Measured in megahertz, the speed of the CPU clock determines how quickly binary instructions are retrieved from memory and processed.

**Internet:** The largest network of interconnected computers in the world and the most common name for the Information Superhighway.

**INTERNIST:** An expert system from the University of Pittsburgh for use in identifying infections in internal medicine, based on a knowledge base of information about more than 500 diseases and their symptoms.

**interpreter:** A computer program that translates a high-level instruction to machine language, line by line, and then executes it before considering the next instruction.

**iteration (looping):** One of the four main constructs in structured programming for executing a series of steps repeatedly in a program, often called looping.

**JAVA:** A programming language now being used to create small, self-contained applications, called applets, suitable for being distributed on the World Wide Web and run on the client machine.

**justifying of lines:** The ability of a word processor to align both left and right margins, such a tedious process with a typewriter that it is never done.

**kerning:** A fine printing feature that overlaps the placement of letter combinations for a pleasant visual effect, available in some full-featured word processors.

**key:** The main identifying field in a data record to which associated information is attached, such as a student number for college records.

**key field:** A main field that can be used to create an index for fast, random-access retrieval of records.

**keyboard:** A common input device for entering data into a computer, similar to a typewriter.

**keyboarding:** The process of inputting data into a computer or word processor at a keyboard.

**killer app:** A slang term for a new and popular software application that is widely accepted and purchased by computer users.

**kilohertz (kHz):** A measuring unit for a sound wave, representing a thousand cycles per second.

**knowledge base:** In an expert system, facts and relations among them gleaned from human experts.

**label:** Adding descriptive information to cells in a spreadsheet or to a graph based on a spreadsheet to make the results more readable and understandable.

**label maker:** A word processing feature making it possible to create labels easily with software and a printer.

**laptop:** A portable computer: small, lightweight, and powered by either batteries or line current.

**laser printer:** A popular nonimpact printer that creates high-quality output by using a laser beam to create an image on an electrically charged drum.

**light pen:** A handheld input stylus that uses a photocell to transmit signals to a computer screen, first used in CAD applications.

**LCD (liquid crystal display):** A liquid-filled display screen that creates images when electrically charged, used in watches, calculators, and portable computers.

**limited domain:** A term that describes how various kinds of success in AI have been achieved in relatively small, constrained areas of application.

**link:** A pointer between nodes in a networked database signifying that they are related in some way.

**LISP:** A language used primarily by artificial intelligence programmers for general string handling and list processing.

**local area network (LAN):** A system of networked computers and other hardware, like printers, that are in relatively close proximity to one another.

**log (audit trail):** A record kept automatically by a computer system of all users, times logged on, and transactions for record keeping and security purposes, especially with distributed access to large databases.

**logic programming languages:** A category of languages like Prolog very similar to symbolic logic, especially applicable to artificial intelligence research and expert systems.

**logical comparison operator:** One of the common logical operations—less than, greater than, equal to, not equal to, etc.—included in most programming languages.

**logical error:** A bug in a computer program in which the logic is faulty—for instance, in which instructions are not in proper sequence or the wrong instructions are used.

**Logo programming language:** An easy-to-use programming language with special graphical features designed for teaching children to do problem solving through an intuitive method. Sometimes Logo is used with a robotic turtle that can be instructed to move around a room with Logo instructions.

**loop:** A series of program instructions performed repeatedly until a certain condition is satisfied, embodying the structured programming construct of iteration.

**Lotus 1-2-3:** One of the most popular spreadsheet programs, a successor to VisiCalc, the first spreadsheet program.

**low-level electromagnetic emissions:** Small amounts of radiation emitted by electronic equipment such as computer screens that may be hazardous to the health of people who work with them for many hours.

**Luddite riots:** Early nineteenth-century revolts by weavers in northern England, when the introduction of weaving machinery into factories led to their being laid off. A famous instance where the introduction of new technology led to unemployment and social unrest.

**machine language:** The basic set of binary operations, specific to each computer brand, that constitute its main power.

**macro:** In a spreadsheet, a programmer-designed function individually developed for a special need. Like functions provided with the spreadsheet program, macro operations are small

programs stored within the spreadsheet itself and accessed by name.

**magnetic ink character recognition (MICR):** An input process used by banks to read the digits and symbols printed in magnetic ink at the bottom of checks.

**magnetic resonance imaging (MRI):** A modern medical imaging technology for diagnosis similar to CAT scanning. MRI employs reflected radio waves to get safe and reliable computer images of internal body organs without x-ray.

**magneto-optical (MO):** Mass storage that combines magnetic and laser technology for safe, portable storage of massive amounts of information in gigabyte quantities.

**mail-merge:** A word processing feature that permits personalizing a form letter by merging the letter document and a name and address file before printing.

**mainframe:** The first commercial computers in the 1950s: large, fast, and of general application. Today they are widely used as central or host computers in large institutions.

**matrix:** An arrangement of data in a grid of rows and columns suitable for storing the pixel layout of a bit-mapped character or graphic in computer memory.

**medical database:** A specialized database of current medical research findings and treatments, such as MEDLINE, well-indexed by categories to offer easy online searches.

**megabyte (MB):** A unit of computer storage, equal to approximately 1 million bytes of storage.

**megahertz (MHz):** A measure of a computer's processor speed equal to 1 million ticks of the computer's internal clock. As a general rule, the more megahertz per second, the faster the computer.

**memory:** The functional component of a computer that stores programs and data before they are processed by the CPU.

**menu:** A list of choices displayed on the screen from which a user can select program operations. A computer with a GUI often presents menus in pull-down form.

**menu-driven:** A technique of presenting command choices in the operating system by giving the user several different options, recently in pull-down menus.

**microprocessor:** The central processor of a personal computer, often called the chip. In the U.S., Intel and Motorola make the most popular ones used in IBM-compatibles and Macintoshes.

**minicomputer:** A computer category between a mainframe and a microcomputer in terms of size, cost, and processing power.

**MIPS (million instructions per second):** One measure of a computer's processing speed, sometimes used to compare how many instructions different microprocessors can execute in a second.

**modem:** A hardware device that enables data to be transmitted over telephone lines by conversion of digital computer signals to analog signals and vice versa at the receiving end.

**Modula2:** A structured algorithmic programming language designed by

Niklaus Wirth as an alternative to Pascal.

**monitor:** A TV-like computer screen that displays information to users. Also called a video display terminal (VDT) or cathode ray tube (CRT).

**monochrome screen:** A computer screen offering one color, typically white, green, or amber, against a black background.

**motherboard:** The main circuit board of a computer containing the microprocessor, memory chips, and other components.

**mouse:** A hand-controlled hardware device that is slid around a desktop for selecting and drawing items on the computer screen, thereby reducing the need to type all commands.

**MPEG:** A standard format for encoding video files in a compressed form.

**multicasting:** An Internet protocol for distributing the same digital files from one computer to multiple other computers at the same time.

**multimedia:** A term for integrating several computer media—text, sound, graphics, and video—together in one application, with some kind of navigation system among them.

**multimedia-machine:** A term for a modern computer, a general purpose symbol-manipulating device, capable of processing and playing a variety of media, such as sounds and video.

**multitasking:** A powerful feature of modern operating systems that allows processors to work on more than one application at a time to achieve faster, more efficient operation.

**multiple-field sorting:** Sorting on two or more fields of information, one primary and the others secondary. For instance, in a mailing list database, a person may sort addresses by states and then within states by ZIP code.

**Musical Instrument Digital Interface (MIDI):** A technology for connecting electronic music instruments and computers. The information that passes between MIDI devices is a condensed description of the composition. On playback, MIDI controls the generation of sound on a synthesizer.

**MYCIN:** An expert system designed at Stanford University to diagnose and suggest treatment for various kinds of bacterial infections.

**nanosecond:** A billionth of a second, the unit of magnitude that personal computer internal speeds are measured in today.

**National Research and Education Network (NREN):** The supernetwork funded by the U.S. government to upgrade the Internet in order to link industries, schools, and private homes across the nation via high-speed fiber optic connections.

**natural language interface:** A search strategy that allows querying a database directly in English, although the way the request is formulated is fairly restricted.

**near letter quality (NLQ):** Fine-quality printing produced by dot-matrix printers in their best resolution, which is almost as good as that produced by fully formed characters.

**netiquette:** A term for acceptable manners on electronic mail.

**network:** A group of computers or other devices, like printers, connected to form a system in which they can communicate with each other directly through a physical link.

**network computer (NC or Web PC):** A new type of stripped-down computer primarily designed to access the World Wide Web, from which users will be able to gather information, write e-mail, and access software through downloading.

**network protocol:** A set of technical specifications that allow different computers to receive and transmit Internet messages through their interconnected communication channels.

**networked model:** A database design for storing information by linking all records that are related with a list of pointers.

**networking:** The process of connecting computers together on a network to that they can communicate among themselves and share resources, such as papers in a writing class.

**neural networks (connectionism):** A computer technique intended to model the human brain's processes in learning, understanding, and remembering.

**node:** A record or field in a networked database with a series of links connecting it to all other associated nodes.

**nonimpact printer:** A printer that produces images without striking the paper, such as ink-jet and laser printers.

**NOT (complement):** A fundamental logical operator that retains only those elements of a set that are not specified. For instance, the NOT of Blue in the American flag is Red and White.

**numeric character:** A number stored as ASCII codes inside a computer, rather than being stored as a binary integer or floating-point real number. A street number or ZIP code as part of an address is an example.

**numeric keypad:** The section of a keyboard containing an arrangement of numbers in a square for easy input of numeric data.

**numerical comparison operation:** A fundamental database operation, also found in programming languages that compares two quantities for a relationship such as "less than" or "equal to."

**object:** In software engineering, an instance of data encapsulated with all its features and possible uses in constructing program applications, like an interchangeable part in manufacturing.

**object code:** The binary version of a program, originally written in a high-level language, having been created as machine language code by the translation process.

**object-oriented database:** A networked database that can link a variety of data objects like text, graphics, photos, video, and sound and associate them with an object, such as a "card" window in HyperCard.

**object-oriented graphics software:** Draw programs that treat graphic constructions as objects suitable for repositioning and resizing as a unit.

**object-oriented programming:** A popular, recent programming technique which offers users a set of predefined objects or tools to construct applications, illustrated by such languages as Smalltalk.

**odd parity:** Indicates that the total number of 1s in the unit of transmitted information must be odd.

**on-line:** A term used to describe a person connected to a computer network, often at a remote location.

**on-line commenting system:** Similar to computer conferencing, a networking setup used for education so that students can read and comment on each other's written work.

**on-line thesaurus:** Computer software including a thesaurus to offer a list of synonyms that can be substituted for a word while the writer is using the word processor.

**open forum:** A computer conference set up on a public bulletin board system that allows anyone who logs on to participate.

**operating system:** The computer's own system software for monitoring all of its operations, such as moving data into and out of storage and coordinating the running of application programs.

**optical character recognition (OCR):** An input process that scans a printed character in a book or reads a number on a check and translates them into computer-readable codes.

**optical disk:** A storage medium read by a laser beam that can store several hundred megabytes of data. CD-ROMs are optical disks that can be read but cannot be erased, but erasable ones are also now available.

**OR (union):** A fundamental logical operator that combines all the elements of two sets of data into one larger set.

**OS/2:** An acronym for Operating System/2, a powerful GUI personal computer operating system owned by IBM.

**output:** Transferring data processed by a computer system to a hardware device like a monitor or a diskette for display or storage.

**output presentation format:** Another term for final formatting and deciding how to present the completed spreadsheet.

**page preview:** A convenient graphical addition to a word processor which shows a small image of what the layout of a word processed page will look like when printed, useful for noting single lines at the top or bottom or adjusting margins.

**paint software:** Graphics programs that allow users to handle prepared shapes or do freehand sketching and manipulate their creations at the pixel level.

**palmtop (hand-held):** A small portable computer weighing one pound or less.

**paperless office:** A term used to describe a totally computerized office where all communications will be handled electronically in soft copy.

**paradigm shift:** A term for a major shift in thinking about an important subject. For instance, if the desktop model of personal computing were replaced with decentralized network computing based on the client/server model of the World Wide Web, computing would have undergone a paradigm shift.

**parallel processing:** A combination of multiple interconnected processors and software techniques that analyze input data simultaneously rather than serially; useful in neural networks.

**parallel transmission:** Method of transmitting data within a computer in which a bundled set of bits is sent over a data bus all at the same time.

**parity bits:** Single bits attached to each byte to check that data are being transmitted correctly through a communications channel.

**parsing:** A linguistic term for breaking up a sentence in a natural language into its syntactical components, such as noun and verb phrases; today a lively subject of computer research.

**Pascal:** A popular structured programming language that is often taught to beginning programmers because it is relatively easy to learn.

**password system:** A software strategy of using a unique, normally secret, code to identify users before granting them access to a computer system or database for multiple users.

**pattern matching:** A computer technique for finding a predetermined pattern, such as a phrase in a long list of clichés.

**pattern matching:** The human ability to recognize underlying patterns of similarity in different contexts, such as handwriting styles and dialects, for which neural networks using fuzzy logic seem appropriate.

**personal computer (microcomputer or PC):** The least expensive but most common type of computer system in use today, built around a microprocessor and used mainly by one person at a time.

**personal digital assistant (PDA):** A new breed of palmtop computer designed to adapt to the user's style of working rather than requiring the person to follow the work pattern of the desktop computer.

**photo-realism:** A term used to describe the increasingly realistic creations of computer graphics made possible by techniques like ray tracing.

**pipelining:** A process to speed up the throughput of a microprocessor by staging different jobs to run concurrently rather than doing them in sequence.

**pirated software:** Programs that have been copied illegally rather than purchased legally.

**pixel:** A term made from the words *picture element* to describe a spot on a computer screen capable of changing color or shade. Modern graphical screens may have more than a million pixels.

**PL/I:** A high-level programming language of the 1960s designed to meet the needs of both business and science by combining the advantages of COBOL and FORTRAN.

**place system:** The basis of any number system, such as decimal or binary integers. A digit in a certain place means that the digit is raised to the power of the base number for that place. For instance, the 2 in the "tens" place in the number 20 must be multiplied by 10 to get its value.

**plotter:** An output device that creates a graphic image by controlling the motion of a pen on paper.

**plugboard:** Before programming languages were invented, programs were individually wired for one application using such a wiring board, and modification required stopping the machine for rewiring.

**portability:** Ability to run the same programs on several brands of computers, one of the attractions of the Unix operating system.

**PostScript:** A software standard created by Adobe Systems for describing a printed document containing a variety of fonts and graphics.

**presentation graphics:** Software that produces graphic representations of information, often used for presentations at meetings.

**primary sort:** The first field to be sorted in a database sorting operation.

**primary storage:** The functional component of a computer where programs and data are stored for processing, normally RAM in PCs.

**printer:** The most common output device for PCs used to create printed reports.

**procedure:** In structured programming, one of a series of independent subtasks that stand alone and can be performed one at a time in a modular fashion.

**process control application:** A process in manufacturing often suitable for installation of robotic machines, such as automated welding on an assembly line.

**processing cycle:** The implementation of the throughput process from input to output, which requires a partnership of hardware and software in carrying out the five functions of all computer applications.

**processing:** Manipulation of data by a computer that results in quick and efficient information.

**processor:** The functional element of a computer system for processing, incorporated in personal computers in the microprocessor chip.

**production rule:** An if/then condition incorporated into the inference engine of an expert system.

**productivity software:** A general term to apply to the most common kinds of applications software to increase a user's productivity: word processors, spreadsheets, database systems, graphics, data communications.

**program:** A set of instructions that tells a computer what to do. Programs are often read from a diskette or a hard drive but sometimes are already resident in the computer's central memory.

**Prolog:** A popular logic programming language for expert systems and other artificial intelligence research procedures like natural language processing.

**proportional spacing:** A fine printing option of variable spacing between letters for a pleasant visual effect, common in typesetting and available with some full-featured word processors.

**prosthetics:** The field of replacing missing body parts with artificial limbs or organs, today being developed with computerized devices.

**pseudocode:** A kind of structured English used to describe the algorithmic steps needed in a program, analogous to a flowchart as a planning tool for programming.

**puff switch:** A small device for people who cannot use their hands on a keyboard or mouse to select items on a computer screen by blowing softly on the switch, used in conjunction with a head pointer.

**pull-down menu:** A menu of command options that is hidden from view until revealed by a combination of keystrokes or depression of a mouse.

**punch card:** Invented for compiling the Census of 1890, an early means of encoding data for computers and other data processing equipment using a code made up of patterns of punched holes in a card.

**public key (PK) cryptography:** A kind of software algorithm based on pairs of numerical keys, one public and one private, for encrypting e-mail and other network transactions.

**query by example (QBE):** A fill-in-the-blanks approach to building a database search, requiring a user to fill out a query form on the screen.

**Qwerty keyboard:** The standard typewriter keyboard layout, named for the first six letters on the top line of characters.

**radiosity:** A software technique to simulate the effects of light diffusion and add shading to objects in computer graphic images that seem sharper than reality.

**random access memory (RAM):** The primary internal storage device of a personal computer, where programs and data are kept during processing.

**range:** A set of adjacent row or column cells treated as a unit, for example, to be placed in a function to get a sum of cell values in a column. Specifying a range of cells eliminates the need to list all of them individually.

**rapid applications development (RAD) tools:** Programming environments with objects, graphical interfaces, and superior debugging features for rapid prototyping of applications. Both Delphi and Visual BASIC fall into this category.

**raster:** A term for the horizontal lines of pixels on a TV or CRT screen, refreshed at a rate of 30 times a second to display an image on the screen.

**raster graphics:** A common method of presenting computer graphic images on a CRT, based on the technology of television, that uses an electron beam to excite phosphor dots (pixels) inside the CRT screen and make them glow.

**ray tracing:** An enhancement technique for computer graphics that simulates the effect of reflected light rays in a three-dimensional scene on a two-dimensional computer screen.

**read-only memory (ROM):** Memory chip that permanently stores instructions and data. Because it can be read from but cannot have new information put into it, manufacturers store important control programs in ROM chips.

**real number:** A positive or negative number, including zero, that can be expressed with fractions, called **floating point** in computers because they are represented with a floating binary point similar to a decimal point.

**real time:** A term used to describe a computer application in which the delay between input of data and completed processing is negligible. When a computer presents results as soon as the data have been received, the process is called a real-time application.

**record:** A collection of related fields comprising one item in a data file, such as a complete book record in an on-line catalog.

**refresh buffer:** In vector graphics, hardware that renews a phosphor-coated display screen with an electron beam to maintain information that would otherwise flicker.

**relational (tabular) model:** A design used in database systems in which relationships are created between one or more flat files or tables based on the idea that each pair of tables has a field in common.

**rendering:** A general term for creating a ray-traced image.

**repetitive stress injury (RSI):** A medical condition resulting in severe arm pain, thought to be caused by sitting long hours at computer keyboards.

**reporting:** The process of printing or displaying information contained in a database, often the last step in database management.

**resolution:** A term referring to the number of pixels on a computer screen. The higher the resolution, the better the characters or images on the screen appear.

**RGB (red-green-blue) monitor:** A term for a color monitor, with the letters of the name standing for the three primary additive colors that combine to make color images on the screen.

**RISC (reduced instruction set computing) chip:** A microprocessor chip with fewer and simpler instructions capable of performing complex tasks by combining simple instructions and reducing processing time.

**robotic machine:** A robot typically engineered with sensors and a gripper arm to carry out an automated industrial process.

**ruler line:** A section of some word processor screens for setting options such as margins, tabs, and spacing between lines of text, resembling a ruler in inches or centimeters.

**scientific visualization:** A process associated with computational science to represent as graphic images the results of complex simulation computations, sometimes involving millions of items of numerical data.

**search and replace:** A word processing feature that searches for a specific pattern like a word or a phrase and replaces it with another, either automatically or after the user approves the change.

**search engine:** Any of the many indexing programs creating for searching for information on World Wide Web pages, usually based on Boolean search strategies.

**searching:** The process of setting up a search request and retrieving information in a database that fulfills the request, a standard feature of all database software.

**secondary mass storage:** A term that applies to the medium in which computer programs and data are stored while not in use, such as on diskettes or magnetic tape.

**secondary sort:** A field in a database used for additional sorting after records have been arranged by the primary sorting operation on another field.

**selection:** The term used in structured programming for the choice represented by a decision box or an if/then/else condition.

**semantics:** The field of linguistic analysis concerned with the meaning component of language, still one of the greatest challenges of natural language processing with computers.

**semiconductor memory:** Another term for RAM chips, based on a semiconductor technology similar to that of microprocessor chips.

**sensory feedback:** The ability of a robotic machine to receive sensory information as data and adjust its behavior accordingly, the highest level of achievement in today's robots.

**sequence:** The structured program construct for a series of statements that are carried out in linear order, one after another.

**sequential search:** A programming strategy of searching for an item in a data file by examining items in the order in which they are stored, often not the most efficient searching method.

**serial process:** The transmission of data in a communications channel like a phone line one bit at a time.

**shareware:** Software distributed free of charge on a trial basis through bulletin boards or among friends. Those who like it are expected to pay a nominal fee in order to receive additional documentation and news of upgrades.

**SHRDLU (BLOCKS WORLD):** A pioneering natural language application designed by Terry Winograd, with features for understanding both the grammar and semantics of instructions for moving a set of blocks around on a plane surface.

**simulation software:** A computer program that imitates a process or set of activities, such as an organic chemical reaction or an environmental disaster.

**site license:** A fee paid to a software company to allow multiple users at a site to access or copy a piece of software.

**slide scanner:** An input device for digitizing color slides directly so that they are suitable for storage in computers.

**Smalltalk:** A pioneering language for introducing concepts of object-oriented programming.

**smart weapons:** Military hardware, like the Tomahawk missile from the 1991 Persian Gulf War, that incorporates computers in its design to carry out its mission.

**smiley:** A set of keystrokes that can be included in e-mail to express emotion in a kind of graphical shorthand.

**snail mail:** Computer jargon for surface mail, which is normally slower than electronic mail.

**SNOBOL:** A string processing programming language, especially popular in humanities computing.

**soft copy:** Computer output presented on a CRT screen rather than being printed.

**software:** The suite of programs that enables a computer system to process data, including both the operating system and a variety of application programs.

**software interface:** A term that describes the way a database user communicates with the software, such as querying by example or using a natural language search strategy.

**software license:** Paying a license fee to software developers for access to a program by a number of users without restriction, common in businesses and institutions.

**software piracy:** Illegal or unauthorized copying of software.

**sorting:** Arranging records in a file according to a specified sequence, such as alphabetically or numerically, from lowest to highest.

**source code:** The statements that make up a computer program in a high-level programming language, ready for an interpreter or a compiler.

**spaghetti code:** A term for a computer program not following structured programming principles, with many "go-to's" that allow unlimited transfer of control between modules.

**special-purpose computer:** A computer dedicated to a single purpose, such as a digital watch.

**speech recognition package:** Software that accepts voice input and recognizes its content for controlling the computer.

**spelling checker:** A computer program that checks a document for misspellings and offers suggestions for correction.

**spreadsheet:** Software that can represent data in a row-and-column format and can manipulate it like an electronic ledger sheet.

**stack:** A term for an individual HyperCard application, analogous to a file.

**stimulus/response:** A common psychological way to

describe the cycle of response in the human body to external sensations as mediated by the brain. Analogous to the throughput process in computers.

**storage:** Another term for memory, a hardware device for storing binary data and programs.

**stored program concept:** The storage of data and instructions in central memory so that instructions can be treated like data. Von Neumann proposed this principle in the 1940s, so that the computer did not have to be hardwired each time a specific task was to be performed.

**Strategic Defense Initiative (SDI):** A defense system begun by the Reagan administration and nicknamed "Star Wars" that combined computerized radar monitoring of incoming missiles and shooting them down with automated interceptor missiles. Controversial from the start about its feasibility, the program is being dismantled in the 1990s.

**string-handling language:** A category of programming languages like LISP and SNOBOL appropriate for lists and textual data, such as natural language.

**structured program design:** The process of designing the components of a computer program as a set of individual self-contained modules that can be interrelated.

**structured query language (SQL):** A technical database search standard recognized by the American National Standards Institute and used by software designers to create their internal computer search criteria. Sometimes ordinary users build search requests in SQL, but most

modern database software hides it from the user.

**style and grammar checker:** A software program that checks for punctuation errors, does limited grammar checking, flags awkward usage, and suggests revisions.

**subsumption architecture:** A design philosophy espoused by some artificial life researchers to create a set of interconnected simple processors that can each carry out basic behaviors, modeling complex behavior with a combination of simple actions.

**subtractive primary colors:** The three primary colors, magenta, cyan, and yellow, defined by the absence of one of the RGB colors, created by eliminating that color from light reflected from a white page. These colors form the basis of color laser printing.

**supercockpit:** A Defense Department research project to create a computerized helmet that resembles a video game and automates many functions for the pilot of the plane.

**supercomputer:** The fastest and most expensive type of computer designed for massive mathematical calculations necessary for much high-level scientific research. Supercomputer speeds today are measured in gigaflops (one billion floating point mathematical operations in a second) and soon in teraflops (one trillion such operations).

**superscalar processing:** A processor strategy similar to parallel processing on the chip that allows the hardware automatically to find instructions that are launched at the same time so that it can maximize their efficient use.

**Super Video Graphics Adapter (SVGA) monitor:** A common type of color computer monitor for graphics display in better IBM-compatibles.

**sweeper:** An element of a raster graphics system that takes information from the frame buffer and updates the display screen.

**syntax:** The field of linguistics concerned with the grammatical relations of words in a sentence.

**syntax error:** An error found in a computer program in the compiling stage because a statement violates the grammatical rules of the programming language.

**synthesizer:** A device that can electronically generate sound, either music or voice, from digital information.

**systems analysis:** A field of analysis that looks at a proposed computer application from the top down and tries to put together an efficient, coordinated system made up of hardware, software, and people to achieve the desired goal.

**table:** Another name for a flat file, an arrangement of data into rows and columns, in relational database design.

**telecommuting:** The use of personal computers and data communications at home to do work without being physically present at the office.

**Telnet:** An Internet protocol that permits a user to log onto a remote computer on the Net and work on it at long distance.

**template:** A cardboard or plastic pattern sometimes packed with software for placement placing on a keyboard, listing the most common commands in the package.

**teraflop (TFLOP):** A trillion floating-point computer instructions per second, a measure of the enormous number of operations carried out by the most advanced supercomputers today (tera = trillion).

**text processing:** A field concerned with text-based applications of computers, including indexing, hyphenation, and concordances.

**throughput:** The computer cycle of inputting data, processing it, and outputting the information produced thereby, analogous to the stimulus/response cycle in the body.

**top-down design:** An approach in structured program design that breaks up a general task into a series of more detailed subtasks, which are further divided until no more detail is necessary.

**touch screen:** An input/output device that allows a user to control the computer by touching the screen, which then displays the output.

**transfer:** Programming statements, like the "go-to" in early nonstructured programming languages, that allow program code to be transferred into and out of modules.

**trash can:** An icon common with graphical user interface systems used for getting rid of files. "Emptying the trash" means deleting files stored there.

**Trojan horse:** An unauthorized program hidden inside a legitimate program, usually doing some harm to the computer system while the host program appears to be performing normally.

**True BASIC:** A modern version of the BASIC programming language, re-created by the developers of the original language (Kemeny and Kurtz) along totally structured programming lines.

**Turing machine:** The concept of the computer developed by Alan Turing, which created a theoretical foundation for computing.

**Turing test:** Alan Turing's 1950 description of a dialogue in which a person tries to guess which of two conversations is being conducted with a person and which with a computer. This test has become a standard model used to judge the "intelligence" of many AI applications.

**twisted-pair wire:** Two copper wires twisted together, often used for home telephone lines and for computer connections in a LAN.

**Unicode:** A new standard coding scheme that allows 65,536 different binary codes because it uses 16 bits to code a character.

**Universal Product Code (UPC):** A bar code printed on most consumer goods that indicates the manufacturer of the good, as well as the product itself. It can be read by a scanner input device for computer processing.

**Unix:** An operating system designed for portability and flexibility among a variety of computers, from microcomputers to supercomputers.

**uploading:** Transferring files to a central computer on a network from a remote machine such as a personal computer.

**USENET:** A general term for the thousands of user discussion groups on the Internet devoted to many subjects, including some that are strictly for adults.

**user interface:** The way a user communicates with the computer.

**value:** The contents of a cell, perhaps a number or a formula.

**value-added network (VAN):** A communications channel leased from a telephone company to offer customers with modems access to network services through a local or toll-free number.

**value-added software:** Software in which additional customized features have been added to a base program, such as a tax preparation program in which a series of tax-form templates and formulas have been added to a basic spreadsheet.

**vector graphics:** The earliest type of computer graphics, in which a set of character-plotting commands activate the phosphors of a computer display with an electron beam.

**video accelerator circuit board:** An optional circuit board for personal computers designed to speed up a personal computer processor's ability to display color graphics on the screen.

**videoconferencing:** A system of computer-monitored two-way video transmission using phone lines that allows viewers at both ends of the session to see and hear one another.

**video game:** One of the most popular and most widely recognized computer graphic applications, available in video arcades and home entertainment software.

**video telephony:** A long-distance telephone conversation with live video and sound.

**virtual classroom:** A distance learning environment in which students and teachers can be physically separated but in contact via a technology supporting remote access like computer networking or videoconferencing.

**virtual reality (VR):** An environment created by computer technology that combines visual, auditory, and tactile interation to create the illusion of realistic objects and sensory experiences for the user. Also called **artificial reality, cyberspace,** and **telepresence.**

**virus checker:** Computer software that monitors the system, looking for computer viruses and correcting or deleting them if they show up.

**VisiCalc:** The first spreadsheet program, developed by Dan Bricklin and Robert Frankston while Bricklin was a graduate student at Harvard.

**visualization systems:** Robotic machines, such as some automated security systems, with television cameras and feedback mechanisms capable of analyzing a scene and carrying out an action based on what is seen.

**voice mail:** A technology that allows a person to send a digitized spoken message to a colleague. The message is stored in a computer and later played back to the recipient when the mail is retrieved.

**voice synthesizer:** A hardware output device that transforms written computer text into synthetic speech, useful for blind people.

**voiceprint:** An audio signature of a person in digital form, useful for allowing a computer system to recognize a person's voice commands.

**Web page:** The name for a document formatted to contain information for distribution on the World Wide Web. It may contain hypertext links to other pages and various multimedia resources.

**what-if scenario:** Using a spreadsheet as a prediction device by making changes to data in some cells to see what impact they have on the overall spreadsheet.

**wide area network (WAN):** A geographically dispersed communications network, with many owners, linking computers for the purpose of communicating with each other, such as a national network for airline reservations.

**window:** A resizable rectangular display area of a computer screen, prominent in systems having a graphical user interface.

**Windows NT:** The upgrading of Microsoft's Windows environment into a full operating system that can be used by all kinds of computers and communications devices.

**Windows 95 (Win 95):** A new operating system introduced in 1995 into the Microsoft family of Windows software for personal computers. It includes numerous improvements over DOS-based Windows 3.1.

**Wintel:** A modern acronym for a computer system containing an Intel microprocessor and a Microsoft Windows operating system.

**wireless infrared remote communications:** The "point and click" technology of the TV remote controller, now being introduced into machines like the Sony Magic Link for transfer of files to another device.

**word processing:** Popular applications software designed for composing, revising, printing, and filing written documents.

**word wrap:** A feature of word processing that allows a person to continue typing beyond the end of a line without pressing the return key. The computer program automatically reformats the material within the margins set by the user.

**worksheet:** A term sometimes used for a spreadsheet.

**workstation:** A category of desktop computers targeted for high-performance specialized applications such as computer-aided design and publishing, modeling, and visualization. Bigger, faster, and, until recently, more expensive than a typical personal computer.

**world knowledge:** Information that people take for granted that must be explicitly stated in computer programs, often as heuristic rules.

**World Wide Web (the Web, WWW):** The most popular part of the Internet today, a method of storing and distributing materials in several media over the network so that it can be viewed with browser software on a personal computer.

**worm:** A program that reproduces itself by creating copies of itself and worming its way into alien operating systems. The infamous Internet worm infiltrated several thousand Unix systems in 1988.

**writing center:** A laboratory found in many colleges and schools offering advice about writing improvement. Today many writing centers are using computers for tutorials and conferencing with students.

**WYSIWYG (What you see is what you get):** The display of information on a computer screen in a form that closely resembles what will eventually be printed, characteristic of word processing or desktop publishing software on computers with bit-mapped screens.

# References

## Chapter 1. Computer Literacy: A Current Perspective

Crick, F. H. C. 1979. "Thinking about the Brain." *Scientific American*, 241 (September): 219–32.

*The New Grolier Multimedia Encyclopedia*. CD-ROM Edition. Version 6. New York: Grolier, 1993.

Hubel, David H. 1979. "The Brain." *Scientific American* 241 (September): 44–53.

Neilsen, J. 1990. *Hypertext and Hypermedia*. San Diego: Academic Press.

Oakman, Robert L. 1987. "Perspectives on Teaching Computing in the Humanities." *Computers and the Humanities* 21: 227–33.

Rosenberg, Jerry M. 1991. *Dictionary of Computers, Data Processing, and Telecommunications*. New York: Wiley.

Springer, Sally P., and Georg Deutsch. 1985. *Left Brain, Right Brain*, rev. ed. New York: W. H. Freeman.

Turkle, Sherry. 1984. *The Second Self*. New York: Simon and Schuster.

## Chapter 2. Computers in Society: The Positives

Crowley, Thomas H. 1967. *Understanding Computers*. New York: McGraw-Hill.

Radlow, James. 1986. *Computers and the Information Society*. New York: McGraw-Hill.

### EDUCATION

Brady, Holly. 1985. " 'Hang on to the Power to Imagine': An Interview with Joseph Weizenbaum." *Classroom Computer Learning* (November/December): 24–27.

Carver, Curtis A., Jr. 1996. "Textbook of the Future." *Abstracts* of the 1996 Annual Meeting of the Association for the Advancement of Science, Baltimore, MD (February): A-18.

DeSieno, Robert. 1995. "The Faculty and Digital Technology." *Educom Review* 30, 4 (July/August): 46–48.

Grady, David. 1988. "Mathematica: Will Mathematics (or Computers) Ever Be the Same?" *Technology on Campus* (Fall): 8–11.

Reinhardt, Andy. 1995. "New Ways to Learn." *Byte* 20, 3 (March): 50–72.

Trollip, Stanley R. 1987. "Issues in Instructional Computing." *Perspectives in Computing* 7, 2 (Fall): 25–31.

Van Gelder, Lawrence. 1995. "Term Papers on CD-ROM Turn Words into Virtual Reality." *New York Times*, 26 April: B8.

Vlahakis, Robert. 1988. "The Computer-Infused Classroom." *Classroom Computer Learning* (November/December): 58–61.

### MEDICAL AND EXPERIMENTAL SCIENCE

Cowley, Geoffrey. 1994. "The Rise of Cyberdoc." *Newsweek*, 26 September: 54–55.

Cowley, Geoffrey, Susan Miller, Rebecca Crandall, and Mary Hager. 1995. "RoboDocs and Mousecalls." *Newsweek*, 27 February: 66–67.

Cox, Donna J. 1990. "The Art of Computer Visualization," *Academic Computing* 4, 6 (March): 20–22, 32–40.

"Federal High Performance Computing Program, The." 1989. *Computing Research News* 1, 2 (Fall): 5–13.

La Breque, Mark. 1989. "What's New in Supercomputing?" *American Scientist* 77, 6 (November/December): 523–25.

Meng, Brita. 1990. "With a Little Help from My Mac." *Macworld* (September): 180–88.

Redington, Rowland W., and Walter H. Berninger. 1981. "Medical Imaging Systems." *Physics Today* (August): 36–44.

"Visualization News: Continuous Forecasting of Lake Erie Water Conditions." 1990. *Pixel* 1, 2 (May/June): 8–9.

Wegner, Peter. 1990. "Computer Science: Achievements and Opportunities." *Computing Research News* 2, 3 (July): 20–22.

## MEDIA

Fisher, Bob. 1988. "Cancelled *Max Headroom* Leaves Legacy." *American Cinematographer* 69, 2 (February): 77–82.

Korzenlowski, Paul. 1985. "USA Today: Satellite Network Delivers Daily." *Computerworld*, 14 October: 1, 6.

Matazzoni, Joe. 1990. "Prepress Progress Report." *Macworld* (October): 168–75.

McGinn, Daniel, and Perri Colley. 1995. "A Walk on the Wired Side." *Newsweek*, 4 September: 50–51.

*San Francisco Examiner.* 1990. "The Examiner Covers the Day in High-Tech," 5 June.

## GOVERNMENT

Bellin, David, and Gary Chapman, eds. 1988. *Computers in Battle: Will They Work?* Orlando: Harcourt.

Boyd, Robert S. 1990. "Privacy Rights Eroding." *Columbia, SC, State*, 5 August: 1D, 5D.

Bradley, Barbara. 1988. "Fingered by the Police Computer." *Christian Science Monitor*, 9 June: 19–20.

Campen, Alan D., ed. 1992. *The First Information War.* Fairfax, VA: AFCEA International Press.

Kraemer, Kenneth L., and John L. King. 1987. "Computers and the Constitution: A Helpful, Harmful, or Harmless Relationship?" *Public Administration Review* (January/February): 93–105.

Laudon, Kenneth C. 1986. *Dossier Society.* New York: Columbia University Press.

Margiotta, Franklin D., and Ralph Sanders. 1985. *Technology, Strategy and National Security.* Washington, DC: National Defense University Press.

Thomas, Evan, and John Barry. 1991. "War's New Science." *Newsweek*, 18 February: 38–39.

Weingarten, Fred W. 1995. "Trying Not to Doubt Thomas." *Computing Research News* 7, 2 (March): 2–3, 12.

Wilk, Charles K. 1987. *Defending Secrets, Sharing Data.* Washington, DC: U.S. Government Printing Office.

## Chapter 3. Computers in Society: The Drawbacks

Altick, Richard D. 1973. *Victorian People and Ideas.* New York: W. W. Norton.

Boyd, Robert S. 1990. "Privacy Rights Eroding." *Columbia, SC, State*, 5 August: 1D, 5D.

Brodeur, Paul. 1990. "The Magnetic-Field Menace." *Macworld* (July): 136–45.

Ishihara, Shintaro. 1991. *The Japan That Can Say No.* New York: Simon and Schuster.

Kantrowitz, Barbara, and Rebecca Crandall. 1990. "Casualties of the Keyboard." *Newsweek*, 20 August: 57.

Kilpatrick, James J. 1990. "Credit Reporting Need Not Tell All." *Columbia, SC, State*, 14 July: 8A.

Kusserow, Richard P. 1984. "The Government Needs Computer Matching to Root out Waste and Fraud." *Communications of the ACM* 27 (June): 542–45.

Montague, Bill. 1996. "Restructuring, and Layoffs, Here to Stay." *USA Today*, 19 February: 1A–2A.

Raspberry, William. 1995. "Is There Any Future in Work?" *Columbia, SC, State*, 10 June: A13.

Rothfeder, Jeffrey. 1992. *Privacy for Sale.* New York: Simon and Schuster.

Rubin, Trudy. 1996. "Government Must Confront Worker Pain." *Columbia, SC, State*, 25 February: D3.

Shadduck, John. 1984. "Computer Matching Is a Serious Threat to Individual Rights." *Communications of the ACM* 27 (June): 538–41.

Simons, Lewis M., and Michael Zielenziger. 1996. "Culture Clash." *Columbia, SC, State*, 31 March: D1, D10–D11.

Slotnick, D., E. M. Butterfield, E. S. Colantonio, D. J. Kopetzky, and J. K. Slotnick. 1989. "Privacy, Security, and Other Concerns." *Computers and Applications*. Lexington, MA: D. C. Heath: 578–603.

*Wall Street Journal Reports.* 1990. "Workplace of the Future," special supplement, 4 June.

## Chapter 4. Computer Hardware

Blissmer, Robert. 1994. *Introducing Computers.* New York: Wiley.

Dvorak, John C. 1992. "Kiss Your ASCII Goodbye." *PC Magazine* 11, 15 (September): 93.

Leeds, Matthew. 1995. "Flexible Storage." *Macworld* (October): 119–123.

Rosch, Winn L. 1993. "The Perfect System." *PC Magazine* 12, 13. (July): 123–45.

Shatz-Akin, Jim. 1995. "A Removables Feast." *MacUser* (February): 94–102.

White, Ron. 1993. *PC/Computing: How Computers Work.* Emeryville, CA: Ziff-Davis.

## Chapter 5. Computer Software

### PROGRAMMING

Baker, F. T. 1972. "Chief Programmer Team Management of Production Programming." *IBM Systems Journal* 11, 1: 56–73.

———. 1972. "System Quality Through Structured Programming." *AFIPS Proceedings of the 1972 Fall Joint Computer Conference* 41. Montvale, NJ: AFIPS Press. 339–44.

Cox, Brad J. 1990. "There *Is* a Silver Bullet." *Byte* 15, 10 (October): 209–18.

Dijkstra, Edsger. 1968. "Go To Statement Considered Harmful." *Communications of the ACM* 11, 3 (March): 147–48.

McCarroll, Thomas. 1993. "Ending the Paper Chase." *Time,* 14 June: 60–65.

Stern, Nancy, and Robert A. Stern. 1996. *Computing in the Information Age.* New York: Wiley.

### COMPUTER VIRUSES

*Christian Science Monitor.* 1989. "How to Protect Computer Programs," 13 October: 12.

Denning, Peter J. 1988. "Computer Viruses." *American Scientist* 76, 3 (May/June): 236–38.

———. 1989. "The Internet Worm." *American Scientist* 77, 2 (March/April): 126–28.

Hafner, Katie. 1990. "Morris Code." *New Republic* 202, 8 (19 February): 15–16.

Markoff, John. 1990. "Computer Intruder Is Put on Probation and Fined $10,000." *The New York Times,* 5 May: A1, A9.

———. 1992. "Feared Computer Plague Passes with Very Few Infections." *The New York Times,* 7 March: A8.

Stefanac, Suzanne. 1988. "Mad Macs." *Macworld* 5, 11 (November): 92–101.

## Chapter 6. Word, Text, and Sound Processing

Bailey, Richard W. 1979. "Authorship Attribution in a Forensic Setting." In *Advances in Computer-Aided Literary and Linguistic Research,* ed. D. E. Ager, F. E. Knowles, and Joan Smith. Birmingham, England: University of Aston Department of Modern Languages. 1–20.

Becker, Joseph D. 1987. "Arabic Word Processing." *Communications of the ACM* (July): 600–10.

Deutsch, Herbert A., et al. 1990. "Teaching Music in the Electronic Classroom." *The Music and Computer Educator* 1, 7: 23–30.

Hardy, Quentin. 1996. "Mass Chinese PC Market Stymied by Massive Keyboard." *Wall Street Journal,* 21 February: B1, B6.

Hutheesing, Nikhil. 1996. "Call It a Strokeboard." *Forbes,* 22 January: 89.

—. 1996. "The Mother of Development." *Forbes,* 22 January: 88–89.

Kiefer, Kathleen E., and Charles R. Smith. 1983. "Textual Analysis with Computers: Tests of Bell Laboratories' Computer Software." *Research in the Teaching of English* 1, 3 (October): 201–14.

Kurzweil, Raymond. 1986. "The Technology of the Kurzweil Voice Writer." *Byte* (March): 177–86.

Macdonald, Nina H., Lawrence T. Frase, Patricia S. Gingrich, and Stacey A. Keenan. 1982. "The Writer's Workbench: Computer Aids for Text Analysis." *IEEE Transactions on Communications* (January): 105–10.

Manes, Stephen. 1995. "You Say 'Internet'; the Spell-Checker Says 'Interment.'" *New York Times,* 5 June: D3.

Meisel, William S. 1993. "Talk to Your Computer." *Byte* 18, 11 (October): 113–20.

Morris, Gloria. 1989. "Strictly Writing." *Infoworld,* 4 September: 43, 50–53.

Oakman, Robert L. 1984. *Computer Methods for Literary Research.* 2nd ed. Athens: University of Georgia Press.

Parker, Roger C. 1988. *Looking Good in Print.* Chapel Hill, NC: Ventana Press.

Rigdon, Joan E. 1995. "Microsoft Word's Spell-Checker Gets Failing Grade in Computerese." *Wall Street Journal,* 15 November: B1.

*The Edinburgh Scotsman.* 1990. "Writing on the Wall for Justice," 3 September: 9.

Shuman, R. Baird. 1995. "Computers and Writing Instruction." *Educational Leadership* 53, 2 (October): 106.

Tanaka, Jennifer, and Adam Rogers. 1995. "Spell Check." *Newsweek,* 23 January: 8.

## Chapter 7. Electronic Spreadsheets

Badgett, Tom. 1987. "Taxes as Easy as 1-2-3." *Personal Computing* 11, 12 (December): 70–74.

Durham, Bill. 1990. "Wet Labs, Computers, and Spreadsheets." *Journal of Chemical Education* 67, 5 (May): 416–20.

Edwards, Paul A., J. Brian McKay, and Charles W. Sink. 1992. "First-Year Chemistry Laboratory Calculations on a Spreadsheet." *Journal of Chemical Education* 69, 8 (August): 648–50.

Hayes, Brian. 1983. "Computer Recreations." *Scientific American* 249, 4 (October): 22–36.

Kantrowitz, Barbara. 1994. "In Quicken They Trust." *Newsweek,* 2 May: 65–66.

Manes, Stephen. 1995. "Now, the Check Is in the Modem." *New York Times,* 31 October: C8.

Slay, Alan L. 1989. "Mac-sumizing Your Money." *Macworld* 6, 2 (February): 206–15.

Yager, Tom. 1990. "What's NeXT after 1-2-3?" *Byte* 15, 10 (October): 147–49.

## Chapter 8. Databases

Blissmer, Robert H. 1994. "Information Systems and Databases." *Introducing Computers.* New York: Wiley.

Boyd, Robert S. 1990. "Privacy: World of Change." Knight-Ridder News Service, 2 July.

Codd, E. F. 1970. "A Relational Model of Data for Large Shared Data Banks." *Communications of the ACM* 13, 6 (June): 377–87.

Hayes, Brian. 1995. "Waiting for 01-01-00." *American Scientist* 83, 1 (January–February): 12–15.

Johnson, Jeff. 1990. "Caller Identification: More Privacy or Less?" *CPSR Newsletter* (Computer Professionals for Social Responsibility) 8, 1–2 (Winter–Spring): 1–6.

Kaplan, Karen. 1996. "Caller ID Service Sparks Battle Over Privacy." *Los Angeles Times,* 25 February: A1, A22.

*The Machine That Changed the World.* 1992. Boston: WGBH. (television series)

Schwartz, John. 1991. "How Did They Get My Name?" *Newsweek,* 3 June: 40–42.
Wallich, Paul. 1991. "Of Two Minds about Privacy." *Scientific American* 264, 6 (June): 27.

## Chapter 9.  Computer Graphics and Video

Bissell, Don. 1990. "The Father of Computer Graphics." *Byte* 15, 6 (June): 380–81.
Foley, James D., and Andries van Dam. 1982. *Fundamentals of Interactive Computer Graphics.* Reading, MA: Addison-Wesley.
Foley, James D., Andries van Dam, Steven K. Feiner, and John F. Hughes. 1990. *Computer Graphics: Principles and Practice,* 2nd ed. Reading, MA: Addison-Wesley.

### HARDWARE

Alford, Roger C. 1991. "Color Printing." *Byte* 16, 10 (October): 149–58.
Bennett, John. 1985. "Raster Operations." *Byte* 10, 12 (November): 187–203.
Demel, John T., and Michael J. Miller. 1984. *Introduction to Computer Graphics.* Monterey, CA: Brooks/Cole.
Lewell, John. 1985. *Computer Graphics.* New York: Van Nostrand Reinhold.

### SOFTWARE

Chao, Julie. 1995. "Adobe Systems Sees Cyberspace as a Brave New Market." *Wall Street Journal,* 25 May: B4.
Fisher, Lawrence F. 1993. "The Tools of a New Art Form" and "Cursor for Hire." *The New York Times,* 19 September: F7.
Guttman, Monika. 1996. "Two Mavericks Become Moguls." *U.S. News and World Report,* 15 January: 48–49.
Papert, Seymour. 1980. *Mindstorms: Children, Computers, and Powerful Ideas.* New York: Basic Books.
Pfortmiller, Larry. 1987. "Data Structures in CAD Software." *Byte* 12, 6 (June): 177–84.
Pitta, Julie. 1996. "Adobe's Brick-Solid Partnership Faces Its Toughest Test Yet." *Los Angeles Times,* 11 February: D1, D14.
Yager, Tom. 1992. "Winning Graphics." *Byte* 17, 6 (June): 131–40.
Young, Jeffrey. 1995. "Standard Bearers." *Forbes,* 27 March: 112–13.

### ADVANCED TOPICS

Arthur, Charles. 1992. "Did Reality Move for You?" *New Scientist* 134 (23 May): 22–27.
Braddock, Paige. 1995. "Computer Animators Log On to 'Toy Story's' Marvels." *Atlanta Journal and Constitution,* 24 November: P13.
Clark, Jim. 1992. "Roots and Branches of 3-D." *Byte* 17, 5 (May): 153–64.
Editors of Time-Life Books. 1988. *The Puzzle Master.* Richmond, VA: Time-Life.
Glassner, Andrew S. 1990. "Ray Tracing for Realism." *Byte* 15, 13 (December): 263–71.
Leonard, Milt. 1991. "You Are There, Virtually." *Electronic Design* 39 (26 September): 18.
Mandelbrot, Benoit B. 1982. *The Fractal Geometry of Nature.* San Francisco: W. H. Freeman.
Prusinkiewicz, Przemyslaw, and Aristid Lindenmayer. 1990. *The Algorithmic Beauty of Plants.* New York: Springer-Verlag.
Rogers, Adam. 1995. "Through a Glass Darkly." *Newsweek,* 23 January: 52.
"A Short Cut into Virtual Reality." 1995. *New York Times,* 23 October: D5.
Sørensen, Peter R. 1984. "Simulating Reality with Computer Graphics." *Byte* 9, 3 (March): 106–34.
Sragow, Michael. 1995. "How the Techies and Toonies Brought 'Toy Story' to Life." *New York Times,* 19 November, Sect. 2: 17, 28–29.
Stewart, Doug. 1991. "Through the Looking Glass into an Artificial World—Via Computer." *Smithsonian* 21, 10 (January): 36–45.
Wallace, John, and John Fujii. 1992. "Radiosity." *Byte* 17, 5 (May): 173–75.
Yares, Evan. 1992. "Photo-Realism." *Byte* 17, 5 (May): 167–70.

## Chapter 10. Computer Networks and Data Communications

Ackermann, Ernest. 1995. *Learning to Use the Internet.* Wilsonville, OR: Franklin, Beedle and Associates.

Bryce, James Y. 1989. "Fiber vs. Metal." *Byte* 14, 1 (January): 253–58.

Crossen, Cynthia. 1990. "Workplace: Where We'll Be." *The Wall Street Journal,* 4 June: R6–R10.

Eisenberg, Anne. 1995. "Doing Business on the Net." *Scientific American* 273, 5 (November): 111.

Elmer-Dewitt, Philip. 1996. "Why Java is Hot." *Time,* 22 January: 58–60.

Flohr, Udo. 1996. "Put the Space in Cyberspace." *Byte* 21, 3 (March): 61–64.

Hafner, Katie. 1995. "A Superhacker Meets His Match." *Newsweek,* 27 February: 61–63.

"Interview with the Cybersleuth." 1996. *Newsweek,* 6 March: 76.

Kantrowitz, Barbara, and Adam Rogers. 1994. "The Birth of the Internet." *Newsweek,* 8 August: 56–58.

Kelly, Kevin, ed. 1988. *Signal: Communication Tools for the Information Age.* New York: Harmony Books.

Krol, Ed. 1992. *The Whole Internet User's Guide and Catalog.* Sebastopol, CA: O'Reilly and Associates.

Levy, Steven. 1984. *Hackers.* Garden City, NY: Anchor/Doubleday.

———. 1995. "The Encryption Wars: Is Privacy Good or Bad?" *Newsweek,* 24 April: 55–56.

———. 1996. "An Indecent Proposal." *Newsweek,* 27 May: 80.

Lofton, Dewanna. 1996. "Browsing, Not Buying At Rackes Site." *Columbia, SC, State,* 19 May: G1, G4.

Markoff, John. 1996. "How a Computer Sleuth Traced a Digital Trail." *New York Times,* 16 February: C13.

———. 1996. "A Most-Wanted Cyberthief Is Caught in His Own Web." *New York Times,* 16 February: A1, C13.

Martin, James. 1981. *The Telematic Society.* Englewood Cliffs, NJ: Prentice-Hall.

McConville, David, Jonathan Migid, and Paul Jones. 1996. "So Wide the Web, So Little Time." *Educom Review,* 31, 3 (May/June): 44–48.

McKeown, Patrick, and Richard T. Watson. 1996. *Metamorphosis: A Guide to the World Wide Web and Electronic Commerce.* New York: Wiley.

Meyer, Michael. 1994. "The 'On-Line' War Heats Up." *Newsweek,* 28 March: 38–39.

———. 1995. "Surfing the Internet in 3-D." *Newsweek,* 15 May: 68–69.

O'Connor, Rory. 1990. "Prodigy's Heavy Hand Squelches Exchange of Ideas." *Columbia, SC, State,* 18 November: 5H.

———. 1993. "Secret Service Fined in Raid on Computer Game Publisher." *Washington Post,* 22 March: WBIZ 12.

Peyser, Marc, Andrew Murr, and Rob French. 1995. "Don't 'Chat' to Strangers." *Newsweek,* 19 June: 42.

Radin, Charles A. 1993. "'Information Highway' Speeds to Completion." *Columbia, SC, State,* 5 January: D1, D6.

Rhodes, Peter D. 1991. *LAN Operations: A Guide to Daily Management.* Reading, MA: Addison-Wesley.

Schwartz, John. 1990. "Hackers of the World, Unite!" *Newsweek,* 2 July: 36–37.

———. 1991. "Sex Crimes on Your Screen?" *Newsweek,* 23 December: 66.

———. 1992. "The Highway of the Future." *Newsweek,* 13 January: 56–57.

"Score One for the Hackers of America." 1990. *Newsweek,* 6 August: 48.

Sterling, Bruce. 1992. *The Hacker Crackdown.* New York: Bantam.

Stoll, Clifford. 1989. *The Cuckoo's Egg.* New York: Doubleday.

Tanaka, Jennifer, and Dogen Hannah. 1995. "A (Free and) Easy Guide to the Web." *Newsweek,* 20 March: 44.

Tanenbaum, Andrew S. 1989. *Computer Networks.* 2d ed. Englewood Cliffs, NJ: Prentice-Hall.

Weise, Elizabeth. 1996. "Internet Purchases Tangled in Fear." *Columbia, SC, State,* 22 January: A1, A10.

"Welcome to the Web!" 1996. *MacUser* (March): 76–82.

"Who's on the Web?" 1995. *Newsweek,* 13 November: 14.

Zazueta, Rob. 1996. "Cybersleuths." *U.: The National College Magazine* (January/February): 13.

## Chapter 11.  Artificial Intelligence

Anderson, James A., and Edward Rosenfeld, eds. 1988. *Neurocomputing: Foundations of Research*. Cambridge, MA: MIT Press.

Arar, Yardena, and Bob Strauss. 1992. "Scientists Miss '2001' HALmark." *Columbia, SC, State,* 12 January: A1, A12.

Baer, Robert M. 1972. *The Digital Villain*. Reading, MA: Addison-Wesley.

Clarke, Arthur C. 1968. *2001: A Space Odyssey*. New York: New American Library.

D'Ambrosio, Bruce. 1985. "Expert Systems—Myth or Reality?" *Byte* 10, 1 (January): 275–82.

Decker, Rick, and Stuart Hirshfield. 1990. *The Analytical Engine*. Belmont, CA: Wadsworth.

Feldman, Maurice I. 1984. *What Every Engineer Should Know about Robots*. New York: Marcel Dekker.

Harmon, Paul, and David King. 1985. *Expert Systems: Artificial Intelligence in Business*. New York: Wiley.

Hofstadter, Douglas R. 1979. *Gödel, Escher, Bach: An Eternal Golden Braid*. New York: Basic Books.

Lenat, Douglas B. 1995. "CYC: A Large-Scale Investment in Knowledge Infrastructure." *Communications of the ACM* 38, 11: 33–38.

Minsky, Marvin, ed. 1985. *Robotics*. Garden City, NY: Omni Press.

Obermeier, Klaus K., and Janet J. Barron. 1989. "Time to Get Fired Up." *Byte* 14, 8 (August): 217–24.

Rogers, Michael, and Yuriko Hoshiai. 1990. "The Future Looks 'Fuzzy.' " *Newsweek,* 28 May: 46–47.

Schank, Roger, and Larry Hunter. 1985. "The Quest to Understand Thinking." *Byte* 10, 4 (April): 143–55.

Schonberg, Harold C. 1989. "Kasparov Beats Chess Computer (for Now)." *The New York Times,* 23 October: A1.

Shapiro, Stuart C., David Eckroth, and George A. Vallasi, eds. 1987. *Encyclopedia of Artificial Intelligence*. 2 vols. New York: Wiley.

Stipp, David. 1995. "2001 Is Just Around the Corner. Where's HAL?" *Fortune,* 13 November: 215–218.

Tazelaar, Jane M. 1989. "Neural Networks." *Byte* 14, 8 (August): 214.

Turing, Alan. 1950. "Computing Machinery and Intelligence." *Mind* 59: 433–60. Rpt. in Edward Feigenbaum and Julian Feldman, eds. 1963. *Computers and Thought*. New York: McGraw-Hill.

Turkle, Sherry. 1984. *The Second Self: Computers and the Human Spirit*. New York: Simon and Schuster.

Van Tassel, Dennis L., ed. 1976. *The Compleat Computer*. Chicago: Science Research Associates.

Weber, Bruce. 1996. "It's Man Over Machine as Chess Champion Beats Computer He Calls Tough Opponent." *New York Times,* 18 February, Sect. 1: 24.

———. 1996. "A Mean Chess-Playing Computer Tears at the Meaning of Thought." *New York Times,* 19 February: A1, B6.

Weizenbaum, Joseph. 1976. *Computer Power and Human Reason*. San Francisco: W. H. Freeman.

Winograd, Terry. 1972. *Understanding Natural Language*. New York: Academic Press.

## Chapter 12.  Computers and the Future

Avalos, George. 1996. "Netscape King of Browsers, Survey Shows." *Columbia, SC, State,* 20 May, Moneywise: 9.

Beer, Randall D., Hillel J. Chiel, and Leon S. Sterling. 1991. "An Artificial Insect." *American Scientist* 79, no. 5 (September–October): 444–52.

Begley, Sharon, and Adam Rogers. 1994. "It's All in the Genes." *Newsweek,* 5 September: 64.

"Byte's 15th Anniversary Summit." 1990. *Byte* 15, 9 (September): 218–367, passim.

"Computer Array Interprets the Human Genome." 1989. *New Scientist* 122 (6 May): 6.

"Computer Revealing Language of Life." 1989. *Science News* 135 (6 May): 284.

Croal, N'gai, and Brad Stone. 1996. "Web PDA." *Newsweek,* 15 April: 12.

Dejesus, Edmund X. 1996. "Toss Your TV." *Byte* 21, 2 (February): 50–64.

Feigenbaum, Edward A., and Pamela McCorduck. 1983. *The Fifth Generation.* Reading, MA: Addison-Wesley.

Frenkel, Karen A. 1989. "HDTV and the Computer Industry." *Communications of the ACM* 32, 11 (November): 1300–12.

Halfhill, Tom R. 1996. "Inside the Web PC." *Byte* 21, 3 (March): 44–56.

———. 1995. "Intel's P6." *Byte* 20, 4 (April): 42–58.

———. 1996. Unix vs. Windows NT *Byte* 21, 5 (May): 42–52.

"Interactive Life, An." 1993. *Newsweek,* 31 May: 42–44.

Lee, Thomas F. 1991. *The Human Genome Project.* New York: Plenum Press.

Lewis, Anthony. 1994. "Prospect of Peace Translates to Economic Boom for Israelis." *Columbia, SC, State,* 5 February: 9A.

Levinson, Marc. 1993. "Cutting Edge?" *Newsweek,* 8 March: 42–44.

Levy, Steven. 1995. "Antitrust and Common Sense." *Newsweek,* 6 March: 78.

———. 1995. "Bill's New Vision." *Newsweek,* 27 November: 54–57.

———. 1996. "The Browser War." *Newsweek,* 29 April: 47–50.

———. 1995. "Computers Go Bio." *Newsweek,* 1 May: 63.

Markoff, John. 1996. "A Quicker Pace Means No Peace in the Valley." *New York Times,* 3 June: C1, C8.

Meyer, Michael. 1995. "Is Your PC Too Complex? Get Ready for the 'NC.'" *Newsweek,* 6 November: 101–102.

Patterson, David A. 1995. "Microprocessors in 2020." *Scientific American* 273, 3 (September): 62–67.

Pollack, Andrew. 1992. "'Fifth Generation' Became Japan's Lost Generation." *The New York Times,* 5 June: D1.

Powell, Bill, and Kay Itoi. 1994. "I Didn't Say That, Did I?" *Newsweek,* 7 March: 47.

Reinhardt, Andy. 1994. "Building the Data Highway." *Byte* 19, 3 (March): 46–74.

Roberts, Leslie. 1991. "GRAIL Seeks Out Genes Buried in DNA Sequence." *Science* 254 (8 November): 805.

Rothman, Stanley, and Charles Mosmann. 1976. *Computers and Society,* 2nd ed. Chicago: Science Research Associates.

Stipp, David. 1995. "2001 Is Just Around the Corner. Where's Hal?" *Fortune,* 13 November: 215–28.

Stix, Gary. 1993. "Domesticating Cyberspace." *Scientific American* 269, 2 (August): 100–10.

"Teaching Minds to Fly with Discs and Mice." 1993. *Newsweek,* 31 May: 47.

Toffler, Alvin. 1990. "Power Shift: Knowledge, Wealth, and Violence at the Edge of the 21st Century." *Newsweek,* 15 October: 86–92. Abstracted from Alvin and Heidi Toffler. 1990. *Power Shift.* New York: Bantam Books.

Udell, Jon. 1993. "Windows, Windows Everywhere?" *Byte* 18, 7 (June): 73–94.

Wallich, Paul. 1991. "Silicon Babies." *Scientific American* 265, 6 (December): 124–34.

Weingarten, Fred W. 1996. "Groups to Challenge Telecom Law in Court." *Computing Research Newsletter* 8, 2 (March): 1–2.

Wolf, Gary. 1994. "The (Second Phase of the) Revolution Has Begun." *Wired* (October): 116–21, 150–54.

Zilber, Jon. 1996. "Prime-Time Player." *MacUser* (April): 64–67.

———. 1996. "Toy Story." *MacUser* (April): 68–73.

# PHOTO CREDITS

**Chapter 1**    Page 7(top): Courtesy of International Business Machines Corporation. Page 7(bottom left): Courtesy Gateway. Page 7(bottom right): Courtesy Compaq. Page 11: Courtesy Intel. Page 12: Courtesy Apple Computers. Page 13: Courtesy Corel Draw Software.

**Chapter 2**    Page 30: Courtesy Microsoft. Page 31(top): Courtesy Lotus. Page 32: Courtesy Micrografx. Page 33: Courtesy Microsoft. Page 37: Reprinted with permission from *Technology and Learning,* ©1988. Page 40(top): Charlie Riedel. Page 40(bottom left): Courtesy of International Business Machines Corporation. Page 40(bottom right): Hughes Medical Division/Peter Arnold, Inc. Page 42: Joseph Rodriguez/Mira. Page 43(top left): Photo by Jeffrey MacMillan, *U.S. News and World Report.* Page 43(top right): Images generated by Stephen Spencer, The Advanced Computing Center for Arts and Design, Columbus, Ohio, after Kempf, Marshall, Yen, *Pixel* Magazine, May/June 1990, p. 8. Page 43(bottom): Courtesy National Center for Atmospheric Research. Page 45(top): Photofest. Page 45(bottom): Courtesy *San Francisco Examiner.* Page 46(left): Mikki Rain/Science Photo Library/Photo Researchers. Page 46(right): Courtesy Apple Computers. Page 47: Courtesy The New York Times Electronic Media Company. Page 51: Courtesy U.S. Air Force.

**Chapter 3**    Page 58(left): David Frazier/Photo Researchers. Page 58(right): Cartoon by Robert Osborn, courtesy John Caffrey, and Charles Mosmann. Page 61: Granger Collection. Page 62: Jeffrey Neubury. Page 63: Courtesy Herman Miller, Inc. Page 64: Courtesy Bob Oakman. Page 65: Peter Freed/Sygma. Page 69: Stacy Pick/Stock, Boston. Page 70: Roger Ressmeyer/Corbis.

**Chapter 4**    Page 76: Courtesy Apple Computers. Page 77: ©Steven Underwood Photography. Page 85: Courtesy Motorola Corporation. Page 86: Courtesy MIT Archives. Page 88: Courtesy Maxtor Corporation. Page 89(top): Courtesy Toshiba/The Benjamin Group. Page 89(bottom): ©Steven Underwood Photography. Page 90(left): Dan McCoy/Rainbow. Page 90(right): Hank Morgan/Science Source/Photo Researchers. Page 91(left): Courtesy Microsoft. Page 91(right): John Brooks/Gamma Liaison. Page 92(top): Image courtesy of Intergraph Corporation. Page 92(bottom left): Courtesy of International Business Machines Corporation. Page 92(bottom right): Courtesy Telxon Corporation. Page 93: Courtesy Xerox Imaging Systems. Page 95: Dick Luria/Photo Researchers.

**Chapter 5**    Page 108(left): Courtesy Institute for Advanced Study, Princeton, NJ. Page 108(right): Courtesy Sperry Univac, Division of Sperry Corporation. Page 111(left): Courtesy Digital Equipment Corporation. Page 111(right): Courtesy Naval Surface Weapons Center. Page 112(top): Dan McCoy/Rainbow. Page 112(bottom and center): Courtesy The Science Museum. Page 112(bottom left): Courtesy of International Business

Machines Corporation. Page 112(bottom right): Courtesy New York Public Library. Pages 116 and 119 (top): Courtesy Microsoft. Page 121: Allan Tannenbaum/Sygma. Page 122: Bob Mahoney.

**Chapter 6**    Page 134: Courtesy Corel Corporation. Page 135: From Stern and Stern, *Computing in the Information Age,* 2nd. ed., Figure 3.9b, p. 71; John Wiley & Sons Publishers. Page 139: Courtesy Softkey International. Page 141: From Stern and Stern, *Computers in the Information Age,* 2e., Figure 3.13, p. 75. John Wiley & Sons Publishers. Page 142: Courtesy University of South Carolina. Page 145: Courtesy Carnegie Mellon University. Page 146: Courtesy University of South Carolina. Page 148: Courtesy Aldus Corporation. Page 149: Lawrence Gartel/Science Source/Photo Researchers. Page 150(top): Courtesy Mark of the Unicorn, Inc. Page 150(bottom left): Hank Morgan/Rainbow. Page 150(bottom right): Courtesy of International Business Machines Corporation. Page 151: Robert Holmgren.

**Chapter 7**    Page 158(left): Courtesy Daniel Bricklin. Page 158(right): Courtesy Apple Computers. Page 160: Courtesy Internal Revenue Service. Page 167: Courtesy Microsoft. Pages 168 and 170: Courtesy Intuit.

**Chapter 8**    Page 177: Courtesy Moore School Computer Museum, University of Pennsylvania. Page 178: M. Grecco/The Stock Shop. Page 193: Courtesy Symantec Corporation. Page 194(left): Laima Druskus/Stock, Boston. Page 194(right): Dan McCoy/Rainbow.

**Chapter 9**    Page 203: Courtesy the MIT Museum. Page 205(top): Focus on Sports. Page 205(bottom): Courtesy Hewlett Packard. Page 212(top): Courtesy Broderbund Software, Inc. Page 212(bottom): Courtesy Adobe Systems, Inc. Page 214: Courtesy Against All Odds Productions. Page 218(top): Courtesy of International Business Machines Corporation. Page 218(bottom left): Image courtesy of Intergraph Corporation. Page 218(bottom right): Courtesy Hewlett Packard. Page 219(left): ©1993 Universal Pictures/ Amblin Entertainment. Photo provided Courtesy of Industrial Light & Magic. Page 219(right): Courtesy IEEE Computer Society and Information International, Inc. Page 220: ©Capital Features/The Image Works. Page 221(left): Courtesy Réunions des Musées Nationaux, Paris. Page 221(right): Water-lilies ©1990 by Deborah R. Flowler, James Hanan, Prezemyslaw Prusinkiewicz and Norma Fuller, from *The Algorithmic Beauty of Plants.* Page 222(top): Courtesy Pixar. Page 222(bottom): Courtesy Exxon Co. USA. Page 223: Peter Menzel/AllStock, Inc./Tony Stone Images/ New York, Inc. Page 224: Fred Ward/Black Star.

**Chapter 10**    Page 230: Peter Sibbald. Page 232: Courtesy U.S. Robotics. Page 233: Loren Santow/Tony Stone Images/ New York, Inc. Page 234: John Walsh/Photo Researchers. Page 235(top): Mark C. Flannery. Page 235(bottom): Photo courtesy of Donna Cox and Robert Patterson, National Center for

Supercomputing Applications, University of Illinois at Urbana-Champaign. Page 239: James D. Wilson/Gamma Liaison. Page 241: Courtesy White Pine Software, Inc. Page 244: Courtesy CompuServe, Inc. Page 245: Jim Cummins/FPG International. Page 248(top): Stephane Compoint/Sygma. Page 248(bottom left): Najlam Feanny/SABA. Page 248(bottom right): Jim Bounds/Sygma. Page 249: M. Ansin/Gamma Liaison. Page 250: Will Van Overbeek.

**Chapter 11**    Page 258: Courtesy The Computer Museum. Page 259: Courtesy Jerry Ohlinger's Movie Material Store. Page 266: Andy Sacks/Tony Stone Images/ New York, Inc. Page 268(top left): James. D. Wilson/Woodfin Camp & Associates. Page 268(top right): Cartoon by Michael Crawford, *Scientific American*, July 1993, Page 77. Reproduced wtih permission of *Scientific American*. Page 268(bottom): James Leynse/SABA. Page 269: Hank Morgan/Rainbow. Page 270: Courtesy The Robotics Institute, Carnegie Mellon University.

**Chapter 12**    Page 279: Peter Menzel. Page 282(top): P. Gontier/The Image Works. Page 282(bottom): Courtesy PointCast News Network. Page 283: Courtesy *Byte* Publications, February 1996, Page 53. Reproduced with permission. Page 284: Lara Jo Regan/SABA. Page 285: Courtesy of International Business Machines Corporation. Page 286: Courtesy *Newsweek*. Reproduced with permission. Page 288: ©Michael Troller Design, San Francisco. Page 289: Courtesy Sony Corporation. Page 290(top): Taran Z Photography. Page 291(top): From *Byte*, March 1995, Page 47: Reproduced with permission of *Byte* Publications. Page 291(bottom): Charles O'Rear. Page 293: Decker/Action Press/SABA. Page 294: Andy Freeberg. Page 295: From *Byte*, August 1995, Page 50. Reproduced with permission of *Byte* Publications. Page 296: Geoffrey Wheeler/Black Star. Page 297: Rick Friedman/Black Star. Page 298: Sam Ogden. Page 300: Alison Seiffer.

# Index

Holgate Library
Bennett College
Date Due

|  |  |  |
|---|---|---|
|  |  |  |
|  |  |  |
|  |  |  |
|  |  |  |
|  |  |  |
|  |  |  |
|  |  |  |
|  |  |  |
|  |  |  |
|  |  |  |
|  |  |  |
|  |  |  |
|  |  |  |
|  |  |  |
|  |  |  |
|  |  |  |
|  |  |  |
|  |  |  |
|  |  |  |
|  |  |  |
|  |  |  |
|  |  |  |